Doron Bar
Yad Vashem

Doron Bar

Yad Vashem

The Challenge of Shaping a Holocaust Remembrance Site, 1942–1976

Translated by
Deena Glickman

DE GRUYTER
OLDENBOURG

The original edition was published in Hebrew by Yad Vashem, Jerusalem: הר הזיכרון: אתגר הנצחת השואה והגבורה ביד ושם 1942–1976 (2021).

This book is published in cooperation with the Schechter Institute of Jewish Studies, Jerusalem

ISBN 978-3-11-126635-0
e-ISBN (PDF) 978-3-11-072148-5
e-ISBN (EPUB) 978-3-11-072161-4

Library of Congress Control Number: 2021944640

Bibliographic information published by the Deutsche Nationalbibliothek
The Deutsche Nationalbibliothek lists this publication in the Deutsche Nationalbibliografie; detailed bibliographic data are available on the Internet at http://dnb.dnb.de.

© 2023 Walter de Gruyter GmbH, Berlin/Boston
This volume is text- and page-identical with the hardback published in 2022.
Cover illustration: Ohel Yizkor. Digital image of a photograph by Yitzhak Amit, from the Judaica Collection of the Harvard Library, Harvard University
Typesetting: Integra Software Services Pvt. Ltd.
Printing and binding: CPI books GmbH, Leck

www.degruyter.com

To the millions who perished in the Holocaust,
To the survivors,
To the ghetto rebels,
To the forest fighters,
To the camp revolutionaries,
To the underground warriors,
To the soldiers in the armies,
To the rescuers of brothers,
To the daring clandestine immigrants,
The heroes of might and sedition.

Preface

One of the State of Israel's most prominent institutions and "a central temple of the Holocaust,"[1] Yad Vashem is a symbol of meaning and unity that has risen in prestige in recent years, especially after the inauguration of the new museum in 2005. But if you ask the country's everyman about the site's very significant history – for example, when Yad Vashem was founded, and why its location in western Jerusalem was selected – you will find that very few have answers. Even scholars of the Holocaust, of the history of Yad Vashem, and of the development and crystallization of the landscape of memory and commemoration in the State of Israel have not dedicated much thought to the institution's physical formation. This book aims to fill the lacuna, depicting the process of the Mount of Remembrance's construction. It begins in the 1940s, when the idea of Holocaust commemoration in the land of Israel was first born, and ends in the 1970s, when Nathan Rapoport's *Warsaw Ghetto Uprising* monument was inaugurated.

I never imagined I would study the history of Yad Vashem; I found the topic daunting. But in recent years my writing has focused more and more on questions of commemoration and remembrance and the shaping of symbols in the form of sacred sites, both popular and national, in the Israeli terrain. At some point, I became interested in the way in which Holocaust commemoration was integrated within Israel's memorial landscape, and the idea of studying the establishment and building of Yad Vashem took root. The turning point came when I was exposed to intriguing material on the bureaucratic dimensions of the institution's founding. While reading the descriptions of the discussions, a fascinating picture appeared in my mind's eye: a complex, extensive, and sometimes painful process, one of disagreement, struggle, and achievement tied to the Remembrance Authority and the construction of the Mount of Remembrance. These discussions returned time and again to the names of a number of prominent figures, people who would later emerge as key figures in the institution's founding. They included Ben-Zion Dinur, the minister of education and chairman of Yad Vashem, and Zerach Warhaftig, later to become minister of religions but during the forties part of Yad Vashem's management. They were joined by a number of other significant figures: architects Munio Gitai Weinraub and Alfred (Al) Mansfeld, along with three additional architects, took part in the planning and construction of Yad Vashem; Mark Uveeler served as representative of the Claims Conference on Yad Vashem's directorate. But most noticeable in the documents was Mordechai Shenhavi

---

[1] Yeshayahu Charles Liebman, "Holocaust Myth in the Israeli Society," *Tfutzot Israel* 19 (1981): 101–14 [in Hebrew].

(Alfenbein), whom I recognized immediately as the conceiver of Yad Vashem as early as 1942; he also had a crucial role in its founding.

The personal, internal process I underwent led me to embark on writing a book on Yad Vashem's construction a number of years ago. It was a journey in which I amassed much material on the subject, primarily documents that had been preserved in different archives. Due to the great scope of the archival sources, I was able to reconstruct the extensive process of the establishment of Yad Vashem. This material facilitates an understanding of a number of dimensions: the development of the memorial and commemorative landscape of "historical" Yad Vashem up until the mid-seventies; the origins of the concept of a square remembrance structure in which the Holocaust was commemorated, with its basalt foundation and concrete top (the Hall of Remembrance); the source of the idea of burying victims' ashes in the soil of the Mount of Remembrance; the reason behind heroism's commemoration in a pillar located atop the highest hilltop on the mount; and the story of the synagogue's location and function.

The study of Yad Vashem's creation, in which these questions and others are addressed, gives scholars of culture, of commemoration and memory, of the Holocaust and its immortalization, an opportunity to examine the bureaucratic mechanism and the process that accompanied the establishment of the site in Jerusalem. In recent years, studies have been written on the Holocaust monuments and museums founded around the world in the last generation – for example, the United States Holocaust Memorial Museum in Washington, the Jewish Museum Berlin, and even Yad Vashem's new Holocaust History Museum.[2] But despite the centrality and significance of Yad Vashem, no study has yet been composed on the chronicles of the Mount of Remembrance's construction. Documents from the time, protocols of the various committees involved in the building of Yad Vashem, detailed correspondence between those involved, maps, and memoirs all made it possible for me to comprehend and examine the intricate and protracted process involved in the formation of one of the world's most vital and important Holocaust remembrance sites.

This book would not have been possible were it not for the documents, photographs, maps, and sketches about the history of Yad Vashem that are preserved in a variety of archives in the State of Israel; the list of archives used in the volume appears at the end of the book. Archive staff perform devoted and crucial work that makes it possible for us, the researchers, to answer our questions

---

[2] Edward T. Linenthal, *Preserving Memory: The Struggle to Create America's Holocaust Museum* (New York: Penguin Books, 1997); Dorit Harel, *Facts and Feelings – Dilemmas in Designing the Yad Vashem Holocaust History Museum* (Jerusalem: Dorit Harel Designers, 2010).

using the boxes and folders in their charge. I wish to thank the employees at the HaShomer HaTzair Archive at the Yad Yaari Research and Documentation Center in Givat Haviva for their assistance. I am also grateful to my friends at the Central Zionist Archives for the many hours of work there and their support. I am indebted, too, to the employees at the Kibbutz Mishmar HaEmek Archive for maintaining Mordechai Shenhavi's personal files and for their commitment to preserving his memory. Thank you to Amos Gitai for generously making available to me the materials from Munio Gitai Weinraub's archive. A special thank you to the staff at the Yad Vashem Archives, where I found a trove that was overflowing with treasures of historical material on the process of the planning and building of Yad Vashem.

This book is published with the assistance of a Schechter Institute of Jewish Studies research grant.

My thanks are also extended to Deena Glickman, who translated the book to English, and to the staff at De Gruyter.

Contents

Preface —— **VII**

List of Illustrations —— **XV**

Introduction —— **1**
    The Book's Structure and Chronological Framework —— **9**

Chapter 1
Yad Vashem until the End of 1948 —— **11**
    Early Concepts —— **12**
    Yad Vashem: A Commemoration Enterprise for a Devastated Diaspora —— **20**
    The National Council and its Involvement in the Establishment of Yad Vashem —— **24**
    The Outline for Yad Vashem —— **26**
    Attempts to Promote the Yad Vashem Plan —— **30**
    The JNF's Misgivings about Holocaust Commemoration —— **32**
    The Yad Vashem Plan near Ma'ale HaHamisha and Neve Ilan —— **34**
    The Difficulty of Adapting the Architectural Plans to the Selected Location —— **36**
    Public Relations for the Memorial Enterprise —— **39**
    Cooperation with the JNF and the Founding of the Yad Vashem Board of Governors —— **41**
    Disagreements about Yad Vashem's Future —— **44**
    "Can a Jewish State be Imagined with a Memorial Enterprise outside of it?" —— **47**
    The Ramat Rachel Plan —— **50**
    Conclusion —— **54**

Chapter 2
From Statehood until the Enactment of the Yad Vashem Law in August 1953 —— **59**
    Yad Vashem Shuttered? —— **60**
    The Ashes of Austrian Jewry —— **64**
    Ashes from the Flossenburg Concentration Camp —— **69**
    The Martyrs' Forest and the JNF —— **72**
    The Yad Vashem Law —— **77**

Finding a Site for Yad Vashem —— 84
Conclusion —— 89

Chapter 3
Building the Mount of Remembrance: First Steps —— 91
Formalizing the Relationship with Yad Vashem's Architects —— 92
Analogous Projects and the Risk of Dividing Holocaust Commemoration —— 95
Yad Vashem Confronts the Ministry of Religions and the JNF —— 97
Funding for Yad Vashem's Construction —— 103
The First Ceremony on the Mount of Remembrance —— 105
The Claims Conference, Mark Uveeler, and Yad Vashem —— 107
Discussions about the Architectural Image of the Mount of Remembrance —— 109
The Dispute about the Construction Plan —— 114
Holocaust and Heroism in the Future Construction of Yad Vashem —— 116
The First Global Yad Vashem Council —— 119
The Symposium for Planning the Mount of Remembrance —— 121
The First Symposium —— 123
The Second Symposium —— 128
Conclusion —— 132

Chapter 4
The Path to the Hall of Remembrance's Construction —— 135
Financial Hurdles and Changes to the Building Plan —— 136
The Martyrs' Ashes and the Mount of Remembrance —— 140
Yad Vashem's Construction Plan —— 149
Deliberations Regarding Yad Vashem's Synagogue —— 153
The Question of Heroism on the Mount of Remembrance —— 157
A Return to the Issue of Martyrs' Ashes —— 163
Toward the Building of the Hall of Remembrance and Another Financial Crisis —— 164
The Heroism Hall Becomes a Heroism Tower —— 168
The Inauguration of the Hall of Remembrance —— 171
Conclusion —— 181

Chapter 5
The Mount of Remembrance: A New Look —— 183
The Heroism Monument —— 184
Yad Vashem's Synagogue —— 193

The Avenue of the Righteous among the Nations —— 196
The Hall of Names —— 199
The Yad Vashem Museum —— 206
The *Warsaw Ghetto Uprising* Monument —— 213
    Initial Ties with Yad Vashem —— 214
    The Monument (or a Copy) to Yad Vashem? —— 215
Critiques of Erecting Sculptures on the Mount of Remembrance —— 217
A Solution —— 221
Conclusion —— 224

Conclusion The Road to Remembrance —— 227
    Mordechai Shenhavi: Visionary and Adversary —— 230
    Dueling Dualities and the Architecture of Remembrance —— 232
    Holocaust Remembrance Meets State Commemoration —— 237
    Holocaust, Heroism, and Yad Vashem —— 240
    National Holocaust Commemoration: A Dream Realized —— 243

Bibliography —— 247
    List of Archives —— 247
    List of Newspapers —— 247
    Secondary Sources —— 247

Index —— 255
    Subjects —— 255
    Names —— 258
    Places —— 260

List of Illustrations

Figure 1 Mordechai Shenhavi, ca. 1930 (KMHA, Unknown photographer) —— 13
Figure 2 Munio Weinraub's 1943 illustration of the pavilion for the lost (HHA) —— 16
Figure 3 Weinraub and Mansfeld's 1946 outline for Yad Vashem (HHA) —— 27
Figure 4 Yad Vashem plan for Ramat Rachel, 1948 (HHA) —— 52
Figure 5 Glass box with thirty vessels of ashes brought from Austria, displayed to the public at the Chief Rabbinate's building, Tel Aviv (NPA, David Eldan) —— 68
Figure 6 Glass box with thirty vessels of ashes displayed in the Chamber of the Holocaust (private collection, Unknown photographer) —— 71
Figure 7 The Yad Vashem Law, passed in the Knesset in August 1953 (YVA, Unknown photographer) —— 83
Figure 8 Map of the Jerusalem area, with the area allocated to Yad Vashem outlined, 1949. This area encompasses what would eventually become Mount Herzl, the military cemetery, the Great Leaders of the Nation's Plot, and Yad Vashem. (HHA) —— 88
Figure 9 Prof. Ben-Zion Dinur, chairman of Yad Vashem, speaks at a memorial ceremony at Yad Vashem (YVA, Unknown photographer) —— 92
Figure 10 Israeli Prime Minister Moshe Sharett speaks at a Holocaust Martyrs' and Heroes' Remembrance Day ceremony in 1954 in the Martyrs' Forest. A sign notes the Yad Vashem Holocaust and Heroism Remembrance Authority's involvement in the ceremony. (NPA, Hugo Mendelson) —— 102
Figure 11 The cornerstone ceremony for Yad Vashem's archive and administration building, July 1954 (YVA, Unknown photographer) —— 105
Figure 12 Mordechai Shenhavi lights a remembrance torch during the cornerstone ceremony for Yad Vashem's archive and administration building, July 1954 (KMHA, Unknown photographer) —— 107
Figure 13 Construction plan for Yad Vashem, 1954 (HHA) —— 110
Figure 14 Model of Yad Vashem, late 1954 (HHA, Unknown photographer) —— 111
Figure 15 The archive and administration building, February 1957 (CAHJP, Unknown photographer) —— 138
Figure 16 Model of Yad Vashem containing the Hall of Remembrance, Pillar of Heroism, and synagogue (CAHJP) —— 152
Figure 17 Arieh Kubovy, chairman of Yad Vashem, 1959–1966 (YVA, Unknown photographer) —— 155
Figure 18 Construction plan for Yad Vashem, late 1950s (HHA) —— 170
Figure 19 Suggestion for placement of the names of twenty-one extermination camps, concentration camps, and sites of murder and transport within the floor of the Hall of Remembrance (YVA, Unknown photographer) —— 172
Figure 20 General appearance of the Hall of Remembrance (NPA, Moshe Milner) —— 174
Figure 21 Gateway to the Hall of Remembrance, designed by David Palombo (NPA, Moshe Pridan) —— 175
Figure 22 Eternal flame designed by Kosso Eloul for the Hall of Remembrance (YVA, Unknown photographer) —— 176

List of Illustrations

Figure 23 The Hall of Remembrance, with the Pillar of Heroism in the background (YVA, Unknown photographer) —— **178**

Figure 24 The winners of the first three places in the competition to design the heroism monument at Yad Vashem. David Palombo and Nathan Rapoport's proposals were rejected and that of Naomi Henrik, winner of the competition, was accepted. (ISA, Unknown photographer) —— **186**

Figure 25 The Pillar of Heroism and the memorial plaza at its base (YVA, Unknown photographer) —— **192**

Figure 26 Yad Vashem's synagogue (YVA, Unknown photographer) —— **195**

Figure 27 Johannes Bogaard, a Dutch farmer who hid Jews on his farm during the Second World War, plants a tree on the Avenue of the Righteous among the Nations, 1964 (YVA, Unknown photographer) —— **198**

Figure 28 The Hall of Names (YVA, Unknown photographer) —— **205**

Figure 29 The *A World Which Was and Is No More* exhibit, the opening portion of the *Warning and Witness* exhibition (CAHJP, Unknown photographer) —— **209**

Figure 30 Yad Vashem's historical museum. The tunnel that symbolized the burrows in which rebels fought against the Nazis led to the third and central wing of the museum, which was dedicated to the Jews' uprising against the Nazis. (NPA, Moshe Milner) —— **212**

Figure 31 Nathan Rapoport's *Warsaw Ghetto Uprising* monument is erected, 1975 (YVA, Unknown photographer) —— **222**

Figure 32 Nathan Rapoport's monument in memory of the ghetto heroes (YVA, Unknown photographer) —— **223**

Figure 33 The *In Thy Blood, Live* monument, the second element in Nathan Rapoport's monument in memory of the Warsaw Ghetto Uprising, 1976 (YVA, Unknown photographer) —— **224**

Figure 34 Nathan Rapoport's *In Thy Blood, Live* monument is inaugurated on Holocaust Martyrs' and Heroes' Remembrance Day ceremony, 27 Nisan 1976 (NPA, Ya'akov Sa'ar) —— **225**

Figure 35 General appearance of Yad Vashem in the mid-seventies (HHA) —— **228**

Introduction

A visitor to the State of Israel's central memorial compound, which includes Mount Herzl, the military cemetery, the Great Leaders of the Nation's Plot, and Yad Vashem, cannot but note a prominent phenomenon: while some parts of the space – Herzl's grave, the Great Leaders of the Nation's Plot, and the cemetery for those who fell in Israel's battles – are near empty, Yad Vashem is overcrowded. Estimates are that nearly one million people visit the site each year. These are not only tourists from overseas, Jews and non-Jews alike, but also Israeli individuals and groups: youth, soldiers, adults, and others, all coming to tour and learn at the Mount of Remembrance.

Why is there such a marked difference between Mount Herzl and Yad Vashem? Why does Yad Vashem enjoy such popularity as an Israeli and Jewish identity and heritage site, and why does it draw residents of the country who find the Holocaust so relevant and significant? Was Yad Vashem always a lodestone for Israelis? What was their attraction to the site over the years?

Sociologists are tasked with answering questions about the Holocaust's status and Yad Vashem's role within twenty-first-century Israeli reality;[1] historians must answer questions related to Yad Vashem's chronicles and the process of the site's establishment and crystallization over the years. But historical geographers must also answer historical questions about dilemmas related to the development of Yad Vashem's memorial landscape, reconstructing the process of the institution's construction – the central topic of this volume.

Thousands of sites around the world, including hundreds of museums, are devoted to Holocaust commemoration. Some of these sites are located in the very places in which massacres and extermination took place, while others are distanced from Europe; some have a universal or national character while others are local, established by survivors, organizations, or the families of those murdered; some target Jewish visitors while others appeal to an international audience. In each, the Holocaust is commemorated in a different way, using a series of symbols, forms, and materials meant to express and exhibit these meanings.

In the land of Israel of both pre- and post-1948, the Holocaust has been commemorated in a variety of physical forms. Monuments, symbolic graves, museums, synagogues, plaques, groves, and forests are some of the ways in which the Holocaust is memorialized in the local landscape.

---

1 Bella Gutterman, *Yad Vashem: 60 Years of Remembrance, Documentation, Research and Education* (Jerusalem: Yad Vashem, 2014), 234–333 [in Hebrew].

But Yad Vashem is unique. It is a state site whose commemoration is pan-Israeli rather than the legacy of only one stream, religion, or tradition – and it is also architecturally distinct. Its memorial landscape is richer and more complex than any other found elsewhere in the country.

Today, Yad Vashem has pride of place in the landscape of symbolic commemoration in Israel; the buildings on the Mount of Remembrance, the monuments, and the sculptures attract much public attention. But, as this book reveals, this was not the case in the three decades that followed the state's establishment. At that time, Yad Vashem had great trouble provoking interest among the country's residents and Diaspora Jewry; only tens of thousands of people visited each year. The state's political leadership did not highlight the site and the events that took place there annually did not draw great crowds.

Yad Vashem's growth and its entry into the heart of the Israeli state was a gradual, drawn-out process. From the establishment of Yad Vashem, the institution's originators and leaders debated how to design a place that would be relevant and meaningful for generations and how to make it a place that would attract a wide audience. At the original Yad Vashem – the one whose cornerstone was laid in 1954, the one in whose center the Hall of Remembrance was inaugurated in 1961, the one in which the historical museum was opened to the public in 1973 – the sight of the Mount of Remembrance and the cultural experience was entirely different from that of today. Today, most visitors to Yad Vashem focus on the Holocaust History Museum, inaugurated in 2005.[2] This constitutes the center of their cultural and emotional experience, and they see almost no other sites. The Hall of Remembrance is especially interesting in this context; in the Mount of Remembrance's modern redesign, it lost its symbolic birthright. In contrast with the first four decades of the Remembrance Authority's activity, when the Hall of Remembrance served as the center of the visiting experience at Yad Vashem, today it is of secondary importance to many visitors.

But the current volume's focus is on the founding and construction of the Hall of Remembrance, and the shaping of the physical memory of the Holocaust at Yad Vashem in general. In the coming chapters, I discuss the process that took place over decades, beginning in 1942, when the idea of commemorating the Holocaust in the land of Israel was first raised, and ending in 1976, when Nathan Rapoport's *Warsaw Ghetto Uprising* monument was completed. Over

---

[2] Stephanie Shosh Rothem, *Constructing Memory: Architectural Narratives of Holocaust Museums* (New York: Peter Lang, 2013); Eran Neumann, *Shoah Presence: Architectural Representations of the Holocaust* (Farnham, UK: Ashgate, 2014).

thirty-four years, the process of thinking, planning, and construction knew ups and downs, achievements and bumps in the road. The book's first section focuses on the attempts to establish Yad Vashem and, in effect, the failure of the conceivers to translate thought into action. For the lion's share of the period under discussion, the institution's leaders were unable to realize the idea, originally formed during the Second World War; it was only in 1961 that the Hall of Remembrance, the center for Israeli Holocaust commemoration, was inaugurated. The book delineates how complex the process was, and how rife with struggles, arguments, and disappointments – but also achievements.

From the early sixties, the site developed; new memorial elements were added on occasion – the Yad Vashem synagogue, the Hall of Names, the Pillar of Heroism – all of which, taken together, formed a homogenous memorial creation. The ceremony for Holocaust Martyrs' and Heroes' Remembrance Day that was held in 1976 at the foot of Rapoport's monument to the Warsaw Ghetto Uprising marked the completion of the process that had begun in 1954, when the cornerstone for the Yad Vashem Archive was laid. Since then, Yad Vashem's landscape has included the Archive and Library Building, memorial and commemoration structures, the museum, and monuments. In the mid-seventies, the heads of Yad Vashem managed to complete the task of establishing a memorial site and, after three decades of struggles, discussions, conflicts, and achievements, its various symbols stood firm – the Hall of Remembrance, the historical museum, the Pillar of Heroism, and others – and signified to the Israeli, Jewish, and international public that the institution's leadership was equal to the task: it had successfully created a memorial and commemorative monument to the Holocaust and heroism.

During the 1970s and 1980s, Yad Vashem's symbolization process continued, and more monuments were integrated into the Mount of Remembrance – the monument to Jewish soldiers and partisans (1985), the Children's Memorial (1987), the Valley of the Communities (1993), and the Cattle Car memorial (1995); new buildings, such as the Holocaust Art Museum (1982), were also built. These components are not part of the current volume, whose focus is on the original Mount of Remembrance. Nevertheless, it is clear that the processes that took place during Yad Vashem's early years are tightly bound up with the integration of these monuments in later years. Taking part in these processes were the institution's heads, its board members, and the architects who planned and oversaw its construction, all part of the political and intellectual elite that birthed Yad Vashem and created the memorial site in its image. These made Yad Vashem an integral and central part of collective Israeli identity, the most prominent memorial site in the state. This process, the book will demonstrate, included the rejection, adoption, and creation of different narratives tied to Holocaust remembrance and commemoration and its architectural and scenic expression until an agreed-upon, unifying version created the "historical," pre-2005, Mount of Remembrance.[3]

***

Early deliberations about the role and responsibility of Yad Vashem as pertaining to the Holocaust, memory, and commemoration took place in the forties, when the idea was first raised and the Zionist agencies began to debate what their obligation was to the subject. In 1948, three years after the Second World War ended, and with Yad Vashem at one of its lowest points, Yehuda Gothelf presented the finer points of the ongoing dilemma regarding the institution, its role, and its future in *Davar*. In an article titled "Our Responsibility to the Living and the Dead," he asserted that had the Jews been like other nations, "we would have no more honorable role than building monuments and pantheons to remember our heroes, marble palaces to commemorate the horror and the heroism." But Gothelf felt that the Jewish nation did not wish to descend into rifling through archives (in which the Holocaust would be documented); it would rather act. The Jewish instinct was not to invest in "images and masks, nor in sanctuaries, towers and pyramids like Assyria, Babylonia, and Egypt, but rather a doctrine of living." Gothelf added that "the initiators of Yad Vashem saw the center of gravity in the stone monument, the series of buildings that will immortalize the heroism and the tragedy. To tell the truth, the waves of stones that were placed on the graves of the dead contained something of the ancient mysterious fear of spirits."[4]

Gothelf, who criticized the plans to develop Yad Vashem in the period before the state's founding, thus presented one of the central dilemmas that has been tied to building a Holocaust memorial site throughout the years: Should the institute's heads stick to traditional Jewish forms of commemoration as they were for generations – prayer, fasting, dedicating books to the memory of the fallen? Or should the dead be immortalized in a form that was different and less accepted at the time, in a plastic, architectural form, building a commemoration site within the land of Israel? Would the intensity of events in Europe and their tragic nature justify a remembrance site that was different than those known until then, using powerful memorial construction within the local landscape?

The decision made by the Zionist institutions and the emerging state's authorities in 1945 was unambiguous. Yad Vashem would not only be tasked with

---

[3] Maoz Azaryahu, *State Cults: Celebrating Independence and Commemorating the Fallen in Israel, 1948–1956* (Sde Boqer: Ben-Gurion Research Institute, 1995), 4–7 [in Hebrew].
[4] Yehuda Gothelf, "Our Obligation for the Living and the Dead," *Davar*, April 4, 1948 [in Hebrew].

collecting historical material about Jewish life in the Diaspora and the annihilation of European Jewry;[5] it would also establish a memorial site which "pilgrims" could visit to remember the events. The institution's heads envisioned a central and impressive monument with memorial structures, dedicated to the millions who had perished and the hundreds of thousands who had fought the Nazis, standing at its center.[6]

Yad Vashem's leaders were occupied with commemoration at a time when the wider world had only just begun to debate the question of the correct way to memorialize the war and the Jews' annihilation. In the forties, hesitant early attempts were made around the world, primarily at the sites of mass murder in Europe, to build and shape war memorials, and this idea developed gradually in the subsequent decades.[7] In Israel itself, both before and after 1948, monumental memorial architectural had still not developed.[8] Architects had almost no experience building large commemorative structures before the mid-sixties, and they certainly had not faced the complex subject of giving comprehensive architectural expression to Holocaust commemoration. The parallels to the institute heads' physical-spatial grappling with Holocaust remembrance were far smaller sites, gradually erected by the State of Israel after its establishment. These were the Chamber of the Holocaust on Mount Zion, the Ghetto Fighters' House Museum, the Yad Mordechai "From Holocaust to Revival" Museum, and the Martyrs' Forest, as well as memorial spaces of a communal or private nature founded in graveyards, synagogues, public parks, and groves.[9]

---

[5] Henry Wassermann, "Nationalization of the Memory of the Six Millions," *Politika* 8 (1986): 6–7 [in Hebrew].

[6] Judith Tydor Baumel, "Commemorating the Holocaust by Communities and Individuals in the State of Israel," *Iyunim Bitkumat Israel* 5 (1995): 364–387 [in Hebrew]; Dalia Ofer, "How and What to Remember: The Holocaust in Israel in the First Decade," in *Independence: The First Fifty Years*, ed. Anita Shapira (Jerusalem: The Zalman Shazar Center, 1998), 171–93 [in Hebrew]; Yechiam Weitz, "Shaping the Memory of the Holocaust in Israeli Society of the 1950s," in *Major Changes Within the Jewish People in the Wake of the Holocaust*, ed. Yisrael Gutman (Jerusalem: Yad Vashem, 1993), 473–94 [in Hebrew]; Boaz Cohen, *Israeli Holocaust Research: Birth and Evolution* (Jerusalem: Yad Vashem, 2001) [in Hebrew]; Maoz Azaryahu, "Innovation and Continuity: Jewish Tradition and the Shaping of Sovereignty Rites in Israel," in *On Both Sides of the Bridge: Religion and State in the Early Years of Israel*, ed. Mordechai Bar-On and Zvi Zameret (Jerusalem: Yad Izhak Ben-Zvi, 2002), 273–94 [in Hebrew].

[7] James E. Young, *The Texture of Memory: Holocaust Memorials and Meaning* (New Haven: Yale University Press, 1994).

[8] Daniel Monk, *An Aesthetic Occupation: The Immediacy of Architecture and the Palestine Conflict* (Durham and London: Duke University Press, 2002).

[9] Mooli Brog, "'The Stone Will Scream from the Wall': Monumental Commemoration of the Holocaust in the Israeli Landscape," *Massuah Yearbook* 32 (2006): 93–109 [in Hebrew].

The aspiration to establish a state memorial that would include symbols of pan-Israeli and pan-Jewish significance, one that could itself become an Israeli symbol, posed a rare opportunity as well as a great challenge for the planners. Their goal in establishing Yad Vashem was not just to pay a moral "debt" to those who had perished but also to use the terrible events that had taken place in Europe to shape and crystallize Israeli society's identity. Yad Vashem's heads wished to intimate that the only legitimate place to commemorate the Holocaust was in Jerusalem, on the Mount of Remembrance, and that the State of Israel and its capital city had priority and privilege over the Diaspora and other Holocaust memorial sites in Israel and around the world. The fact that the years that followed the Second World War overlapped with the battles of the War of Independence and the establishment of the State of Israel only served to underscore the dilemmas related to the link between the Holocaust and heroism and the link between the Holocaust and the establishment of the state. IDF soldiers, underground fighters in the land before the state's birth, ghetto uprising fighters during the war, partisans, and Allied soldiers were all oftentimes presented as worth identifying with, models that one should strive to live up to.[10]

But Holocaust commemoration was not always the subject of national agreement; uniting with the memory of the millions who had died was not the cleansing and purifying experience for all of Israeli society that had been anticipated. Rather, beginning in the forties with the end of the Second World War and throughout the years studied in this volume, it was accompanied by endless political disagreements. These conflicts – arguments about the date of the day of remembrance for those the Holocaust's victims, the question of compensation from Germany, the debate about how and by whom the Holocaust would be commemorated – were always fierce, emotionally charged, bitter, and laden with tension.[11] Many of those active in the pre-state Yishuv's national institutions, leaders of parties, and Knesset and government members vacillated at the time between lip service to the memory of the Holocaust and engaging in an honest and painful struggle with its aftermath.[12] The true tension and challenge for the nation's leaders was successfully

---

[10] Eliezer Don-Yehiya, "Statehood and Holocaust," in *In the Paths of Renewal: Studies in Religious Zionism*, ed. Avraham Rubinstein (Ramat Gan: Bar-Ilan University Press, 1983): 167–88 [in Hebrew]; Yael Zerubavel, "The Death of Memory and the Memory of Death: Masada and the Holocaust as Historical Metaphors," *Representations* 45 (1994): 72–100; Don Handelman and Lea Shamgar-Handelman, "The Presence of Absence: The Memorialism of National Death in Israel," in *Grasping Land: Space and Place in Contemporary Israeli Discourse and Experience*, ed. Eyal Ben-Ari and Yoram Bilu (Albany: SUNY Press, 1997), 85–128.
[11] Yechiam Weitz, "The Political Connection: Israeli Political Parties and the Memory of the Holocaust in the 1950s," *Iyunim Bitkumat Israel* 6 (1996): 271–87 [in Hebrew].
[12] Ofer, "How and What."

integrating the Holocaust's story in contemporary memory and identity within the interpretation given at the time to the Holocaust's meaning and lessons in the Jewish nation's everyday life.

These questions had ramifications for events at Yad Vashem. The institution's "agents of memory" – Mordechai Shenhavi, who originated the idea of Yad Vashem; Dinur; Mark Uveeler, who represented the Claims Conference on Yad Vashem's directorate; architects Arieh El-Hanani and Arieh Sharon; and many others who were active over the years in establishing and building the Mount of Remembrance – all acted within the state's historical reality in its early years. After confronting many complications, they were ultimately able to integrate a memorial to the Holocaust, one that contained their interpretation of what had taken place and its ramifications for the State of Israel's values, within the Israeli landscape. Their interpretation made it necessary for them to face many loaded questions and conflicts about the prevailing view of Holocaust commemoration at the time and to clarify the relationship between Holocaust and heroism; between victims and heroes; between Holocaust and a Jewish state as an entity ostensibly representing the Jewish Diaspora. The Martyrs' and Heroes' Remembrance (Yad Vashem) Law, passed in August 1953, was also, to a great extent, the most significant catalyst in Yad Vashem's construction. It reflected the quandary of the nation's leaders regarding Holocaust commemoration. The law expressed the Israeli legislators' and the heads of Yad Vashem's – and perhaps all of humanity's – continued inability to understand what had happened "there"; what the role of a Remembrance Authority should be; and how it should deal with the task of immortalizing six million people who had died. How was it even possible to find and invent significant ways to facilitate remembering such a deviation from human behavior and human understanding?[13]

This deliberation, of course, also had architectural implications, and these were expressed in the many different plans proposed to Yad Vashem over the years, which will also be discussed in this volume. But the center of the debate was the extensive, agonizing struggle of the Remembrance Authority's heads regarding the memorial site's look and development, ultimately expressed in the site's appearance. Complex issues of the crystallizing Zionist and Israeli identity against the backdrop of the Holocaust; various political needs; the culture of commemoration and memory – that is, the question of what form commemoration would take

---

[13] Amos Elon, *The Israelis: Founders and Sons* (London: Weidenfeld and Nicolson, 1971), 207–209.

and how it would be expressed in plastic and spatial form[14] – all were decisively influential within Yad Vashem's process of planning and construction. As we will see, the original idea of designing Yad Vashem as a large site with two central memorial buildings – a Holocaust sanctuary, dedicated to the annihilation of the Jews and, across from it, a Heroism sanctuary, immortalizing Jewish fighting – was replaced in time with the idea of building the Hall of Remembrance. Yad Vashem's plans were redesigned such that ultimately the memorial compound contained one powerful, though not particularly large, building, devoted exclusively to memorializing the six million Jews murdered in the Holocaust; its power derived from the fact that it contained nothing but the names of the concentration and death camps, an eternal flame, and a symbolic grave in which ashes of those who had perished, brought from Europe, were buried.

The chronicles of building Yad Vashem are tied, of course, to the wider question of Holocaust commemoration in Israeli society, to the way in which it formed during the critical decades that followed the Second World War, and especially to how Holocaust commemoration evolved after the founding of the state. Collective memory has taken a growing place in academic research in recent years, not only within sociology and other humanities but also for historians and geographers who study the influence of culture on landscape. Collective memory is the image of the past being shaped through a struggle between different, sometimes conflicting, agents of memory.[15] Conflicting ideological and political interests lead to the creation of myths, to the erection of symbols and monuments, to different ceremonies that are exploited to influence the national agenda. The construction of Holocaust memory in the years that followed the Second World War made similar use of symbols, myths, and monuments and reflected the changes that took place in the State of Israel's public and political approach toward the Holocaust and its lessons. This memory changed often over the years and serves as a reflection of the processes that shaped Israeli society and defined its collective identity. The process of construction of the Mount of Remembrance is unparalleled in its relevance and significance; it reflects many years of deliberations about the correct and most significant way to commemorate the Holocaust.

---

14 Maoz Azaryahu, "(Re)locating Redemption – Jerusalem: The Wall, Two Mountains, a Hill and the Narrative Construction of the Third Temple," *Journal of Modern Jewish Studies* 1 (2002): 22–35.
15 Daniel Gutwein, "The Privatization of the Holocaust: Memory, Historiography, and Politics," *Dapim – Studies on the Holocaust* 15 (1998): 7–52.

The Book's Structure and Chronological Framework

The book spans one generation, some three decades, between the mid-forties and the mid-seventies. During this time, the State of Israel was founded at the end of a prolonged military struggle, Israeli society developed, and patterns of government, society, and culture were established. But these general processes had nearly no effect on the evolution of Yad Vashem; the Remembrance Authority's milestones were different: in 1945, Yad Vashem's secretariat was appointed; in June 1947, the board of governors, the body in which the representatives of the different bodies that established Yad Vashem sat, assembled. Between these two events, in 1946, the first outline for the memorial site was prepared. In 1953 the Yad Vashem Law was enacted. One year later, in 1954, an agreement was signed between Yad Vashem and the Claims Conference, and the cornerstone for the first building on the Mount of Remembrance was laid. In 1956, two symposia were convened to discuss the architectural future of Yad Vashem, and, on 27 Nisan 1961, the Hall of Remembrance was inaugurated. These are only a few of the important landmarks in the history of Yad Vashem and the Mount of Remembrance, but they demonstrate that the development of the Remembrance Authority, despite the influence of "external" events taking place at the time in the world and in the State of Israel, occurred almost independently and nearly isolated from them. The same can be said of the Eichmann trial's marginal influence on Yad Vashem's development: in researching this volume, no evidence was found that the dramatic trial, which had such a far-reaching effect on Israeli society's Holocaust consciousness, contributed in any way to the building of Yad Vahem. This book's validation and chapter structure are therefore interior to Yad Vashem and reflect the place's internal development. The book opens in 1942, when Mordechai Shenhavi proposed establishing a Holocaust memorial site in the land of Israel, and closes on 27 Nisan 1976, with the inauguration of the second part of the *Warsaw Ghetto Uprising* monument by Nathan Rapoport. During those thirty-four years, the Mount of Remembrance was built, its landscape was designed, and other buildings, monuments, and symbols were added to it.

Aside from its introduction and conclusion, this book contains five chapters that move chronologically and span the story of the planning and building of Yad Vashem from the forties until the mid-seventies.

The first chapter is occupied with the period between 1942, when Mordechai Shenhavi first raised the idea of establishing a Holocaust memorial site in the land of Israel, and 1948, with the state's founding. It was during these years that great efforts were made to establish Yad Vashem, both organizationally and in terms of building the memorial compound. The question of the site's location remained open and a number of plans were made to build it in the Hula Valley, the western Jezreel Valley, the Ma'ale HaHamisha area, Ramat Rachel, and Jerusalem.

The book's second chapter focuses on the period between 1948 and 1953, a low point in the institute's history; it was, in effect, closed due to its failure to establish itself in the late Mandate period. The dramatic change for Yad Vashem came in 1953, when the Knesset enacted the Yad Vashem Law, resolving that a state authority would be founded, charged with commemorating the Holocaust and heroism and preserving its legacy.

Chapter 3 examines the years of founding Yad Vashem, with Dinur at the helm, from right after the Yad Vashem Law's enactment in 1953 until after the two symposia met in 1956, symposia that to a large extent determined the construction plan for Yad Vashem and grounded the institution's future.

The book's fourth chapter focuses on the years 1956–1961, emphasizing the complicated and extensive process that the institute's heads and the team of architects that took part in the planning and building of the Mount of Remembrance underwent before the inauguration of the Hall of Remembrance on 27 Nisan 1961.

The fifth chapter examines the fifteen years that elapsed between 1961 and 1976, from the opening of the Hall of Remembrance to the final inauguration of Nathan Rapoport's *Warsaw Ghetto Uprising* monument. This time period was critical in the shaping of the memorial landscape of "historical" Yad Vashem, before the big change that took place in 2005, showing how and when the historical museum, synagogue, heroism monument, and other memorial elements were integrated.

Finally, the book's conclusion puts Yad Vashem's construction in historical perspective and underscores the singularity of the institute and its construction process.

While the book presents the history of Yad Vashem chronologically, from 1942 to 1976, it also examines a number of ideas that are woven throughout all of the chapters – the deliberations about the proper way to commemorate the Holocaust in the State of Israel; the question of the relationship between Holocaust and heroism and its ramifications on constructing a memorial; the link between architecture and Holocaust remembrance, a subject that occupied people both in Israel and abroad; and the question of Yad Vashem's location. The ultimate resolution of these dilemmas and questions led to the creation of one of the world's most powerful and emotional commemorational sites, a place dedicated to the memory of the Holocaust and the annihilation of six million Jews.

Chapter 1
Yad Vashem until the End of 1948

In developing the first plans for a Holocaust commemoration site in the land of Israel in the period before the founding of the state, its proponents confronted crucial questions: What must remembrance look like? How can an event that was so unprecedented in this history of the Jewish nation be most fittingly immortalized? The challenge of building a Holocaust commemoration site in the land of Israel compelled Yad Vashem's organizers to confront profound questions about their own perceptions of the horrors of the war and the physical expression of remembrance, with the erection of buildings, monuments, towers, and plazas.

The deliberations about Holocaust commemoration in the years that preceded the founding of the State of Israel and the enactment of the Yad Vashem Law (1953) have already been the subject of research. Scholars have studied the attempts made to establish the institution and the many difficulties involved.[1] The present chapter focuses on the different plans and ideas for giving physical and spatial form to Holocaust commemoration in the local landscape that arose in the forties, focusing on the circumstances surrounding Yad Vashem's founding and its ultimate failure to erect a memorial site. Aside from examining the issue of the site's location, the chapter discusses the institution's debate about the appropriate way to memorialize the Jews' extermination and the heroism of those who fought the Nazis, framing the issue within the deliberations over the plans for commemoration that were proposed at the time.

Yad Vashem's planners confronted these questions following the end of the war, at a time when the world at large was also pondering the proper forms for Holocaust commemoration.[2] Zionist bodies in the land of Israel had not yet developed monumental memorial architecture,[3] and local architects had next to

---

[1] Tydor Baumel, "Commemorating the Holocaust"; Roni Stauber, *A Lesson for this Generation – Holocaust and Heroism in Israeli Public Discourse in the 1950s* (Jerusalem: Yad Izhak Ben-Zvi, 2000) [in Hebrew]; Cohen, *Holocaust Research*; Mooli Brog, "'In Blessed Memory of a Dream': Mordechai Shenhavi and Initial Holocaust Commemoration Ideas in Palestine, 1942–1945," *Yad Vashem Studies* 30 (2002): 241–69 [in Hebrew]; Mooli Brog, "A Memorial for the Fighters and Commemoration of the Victims: Efforts by the Va'ad Haleumi to Establish Yad Vashem, 1946–1949," *Cathedra* 119 (2006): 87–120 [in Hebrew]; Mooli Brog, *Who Should Be Remembered? The Struggle for Commemorative Recognition at Yad Vashem* (Jerusalem: Carmel, 2019) [in Hebrew].
[2] Young, *The Texture*.
[3] Monk, *Aesthetic*.

no experience building large memorial structures; they certainly had not faced a subject so complex as giving comprehensive architectural expression to the memory of the Holocaust. Moreover, Jewish heritage had, for generations, preferred to immortalize devastation in more traditional forms.[4] This further underscores the unique nature of the proposals raised beginning in 1942, at the height of the Second World War and when the true proportions of the destruction were not yet clear; it was then that an attempt was made to commemorate the Holocaust architecturally, quantitatively, and symbolically by building a memorial site. These attempts were doomed to failure. It was only in 1953, after the passing of the Martyrs' and Heroes' Remembrance (Yad Vashem) Law, that Yad Vashem was born. Nonetheless, the early attempts served as the foundation for the building of the institution, erected in the fifties, for the inauguration of the Hall of Remembrance in 1961, and for the Mount of Remembrance's development in later periods.

Early Concepts

The idea of establishing a memorial in the land of Israel for the Jewish victims of the Holocaust was first raised in the summer of 1942. The initiator of the commemoration endeavor was Mordechai Shenhavi who, among other things, worked at the Jewish National Fund – or JNF – at the time.[5] Shenhavi drafted a document titled "The Idea of Immortalizing All of the Losses at the Feet of the Jewish Nation's Catastrophe in light of the Horrors of the Nazis and the War."[6]

In his mind's eye Shenhavi saw a "garden," extending some dozens of acres, devoted to this memory. He was inclined to situate the undertaking in proximity to kibbutzim and pioneering settlement spaces. Initially, he suggested building it close to the kibbutzim of Metzudat Ussishkin in the northern Hula Valley, feeling

---

4 Yosef Haim Yerushalmi, *Zakhor: Jewish History and Jewish Memory* (Seattle and London: University of Washington Press, 1982).
5 On Shenhavi's biography see: KMHA, Mordechai Shenhavi's file; David Zait, *Visions in Action: The Life Story of Mordechai Shenhabi* (Givat Haviva: Yad Yaari, 2005) [in Hebrew]; Izhar Ben Nahum, *Visions in Action: The Life Story of Mordechai Shenhabi* (Dalia: Yad Yaari, 2011) [in Hebrew]; Brog, "In Blessed Memory." Archival sources are in Hebrew unless otherwise indicated. The Jewish National Fund, known in Hebrew as *Keren Kayemet le-Yisrael*, is referred to in this book by its English name or the initialism JNF; however, the archival sources used in footnotes give KKL, as per the name of the archive.
6 Stauber, *A Lesson*, 14–33.

Figure 1: Mordechai Shenhavi, ca. 1930 (KMHA, Unknown photographer).

that the center of commemoration would be in Safed, where a "pavilion containing the chronicles of the suffering and the victims" would be established.[7]

Shortly thereafter, Shenhavi prepared a more coherent and detailed plan for the commemoration enterprise, this time under the title "Outline of a National Enterprise." This he submitted to the head office of the JNF, the body he hoped would take on Holocaust remembrance in the land of Israel, in September 1942. He believed that the JNF could be incentivized to participate in the enterprise due to its need for a "new slogan" that could easily make it a "pipeline for significant funds."[8] Shenhavi was certain that if his plan had a basis for substantial funding, the JNF's management could be convinced to adopt it and execute it over five years.

Jewish tradition prefers to commemorate tragedies in time-honored forms, usually through prayer or publishing religious tomes.[9] Shenhavi's proposal, then, was a singular one, bold in its vision of Holocaust commemoration in architectural, quantitative, and symbolic terms, to be executed through the building of a memorial compound in the local landscape. He proposed declaring a national enterprise for the fallen and allocating thousands of acres upon which "Gan Am" (the nation's garden) would be founded.[10] The center of the commemoration enterprise, he determined, would be a "built institute, containing

---

[7] YVA, AM1 288; Brog, *Who Should*, 64.
[8] Yoram Bar-Gal, *Propaganda and Zionist Education: The Jewish National Fund, 1924–1947* (Rochester, NY: University of Rochester Press, 2003).
[9] Yerushalmi, *Zakhor*.
[10] YVA, AM1 287, Shenhavi, "The Outlines of a National Enterprise," September 1942.

within it the names of all of the fallen and murdered Jews around the world." Inside the building and nearby would be pavilions devoted to describing Jewish heroism throughout history, a museum, and a symbolic cemetery for those who had died overseas,[11] which should serve to resolve the dilemma of the lack of a true grave for those who had been murdered.[12]

This was the first time that this duality – not just destruction, but heroism, too – was raised in the discussion of physical Holocaust commemoration. Shenhavi's wish, a wish that grew as news of the devastation in Europe grew and as the struggle against the Nazis intensified, stood at its core: to immortalize the millions who had died and to highlight the Jewish heroism and combat that had been displayed during the war.

Shenhavi's proposal was submitted to the JNF's management and discussed by its members a number of times. Opinions were mixed, and largely negative. The JNF was uncertain whether the proposal contributed to the Fund's goal – collecting resources for the purchase of Zionist land. "Can the suffering of Israel be used as a tool?" JNF director general Abraham Granovsky (Granot) asked, determining that "we are not a Fund for educating the nation." This statement set the tone for the discussion; most of the participants opposed Shenhavi's proposal, including Jacob Tchernowitz Tsur, director of the Public Relations Department, who said that "a nice garden, a center with memorial plaques, a cemetery [the things that Shenhavi proposed to include] – are all well and good for satiated Jews who rest on their laurels, but not for hungry Jews [like the survivors after the war]." He felt that instead of the commemoration proposed by Shenhavi, the purchase of property for settling the land of Israel should be expanded for the benefit of the orphans and survivors who would soon be arriving from Europe, adding that "for a symbol alone – we do not have free time." Abraham Epstein, another participant in the discussion, also had reservations. He felt that interest in the "pantheon" Shenhavi proposed would wane over the years, suggesting, instead, a simple memorial monument in the Jewish cemetery on the Mount of Olives and a focus on purchasing land for the Jewish soldiers who would be released at the end of the war and settle in the land of Israel. Ultimately, the JNF, while not rejecting Shenhavi's proposal, had "strong criticism of its organizational and psychological foundations." Shenhavi was asked to rework the plan and submit it for reexamination.[13]

---

11 Ibid.
12 CZA, KKL5/12925, Shenhavi, "Nations' Monument Dedicated to the Memorialization of the Victims of the Diaspora and a Memorial for the Jewish Fighter," December 7, 1944.
13 HHA, 3–95. 14 (6), Shenhavi's proposal for the JNF (September 10, 1942): "National Enterprise for the Commemoration of the Destroyed Diaspora, Negotiations and Debates," August 1946;

Shenhavi indeed revamped the proposal. In order to do so, he met with members of JNF's management and searched for a fitting location for the enterprise. The idea of situating it in the northern Hula Valley was struck from the agenda due to the region's relative distance, and he sought other locations – for example, in the western area of the Jezreel Valley and near his kibbutz, Mishmar HaEmek. Granot and Shenhavi agreed that the area had many advantages. Jewish settlement there was widespread, "containing natives from most of the lands in Europe and America"; the distance to Haifa and to Jewish settlement in the Galilee and the Jordan Valley was small; and travel from Jerusalem and Tel Aviv was relatively easy. Shenhavi suggested that aside from erecting memorial structures, accommodations and educational buildings could be built there as well – a university for the people and hotels in which Diaspora Jewry, as well as "the public from the land of Israel looking for rest and respite," could be hosted, making the site a regional center for travel.[14]

In January 1943, Shenhavi proposed a two-stage plan for the memorial site.[15] It focused first on activities that should be held at the site and then on the physical dimensions of the memorial venue and the institutions and endeavors it housed. In the center, he proposed building a "garden of the nation" or a "rebirth garden," a spot dedicated to the establishment of a homeland in the land of Israel. Another space in the memorial enterprise would contain the "pavilion to the missing," dedicated to those who had perished in the Holocaust, where memorial books would preserve their names; it would include "special markers" commemorating the missing. The monumental structure must express "the magnitude of the Holocaust that has come upon us and serve as a sign for generations of the will power to exist that lives among the people." Shenhavi proposed that the site serve as "a center around which institutions and enterprises serving as additional pipelines for reinforcing the national spirit and the capacity of the JNF can operate."[16]

The personal relationship between Shenhavi and Haifa architect Munio Weinraub (Gitai)[17] led to Weinraub's preparation of an architectural illustration of the pavilion for the lost at Shenhavi's request. It was a three-story, round tower

---

HHA, 3–95.14 (1), meeting concerning Shenhavi's proposal with the participation of Granovsky, Epstein, and HaEzrahi, November 21, 1942.
14 HHA, 3–95. 14 (1), Remarks about the proposed plan, following a conversation with Granovsky, November 9, 1942.
15 KMHA, S-29, 1, Shenhavi's proposal for the JNF, January 18, 1943.
16 Ibid.
17 Richard Ingersoll, *Munio Gitai Weinraub: Bauhaus Architect in Eretz Israel* (photographs by Gabriele Basilico; Milan: Electa, 1994), 228–35; Winfried Nerdinger, ed., *Munio Weinraub Amos Gitai Atchitektur und Film in Israel* (Munchen: Edition Minerva, 2008), 10–17.

located atop a hill, neoclassical in style and made of stone. The ground floor of the memorial structure was comprised of stone arches and above it was a tall, narrow, cylindrical space split into strips, with long, narrow windows at the top. At the height of the tower was a dome with a large round opening at its center. The tower's internal space was simple and devoid of ornamentation, except for a symbolic Star of David sketched in the middle of the round floor, at the center of which burned an eternal flame. Further within the round hall, Weinraub placed a long monument, hinting perhaps at the "grave of the anonymous victim."[18]

Figure 2: Munio Weinraub's 1943 illustration of the pavilion for the lost (HHA).

In February 1943, Shenhavi submitted another letter to the JNF's central office, which included clarifications of his previous proposal as well as additional details. He expressed his wish to find a fitting name for the enterprise and to declare Hebrew its first language. He also emphasized the importance of immortalizing

---

18 HHA, 3–95. 7 (1), Sketches (on transparent paper), unsigned, 1943.

Jewish combat and soldiers in the Allies' struggle against the Nazis, both those who were feared dead and those who he hoped would achieve victory over Germany and soon return home. He predicted that the "pavilion of the Jewish soldier," and, around it, the "grove of the Jewish soldier," would become a site for pilgrimage from around the world, including delegations from military federations and soldiers' organizations coming specially to the remembrance site.[19] As we will see, the struggle against the Nazis would soon become a central component in Shenhavi's understanding of the memorial enterprise, part of his perception that while the Jews' extermination must be remembered, so must the heroism displayed during the battle against the Nazis in Europe. This was tied to the way in which his movement, HaShomer HaTzair, perceived the events of the Holocaust and the emphasis it placed on ghetto uprisings and revolts against the Nazis in contrast with the terrible devastation.[20]

Shenhavi's new proposal was discussed by the heads of the JNF; a special committee was even convened to deliberate. Nonetheless, it was once again rejected. It was not just that "[Shenhavi's] proposal looks to the past while the JNF looks to the future," it stated, but also that his plan to establish a cultural-national enterprise was entirely outside of the JNF's central goal, the redemption of land.[21] The challenge to the JNF's financial appeals was only one problem; there were also practical reasons for rejecting the plan. At that time, the JNF was considering planting a "forest of the Jewish soldier" near Kibbutz Ma'ale HaHamisha, dedicated to the Jews who fought against the Nazis in Allied armies;[22] this conflicted with Shenhavi's proposal to establish the "pavilion of the Jewish soldier." However, some members of JNF's management did feel that the organization should establish a memorial to the Diaspora and the Holocaust in the land of Israel, unrelated to Shenhavi's proposal. "There is a national necessity to establish a type of *memento mori* for generations which will tell each Jew, and especially each Jew still living in the Diaspora, the shocking chronicles of a group of millions of exiles," determined Idov Cohen, editor of the JNF's monthly magazine, *Karnenu*, after Shenhavi's proposal had been rejected. He felt that a garden should be established, with an "architectural" feature at its center, and serve as a pilgrimage destination. An architectural competition should be held that would constitute a "cooperation of Jewish thought and

---

19 KMHA, S-29, 1, Shenhavi to the JNF, February 21, 1943.
20 KMHA, S-29, 1, Shenhavi, "A Proposal for Registration and Commemoration of the Pogroms' Victims and Those Who Fought War and Its Victims," n.d.
21 HHA, 3–95. 14 (2), protocol of a meeting held in the JNF offices, April 1, 1943.
22 HHA, 3–95. 14 (6), Shenhavi's proposal for the JNF (September 10, 1942): National Enterprise for the Commemoration of the Destroyed Diaspora, Negotiations and Debates, August 1946.

imagination from all lands"; the memorial building would "serve as an expression of a symbol of the spiritual-religious life of the land and the nation reborn." One significant innovation in his words was the suggestion that the memorial site should be located in Jerusalem's vicinity, a city that had, until that point, not held a prominent place in the Jewish remembrance landscape.[23]

The JNF's renewed rejection did not weaken Shenhavi's stance, and he persisted in his efforts to found a memorial enterprise. In June of 1943, he once again petitioned Granot, expressing the wish that the JNF discuss his idea another time. He may have hoped that the distressing news about the methodical extermination of the Jews that was emerging from Europe with greater frequency would persuade the Fund's heads. He also attempted to recruit other bodies to take part in the commemoration efforts, for example, the Youth Aliyah (*aliyat hanoar*). He felt that the fusing of "his" memorial site with an organization that focused on saving children and youth and organizing their immigration to the land of Israel might succeed.[24] The death of Henrietta Szold in early 1945 brought the potential collaboration to a halt.

What further spurred Shenhavi was the fact that he was not the only one occupied with Holocaust commemoration. With the end of the Second World War and the ever-clearing picture of the genocide that had taken place, other agents began to focus on commemoration as well. In November 1944, the World Jewish Congress (WJC) discussed the subject and charged two of its members, Baruch Zuckermann, responsible for the Congress's Organization Department, and Jacob Helman from South America, with the task of creating a plan on the subject to present to the Congress. In February 1945, they submitted their proposal to build "a monument in memory of our pure and saintly" at Mount Carmel, where they would establish a building whose rooms would be devoted to the Jewish communities in the lands of devastation. At the center of the complex, in one of the memorial building's rooms, they proposed placing "an artistic symbol of a mass grave." Aside from that, it would also contain "gas chambers," "a train car of the transported," a room containing the names of those murdered, a room devoted to the ghetto fighters, and rooms dedicated to the different lands of destruction.[25]

---

[23] HHA, 3–95. 14 (1), Idov Cohen, "Remarks and Counter Proposals," April 1, 1943.
[24] HHA, 3–95. 14 (1), "Proposal for the Initiation of National Commemoration Enterprise for the Memory of the Victims Killed by the Nazis and Those Who Lost Their Life in Battlefields," July 1944.
[25] KMHA, S-29, 1, Baruch Zuckermann, "Eternal Memory," February 1945 [in Yiddish]. For a Hebrew version see: Baruch Zuckermann, "Yad Vashem's Idea," *Gesher* 4, no. 2 (1958): 71.

Hebrew University also initiated a Holocaust memorial project. The institution's leadership elected to dedicate some of the land on Mount Scopus to a "monument to the Diaspora," an institute devoted to researching European Jewry's past. According to the plan, a building would be constructed to include a lecture hall, a museum with the remains of Jewish culture and history, and a "collection building" for memorial items "that remained after the destruction of the European diaspora."[26]

The interest that Holocaust commemoration provoked in the land of Israel was evident in the newspapers at the time. *Yedioth Ahronoth* devoted an entire page to the question "How Should We Commemorate Our Martyrs?" in which it brought different opinions on the subject.[27] Private suggestions included establishing a memorial monument "in the style of the Old City wall" for the diaspora's children;[28] inaugurating a monument on the shores of Tel Aviv;[29] building a "Jewish military memorial hill" or a stone monument of "Jews who fought and fell in the campaign"; and "names engraved on stone plaques and distributed on one of Jerusalem's hills creating a sort of 'settlement' of great political importance."[30]

These proposals agitated Shenhavi, stirring his concern that they would predate his own enterprise. He warned that "different proposals are arising and advancing slowly, committees are being formed, people with 'interests' are appearing, and the holy goal and all that is hidden within it will be ripped to pieces." He adamantly insisted that Granot allow him to publicize his proposal – which had only been discussed within the JNF until that point – within the Jewish public in the land of Israel.[31]

Granot took his time; it was only in February of 1945 that he convened another discussion about the question of commemoration. This time, too, most were opposed to Shenhavi's plan, primarily because it undermined the Fund's goals. "If we name Kfar Baruch [a settlement founded in 1926 in the western Jezreel Valley named for the philanthropist Baruch Kahane] for a Jew who gave a certain amount of money," Tchernowitz claimed, "it constitutes a terrible disproportionality when next to that village stands the village of Warsaw," which

---

26 "Memorial for the Diaspora on Mount Scopus," *Haaretz*, February 12, 1945. All newspaper articles are in Hebrew unless stated otherwise.
27 "How Should We Commemorate Our Martyrs," *Yedioth Ahronoth*, May 15, 1945; "All Those Who Want to Erect a Memorial for the Diaspora – Unite!" *Yedioth Ahronoth*, May 25, 1945.
28 YVA, AM1 396, T. Dostovski to Yosef Sprinzak, February 27, 1945.
29 Y. Beham, "A Letter to the Editor," *Davar*, May 16, 1944.
30 YVA, AM1 396, "A Few Notes about a 'Hebrew Military Memorial Monument.'"
31 HHA, 3–95. 14 (3), Shenhavi to Granovsky, February 12, 1945.

made no contribution to the JNF and its goals. "The Yishuv must establish a monument to the devastated Diaspora, symbolic and simple"; nonetheless, the truism that "a Jew prefers purpose over sentiment" was stated with great confidence, rejecting the possibility that the Yishuv would want to commemorate the Holocaust's victims widely. Others feared the too-broad scope of Shenhavi's plan, feeling that a nation that preferred to support Holocaust survivors would be offended when the JNF focused on symbols. There was a need to reinforce the JNF's call for "land, land, land," the JNF circles claimed, as "we will not build it all on tears."[32]

Yad Vashem: A Commemoration Enterprise for a Devastated Diaspora

When Shenhavi was informed of his ideas' rejection anew, he demanded that they be circulated in the public, feeling that the pressure that would be generated by public opinion would convince the JNF's heads to execute his plan. Shenhavi managed to hold off for a few more weeks, but "the need to keep the secret ended once the JNF feigned an inability to take on such a large project on its own," he later said.[33] In early May 1945, after he had reformulated his ideas in a document that was more than twenty pages long, which he distributed to various bodies within the Zionist movement,[34] he also published a short version in the local newspapers. The document's name was "Yad Vashem – Enterprise for the Commemoration of the Destroyed Diaspora." Shenhavi had originally suggested naming the enterprise *Yad la-Gola ha-Nehrevet* (memorial to the destroyed Diaspora) but, later in 1945, the name had been changed to *Yad va-Shem la-Gola ha-Nehrevet* (a memorial and name to the destroyed Diaspora). The name was taken from the book of Isaiah (56:5): "To them I will give within my temple and its walls a **memorial (*yad*) and a name (*va-shem*)**" [my emphasis]. The name was suggested by Rabbi Moshe Burshtein, head of the JNF's Religious Department.[35] In Shenhavi's document, he emphasized how

---

32 HHA, 3–95. 14 (1), "Summary of Referents Meeting on the Subject of Commemoration Enterprise," February 19, 1945.
33 HHA, 3–95. 2 (6), "On the History of Yad Vashem."
34 CZA, S25/5204, "'Yad Vashem' – Enterprise for the Commemoration of the Destroyed Diaspora: Outlines for a Plan to Commemorate the Memory of the Diaspora," May 2, 1945. Quotes are taken from this source.
35 "Personal notice by M. Shenhavi," *Al HaMishmar*, January 18, 1960; Brog, *We Should*, 78.

the nation will establish a testament-monument in memory of its destroyed communities and its sons who were killed and devastated, in memory of its heroes who fought its war, a war of honor and daring never before seen. This testament-monument will be a teacher and guide for the coming generations, a sign and a warning to us, and a certificate of faith and commitment to the world around us. This testament-monument will protect the memory of every single victim who fell and allow all people of Israel to sanctify the memory of its victims.[36]

Aside from the many organizational dimensions Shenhavi discussed in his document, he also referred to the site's physical outline. He planned a "remembrance hall" standing at the center of Yad Vashem, in which the "pavilion of the Jewish soldier" would be dedicated to the Jewish fighters who took part in resisting the Nazis and to those who fell during the war. The remembrance hall would curate memory books and "special stone markers" on which the names of those who had perished would be inscribed. This shrine, Shenhavi emphasized, must be

monumental in scope and shape. Symbols are not enough for us this time. It is not enough to give the names of ruined communities to new communities [as the JNF had suggested]. It is not enough to plant groves [as the JNF had intended], or [create] boulevards in memory of those fallen. It is not enough to establish archives to the Diaspora [as others suggested], nor to commemorate select communities or great personalities in special "memorial books."

In contrast with all of these, Shenhavi proposed building a "monument to the anonymous victim," dedicated to the memory of the unidentified, those whose names would not be commemorated in the aforementioned memorial books. Shenhavi, who continued to be aided by Munio Weinraub, created a detailed written description of the remembrance hall and the complex around it. His proposal had it as a "closed, round hall" at whose center stood "the monument to the anonymous victim." The hall would be divided into twenty commemoration cells, devoted to the countries of destruction, on whose walls would be plaques with the names of the millions of victims, divided geographically. In order to overcome the symbolic and geographic gap between the land of Israel and the

---

36 YVA, AM1 287, Shenhavi, "Yad Vashem for the Diaspora," May 2, 1945; "A Monument and a Name (*yad va-shem*) for the Destroyed Diaspora," *Davar*, May 25, 1945. Later, it was Shragai who suggested that the name of the institute be "Yad Vashem," while its subtitle would be "To the Annihilated Diaspora and to the War of Independence." This proposal was accepted on February 25, 1946. It was decided that the official name of the institute would be "Yad Vashem: To the Victims of the Extermination, to the Ghetto Fighters, to the Destroyed Communities, to Those Who Lost Their Lives during Fighting, and to the Volunteers." See: HHA, 3–95. 18 (5), Protocol of Yad Vashem management meeting, February 25, 1946.

lands of extinction in Europe and to guarantee Yad Vashem a monopoly on Holocaust commemoration in the Jewish world, he suggested making the monument a model that could be reproduced in Jewish cemeteries around the world and erected in the places in which extermination had taken place. Shenhavi also suggested creating "supplementary undertakings" for the remembrance hall – a pavilion dedicated to the chronicles of "heroism of the nation throughout generations, especially the ghetto fighters"; a central archive of the chronicles of the Diaspora, including a collection of photographs, pictures, and documents; an archive of the history of the land of Israel and the Zionist enterprise in particular; an exhibition hall and library; and a research center devoted to Diaspora history. Aside from these "content" buildings, he also hoped Yad Vashem would hold a hall and plazas for large assemblies; a synagogue for observant visitors; a hotel; accommodations for youth; and more.[37]

Shenhavi continued his feverish search for an appropriate site, now in Jerusalem and its surroundings. In the second half of the forties, the Zionist movement's efforts were focused on defining Jerusalem as the future capital city of the state that would be founded in the land of Israel,[38] and the city looked to many to be a fitting place for the establishment of Yad Vashem. In early June 1945, the board of the Jewish National Council met with representatives of other Zionist bodies to consult on commemoration of European Jewry and, within this framework, also discussed the establishment of a memorial site in the land of Israel. Aside from the fact that they felt that "we must depart from private plans and make the subject the purview of an accredited national authority," Jerusalem was suggested as the site for commemoration.[39] David Remez, chair of the Jewish National Council, was adamant: "It appears that we must make the initial assumption that any memorial to the Diaspora that we wish to build – its center will be in Jerusalem, because it [Jerusalem] will illuminate for generations," he said, and proposed establishing the memorial on Mount Scopus, "the highest peak we have close to the Hebrew University," the most prominent Jewish-Zionist symbolic center in Jerusalem.[40] The Hebrew University on Mount Scopus had been,

---

[37] CZA, J1-3610, Shenhavi, "A Hand (*yad*) and Name (*va-shem*) to the Destroyed Diaspora," July 22, 1945.
[38] Motti Golani, *Zion in Zionism: Zionist Policy and the Question of Jerusalem, 1937–1949* (Tel Aviv: Tel Aviv University and the Ministry of Defense, 1992) [in Hebrew]; Yehoshua Ben Arieh, ed., *Jerusalem and the British Mandate, Interaction and Legacy* (Jerusalem: Mishkenot Shah'ananim and Yad Izhak Ben-Zvi, 2003) [in Hebrew].
[39] "Conference Dedicated to the Building of a Memorial for the Diaspora," *Davar*, June 5, 1945.
[40] YVA, AM1 372, "Consultation on the Building of a Memorial for the Diaspora," June 4, 1945.

since its establishment in 1925, the Jewish-Zionist symbolic center in Jerusalem. The site's advantages were obvious – its height, 820 meters above sea level, visible from all parts of the city, as well as the ability to integrate the memorial enterprise within a university campus.[41] A memorial book recording the names of those who had perished would be preserved in a memorial tower built on Mount Scopus, the center of commemoration.[42] The National Council, it was decided, would take on the responsibility for putting together the different proposals for Holocaust commemoration and prepare recommendations in advance of a session of the Zionist General Council slated to take place at the Zionist Congress in London later that year.[43]

In parallel to the National Council's activity, other bodies raised proposals about the look and location of the monument to the Holocaust. The heads of Jerusalem's Hevra Kadisha (burial society) suggested establishing a monument in the Jewish cemetery on the Mount of Olives, where the ashes of the Holocaust's victims, they proposed, could be buried once they were brought from Europe.[44] Others felt that the commemoration site should be located in Jerusalem's Old City, or in Ramat Gan, where it had been suggested that a Jewish museum, focusing on annihilation and combat during the Second World War, would be established.[45]

Behind the scenes, the struggle between Shenhavi and the JNF about the Fund's involvement in the memorial enterprise – involvement that Shenhavi felt was critical – continued. The JNF heads, on the other hand, chose to make an announcement in mid-1945: a memorial forest with five million trees would be planted and thirty settlements would be established and dedicated to the memory of those who had perished[46] – a place that would become, during the early fifties, the Martyr's Forest.[47]

---

41 Diana Dolev, "The Hebrew University's Master Plans, 1918–1948," in *The History of the Hebrew University of Jerusalem: Origins and Beginnings*, ed. Shmuel Katz and Michal Heyd (Jerusalem: Magnes Press, 1997): 257–80 [in Hebrew].
42 YVA, AM1 372, "David Remez on the Building of a Monument for the Diaspora," June 4, 1945. On the Hebrew University during the Mandate Period see Yair Paz, "The Hebrew University on Mount Scopus as a Secular Temple," in Katz and Heyd, *History of Hebrew University*, 281–308 [in Hebrew].
43 YVA, AM1 290, Shenhavi, "London Decision about Yad Vashem," n.d.
44 YVA, AM1 396, Israel Bardaky and Avraham Haim Zwebner to the Jewish National Council, July 12, 1945.
45 YVA, AM1 396, Asher Bavli to Avraham Krinitzi, November 16, 1944.
46 CZA, KKL5/12925, Zeev Shertok, "Memo," June 10, 1945.
47 Doron Bar, "The Martyrs' Forest, the JNF and Yad Vashem and the Commemoration of the Holocaust," *Cathedra* 140 (2011): 103–30 [in Hebrew].

The National Council and its Involvement in the Establishment of Yad Vashem

During a Zionist convention that convened in London in August 1945, a session of the Zionist General Council discussed the various proposals for Holocaust commemoration, and the plan of establishing Yad Vashem in the land of Israel within five years was adopted. "The Congress," it stated, "joins the initiative of the *Yad la-Golah* (memorial to the Diaspora) enterprise that will gather all of the heritage of the devastated Diaspora in the land of Israel and establish a fitting memorial monument to the nation's sons who fell as victims, sanctifying the name of Israel, and on the battlefields and the revolts in the days of horror."[48] The Congress decided that the memorial enterprise would be devoted to immortalizing the Jewish communities that had been destroyed in the Holocaust and emphasized that the proposed site would include a garden plot in the shape of the European continent, with flowerbeds marking the annihilated communities in a symbolic manner. It further concluded that the site would include a monument to the ghetto fighters and that a memorial tower would be dedicated to those who had fought against Hitler, including volunteers from the land of Israel who fought in the Allies' lines. It noted that "the death camps and ovens and instruments of torture [would] be presented in their eternal disgrace" and that "the human acts of the righteous among the nations [would] be noted and emphasized." At the end of the discussion, an "active secretariat" (management) was chosen to manage the memorial enterprise, headed by David Remez, chair of the National Council.[49] Elected to the secretariat were Mordechai Shenhavi; Shlomo Zalman Shragai, a Mizrachi man and member of the board of the Jewish Agency and the National Council; and Baruch Zuckermann, who was later replaced by Dr. Arieh Tartakover, a sociologist who also served as a representative in the World Jewish Congress. Their job was to establish a managing body for Yad Vashem that would include groups such as the National Council, the Jewish Agency, the JNF, the Hebrew University, the Chief Rabbinate, various veterans' organizations, and representatives of the World Jewish Congress. The joint task of all involved would be to establish and build Yad Vashem.

The JNF, being the oldest body and the most experienced at raising funds, appeared to be the natural candidate to shoulder the responsibility for the commemoration initiative, even if the National Council would be responsible for its

---

[48] CZA, S5/111351, "Decisions of World Zionist Council, Chapter 3, Decision 3"; CZA, J1/6442, "Yad Vashem"; Brog, "A Memorial."
[49] HHA, 3–95. 14 (6), Yad Vashem, London meeting, August 15, 1945.

image and content. Shenhavi was concerned about the continued opposition on the part of the national foundations, JNF and Keren Hayesod, and attempted to induce their heads to change their approach toward Yad Vashem. Aware as he was of the JNF's sensitivity to financial matters and with his desire to guarantee Yad Vashem's financial success, Shenhavi decided that the first phase would include collecting funds, primarily through recording names of victims, accompanied by a financial commitment on the part of their families, and by rescuing valuables from Europe, which would be transferred to the institution. Only later, when the necessary funds had been secured, would the planning of the area and the erection of buildings at the site take place.[50] Shenhavi attempted to recruit David Ben-Gurion, head of the Jewish Agency, in order to convince the JNF's heads; he even met with Prof. Chaim Weizmann, president of the World Zionist Organization, and suggested that he helm the project.[51]

In reality, the JNF and Keren Hayesod continued to give Shenhavi and the rest of Yad Vashem's management the cold shoulder. Granot felt that the enterprise would be possible only "if we can descend from the high peak of millions [of Palestine pounds necessary for founding the enterprise] and do something smaller that can be a memorial enterprise."[52] Keren Hayesod also fiercely opposed the direction taken for Yad Vashem's commemoration. "This idea [of Yad Vashem] must be uprooted from the world . . . it is not Jewish. To an extent, it approaches the cult of the dead, which goes against the foundations of Judaism," its people felt. Aside from asserting that the money should be dedicated to more pressing national needs in the land of Israel than Holocaust commemoration, the group raised another point: "for the second generation, the names that we collect there will mean nothing." There was a further objection to "presenting the gas chambers and immortalizing those instruments." Yosef Sprinzak, secretary of the Histadrut (General Organization of Workers) and a member of both the National Council and Keren Hayesod, slightly offset the tone: "These are not dead but martyrs," he claimed. Moreover, he noted, "This is historical commemoration for the coming generations," adding that

> it cannot be that in the land of our forefathers, in the land of our future, no great memorial will be erected to shock the generations of Jews and non-Jews. As there is a Western

---

50 MGWAA, "Incomes and Expanses of Yad Vashem," February 1946; HHA, 3–95. 14 (6), "Negotiation with the JNF on Yad Vashem," July 1, 1946.
51 KMHA, S-29, 1, Memorandum of a meeting between Shenhavi and Prof. Weizmann, April 23, 1946.
52 HHA, 3–95. 15 (6), Meeting about Yad Vashem, May 27, 1946.

Wall to commemorate the destruction of the state, so there should be a memorial to the destruction of the nation for our generation and our children and for all of the generations.[53]

The Outline for Yad Vashem

The discussions among Yad Vashem's management about the initiative's funding and form went on throughout 1946. Shenhavi, for his part, continued to search for a fitting place, examining the possibility of building in Anatot, north of Jerusalem, as well as in Ma'ale HaHamisha, Ramat Rachel, Safed, and the Negev region.[54] He also strengthened his relationship with the architects Weinraub and Alfred (Al) Mansfeld, partners in a Haifa architectural firm who were working diligently to prepare an architectural outline for Yad Vashem.[55] The management was won over by Shenhavi's enthusiasm and adopted his plans for a commemoration site,[56] despite the warning that "the professionals [architects] will still need to work a lot before the final form of the entire enterprise's plan and the 'remembrance hall' in particular will be final."[57] They continued to debate whether to distinguish between "the soldier and the slain" in Yad Vashem's commemoration. Shenhavi felt that this separation, between commemorating Jewish fighters in the Second World War and immortalizing those who had perished in the Holocaust was justified, necessary, and unavoidable, as "one act will swallow the other."[58] He succeeded in convincing his colleagues in Yad Vashem's management to support his vision and separate Holocaust from heroism, extermination from engaging battle – a vision that was expressed in the plans for the place.

In May 1946, Weinraub and Mansfeld presented their outline for Yad Vashem;[59] following an effort that had extended for four years, Shenhavi held in his hands a general plan for the commemoration site. And, despite the fact that a location had not yet been selected for the institution, the feeling was that this

---

53 CZA, S53/1671, Keren Hayesod directorate meeting, September 16, 1946.
54 KMHA, S-29, 5, Shenhavi, Items to discuss with Remez, November 12, 1945.
55 Weinraub and Mansfeld became partners in 1937 and cooperated until 1959. It seems that at the beginning the ties between Weinraub and Shenhavi were personal and only later, with the growing need to design and build Yad Vashem, Mansfeld became involved with the enterprise.
56 HHA, 3–95. 15 (6), "Yad Vashem: Basis of the Plan (a Proposition for a Discussion following Zuckermann, Shenhavi, and Shragai's Work)," n.d.
57 HHA, 3–95. 18 (5), Yad Vashem executive meeting, February 25, 1946.
58 HHA. 3–95. 14 (6), Shenhavi, Outlines of the operation and its mechanism, March, 1946.
59 HHA, 3–95. 7 (1), Weinraub and Mansfeld, "Yad Vashem: A Diagram of the Enterprise," 1:5,000, May 1946.

was a great achievement, bringing the complex ideas of Holocaust and heroism remembrance to architectural expression.

The plans had Yad Vashem spread across a vast area of roughly five hundred acres. At the time, the few physical memorial sites that existed were far smaller. Zionist commemoration was expressed in Abraham Malnikov's statue of a roaring lion, which stood in Kfar Giladi, or Alexander Zaïd's sculpture in Sheikh Abreik.[60] Yad Vashem's plan was immense in scope and was of a scale that, were it to be executed, would make it one of the largest memorial spaces in the land of Israel.

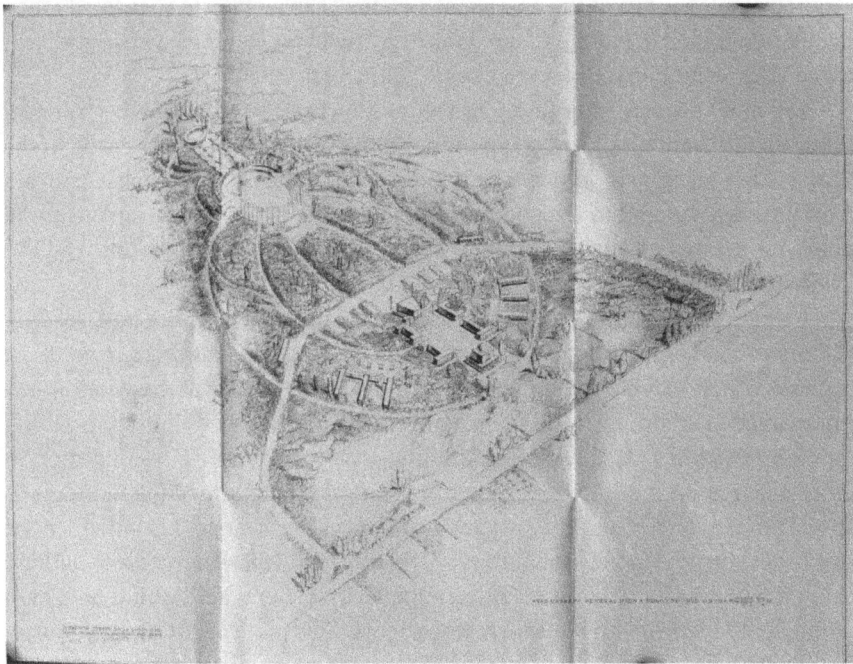

Figure 3: Weinraub and Mansfeld's 1946 outline for Yad Vashem (HHA).

Weinraub and Mansfeld's plan was based on round shapes, pathways, and routes that took visitors between its various components. The space was divided between the "educational" area, situated at the lower part of the site, and the "sacred," commemorative space, at the top. Most of the building was planned for the site's lower end, which included the supplementary ventures – the convention

---

[60] Gideon Ofrat, *Origins of Eretz-Israeli Sculpture: 1906–1939* (Herzliya: Herzliya Museum, 1990) [in Hebrew].

hall; offices; a building containing the names of the victims; the Diaspora archive; the history of Jewish heroism pavilion; the research centers; the hotels; the neighborhood for the institution's employees; and the synagogue. The area between the two spaces would be planted with trees, the JNF's planned memorial forest.[61]

On the upper part of the compound, an oval plaza, baroque in shape, elongated and of large dimensions, would house assemblies of tens of thousands of people. On the plaza's sidelines, a series of tall columns defined its boundaries; on one side, there was a rectangular monument placed on a raised platform, symbolizing the grave of the anonymous victim. The architects suggested erecting a torch there, an eternal flame flanked by two vast columns whose goal was to focus the attention on the ceremonies taking place there.[62]

The most prominent building in the architectural outline was the "remembrance hall," built on the outskirts of the square, spread across the slope in the shape of a semicircular portico. The building was made up of separate cells, memorial rooms devoted to the countries of extermination in which the memorial books for the destroyed communities – with the millions of names that Yad Vashem would collect over the years – would be kept.

A monumental staircase was planned above the remembrance hall, leading visitors to memorial structures dedicated to the righteous among the gentiles, to those who fell in battle, to the underground fighters, and to the ghetto revolutionaries. In addition, at the site's highest area, hinting at its importance, was the hall of fighters. This elliptical building, open to the skies, was devoted to those who fought the Nazis – whether in the armies that battled the Germans or as warriors in the forests, ghettos, and other loci of resistance. Also planned for this space was the "homeland field," an open garden whose border was defined using a boulevard of cypress trees, forming a circle; here there would be a map of the land of Israel with its Jewish settlements. This part constituted a counterweight to the "Europe field," highlighting Jewish pioneering and realization in contrast with the destruction in Europe.

Weinraub and Mansfeld's plan was prepared before Yad Vashem had identified a fitting location. This was a conceptual plan which, Shenhavi hoped, would be adapted to the place chosen. While the architects' worked, he maintained his efforts to find an appropriate place for a memorial site, helped by the JNF and the Palestine Land Development Company, who were asked to check

---

61 MGWAA, Schematic Diagram, 1:2,000, n.d.
62 Harold Marcuse, "Holocaust Memorials: The Emergence of a Genre," *American Historical Review* 115 (2010): 53–89.

the land inventory of Jewish or other ownership, in Jerusalem and around it. This was all done with great secrecy, primarily due to the fear that interest in purchasing land would raise its price.

A number of possibilities for appropriate plots of land in the areas around Jerusalem were raised. To the city's north, plots near Anatot (a location tied to the prophet Jeremiah) and near a number of Arab villages were examined. Gibeah, a biblical hilltop, appeared to be the most fitting, primarily due to its height and its visibility from certain areas in Jerusalem. The possibility of establishing the site near the grave of Samuel the prophet, at one of the highest peaks in the city's vicinity, arose. Another place considered was found to the west of Jerusalem, near Kibbutz Kiryat Anavim,[63] a proposal that would be seriously considered later on.

The chances of finding a location that was fitting for Yad Vashem in Jerusalem itself were smaller. The Hebrew University on Mount Scopus was a significant Jewish-Zionist stronghold, and the possibility of building Yad Vashem there had been examined earlier. But aside from Mount Scopus, the Palestine Land Development Company did not hold significant and large plots of land in the city. With the restrictions the British had placed on purchasing territory, the chances of winning their cooperation to identify a large plot of land in Jerusalem and execute Yad Vashem's extensive plan were negligible.[64]

In early May 1946, a year after the war's end, and against the backdrop of the publication of the architectural outline for Yad Vashem, the Jewish National Council convened to hear about the detailed plan that the secretariat had formulated. Remez noted that Jerusalem had been chosen for the memorial site, but could not give a specific location. On the basis of the plan that had just been prepared, he added that two halls would stand at the center of Yad Vashem, the remembrance hall and the heroism hall, and these would be tied together architecturally, complementing and contrasting with one another. According to the plan, the goal of building the Jewish heroism hall was to emphasize the participation of the land of Israel's Jews in fighting the Second World War and the spirit of volunteering displayed by the Yishuv. In the remembrance hall, on the other hand, an eternal flame would be kindled, dedicated to those who had perished. The focus of this room – and, in essence, the focus of Yad Vashem – would

---

[63] YVA, AM1 289, Land Development Company, "On the Search for a Site for Yad Vashem in the Area of Jerusalem," March 14, 1946.
[64] HHA, 3–95. 15 (7), Summary of a meeting with Thon [Yehoshua Thon] (manager of the Land Development Company), May 15, 1946.

be the monument, "a monument that Yad Vashem would orient to the Diaspora," which would be selected from all of the artists' proposals.[65]

Attempts to Promote the Yad Vashem Plan

Yad Vashem's heads made noticeable efforts to recruit people from among the Zionist bodies and to disseminate the tidings of Yad Vashem and the construction plans among various bodies and agencies – for example, the *Landsmannschaften*, associations of European communities. Their participation in Yad Vashem felt crucial to the success of the enterprise, and Yad Vashem's people laid out their plans and intentions in detail.[66] In contrast with the "captive audience" that were the *Landsmannschaften*, the question of the religious public in the land was more complex. When Shenhavi published his plan for Yad Vashem in early May 1945, he suggested building a "synagogue to meet the needs of religious visitors" there.[67] The primary reason for this was Shenhavi and others' wish to tie the land's religious community to the memorial site. This was a time in which observant Jews were debating how to fittingly commemorate the ruin of Jewish communities. They were less enthusiastic about the news of Holocaust memorialization emerging from the National Council and about Yad Vashem.[68] "The nation of Israel does not see eternal commemoration in man-made monuments, in stone, which will be eroded by time or destroyed by explosives, which can be desecrated and complicit in changing fate and times," *HaTzofe*, the Mizrachi movement's newspaper, asserted.[69] In contrast with the inclination of Shenhavi and others to ground reemembrance in Yad Vashem in building and monuments, rabbis wished to commemorate the murdered communities in a traditional Jewish form, in prayer, writing memorial books, and holding memorial ceremonies, Mishnah learning, and organized prayers at holy sites in the land of Israel.[70]

---

[65] CZA, J1/6442, Jewish National Council executive meeting, May 6, 1946.
[66] CZA, J1/6442, Memorandum of a meeting between Warhaftig and Shenhavi, February 4, 1947.
[67] YVA, AM1 287, Shenhavi, "Yad Vashem for the Diaspora," May 2, 1945.
[68] Hava Eshkoli, "Destruction Becomes Creation: The Theological Reaction of National Religious Zionism in Palestine to the Holocaust," *Holocaust and Genocide Studies* 17, no. 3 (2003): 430–58.
[69] Dr. Yaakov DeRabi Natan, "Holocaust Commemoration," *HaTzofe*, August 5, 1945.
[70] Azaryahu, "Innovation and Continuity"; Michal Shaul, *Beauty for Ashes: Holocaust Memory and the Rehabilitation of Ashkenazi Haredi Society in Israel 1945–1961* (Jerusalem: Yad Vashem and Yad Izhak Ben-Zvi, 2014), 256–59 [in Hebrew].

The anticipated founding of Yad Vashem aroused noticeable and serious deliberations among the leaders of the religious community. Given their concerns and hesitations, those involved in Yad Vashem made great efforts to endear the project to the group, for example, with the promise that all of the food served there would be kosher or by raising the possibility that a yeshiva would be built there.[71] To these they added a possible synagogue, a place that could house symbolic Torah learning and in which visitors could pray.

Yad Vashem's representatives created a "campaign" to market their plan within the religious public, attempting to generate interest through a combination of articles about Yad Vashem in religious newspapers.[72] They also held meetings with various rabbis and representatives of the religious community, hoping to gauge the religious population's attitude toward Yad Vashem.[73] In the meetings, the institution's people repeatedly reiterated their commitment that a synagogue would be built in the center of the memorial site, close to the "monument to the anonymous victim," and that an eternal flame would serve as a traditional memorial candle.[74] The religious representatives, in contrast, asserted that Yad Vashem would have a secular-Zionist nature, and claimed "What are [planted] trees and houses good for? [We] need rabbis and Talmud Torahs [children's religious schools]." "Compare this enterprise to the holy religious way of Torah?" one of the rabbis asked, wondering, "Will they bring all of the arguments in here? This place should be a place of holiness for the entire nation." He added that "a synagogue without content has no value. It must have content ... there must be Torah there."[75] The religious community's fear that Yad Vashem would take on a secular form and content and that acts that ran counter to Jewish tradition would take place there was compounded by the question of the place's location. The Jezreel Valley, Mount Scopus, and the other sites being considered for the establishment of Yad Vashem were all neutral from a Jewish perspective, devoid of "heritage," which made some of the rabbis and religious leaders uncomfortable and reticent. The consensus was that if a memorial site must be built, it should be in a place with Jewish symbolism and meaning, for example, the Jewish cemetery on the Mount of Olives or the Old City, near the Western Wall.[76]

---

71 YVA, AM1 289, Shragai to Zuckermann and Shenhavi, March 21, 1946.
72 KMHA, S-29, 1, Y. Ariel, Suggestions for consideration, May 27, 1946.
73 YVA, AM1 107, Summary of meetings and discussions with haredi rabbis, September 17, 1946.
74 Ibid.
75 YVA, AM1 107, Summary of a meeting between Ariel and Rabbi Kovner, August 15, 1946.
76 YVA, AM1 107, Summary of a meeting between Ariel and Rabbi Natan Ra'anan, August 18, 1946.

The JNF's Misgivings about Holocaust Commemoration

When Shenhavi suggested that a memorial for European Jewry be established in September 1942, he submitted his proposal to the JNF's administration. He did so not only because he worked there but also because he felt that the Fund was well-suited and fitting for the task, as almost the only option.

The JNF's heads were themselves debating how to respond to the shocking news emerging from Europe.[77] In 1944, the Fund put out a call for proposals to the Yishuv, indicating the role it had taken upon itself relating to the Holocaust: "the great Holocaust that has come upon our nation demands of us a supreme national effort in order to maintain a torch in our land to the nation of Israel's survivors," it said, noting that

> we are charged with readiness for the great days that will soon be upon us, when we will greet our brothers, brands plucked from the fire of destruction. We will prepare wide swaths of land for the Diaspora's refugees . . . the yearning for freedom lighted in our masses' hearts through the sea of flames of the Diaspora's destruction will find expressions in real actions, in creating new positions of conquest in the campaign of a people fighting for its resurrection and future.[78]

The JNF's management felt that the Fund must base Holocaust commemoration on its traditional activity, purchasing and preparing land, which would be at the disposal of the survivors arriving in the land of Israel. At the same time, there were those in the JNF who claimed that the Fund should nonetheless establish a "memorial garden," dedicated to the soldiers and those who had been killed in the Holocaust:

> The trees that will be planted on the national remembrance day or other opportunities will be planted in this garden and the names of those who were murdered and the fighters will be preserved in a special book called "The Martyrs' Forest Ledger." An appropriate piece of land, preferably in the Jerusalem area, will be apportioned by the JNF and hundreds of thousands of trees will be planted in it. The central boulevard will carry the name of the communities that were destroyed in the Holocaust . . . .. In the memorial garden, a building will be established for preserving sancta and notes and documents will be saved and collected. The communities registered in the martyrs' book will be given a place in the memorial building and a memorial plaque will be placed there. The chronicles of the destroyed communities will be preserved in this place.[79]

---

[77] CZA, KKL5/19079, a letter (no author) to the JNF, January 10, 1944.
[78] *Karnenu*, 21, no. 1 (Kislev 1944): 5.
[79] CZA, KKL5/17352, Hanan R. Yarden, "'Memorial Garden' and 'Martyrs' 'Book,'" June 26, 1944.

This idea was adopted and, in mid-1945, immediately with the end of the Second World War, the JNF chose to plant a memorial forest with five million trees, the estimated number of those who had perished. The forest, it was determined, would spread over an area of thousands of acres and thirty settlements would be founded in its territory, carrying the names of the lands of destruction.[80] An index was created according to the number of Jews who had been murdered, and it was decided that three settlements would be named for Polish Jewry, two settlements for Russian Jewry, and so forth. The forests were meant to hold watchtowers that would "serve to present material and details related to the memory of those in whose name the forests were planted."[81]

There were many in the JNF who still had their hesitations about commemoration. "Slogans such as reviving the land of Zion or the establishment of a Jewish state may arouse enthusiasm and amass millions far better than the slogan of commemorating the Diaspora," one asserted. The concern was raised that if the JNF needed to choose between Diaspora and a Jewish state, it would "ultimately be proven that we must set aside one of them in order to focus our efforts on the essence: redeeming land, preparing it, and afforesting it." It was Idov Cohen who wondered whether the JNF even could, with symbolic commemoration, compete with another institution or committee proposing "substantive commemoration."[82] Others worried that "here, too, there are those who will say that the JNF wanted to profit for itself off of the nation's calamity," and determined that

> it is clear that this claim is founded on a lack of understanding and distinction between a great national enterprise and the collection of charity. This proposal should not be confused with other proposals for commemorating the communities and the victims through enterprises [most likely Shenhavi's proposal] whose aim is outside of the JNF's activity and whose realization entails large expenditures. Here [the enterprise of the forest combined with settlements] is a clear-cut JNF enterprise, but it can be tied to the great national grief and sadness and give some relief to the mourning in the form of national revival and national creation and this enterprise does not require excessive expenditures.[83]

The publication of the JNF's plan to plant a memorial forest for the victims aroused Shenhavi's concern that it would render the establishment of Yad Vashem redundant. He appealed to Granot, saying that "a tree, in and of itself, cannot serve as a direct means of commemoration," and added that as the JNF

---

80 CZA, KKL5/12925, Zeev Shertok, Memo, June 10, 1945.
81 CZA, KKL5/12925, Yosef Weitz, "Schematic Proposition for Afforestation as a Commemoration for the Diaspora," June 4, 1945.
82 CZA, KKL5/12925, Idov Cohen to Granovsky, June 3, 1945.
83 CZA, KKL5/19079, Letter (no author) to the JNF, January 10, 1944.

had been using tree-planting from its inception, it would be inappropriate to use it for the purposes of commemorating the Holocaust. Shenhavi also expressed the concern that "the act for the benefit of the tree will eclipse the rest of the JNF's fields of operation and collection. Its losses will exceed its profits," warning of the possibility that the JNF would squander its chance to be the one responsible for the national Holocaust commemoration plan, as he had hoped it would be.[84]

During the Zionist Congress that took place in Basel in late 1946, an effort was made to include the JNF within the general, binding framework and to urge it not to carry out its plans separately from the other bodies. While the JNF was given permission to plant memorial trees, it was agreed that it was preferable for commemoration to be included within Yad Vashem's activities and that it should take place in complete coordination. At the end of the Congress, an understanding was signed with the Fund, which agreed to actively cooperate in the establishment of Yad Vashem.[85]

The Yad Vashem Plan near Ma'ale HaHamisha and Neve Ilan

The National Council's plan to establish Yad Vashem in Jerusalem did not move forward; aside from the fierce disagreements between the Zionist bodies, Shenhavi had a hard time identifying a fitting place for establishing the memorial site in the city. "Jerusalem is not an agricultural periphery city, it is not part of the working land of Israel. It is not a city of Zionist activity," Zvi Lurie, a member of the National Council and of the national kibbutz movement, explained, suggesting that Yad Vashem instead be located in the Jordan Valley or Beersheba.[86]

With the absence of a fitting place for the construction of the institution, the pressure on Shenhavi grew; he felt that other bodies might beat him to the punch. He prepared a list of more than forty initiatives that were competing with Yad Vashem overseas – in the United States, Argentina, Poland, and Czechoslovakia – alongside another list of eleven similar initiatives that had been announced in the land of Israel. He presented the lists as proof of the urgency of beginning to build Yad Vashem.[87] "That which we feared – has happened,"

---

[84] CZA, KKL5/12925, Shenhavi to Granovsky, June 13, 1945.
[85] CZA, KH4/3939, Wording of the agreement from December 12, 1946; Brog, "A Memorial," 100–102.
[86] YVA, AM1 287, Memorandum of a meeting with the HaShomer HaTzair executive, June 18, 1946.
[87] YVA, AM1 287, "Competing Enterprises for Commemorating the Holocaust in the World."

he said to Eliezer Kaplan, a member of the Jewish Agency and its treasurer. "Everyone is holding a part of the staff. There is no day that will not bring the crumbs of the split. Who benefits from this? Why are the foundations not objecting? And the investments in the divided enterprise are far greater than any investment we demand in its privatization." He warned that "the public has given up. More correctly – it will not take our existence into account."[88]

In mid-1946, it appeared that a solution had been found for Yad Vashem's location when a plan was formed to build Yad Vashem west of Kibbutz Ma'ale HaHamisha. A space of approximately 350 acres was found and deemed appropriate. It was an offshoot that extended from Ma'ale HaHamisha westward toward the Arab village of Bayt Thul, in an area where the JNF had purchased a sizeable portion of land.[89]

In September 1946, Shenhavi, Weinraub, and Mansfeld held an excursion at the site to determine its suitability to the enterprise and the plans that had been prepared. The first question they faced was whether the site, situated some fifteen kilometers from Jerusalem, could be considered part of "greater Jerusalem," a symbolic element that was considered essential for the project's success. The architects took note of the difficult surface conditions – the channels and high hilltops (the highest peak was 761 meters above sea level), the differences in height of 250 meters within the area, and the steep slopes with severe inclines that in some places reached 45 percent. There was also no permanent source of water and the rock seemed problematic. Nonetheless, they were prepared to take comfort in the advantages that they noted – the proximity of the site to the Jerusalem–Tel Aviv road and the availability of the land. They mentioned the "panorama" at the place, which looked promising, and the beautiful view from there, primarily toward the coastal plain. Regarding the question of its link to Jerusalem, the architects considered overcoming it with elevated construction. Despite the site's many disadvantages, they determined that it was possible "to adapt it to the role of the enterprise that will be erected and upraised in surroundings that are full of beauty and glory and will be seen from a great distance."[90]

---

[88] CZA, J1/6442, Shenhavi, Summary of a discussion with Eliezer Kaplan, September 12, 1946.
[89] CZA, KLM5/5591, Map of Neve Ilan, 1:20,000, n.d. Later, this area would be known as *Har ha-Ru'ah* (the wind mountain).
[90] YVA, AM1 289, Weinraub and Mansfeld to Yad Vashem, September 24, 1946.

The Difficulty of Adapting the Architectural Plans to the Selected Location

The selection of the site for Yad Vashem was a significant step toward the establishment of a memorial enterprise; all that was needed was to adapt Weinraub and Mansfeld's conceptual plan to the territory.[91] However, the Association of Engineers and Architects in Palestine appealed to Yad Vashem's management at the end of 1946, demanding that it announce an architectural competition for the planning of the memorial enterprise.[92] Weinraub and Mansfeld were inclined to concede to the request, but advised Shenhavi to preserve Yad Vashem's independence by maintaining selective choice of the proposals submitted and inviting well-known architects to take part in the competition. They themselves meant to compete.[93]

But Shenhavi firmly dismissed all possibilities of announcing an architectural contest for Yad Vashem, primarily because he worried that the project would be taken out of his hands. In order to expedite the construction, he prepared, with the help of the architects, a document titled "Assumptions and Numbers for Clarification of Yad Vashem's Plan" in February 1947, which explained how he and the architects viewed the outline for the memorial site.[94]

At the center of the memorial enterprise, Shenhavi, Weinraub, and Mansfeld positioned the remembrance hall, a monumental building containing twenty commemoration cells, the number of the lands of destruction. The façade, some 20 meters high and 250 meters wide, was meant to open toward Yad Vashem's central square, with its cells containing the communities' books with the names of the dead and important "notations" engraved on the walls. While for individuals, families, institutions, and organizations, the registration of the victims would be on "pages" kept there, the "books" would curate the information on the Jewish communities that had been annihilated.

The square itself was meant to spread over 25,000 square meters, surrounded by a wall with fresco pictures that would artistically illuminate the Holocaust and its various expressions. At the center of the wall, a mosaic would be dedicated to the children who had perished. A covered colonnade stretching the length of the semi-circular building would connect the commemoration cells and allow for movement between the remembrance hall's different sections. Yad

---

91 YVA, AM1 72, Weinraub to Shenhavi, January 20, 1947.
92 YVA, AM1 289, Baruch Beg to the Jewish Agency, October 22, 1946.
93 YVA, AM1 72, Weinraub and Mansfeld to Yad Vashem, November 11, 1946.
94 KMHA, S-29, 1, Shenhavi, "Assumptions and Numbers for Clarification of Yad Vashem's Plan," February 16, 1947.

Vashem would have a heroism hall as well, known also as the hall for the Jewish soldier. This would be another monumental building that would serve to complement the remembrance hall, "giving expression to the nation's activity in the war for its existence and the war of its humanity," dedicated to the soldiers who had taken part in the war.

The "field of Europe" also underwent a change in the new plan. In the past, the proposal had an immense garden in the form of Europe that included a kind of flowerbed dedicated to the lands of destruction and the different communities. Shenhavi now suggested substituting the garden with a relief, large and topographical and in the form of the continent, which would be positioned on the walls or on the complex's floor, a type of model upon which the names of the communities and their sizes before the destruction would be engraved. "The homeland garden" preserved its original look in the new plan – a large garden shaped in the form of the land of Israel noting the existing Jewish settlements and new settlements that would be formed. Another important component in Yad Vashem's plan, in cooperation with the JNF, was the Diaspora forest (or "Martyr's Forest"), which would be planted over about 250 acres around the memorial enterprise.

Shenhavi was not content with this architectural surplus; he related to other components as well, such as the relics that would be integrated in the remembrance mount, illuminating for visitors the terrible events that had taken place in the war. These were "a gas chamber in its image and form," an oven, "a collection of strangulation and torture tools from the extermination camps," and a gas van similar to the ones used by the Nazis to murder Jews. Another proposal was to bury the ashes of the martyrs, brought from the extermination sites, at the remembrance hall. Supplementing all of these components, Shenhavi proposed establishing an archive of the Diaspora at Yad Vashem, an institute that would focus on the lives of Jews in the Diaspora, as well as two museums, the museum for Jewish heroism during the Second World War and the museum for the chronicles of settlement in the land of Israel. All of these were meant, in his vision, to reinforce the experience of visiting Yad Vashem, to expand it, and, primarily, to influence the Jewish and Zionist identity of the visitors.

The plan was impressive and extensive, but it also deterred some. Yad Vashem's management discussed it a number of times, focusing on the enterprise's priorities and whether it should adopt the monumental building. Warhaftig, who had become a central figure in the management of the memorial enterprise, emphasized the need for the "emergency project" and claimed that the documents and books that were getting lost and spread throughout Europe must be saved first, and that a building to house them must be erected at Yad Vashem. At the same time, he asserted that it was only later that the "splendored" construction should take place. He further added: "first refugees and not the commemoration of the dead"; the national institutions must care for the Holocaust survivors knocking at the gates of the land and not necessarily focus on the commemoration of those who had perished. When Shenhavi tried to counter that Yad Vashem would soon become a center and a symbol that the Jewish world would turn to, Warhaftig stated that it was impossible to artificially create sanctity and that "religion cannot be replaced with logic."[95]

But it appeared that Shenhavi's enthusiasm was contagious, and influenced the members of Yad Vashem's board; they emphasized that "an important, strong element will be added to the event itself as soon as we can find a specific place that belongs to the enterprise [i.e., the Ma'ale HaHamisha area]."[96] The management was asked to visit the planned site and examine its unique qualities in order to come to a decision about building the memorial there. The architects were also asked to reexamine the degree of the site's monumentality and the question of the architectural expression of the relationship between Holocaust and heroism. This subject became significant, and it was not for nothing that Remez emphasized in one of the Yad Vashem management meetings the importance of the heroism hall, which was, in his opinion, "the Mecca stone [i.e., the Kaaba stone at Mecca]" – the hall would be the heart of the memorial site and the central attraction drawing visitors to Yad Vashem. He added that "there have been occasions of Jewish heroism and heroes throughout Jewish history in the land of Israel and in the Diaspora. For each era, there should be a pavilion – or a book – that gives expression to each." Shenhavi warned that "it is no coincidence that the subject of the heroism hall [in the crystallizing plan] is not so clear to us."[97]

Yad Vashem's management was also occupied with the question of the monument that would be built there; the plan was to make it the site's most prominent symbol.[98] A decision was made to announce an architectural competition for planning it so that copies of the monument could be sent to Europe and to the various Jewish communities. According to the plan, the monument's stones

---

95 ISA, G-18/4722, Discussion between Warhaftig, Tartakover, and Remez, February 2, 1947; for Warhaftig's autobiography, see Zerach Warhaftig, *Refugee and Remnant during the Holocaust* (Jerusalem: Yad Vashem, 1984) [in Hebrew].
96 YVA, AM1 287, Assumptions and propositions to be discussed during executive meeting, February 20, 1947.
97 CZA, J1/6442/1, Executive meeting, February 24, 1947.
98 YVA, AM1 110, JNF directorate sub-committee on Yad Vashem, April 1, 1947.

would be quarried from the land of the remembrance mount and Yad Vashem would have a monopoly on selling them.[99]

Public Relations for the Memorial Enterprise

Shenhavi continued to promote Yad Vashem and met for consultations with different figures and organizations in order to garner their support and cooperation.[100] So, for example, the suggestion that Yad Vashem be founded in partnership with B'nai B'rith, which at the time was attempting to establish an educational undertaking in the land of Israel, was raised in 1947. Shenhavi proposed uniting and connecting the memorial forest that the JNF planned to plant around Yad Vashem with the B'nai B'rith forest.[101] Another idea put forward was to tie Yad Vashem to the Garden of the Prophets and Sages, which Ephraim Hareuveni had worked toward for years. The latter had conducted negotiations with the heads of the JNF about founding the garden and Yosef Weitz, who was involved in both initiatives – Yad Vashem and the Garden of the Prophets and Sages – suggested merging the two.[102]

During this period, many artists turned to Shenhavi and Yad Vashem's management to take part in the enterprise. David Polus, who had sculpted, among other things, the sculpture of Alexander Zaïd, offered to make a piece for Yad Vashem on the ghetto uprisings.[103] Nathan Rapoport, while working on his monument to the Warsaw Ghetto Uprising, also offered to take part in preparing Yad Vashem's "mausoleum" and erecting statues there.[104] He was bothered by the "problem of monumental sculpture in open space in relation to the religious prohibition against erecting sculptures."[105] Rapoport's appeal was the beginning of his long-standing relationship with Yad Vashem's management, which ended in

---

99 HHA, 3–95. 14 (6), Shenhavi, Proposal for a memorial, February 15, 1947.
100 YVA, AM1 209, Memorandum on a meeting between Shenhavi and Avraham Herzfeld, February 24, 1947.
101 YVA, AM1 435, Shenhavi to Gad Frumkin, April 22, 1947.
102 YVA, AM1 349, Memorandum of a meeting between Weitz and Shenhavi, March 30, 1947; on the "Garden of the Prophets," see Yair Paz, "The Botanical Garden and the 'Garden of the Prophets': Two Educational Projects in the Early Years of the Hebrew University," in *The History of the Hebrew University of Jerusalem: A Period of Consolidation and Growth*, ed. Hagit Lavsky (Jerusalem, Magnes Press, 2005): 443–72 and especially 465 [in Hebrew].
103 YVA, AM1 16, "B. Ben Aharon," May 7, 1947.
104 YVA, AM1 15, Rapaport to Shenhavi, September 2, 1947.
105 YVA, AM1 16, Rapaport to Shenhavi, January 24, 1948.

1975, when his Warsaw Ghetto Uprising sculpture was unveiled on the Mount of Remembrance.

Attempts to recruit the religious community to the Yad Vashem enterprise continued. Shenhavi met with Rabbi Yitzhak-Meir Levin, the leader of the ultra-Orthodox political party Agudat Yisrael, in order to convince him that his community should be part of Yad Vashem. Shenhavi asserted that "as the oppressor and foe did not distinguish between enemy and enemy," so "the framework of the enterprise must be a general one, encompassing all circles in Judaism."[106]

Remez, Warhaftig, and Shenhavi met with the chief rabbis, Rabbi Yitzhak Halevi Herzog and Rabbi Ben-Zion Meir Hai Uziel. The rabbis were not content with the plans including a synagogue, which to them felt like lip service rather than a materially religious element. Aside from their concerns about Yad Vashem being open on the Sabbath and visitors desecrating the Sabbath, they were bothered by another issue – the statues at the memorial site. This was a kind of code word that concealed the rabbis' fears regarding what they considered the too-monumental architecture at Yad Vashem, unprecedented in modern Jewish history, which to them felt foreign and alien.

Remez promised both rabbis that Yad Vashem's people would follow the halakhic prohibition and the Jewish proscription and custom of not making statues, adding that in building the site, the architects would take the religious community's sensibilities into account. "My idea is to establish fixed learning, [chanting the] Kaddish, [and] prayers, and to obtain [religious] books from the Diaspora," Remez said, adding that "I do not want a museum to somehow preserve the survivors' religious objects. We began not with tree and stone but rather with collecting the names of those who were burned. The central content is in establishing a name for individuals and communities." Regarding the Sabbath, he also stressed that there would be no "authorized" desecration, but, on the other hand, he did not agree to the request to close the site on the Sabbath; he saw it as a "synagogue" that should remain open to the public on all days. He concluded that "there will be no desecration of the Sabbath within the walls of the institution; the restrictions can be negotiated during the work from a desire to preserve the religion and its boundaries and not offend the ultra-Orthodox community's feelings."[107]

---

[106] YVA, AM1 103, Shenhavi to Rabbi Yitzhak Meir Levine, May 28, 1947.
[107] CZA, J1/6448, Meeting about Yad Vashem in Chief Rabbi Herzog's house, December 3, 1947.

Cooperation with the JNF and the Founding of the Yad Vashem Board of Governors

Shenhavi was now busier than ever adapting the architectural plan that had been prepared in 1946 to the selected site, close to Ma'ale HaHamisha and Neve Ilan. He estimated that the entire initiative would cost 2 million Palestine pounds, an immense, unprecedented sum for the time. "The topographical map of Neve Ilan makes it possible to examine, for the first time, a sketch of a plan that is fitting for the territory," he said to Weinraub and Mansfeld, and asked them to update the data they had used for the earlier planning of the memorial initiative in order to prepare an architectural plan for the site. They agreed that this would be a modular plan, with three stages, making it possible to build Yad Vashem gradually and to move from the minimal plan (focusing on the remembrance hall and the heroism hall) to the maximal one.[108] He requested that they create "three circles of architectural elements, each of which constitutes a certain wholeness, and each of which complements the remainder to achieve the wholeness of the enterprise."[109]

The JNF continued purchasing territory in the Ma'ale HaHamisha area, and the possibilities of allocating a specific site for Yad Vashem grew. An agreement was formed to abandon the plan to establish Yad Vashem on the "wind mountain" and to focus on a plot closer to Kibbutz Ma'ale HaHamisha. Weitz and Shenhavi felt that some of the broad territory intended for Yad Vashem could be dedicated to planting groves and thus supporting the initiative financially,[110] and, in late April 1947, the JNF decided as much. The Fund's heads may have determined that Holocaust commemoration in the land of Israel was a matter of special national importance, but they did not forget to emphasize that the proposal must be carried out in the appropriate "framework," in which the "memorial forest" would hold a place of honor. They were referring to the Martyrs' Forest, the founding of which they were working on at the time. They wished to guarantee that funds raised for Yad Vashem would not impede the Fund's income, and that some of the funds earmarked for Yad Vashem would be devoted to planting their forest. The territory, it was decided, would be preserved for a memorial initiative for three years, until the conclusion of the global appeal.[111]

The JNF may have agreed to support Yad Vashem but, at the same time, it continued to work independently, initiating the planting of forests in memory

---

108 YVA, AM1 287, Meeting of Weinraub, Mansfeld, and Shenhavi, March 14, 1947.
109 YVA, AM1 110, JNF directorate sub-committee on the issue of Yad Vashem, April 1, 1947.
110 YVA, AM1 349, Memorandum of a meeting between Weitz and Shenhavi, March 30, 1947.
111 YVA, AM1 110, JNF directorate sub-committee on the issue of Yad Vashem, April 1, 1947.

of Holocaust victims in other places around the land of Israel and even around the world. In mid-1947, Shenhavi began to hear that the JNF was raising funds in England for the planting of a memorial forest there.[112] It quickly became clear that the JNF's endeavor in England was only the tip of the iceberg; its activity was far more widespread. The JNF had begun to partner with Jewish communities in Europe, South Africa, and America, collecting money to plant forests in memory of Holocaust victims. This was a combination of the JNF political activists' desire to expand its activity and raise funds for its purposes and the growing demand on the part of survivors that their relatives be immortalized at a time when no fitting memorial enterprise yet existed. The JNF created an independent channel of Holocaust commemoration, competing with Yad Vashem.

In early June 1947, the first and festive meeting of Yad Vashem's board of governors took place. This body held representatives from the different organizations that founded Yad Vashem, including the JNF.[113] This meeting was the peak of the prolonged and extensive negotiations that had taken place since 1945, and was occupied with the Zionist institutions' and national foundations' involvement in the founding of the enterprise.

At the beginning of the meeting, warm words of greeting were read by Prof. Chaim Weizmann;[114] representatives of the different bodies also read impassioned statements and then the discussion about the future of Yad Vashem began. The board of governors considered Yad Vashem's methods of work and decided that the institutions taking part in the initiative could not work separately on Holocaust commemoration.[115] This decision may have been connected to Shenhavi's concern about the JNF's negative impact on the enterprise's success; among other things, he feared that the JNF would take upon itself the historic role and in so doing "minimize its [Yad Vashem's] image and reduce it to nothing."[116]

The building plan was presented to the participants:

> On the remembrance mount, three central buildings will be founded: the remembrance hall, in which the names of the dead will be collected; a solid hall in which the names of the "Jewish soldiers who took part in the last war" will be recorded; and the library (*beit akad*) of Yad

---

112 YVA, AM1 110, Shenhavi to Shragai, May 29, 1947.
113 "Yad Vashem's Board of Governors Established," *HaTzofe*, May 13, 1947; HHA, 3–95. 14 (2), "Instructions for Examining Yad Vashem Plan," February 19, 1947.
114 KMHA, S-29, 5, Memorandum of a meeting between Shenhavi and Prof. Weizmann, April 14, 1947.
115 CZA, KH4/3/3939, Memo for the board of governors, May 29, 1947.
116 YVA, P20/19, Meeting between Warhaftig and Shenhavi, February 6, 1947.

Vashem, in which the books of the fallen Jewish communities and all of the documents related to the destruction and the Jewish participation in the war will be collected.[117]

Shenhavi distributed a kind of "dictionary" of terms for the symbolic and architectural elements of the plan to the participants. The pavilion of Jewish history was called the "revival hall"; the remembrance hall was called the "hall of might"; and the monument in honor of the righteous among the nations was called "redemption and recompense."[118]

The presentation of the site's plan to those present, many of whom were seeing it for the first time, aroused much interest and diverted the discussion to remembrance and Holocaust commemoration. David (Werner) Senator of the Hebrew University expressed a concern about the excessive integration of symbolic elements in the architectural plan. Rabbi Shmuel Aharon Shazuri (Weber), secretary of the Chief Rabbinate, focused on the prohibition of other institutions to operate in the area of Holocaust commemoration. "There is plastic commemoration in creating a mount of memory. But there is also transcendent, spiritual commemoration. And how can we say that no institution [besides Yad Vashem] can do anything in the sphere of commemoration?" he asked, referring to the religious commemoration taking place in the land at the time. Remez, who was leading the discussion, summed it up with lofty words: "I believe only in the real thing," he claimed,

> that a Jewish family and a soldier who fought in the war sitting in Boston or Australia, in Hungary, has in one place in the land of Israel, on one of Jerusalem's hills, the fact or the relative who fell will be recorded, as a supreme historic grave for his son's generation and that of his son's son, . . . They will not go anyplace in Europe to bury the ancestors; this will be the grave, the ancient tomb in the land of Israel.[119]

At the end of the meeting, which approved the commencement of the Yad Vashem enterprise, the plan for the site, and the partnership between the different Zionist bodies, Shenhavi hastened to commend Weinraub and Mansfeld again: "I am confident that your role in the activity in the field, charged as you are with determining the image of the enterprise, will not be lost. Along with the professionals and artists, the nation's outstanding professionals and inspirational figures, join hands, give from your abilities, and succeed."[120] Weinraub and Mansfeld answered Shenhavi in kind, blessing him on the beginning of activity, but they also wished to guarantee their continued involvement in planning the

---

117 HHA, 3–95. 14 (6), Draft of a letter (presumably sent in 1947 to Tartakover).
118 YVA, AM1 27, "List of Term Used in Yad Vashem Plans," April 6, 1947.
119 ISA, G-6/4726, Yad Vashem board of governors' first meeting, June 1, 1947.
120 YVA, AM1 72, Shenhavi to Weinraub and Mansfeld, June 2, 1947.

memorial site. "We are certain that our rights, stemming from our involvement as architects over the years, will be recognized by you also during this stage of executing the initiative," they half requested, half demanded.[121]

Disagreements about Yad Vashem's Future

Yad Vashem's management planned to hold a symbolic planting ceremony in July 1947 on Ma'ale HaHamisha's remembrance mount, and to invite not only the representatives of national foundations and the other Zionist bodies but also members of UNSCOP (United Nations Special Committee on Palestine), who were in the land at the time. According to the plan, the JNF's directorate was meant to symbolically transfer the land to Yad Vashem's representatives during the ceremony. It was suggested that Prof. Chaim Weizmann plant the first tree in memory of his son, a pilot who had been killed during the Second World War.[122] The desire to emphasize the heroism displayed during the Holocaust was also expressed in the decision to integrate symbolic trees and groves in memory of the ghetto fighters and partisans, Jewish Brigade soldiers, paratroopers who landed in the enemy's hinterland, and righteous among the nations in the memorial forest.[123] With the date of the inaugural ceremony approaching, Shenhavi met with representatives from Ma'ale HaHamisha, Kiryat Anavim, and Neve Ilan, all bordering the site slated for Yad Vashem, in an effort to guarantee their cooperation with the enterprise. The meeting ended with the residents expressing satisfaction that Yad Vashem would be established nearby and with emphases on their "preparedness to shoulder the burden of the roles and duties."[124]

The planting ceremony, meant to signal the commencement of Yad Vashem's construction, never took place, a symptom of the many organizational problems Yad Vashem's heads confronted and the lack of enthusiasm on the part of the organizations that comprised the board of governors. On one hand, the fact that the institution's offices already resided in a three-room apartment in Jerusalem attested to its institutionalization. A handful of Yad Vashem employees worked there, planning activity and collecting and cataloging archival materials, and they had begun to compile a list of the communities that had been devastated. On the other hand, among some on the board of governors, question marks about

---

[121] HHA, 3–95. 14 (5), Weinraub and Mansfeld to Yad Vashem, July 5, 1947.
[122] YVA, AM1 287, "Symbolical Planting Ceremony on the "Mount of Remembrance," June 23, 1947.
[123] YVA, AM1 92, "Letter from S. Friedlander," June 11, 1947.
[124] YVA, AM1 39, Secretariat Diary 11, May 27, 1947.

the immense size of the enterprise and its huge financial scope were growing. Arieh Leib Yaffe, director general of Keren Hayesod and a prominent opponent of the Yad Vashem plan, demanded that the scope of building be reduced. "Perhaps do not build three buildings," he requested, "but one building with two parts."[125] He warned that Yad Vashem was doomed to abject failure and that failure "would be attributed to the National Council and the central institutions that were tied to it."[126] Shenhavi wrote, sarcastically, of Yaffe's "bitter weeping . . . about the rise of enemy number one [Yad Vashem] to destroy what had been established over a generation. And it is not simple: to demand of a Jew ten dollars once in his life for commemorating his parents or relatives, those same ten dollars that were meant for him, for Keren Hayesod."[127]

Criticism of the Yad Vashem plan was heard from a number of directions. When Abba Kovner spoke before participants at the July 1947 conference on Holocaust and Martyrdom in Our Time, he wondered what "feeling a Jewish pilgrim would feel upon entering and exiting the heroism hall on the remembrance mount in Jerusalem." What would the feeling of a "native of the land" visiting there be?

> Will he be happy that across from the house of the Holocaust a corner of light, of sovereignty, has been established? Will his heart expand with pride? Or might the heroism hall, if it is established as I see it in my mind's eye, over-suppress the heart of a person leaving the house of the Holocaust and entering the heroism hall? Perhaps someone will leave there with great sadness because before him will be the affair of the neglected rebellion, because this tent will be a tent of a very orphaned heroism.[128]

In *Haaretz*, one writer hoped that the "vulgar" plan would be abandoned. Aside from the waste of money in building Yad Vashem there – money that could be put toward "constructive" purposes – the newspaper protested the possibility that the place would become "a center for worship of ancestors, like the houses of worship of idolatrous tribes in Africa. Groups of schoolchildren and other pilgrims will visit there. They will look at the lists of names and surrender to a kind of sick worship of the dead." The article also described the form of commemoration chosen; it was "against all Jewish tradition to establish this type of monument to the dead." Yad Vashem was even compared to the "German 'Valhalla' – one of the most vulgar and tasteless buildings ever built."[129] The writer

---

125 CZA, S5/111351, Protocol of a meeting about Yad Vashem, June 10, 1947.
126 CZA, S53/1671, Leib Yaffe to Eliezer Kaplan, August 11, 1947.
127 CZA, J1/6449, Shenhavi to Granovsky, August 23, 1947.
128 Abba Kovner, "Mount of Remembrance – Mountain of Warning," *Mishmar*, July 25, 1947.
129 Hanske Horst and Jörg Traeger, *Walhalla. Ruhmestempel an der Donau* (Regensburg: Buchverlag der Mittelbayerischen Zeitung, 1992).

concluded that the place might "encourage the oversensitivity that we suffer from more than enough. These will be large, empty memorial monuments," and "this monument should be given a constructive image that will accord with the spirit of the Yishuv – and not a form that opposes common sense and the Jewish treatise as one."[130] A similar opinion was expressed by Sinai Ucko in *Haaretz*, who determined that "the hunger poems of Yitzhak Katznelson [and] the memories of Yitzhak Zuckermann" should be preferred to a future visit to Yad Vashem.[131] He opined that their call would be equal to "pilgrimage to this 'not-small temple' when built." His fear was of "automobiles of travelers, a tourist center, the sale of souvenirs (only in the secular section, of course!), columns covered in names of people who 'were there,'" and he expressed his doubts as to their necessity.[132]

Prof. Simha Assaf, the head of the Hevra Kadisha in the land of Israel and, later on, rector of the Hebrew University and a supreme court justice, joined the critical voices, claiming that the "unusual and strange" plan had no ties to Jewish heritage or Jerusalem. He suggested focusing on building a synagogue as a commemoration center and supplementing it with the establishment of a historical archive on Mount Scopus and a museum to preserve the antiquities that remained from the lands of devastation. He also critiqued the site chosen for the erection of Yad Vashem, "far from man and city. 'A hand and a name (*yad vashem*) **in my home** and in my walls' – it says," he stated [my emphasis].[133]

Harsh criticism was also voiced during the joint meeting of Yad Vashem's management with the representatives of the national foundations, the JNF and Keren Hayesod, where the disagreements about funding for the enterprise – and also its goals – were expressed full force. Shmuel Zuchovitzky (Zakif), a member of the JNF's directorate, firmly asserted that they "want to include in it [Yad Vashem] an old-fashioned cult. We are for the revival of the land and not minimizing the ties to the land of Israel with our forefathers' graves. That was [the case] once and the Zionist movement changed it," Zachovitzky asserted, suggesting "communing with the land of Israel through commemorating the dead in a more modern way." Shenhavi responded that the character of the institution was dependent solely on the employees of Yad Vashem, who would

---

130 "Yad Vashem," *Haaretz*, June 26, 1947.
131 Shlomo Even Shoshan, *Itzhak Katznelson, Lament of the Holocaust* (Jerusalem: Ministry of Education, 1964) [in Hebrew]; Pua Hershlag, *The Story of Yitzhak Zuckerman (Antek)* (Jerusalem: Yad Izhak Ben-Zvi, 2006) [in Hebrew].
132 S. Ucko, "Some Thoughts about a Mighty Idea," *Haaretz*, July 24, 1947.
133 S. Asaf, "Yad Vashem Plan," *Haaretz*, July 3, 1947.

determine its character "to preserve the line and foundation so that it will not become a cult temple."[134]

"Can a Jewish State be Imagined with a Memorial Enterprise outside of it?"

The second day of the International Conference on Holocaust and Martyrdom in Our Time – convened by Yad Vashem and the Hebrew University's Institute of Jewish Studies in July 1947 at the end of a conference on Jewish Studies – was devoted to discussing Yad Vashem and its objectives. Some of the participants visited the remembrance mount near Ma'ale HaHamisha. However, the decision they took was to recommend the establishment of Yad Vashem "within Jerusalem."[135]

In July 1947, Yad Vashem's secretariat went back to discussing the location of Yad Vashem and, against the backdrop of the doubts raised about the selected site at Ma'ale HaHamisha, Remez asked that the possibility of building Yad Vashem on Mount Scopus be considered after all.[136] "Why are we suddenly put off by the attack of twenty-three professors who cannot see beyond their corner of activity?," Shenhavi railed, referring to the opposition raised during the conference to Yad Vashem's modus operandi and to the overemphasis placed there, in his opinion, on Holocaust research rather than commemoration. "Yad Vashem should first deal with the elementary, natural pathos of commemoration of martyrs," *HaTzofe* wrote. "Commemoration and research – commemoration comes first."[137]

Shenhavi strongly opposed the possibility that Yad Vashem would be built near "the bustling lives of thousands of students," and wondered if the university's administration would agree to reduce the area dedicated to developing a campus for Yad Vashem. "Is there really no one who discerns what proximity to the sports fields, swimming pools, and bustling lives of thousands of students, a city that spreads over two thousand [dunams; five hundred acres], means?" he asked, and wondered what would happen if, after Yad Vashem was forced to make do with few acres, the need to expand the enterprise would arise later.

---

134 CZA, J1/G449, Summary of Budget Committee meeting, June 24, 1947.
135 CZA, S26/1326, "Decisions of the International Conference on Holocaust and Martyrdom in Our Time, Convened by Yad Vashem and the Hebrew University's Jewish Studies Institute," July 13–14, 1947; on the conference: Cohen, *Holocaust Research*, 99–122.
136 ISA, G-6/4726, Secretary meeting (3), July 17, 1947.
137 "Holocaust Research and Commemoration," *HaTzofe*, July 20, 1947.

"Would they then go to a third remembrance mount? I caution us against this route. If the professors want, they will come to the enterprise even when it's some distance from the city – which will still always be smaller than the distances within the city of London."[138]

Shenhavi maintained his efforts to promote the memorial site's construction near Ma'ale HaHamisha. Neither he nor Remez shared the doubts about the chances of establishing the initiative there with the architects. In August 1947, architects Arieh El-Hanani and Arieh Sharon joined Weinraub and Mansfeld; the planning team for Yad Vashem now numbered four architects and three offices, all of which were advancing the construction plan for Ma'ale HaHamisha.

It is clear that the partnership between the four architects was not a naïve one. Weinraub and Mansfeld, the veterans on the project, understood that the addition of two well-known architects would raise their chances of continuing to work on the institution's planning and construction. In the background, it appears, stood the Association of Engineers and Architects in Palestine's demand that a competition be opened for planning the site.[139]

Indeed, the agreement signed between the four architects stated that despite the seniority of Weinraub and Mansfeld's office in planning Yad Vashem, all three offices would have equal rights on the project. Weinraub and Mansfeld committed to handing all of the materials they had to their new partners and agreed that work on Yad Vashem would only be carried out in full partnership between all of the offices.[140]

In early September 1947, the concern was raised that the Ma'ale HaHamisha site must be abandoned. The UNSCOP committee had just completed its work and submitted its recommendations for discussion at the UN's General Assembly. These recommendations included, inter alia, the possibility that two states, one next to the other, would be established in Palestine – a Jewish one and an Arab one. There was a concern that the location selected for Yad Vashem, next to Ma'ale HaHamisha, would be part of the future Arab state's territory.[141] Shenhavi asked Weitz for assistance in locating an alternate place for the memorial enterprise and stated that "Yad Vashem must know the alternate possibilities already now, for any possible scenario."[142]

---

138 CZA, J1/6449, Secretary meeting (4), July 22, 1947.
139 HHA, 3–95. 14 (5), Weinraub and Mansfeld to Shenhavi, July 5, 1947.
140 HHA, 3–95. 15 (7), Agreement, n.d.
141 CZA, KKL5/29839, Map of Ma'ale HaHamisha, no scale, n.d.
142 YVA, AM1 146, Memorandum of a meeting between Shenhavi and Weitz, September 7, 1947.

In an October 1947 meeting of Yad Vashem's management, a crucial discussion was held about the location of the memorial site. Now Britain's announcement regarding its withdrawal from Palestine colored the deliberations, with the uncertainty about the future of Jerusalem and its environs, and in particular about its internationalization, intensifying. Remez was adamant that "it is important to concentrate great Jewish enterprises in Jerusalem now as much as possible. To give an opportunity for Jewish settlement in Jerusalem, for more Jewish livelihood in Jerusalem, and to reinforce the ties with the past by the nation's additional ties to Jerusalem," he concluded, Yad Vashem must be brought to fruition in Jerusalem and not in Ma'ale HaHamisha. Remez also raised the critical question of how "we can now come and turn the eyes of the Jews to this place [i.e., Ma'ale HaHamisha]. Yad Vashem can be consistent with Jerusalem, even if it is international [referring to the internationalization plan for the city], but not in territory that is not Jerusalem, in the Arab state." Shenhavi, too, realizing that the chances that the institution would be established at the Ma'ale HaHamisha site were dwindling, asked: "Can a Jewish state be imagined with a memorial site outside of it?" Remez responded that he was

> hopeful that the Jewish state would by no means surrender pulling together Yad Vashem in the land of Israel, and on a great scale. I have no doubt of this. It is one of the things that ties the nation and tied the nation to its generations and I have no doubt that Yad Vashem will be supported by all who care for the ties of the nation and the state, the ties of the nation and the land.[143]

If not in Ma'ale HaHamisha, those debating the question asked themselves, where would Yad Vashem be established? Remez again turned to Mount Scopus, stating that "there is no doubt that the subject of the college [Hebrew University], even if Jerusalem is international" was the fitting one. He added that "there will be a large Jewish domain [on Mount Scopus], full of wisdom and a library, and antiquities institutes, and also a large city generally. A large area." Granot explained that if Yad Vashem were built on Mount Scopus, it would be necessary to pare down Shenhavi's grandiose plans, which demanded a vast area. "Even a small thing can be beautiful," he reassured the group, describing how "we will sit within our nation. It will be more secure and will also add something to the great plan of a college compound." But Warhaftig emphasized the disadvantages both of the modifications and of the connection between Yad Vashem and Hebrew University. When "two institutions, each of which has its own individual consecration on its own, are brought together, a Jew will get the impression of the enterprise – and will remain with only one impression," he

---

143 CZA, KKL5/16006, Yad Vashem board of governors' second meeting, October 26, 1947.

claimed. He repeated his proposal that Yad Vashem be built in the Old City, in Jewish-owned buildings that had been abandoned due to the national tension between Jews and Arabs.[144] Shenhavi also continued to oppose the university plan; his ire grew when he learned of negotiations that had taken place behind his back with a number of the university's professors (one of whom was Ben-Zion Dinur, later the chairman of Yad Vashem, with whom Shenhavi would often spar) about integrating the memorial enterprise there.[145] The meeting ended with a resolution to convene a committee to discuss the subject whose members would be Senator, Granot, Shenhavi, and Remez – but the committee was never formed.[146]

The Ramat Rachel Plan

At the beginning of 1948, against the backdrop of the military situation in the land with the outbreak of the War of Independence, Yad Vashem's heads elected to abandon the plot of land slated for the institution near Ma'ale HaHamisha.[147] The JNF promised that in exchange, a fitting territory would be put aside in Jerusalem, where the planned memorial forest would be planted.[148]

The decision intensified Shenhavi's efforts to find a fitting alternative location, and he initiated a renewed assessment of the different options for Yad Vashem in Jerusalem and its environs, against the backdrop of the emerging political and military reality at the time. The result of this evaluation was the document "Opinion regarding the Appropriate Site for the Yad Vashem Enterprise," submitted to him in February 1948.[149]

"Architecturally speaking, the enterprise requires a special place, high, broad, self-expressed in the space, and with fitting opportunities in the territory," determined the report's writers. They added that "topographically speaking, the territory must be visible in Jewish Jerusalem and surround it by virtue of its status. Geographically, the place must be atop a high mountain with its own independent surroundings," and went on to assess the various options.

---

144 CZA, J1/3610/2, Jewish National Council to Zerach Warhaftig, February 24, 1947.
145 Arieh Bauminger, "Cathedral Dedicated to the Annihilation of European Jewry," *Davar*, October 8, 1947.
146 CZA, KKL5/16006, Yad Vashem Board of Governors' Second Meeting, October 26, 1947.
147 YVA, AM1 325, Neomi (no surname) to Shenhavi, January 19, 1948.
148 CZA, KKL5/16006, Granovsky to Yad Vashem, February 15, 1948.
149 YVA, AM1 27, "Opinion regarding the Appropriate Site for the Yad Vashem Enterprise," February 1948.

The report rejected the possibility that Yad Vashem be built in Ma'ale HaHamisha or Mount Scopus. The claim was that the space allocated for it at the university, most likely in the campus's western area, did not suit the objective, and that "architectonically, there is a danger that Yad Vashem, with its architectonic dimensions and blocs, will reduce the architectonic value of the university's buildings themselves." The report's writers also warned of the risk that "the content of Yad Vashem would be swallowed up by its location within the multi-hued and multifunctional bloc of university buildings," and that "it should be borne in mind that Yad Vashem needs extensive and open spaces, because only by integrating architectonic stones and green fields will it be possible to find architectonic expression for the Yad Vashem enterprise. A small area will force Yad Vashem to plan its buildings more densely than desired and will not allow for open planning."

After rejecting other possibilities, the surveyors recommended a plot south of Kibbutz Ramat Rachel as best suited to the establishment of Yad Vashem: "topographically, in this plot we can attain visual control over Jerusalem by establishing a tall building at the highest spot in the territory." They added that "the territory is free and expansive. Its dimensions allow for free and open planning of all of the architectonic elements of Yad Vashem in integration with nature adapted to independent architectonic perfection." The surveyors related to the complex geopolitical situation of the time and the prediction that the city would be divided or given special international status; they felt that "geographically, this strong, prominent spot could be the important link in the chain of enterprises and institutions in Jerusalem's south." It appeared that the area was marked by Shenhavi as a possible place for the establishment of Yad Vashem as early as late 1947. He held a tour there and located, with Weitz's help, an area of two hundred acres that could be used.[150] Apparently, the "territory next to Ramat Rachel" that was found by the surveyors was Jabel Abu Ghuneim, south of Kibbutz Ramat Rachel, east of the Mar Elias Monastery, and north of the village of Beit Sahur. It was a spacious hilltop, about a kilometer square, on which the neighborhood of Har Homa would later be built.[151]

The attempt to find a fitting place for Yad Vashem in this area was not without meaning. As early as 1937, a number of plots in that area had been bought by the Palestine Land Development Company, and there was even an intent to

---

150 HHA, 3–95. 14 (5), Shenhavi to Zuckermann, November 5, 1947; for a possible mention of this site, see Aminadav Eshbal, *Hakhsharat ha-Yishuv* (Jerusalem: Hakhsharat ha-Yishuv, 1976), 66 [in Hebrew].
151 HHA, 3–95. 15 (7), Transparent sheet of paper stamped December 25, 1947 which includes pencil-drawn lines, coordinates, and the shape of a polygon.

Figure 4: Yad Vashem plan for Ramat Rachel, 1948 (HHA).

establish a neighborhood there called "Efrata."[152] Aside from these plots, more land was purchased in the area by private buyers.

The disadvantages of this site were no doubt many, and it is difficult to understand why it was even considered by Shenhavi and his colleagues. The site was near Arab Bethlehem, distanced from the Jewish neighborhoods of southern Jerusalem. Kibbutz Ramat Rachel was the Jewish settled Jewish space and it, too, was some hundreds of meters away. The hilltop being considered may have towered over its environs (at 774 meters above sea level), but it had no visual or physical link to Jerusalem and no roads led there. In contrast, the place's central advantage was that many plots of land there had been purchased by various arms of the Zionist Organization; these could be given over to the disposal of the enterprise. The visibility of the hilltop from the Jerusalem–Bethlehem road, one kilometer to its west, and from the area of Rachel's Tomb were also advantages. It is possible that these were the reasons that led the heads of Yad Vashem to consider the possibility of founding the memorial enterprise there in any event, and they even asked the architects to prepare a new plan for the area.[153]

A new outline for Yad Vashem was prepared for the site near Ramat Rachel in 1948 by the joint team of four architects.[154] This was to a great degree an outgrowth

---

152 Eshbal, *Hakhsharat ha-Yishuv*, 64–70.
153 HHA, 3–95. 7 (1), Yad Vashem, 1:2,000, 1948?.
154 HHA, 3–95. 7 (1), Yad Vashem, Isometric color draft; HHA, 3–95. 7 (1), Yad Vashem, 1:500, folded paper plan; HHA, 3–95. 7 (1), Yad Vashem, 1:500.

of the plan that had been prepared in 1946 by Weinraub and Mansfeld, influenced by Shenhavi's suggestions and outlook on commemoration and memorialization of Holocaust and heroism, but at the same time it was a new architectural creation. Almost all of the memorial buildings that had appeared in the earlier plan were copied to the new outline, but its innovation was in its different architecture and the form of situating the buildings. These differences were tied, most likely, to the involvement of the new partners, Arieh Sharon and Arieh El-Hanani, in planning the memorial enterprise; they infused a new, modern architectural line and style.

In contrast with the 1946 outline, whose rounded lines and, most noticeably, immense dimensions stood out, the 1948 plan was characterized by a more modest scope and more restrained architectural lines. This plan took about one fifth of the space that the previous one had; the memorial site was more "compact" and less "romantic" than the 1946 version, with straight lines rather than the original rounded ones. In both plans, the separation between the educational space and the memorial space, the heart of the commemoration, stood out.

The Ramat Rachel version of the memorial enterprise had a wide boulevard leading to it from the north, possibly hinting to a road from Jerusalem. A gate indicated the entrance to the site and a building stood nearby; it would contain a card catalogue with the names of those who had perished in the Holocaust, the foundation for what would later become Yad Vashem's Hall of Names. Both sides of the wide entrance boulevard, some six hundred meters in length, were adorned with trees; beyond them was the Diaspora forest.

The boulevard led to the commemoration compound, a sort of raised temenos of about 1,500 square meters, square and separated from its surroundings. On both sides of the plaza, to its east and west, were two of Yad Vashem's central structures, the heroes' hall and the remembrance hall, a significant enhancement from the previous plan. While in the previous outline, the structures were spread over an extensive territory and situated one above the other on the hill's incline, here the architects chose to situate them across from one another, emphasizing the importance of one over the other through architecture – the larger, higher heroes' hall stood across from the remembrance hall, devoted to the memory of the Holocaust's victims.

The remembrance hall was planned as a two-story, square building, decorated with many openings, above which was a large dome. The ground plan of the structure included a large central space off of which were openings to long, narrow rooms, nineteen in total, which, we can assume, were meant to fill the role of holding the martyrs' books with the names of those who had perished. Across from the remembrance hall, on the eastern size of the plaza, a heroes' hall, dedicated to the heroism displayed during the war, was planned. This was a long, tall building that was meant to rise above all other parts of the compound.

The entrance to it was through a ramp taking the visitors from the plaza to the building's entrance, with its sharpened, oriental arch, similar to the entrances surrounding the remembrance hall. The inner space of the heroism hall rose its entire height, some twenty meters, and was divided into two main spaces, whose content was unclear.

The central plaza of Yad Vashem was meant for gatherings of thirty thousand people, and separated the two main buildings. This space was left empty of structures aside from a monument placed near the remembrance hall. In this plan, as in the previous one, the architects did not detail the appearance of the monument or its plan and it appears as an undefined square, apparently based on the assumption that this element would be shaped in the future as the outcome of an architectural competition. Aside from the ceremonial plaza, a covered walkway, made up of a series of columns, also connected the remembrance hall and the heroes' hall. Along the walkway, facing north, were four small buildings. These were the four memorial structures dedicated to ghetto revolutionaries, underground fighters, the military's fallen, and the righteous among the nations.

On the eastern side of the site was the educational compound, a place that took up the lion's share of Yad Vashem. This area was saturated with greenery and at its center was the domed synagogue and, next to it, the archive and research centers. At the easternmost point of the area were five additional buildings, hotels and homes for Yad Vashem's staff.

This blueprint was not publicized; the only evidence of it (that I have found) was the plan prepared by the architects, preserved by Shenhavi at the Yad Yaari Research and Documentation Center. This ostensibly attests to the fact that they were never adopted by the institution's heads. Perhaps the reason for this was that the area selected for the enterprise was in the hands of the Hashemite Kingdom of Jordan from 1948. Nevertheless, it is clear that the Ramat Rachel plan constituted a leap in terms of the planning process. It served as the foundation for the later process of planning Yad Vashem in Jerusalem's west, and some of its elements were integrated in the Mount of Remembrance.

Conclusion

The desire to build a memorial to the Holocaust and heroism in the land of Israel compelled Yad Vashem's heads to deal with three central issues: commemoration – what would be memorialized and commemorated at Yad Vashem –

Holocaust, heroism, or both;[155] the way in which the remembrance of the Holocaust and heroism would be shaped – giving architectural expression to the terms and building a commemorative compound dedicated to memory; and the question of the correct, most accurate space for the memorial within the land of Israel. The last two questions – the institution's location and the form of Holocaust and heroism remembrance in the landscape of the land of Israel – were the focus of the current chapter.

The first years after the war, when the Nazis' horrors toward European Jewry were becoming clear, were characterized by the search for a fitting way to memorialize the events. It seemed that the Holocaust should be related to as Judaism had related to traumatic events in the past, through prayer; writing memorial books; holding memorial, Mishnah-learning, and prayer services; or through assemblies, rallies, and protests. But the aspiration of many in the land of Israel and overseas – private institutions, within the Zionist movement's bodies and outside of them – was to underscore that the Holocaust was different from all other events in Jewish history. In mid-1946, roughly a year after the war's end, Shenhavi made a list of over fifty initiatives that competed with Yad Vashem, forty of them overseas and eleven similar ones in the land of Israel. The list, presented as proof of the urgency to act in founding and building Yad Vashem, highlights the scope and intensity of this phenomenon.[156]

Shenhavi wished to guarantee a monopoly over Holocaust remembrance in the land of Israel in having the Zionist bodies establish Yad Vashem. But the attempt to shape collective memory for the Holocaust and heroism, commemoration that would be based on the future state's institutions' shared Zionist-national identity, turned out to be too complex and problematic. The many conflicts surrounding emerging Zionist-Jewish identity, which were part and parcel of the disagreements about the issue of Holocaust and heroism commemoration, led to the fact that no agreement or unanimity about the proper way to memorialize and commemorate the Holocaust materialized. Shenhavi's interpretation of the Holocaust, his attempts and those of Yad Vashem's management to negotiate between the horrors of Europe and the land of Israel, between a terrible past and a present of pioneering and establishing a Jewish state, between a rejected Diaspora and a predetermined state were doomed to failure. Shenhavi and his colleagues were ultimately unable to overcome the gaping abyss – not only geographical but primarily

---

155 Doron Bar, "Holocaust and Heroism in the Process of Establishing Yad Vashem 1942–1970," *Dapim – Studies on the Holocaust* 30 (2016): 1–25.
156 YVA, AM1 287, "Competing Enterprises for Commemorating the Holocaust in the World."

political – between these concepts, and the vision of establishing a memorial site collapsed.

Politics and poetics are two of the most influential factors related to commemoration in landscape. The politics of memory determines what and whom should be commemorated, while the poetics deal with form and style.[157] Despite the fact that Shenhavi and the other heads of Yad Vashem attempted to advance both of these subjects and obtain wider agreement for building a memorial site for the Holocaust and heroism in the land of Israel from the heads of the national foundations, the current chapter indicates, politics here annihilated poetics, precluding the possibility of the plan becoming reality. Shenhavi and his colleagues in Yad Vashem's management were unable to overcome or bridge the essential conflicts that erupted between the different agents and the objective problems tied to the place, and the building of the commemoration site was not executed. This failure was tied not only to the enormity of the commemoration Shenhavi proposed, nor to its extraordinary financial scope, but primarily to his inability to unite the different forces around his vision. With his singular personality and his zealous passion for the project, he aroused great antagonism. It was not the objective difficulties of establishing a memorial site that impeded him, but primarily the lack of agreement and the great division that emerged around Holocaust and heroism remembrance.

In the six years covered in this chapter, proposals were raised for founding Yad Vashem in various places around the land of Israel. Initially, these were the pioneering landscapes of the northern Hula Valley and the western Jezreel Valley, and, later on, the Zionist bodies and heads of Yad Vashem focused on Jerusalem and its environs. Here, too, different proposals were raised about the enterprise's location, whether it was Mount Scopus, west of the city, or in its south. These moves from place to place serve to illuminate the difficulties tied to the institution's establishment. It was not just finding the land that was problematic; the mobilization and unification around the idea of Holocaust and heroism commemoration was what emerged as most troublesome.

Ultimately all of the plans failed. The differences of opinion that characterized the institution's activity in those years thwarted its establishment, accompanied as they were by the struggle to establish a state and the military challenges that abounded during the second half of the forties. Even Shenhavi's unending dedication to the idea of Yad Vashem and adherence to the task were not sufficient to realize the idea of establishing the institution, and he was forced to make

---

157 Maoz Azaryahu, "Memory in the Landscape: Invisible Memorials – Three Test Cases," *Cathedra* 150 (2013): 211–38 [in Hebrew].

do with small offices in Jerusalem and Tel Aviv, few and limited achievements when compared to his grand vision.

But Shenhavi's ideas did not fade into nothingness. In contrast with other commemoration plans that vanished, leaving behind nothing but sketches and correspondence, it became clear after the fact that Yad Vashem's destiny was unique. Shenhavi's ideas and the plans generated by the architects with whom he worked served as the basis for the foundation of Yad Vashem after 1953 and the passing of the Yad Vashem Law. As we will soon see, Shenhavi continued to accompany Yad Vashem in this period as well, first as its director and later in opposition, fighting against the institution's administration and architects, the realizers of the path he himself had begun to lay out in 1942.

Chapter 2
From Statehood until the Enactment of the Yad Vashem Law in August 1953

The period of time between May 1948, with the establishment of the State of Israel, and August 1953, when the Yad Vashem Law was passed in the Knesset, was no less than dramatic. Its influence on the establishment of Yad Vashem, in retrospect, was most significant. The beginning of the period was characterized by great distress for the heads of Yad Vashem, a sense that the curtain had fallen on the body they had labored to establish; it seemed the institution would never be built. The end of the period, however, was far more uplifting – a decision was made to establish an Israeli national authority for Holocaust commemoration and a memorial site in Jerusalem.[1]

During these five years, a low point for Yad Vashem, other bodies in the State of Israel filled the vacuum that surrounded Holocaust memory and commemoration. In 1949, Kibbutz Lohamai HaGeta'ot opened a museum that focused on the fight against the Nazis and founded an archive and library; the JNF began to plant the Martyrs' Forest in the mountains west of Jerusalem in 1951; and the Ministry of Religions founded the Chamber of the Holocaust on Mount Zion. During this period, funerals were also being held for ashes of Holocaust victims that were brought to the land of Israel. This vigorous activity only served to highlight Yad Vashem's crisis; what had, in the years leading up to the founding of the state, been the Zionist body tasked with Holocaust commemoration had now lost its monopoly.

Shenhavi had been a key figure in the process of establishing Yad Vashem in the period before the state was founded; he continued to be central during this era as well. Despite the bleak atmosphere that characterized his colleagues on Yad Vashem's management, and against the backdrop of the emerging competition surrounding Holocaust commemoration, Shenhavi continued his work – for example, on the question of the institution's location. After the search for a fitting site, Yad Vashem, with his help, finalized its location on a desolate hilltop in Jerusalem's west. Shenhavi was also responsible for the May 1950 idea of giving symbolic Israeli citizenship to Holocaust victims, a concept that ultimately, at the end of a long political process, was translated into the legislation of the Martyrs' and Heroes' Remembrance (Yad Vashem) Law. This law defined the many and

---

[1] Stauber, *A Lesson*, 61–95.

varied goals of the authority that would now be established and constituted the basis for the building of Yad Vashem on the Mount of Remembrance.

Yad Vashem Shuttered?

The different plans for building Yad Vashem in Ma'ale HaHamisha and Ramat Rachel, developed in the period that led up to the establishment of the State of Israel, were never realized. The disagreements that characterized the institution's activity at the time, along with the struggle to found the state and the concurrent military issues, thwarted its creation. In early 1948, before the founding of the state, Remez still felt that Yad Vashem should be insisted upon, as it would "have great value precisely at a time like this, when the existing humanities institutes would have added another in the midst of Jerusalem."[2] The press still mentioned the Yad Vashem plan as a solution for the "apathy" that had spread among the land's residents and survivors regarding Holocaust commemoration.[3] Nothing happened, and the curtain came down on the body that so many had toiled for since 1942.

But even during this period, against the backdrop of the political uncertainty in the land of Israel at the time and the growing military-existential threat, Shenhavi continued to work on the idea of Yad Vashem. He was driven by the fear that some actor in Israel or abroad would precede him and establish a Holocaust commemoration site. "Do we not know," he asked in mid-1948,

> that establishing a memorial monument for the six million on one of the streets of New York – with the help of foreign governmental institutions – keeps Jerusalem from building a single center for the enterprise of national remembrance? Does the incident of the monument in Warsaw, though we are grateful for its dimensions, not come to turn the eyes of the nation in the Diaspora away from Jerusalem? And if a global center for documents of the period is established in Paris – despite the existence of such a center in Jerusalem – is it really only coincidence?[4]

Shenhavi was speaking of an initiative to establish a monument to the Holocaust in New York, planned by Richard Kauffmann, and the memorial to the Warsaw Ghetto Uprising inaugurated in April 1948 (see below). More than anything, Shenhavi was concerned about the spirited activity of Isaac Schneersohn, who at that time was working on establishing a center for the commemoration and

---

[2] YVA, AM1 322, "Meeting of Representatives of Immigrants' Associations and Soldiers' Unions," February 19, 1948.
[3] "It Happened in the Forest, following the Revolt," *Yedioth Ahronoth*, April 23, 1948.
[4] YVA, AM1 27, "Meeting of the Histadrut General Council," May 10, 1948.

documentation of the Holocaust (Centre de Documentation Juive Contemporaine) in Paris.⁵ "Throughout the Diaspora, the belief that the large, central national monument will still be established in the homeland is waning and each place and each land is beginning to think of establishing local and separate monuments."⁶

Yad Vashem found itself in grave financial distress at the time. The office in Jerusalem was in danger of closing and different creditors threatened to sue the members of the management.⁷ One expression of the organization's state was its inability to raise funds in order to release dozens of crates of documents sent by Jewish Agency representatives in Munich from customs. The crates stood untouched at the Tel Aviv port for many months, just one component of the much more extensive historical material that had been collected at the time in Yad Vashem's offices that could not be examined or catalogued.⁸

At first, Yad Vashem's leaders believed that the continued existence of the institution should be guaranteed at all costs, and sent letters requesting financial support, for example to the heads of the Jerusalem Development Department at the Jewish Agency or the Zionist Organization.⁹ "The national and Jerusalem remembrance enterprise can and should become important financial leverage through the stream of tourists and visitors which it will have the power to attract," they explained, adding that "a national and popular instrument will grow at Yad Vashem for the Zionist movement, which will serve as a unifying force for all strata of the nation around the national and central rehabilitative enterprise in Jerusalem."¹⁰ Positive responses to these appeals and declarations of the Zionist bodies about the importance of Yad Vashem were in abundance. In late August 1948, the Zionist General Council resolved that the Zionist movement must see itself as devoted to the enterprise and called

---

5 On Erich Mendelsohn's New York monument: Young, *The Texture*, 290–92; on the Warsaw monument: Young, *The Texture*, 155–84; on the center in Paris: Laura Jockusch, "Breaking the Silence: The Centre de Documentation Juive Contemporaine in Paris and the Writing of Holocaust History in Liberated France," in *After the Holocaust: Challenging the Myth of Silence*, ed. David Cesarani and Eric J. Sundquist (Abingdon, Oxon: Routledge, 2011), 67–81; Shaul Krakowski, "Memorial Projects and Memorial Institutions Initiated by She'erit Hapletah," in *She'erit Hapletah, 1944–1948: Rehabilatation and Political Struggle*, ed. Yisrael Gutman and Adina Drechsler (Jerusalem: Yad Vashem, 1990), 354–55 [in Hebrew].
6 "We Will Build Yad Vashem for the Martyrs and Heroes," *Davar*, March 11, 1949.
7 HHA, 3–95. 15 (6), Tartakover to Remez, October 17, 1949; CZA, S21/301, D. Baharal to Yitzhak Ernst Nebenzahl, March 9, 1949.
8 HHA, 3–95. 15 (6), Tartakover to Shenhavi, June 22, 1949.
9 CZA, S21/301, Warhaftig and Shenhavi to Ze'ev Gold, November 22, 1948.
10 HHA, 3–95. 15 (6), Yad Vashem to Berl Locker, n.d.

on the movement's institutions to step up.[11] But in practice, none of the bodies showed enough interest, power, or motivation to aid Yad Vashem financially.

Near the end of 1948, against the backdrop of the fierce battles of the War of Independence, some of the management expressed the feeling that Yad Vashem should be put to rest and its failure acknowledged.[12] The chairman, Remez, wished to freeze the institution's activities until the end of the war, and wait until a determination was made about Jerusalem's future. Shenhavi, after opining that "the war and the founding of the state only increase the need for establishing the enterprise," maintained that the management should concede defeat, resign, and "hand the keys over to a supreme national institution."[13] Others, in contrast, were more moderate. Warhaftig and Tartakover suggested separating Yad Vashem from the documentation enterprise and continuing it independently, perhaps under the auspices of the newly formed Ministry of Education. Another proposal was that the JNF take responsibility for funding the institution. The Fund's chairman, Granot, vehemently disagreed, demanding that the enterprise's demise be declared post-haste. "The disaster of Yad Vashem," he said, "stems from the fact that they began with plans that were too large and did not limit them to something modest," aiming his allegations, indirectly, at Shenhavi. Granot proposed that Israel's government, when it was established, take the mission on itself. "In any event, the role of commemoration and memorialization is one of the government's first jobs," he stated, adding that "I cannot imagine that there would be a government in our state that would shirk such a responsibility."[14] In another meeting, a suggestion to transfer Yad Vashem's activity to Paris and thus compete with Schneersohn's enterprise there was raised. Shenhavi cautioned of wasting a "valuable and singular national element," energy, nerves, and public enthusiasm,[15] and suggested trying to convince various agents that the establishment of the institution in Jerusalem, especially at a trying time, when the city's future was uncertain, was of utmost importance. A letter to the Zionist Organization claimed that "special importance and weight are destined for the national memorial enterprise within the set of tools that will reinforce and broaden Jerusalem's strength. The natural,

---

[11] YVA, P.20/19, "Zionist General Council Decisions on Yad Vashem," August 30, 1948.
[12] HHA, 3–95. 15 (6), Warhaftig and Tartakover to Remez, November 6, 1949.
[13] CZA, KK5/16006, "Yad Vashem Meeting," October 11, 1948; CZA, KK5/16006, "Yad Vashem Meeting," November 26, 1948.
[14] Ibid.
[15] CZA, KK5/16006, "Yad Vashem Meeting," November 26, 1948.

organic link between the national memorial enterprise and Jerusalem can and should become important financial leverage through the stream of tourists and visitors which it will have in its power to attract."[16]

Even with the end of the war in 1949 and the stabilization of the political situation, the State of Israel's leaders were in no hurry to focus on Yad Vashem; it was unclear which of the state authorities was responsible for it. The board members turned time and again to Remez and stated that it was not possible "that the issue of Yad Vashem would be frozen for some time without the breath of life and without disassembling,"[17] and demanded that a decision be made in one direction or another.

The vacuum created in Holocaust commemoration and the lack of a central body that would be occupied with it led different actors, both public and private, to attempt to step in. One prominent example of this was the Holocaust commemoration activity at Kibbutz Lohamei HaGeta'ot in the western Galilee. Immediately with the establishment of the kibbutz on April 19, 1949 (on the sixth anniversary of the outbreak of the Warsaw Ghetto Uprising), its members began to work on Holocaust commemoration, founding an archive and library and even a small museum. In the early fifties, an exhibit on Jewish resistance and uprisings against the Nazis opened there; it attracted great crowds.[18]

Private individuals also developed independent ideas regarding Holocaust commemoration. One proposed establishing a "City of the Slain" that would be dedicated to the memory of IDF soldiers, "pioneers of Jewish defense, and survivors of the Nazi horrors." This place would contain a museum, halls with names of victims engraved on their walls, a park, monuments, but also a house of religious study (*beit midrash*) and a hotel.[19] Another citizen, a resident of Tel Aviv, suggested establishing the memorial to the six million in one of the squares close to the Tel Aviv coastline – a large building in the form of a hexagon, topped with a six-armed Menorah, in which martyrs' ashes would be placed.[20]

---

16 HHA, 3–95. 15 (6), Yad Vashem to Berl Locker, January 1, 1949.
17 HHA, 3–95. 15 (6), Warhaftig and Tartakover to Remez, November 6, 1949.
18 Maoz Azaryahu and Batia Donner, *Beit Lohamei HaGeta'ot: The Yitzhak Katzenelson Holocaust and Resistance Heritage Museum, 1949–1999* (Lohamei HaGeta'ot: Beit Lohamei HaGeta'ot, the Yitzhak Katzenelson Holocaust and Resistance Museum, 2000), 1–10 [in Hebrew].
19 ISA, G-3/5564, Zvi Shapira to Ben-Gurion, July 19, 1951.
20 ISA, G-3/5564, Haim Pismolt to various addresses, November 1951.

The Ashes of Austrian Jewry

The burial of the ashes of Austrian Jewry in 1949 in the Sanhedria cemetery constituted a significant test for Yad Vashem. This was a time when Torah scrolls and religious objects – but also human remains – were being transferred from the devastated communities to the State of Israel. These types of remains were brought by the survivors who streamed into the state after the end of the Second World War; in many cases, the remains were buried by community members in various cemeteries in the country and even on the Mount of Olives.[21]

The "delivery" of martyrs' ashes from Austria in the second half of 1949 constituted a turning point for these types of remains in the State of Israel. A glass box with some thirty urns was sent to Israel; in the urns were ashes belonging to Austria's Jews who had been killed in the camps. The box found itself at the center of a burial journey that infused Israel's public with the Holocaust and its meaning with great intensity. Later on, during the fifties, Yad Vashem made a major effort to transfer the ashes of the European victims to its auspices, as part of its attempt to bury the remains on the Mount of Remembrance and thus demonstrate the site's importance and sanctity. Despite the fact that the ashes coming from Austria in 1949 could have become the symbolic foundation for Yad Vashem, the institution's weakness in the years that followed the state's establishment led to the Ministry of Religions' takeover of the funeral ceremony and of the box of ashes, which was ultimately brought to the Chamber of the Holocaust on Mount Zion. This act established the Ministry of Religions' site as a commemoration locus of traditional Jewish character, and led to a protracted state of overlapping and competition with Yad Vashem.[22]

In early 1948, a proposal by Rabbi Shimon Efrati, formerly the head of the religious court (*av beit din*) in Warsaw, was submitted to Yad Vashem, suggesting that the institute take on the collection of the remains of Holocaust victims and their transfer to Israel, an endeavor that he called "the martyrs' bones." Having garnered approvals and recommendations from rabbis, Efrati suggested that after a fitting place was found for the burial of the bones – a site whose

---

[21] "Martyrs' Ashes' Funeral," *HaTzofe*, June 10, 1957; "In the Memory of Lyda's Martyrs," *Davar*, September 1, 1947; see also: Shimon Efrati, *From the Valley of Tears: Questions and Answers* (Jerusalem: Mossad Harav Kook, 1948) [in Hebrew]; idem, *From the Valley of Death: Responsa* (Jerusalem: Yehuda, 1961) [in Hebrew]; Rivka Parciack, *Here and There, Now and on Other Days: The Holocaust Crisis Seen through the Material Culture of Cemeteries and Monuments in Poland and Israel* (Jerusalem: Magnes Press, 2007), 63–66 [in Hebrew].

[22] Doron Bar, "Holocaust Commemoration in Israel during the 1950s: The Holocaust Cellar on Mount Zion," *Jewish Social Studies* 12, no. 1 (2005): 16–38.

entrance would be a "Mourning Gate" inscribed with the names of the victims – a special envoy would be sent to Europe to clarify the number of those buried there; then the remains would be brought to Israel under the auspices of Yad Vashem.[23]

At the same time, Yad Vashem received information about ashes of Austrian Jewish victims. Simon Wiesenthal, representative of the historic Linz committee, wished to bring the ashes to Israel, and the community members planned to bury them in a unique mausoleum of their own creation, at whose center a copy of the entrance gate to the Austrian concentration camp, Mauthausen, would stand.[24]

The establishment of the mausoleum threatened Yad Vashem's chances of being established,[25] and the suggestion that the commemoration of Austria's Jews be integrated within the JNF's Martyrs' Forest (though separately) gave Shenhavi's mind no rest.[26] Fearing that the Austrian Jews' initiative would weaken Yad Vashem and even topple the faltering enterprise entirely, he demanded that Wiesenthal transfer the ashes to Yad Vashem and then "what is fitting and appropriate within the framework of the enterprise will be done with it, as we will decide about the martyrs' ashes from different mass graves brought to the land."[27]

The Jewish community in Austria abandoned its wish to establish a separate site; it was willing to suffice with burying the ashes anywhere in the State of Israel. Now the dispute related to where that place would be. At first, in November 1948, Wiesenthal acted to transfer the ashes for burial in Tel Aviv, perhaps due to the wish that it be buried in the first Jewish city or perhaps because of the uncertainty of Jewish Jerusalem's future. Wiesenthal's appeal to Tel Aviv's municipality led Mayor Israel Rokach to respond: "It is with the trembling of holiness and appreciation that we received your proposal for Tel Aviv and its municipality to receive the trust and preservation of the box containing the thirty vessels of our martyrs' ashes," but he emphasized that the trust would be temporary. The box would remain in Tel Aviv

---

23 See, for example, "Martyrs' Ashes Funeral," *HaTzofe*, June 10, 1947; "In Memory of Lyda's Martyrs," *Davar*, September 1, 1947. For a discussion of the burial of ashes in Judaism, see Rivka Parciack, *Here and There*, 63–66 [in Hebrew].
24 YVA, M9 69, "Draft of the Mausoleum for 200,000 Jews Who Died in the German Concentration Camps in Austria," architect: S. Wiesenthal.
25 YVA, AM1 325, Neomi (no surname) to Shenhavi, January 19, 1948.
26 YVA, AM1 39, "Leaflet to Members of the Central Committee," February 27, 1948.
27 YVA, AM1 27, Shenhavi to members of the secretariat, March 14, 1948; CZA, KKL5/16006, JNF to Yad Vashem, April 6, 1948.

until a body was established that could determine the place of "preserving these ashes for eternity."[28]

Shenhavi recognized the danger in the proposal and understood both how important the burial of the ashes in Jerusalem was and the link between this occasion and the future of the remembrance enterprise: "from many serious and weighty perspectives, the martyrs' ashes should be transferred to the city in which our national memorial enterprise will be erected – Jerusalem," he demanded of Wiesenthal, adding that "in light of the situation . . . until Yad Vashem is founded and built, the place [of the ashes' burial] will be temporary. This will be a supreme expression of the entire nation's feelings, our giving the place to this holy city to which we will merit to bring the martyrs' ashes."[29]

Wiesenthal approved Shenhavi's appeal at the beginning of 1949. "We have requested of the Tel Aviv municipality that it preserve the box until a fitting time, when Yad Vashem settles on the place to memorialize the 'holy ashes',"[30] he apologized, and conveyed that "we also believe that for political and national reasons in the current time period we must do all we can to focus everything in Jerusalem and the enterprise that symbolizes our nation's Diaspora's link with the State of Israel."[31] Wiesenthal was relating, of course, to the question of Jerusalem's international future and the "danger" of internationalization hovering over it as well as to the importance the state attributed to firmly grounding the Israeliness of the western side of the city.

Shenhavi wanted the funeral for the ashes to be an occasion on a large scale, hoping that it would help instill Yad Vashem's concept among the public and the nation's leaders. He suggested postponing the transfer of the ashes so that Yad Vashem could organize the event. State authorities at the time were occupied with Theodor Herzl's second burial in Jerusalem, with his funeral scheduled for August 1949, lending further support to Shenhavi's request.[32]

At first, the ashes' funeral was meant to take place under the joint auspices of Yad Vashem and the Jewish Agency. In June, Yad Vashem initiated a special committee that included the Jerusalem municipality, the World Jewish Congress, and the Ministry of Religions.[33] The press referred at length to the expected arrival of the box and reflected the commonly held beliefs about Holocaust commemoration.

---

[28] ISA, G-2/8023, Committee of Austrian Jews to Tel Aviv Municipality, November 11, 1948; YVA, AM1 138, Tel Aviv Municipality to Simon Wiesenthal, November 12, 1948.
[29] ISA, G-2/8023, Shenhavi to Wiesenthal, December 19, 1948.
[30] ISA, G-2/8023, Wiesenthal to Shenhavi, January 10, 1949.
[31] ISA, AM1 138, Wiesenthal to Tel Aviv Municipality, January 10, 1949.
[32] ISA, AM1 138, Shenhavi to Wiesenthal, February 12, 1949.
[33] ISA, G-2/8023, Tartakover to Bergman, February 22, 1949.

Herzl Rosenblum gave the treatise he wrote on the subject the title "The Victims of Christian Civilization – in Jars."[34]

When the ashes arrived in Israel in June 1949, the Knesset communed with the memory of the six million,[35] but then, too, Yad Vashem's weakness and the different bodies' lack of interest in taking part in and funding the funeral was exposed. The Ministry of Religions, and, in effect, its director Shmuel Zanvil Kahana, was the only body to accept the challenge, taking the ceremony almost entirely under its own patronage. The religious Zionist community and the Chief Rabbinate turned the remains' burial into a powerful ceremony.

The ceremony of the transfer of the ashes began in the Ebelsberg Displaced Persons' Camp near the city of Linz in Austria. The central speaker was Menashe Opozdower, who at the time served as general secretary of the Zionist Federation in Austria. He stood with the crowd across from the container of ashes while community members transferred them symbolically to Wiesenthal's hands, and he departed for Israel.[36] The box contained thirty ceramic urns, painted in blue stripes with the word "Mauthausen" in German. On the lids, the names of the concentration camps in Austria, such as Amstetten, Gussen II, and Linz, were added (in all probability later on). The jars had a red triangle, pointing downward, painted on them, and they held ashes most likely collected from the sites of extermination in Austria. According to some, the jars held written confirmation of the authenticity of the ashes they contained.[37]

When the plane with the ashes touched down at the Lod airport, a few dozen public figures awaited, foremost among them the chief rabbis and Deputy Speaker of the Knesset Yosef Burg. The box was stationed in the hall of the Chief Rabbinate in Tel Aviv for the masses to see and afterwards moved to the Great Synagogue, where many passed before it; it was then moved to Jerusalem, covered in a flag of Israel and *tallit* (prayer shawl), and accompanied by members of the Hevra Kadisha and police officers. At the entrance to Jerusalem, a ceremony was held with the participation of a military honor guard; from there the participants continued to

---

34 *Yediot Ahronoth*, June 22, 1949.
35 "The Knesset Commemorates the Memory of the Millions," *Al HaMishmar*, June 23, 1949.
36 BLHA, 28776 א.
37 It is logical that the jars containing the ashes of Jews murdered in Austria would be marked with a double triangle in the form of a Star of David, the one used by the Nazis to mark Jewish prisoners. But the fact is that the symbol used by the Nazis to identify political prisoners, both communist and socialist, in the concentration camps is what appears on the jars. I have not been able ascertain how the ashes were collected and from where exactly, and why it was said that the jars contained the ashes of 200,000 Jews. It appears that the use of this number is fundamentally flawed and that, in fact, that was the number of Jews living in Austria right before its annexation to Germany in 1938.

Figure 5: Glass box with thirty vessels of ashes brought from Austria, displayed to the public at the Chief Rabbinate's building, Tel Aviv (NPA, David Eldan).

the Yeshurun Synagogue, another site of religious Jewish symbolism. The ashes were brought to the Jewish cemetery in Sanhedria and buried in one of its corners, in a section named the "Martyrs' Square." Some individuals took advantage of the opportunity to bury other remains that they had brought to Israel within the open grave, such as pieces of soap – popular opinion was that they had been produced by the Nazis from the remains of those who were killed.[38]

The burial in Sanhedria was considered temporary; many hoped that someday the ashes would be reinterred in the Jewish cemetery on the Mount of Olives, which was, at that time, across a border and under Jordanian control.[39] As we will see, six months later, on the traditional day for Holocaust commemoration, 10 Tevet 5710 (1949), the ashes were removed and taken to the Chamber of the Holocaust, where they served as the place's most prominent symbol and a significant component in the shaping of memory at the site.

---

[38] ISA, G-2/8022, "Ashes Funeral"; "Death Camp Victims Ashes Laid to Rest in Jerusalem," *Palestine Post*, June 27, 1949.
[39] CZA, KKL5/16006, Arieh Leo Lauterbach to Locker, June 21, 1949.

Ashes from the Flossenburg Concentration Camp

Shenhavi may have lost the opportunity to use the burial of the Austrian ashes for the founding of Yad Vashem, but later in 1949 another opportunity arose. In March 1949, Reuben Hecht, a Jewish shipping man of German extraction living in Germany after the Second World War,[40] sent a letter to Prime Minister David Ben-Gurion, announcing his intent to transfer a glass case with ashes from the German concentration camp Flossenburg, in the Bavaria region. He had a letter attesting to the ashes' authenticity, given to him by Philipp Auerbach, a Jew serving as special commissioner to the victims of Nazi persecution in Bavaria's government.[41] The letter stated that the container held "the ashes of those killed in the Flossenburg concentration camp, where more than eighty thousand people were sent to their deaths in the crematorium, including twenty thousand Jews from various lands."[42]

Yad Vashem was meant to be the body charged with burying the ashes but Hecht, who brought the box to the country, had other plans. He suggested to Ben-Gurion that the ashes be buried in a mass grave in a "national pantheon," in which Theodor Herzl would be reburied. This memorial monument would be built, in his vision, as two immense Tablets of the Law, "larger than the pyramids," which would be seen from afar: "any Jews in the world struck over those killed from his family who does not know their place of burial can lift his eyes to the grave in Jerusalem in emotion, as here no doubt are buried the bones of his family members."[43]

Tartakover, representing both the World Zionist Congress and Yad Vashem, asked that a committee be formed to organize the ashes' burial.[44] For Shenhavi, Hecht's initiative once again aroused a sense of danger.[45] It also appears that the fact that Hecht belonged to the Revisionist camp deterred Shenhavi. He quickly dispatched a letter to the Prime Minister's Office in which he cautioned Ben-Gurion against national interference in the ashes' burial. He claimed that there was no uniqueness to this cargo of ashes, and similar ones were arriving in Israel and all must be cared for. He emphasized that "it is necessary that our

---

40 Reuben R. Hecht, *Last Gentleman: Autobiography* (Or Yehuda: Zmora-Bitan, 2007) [in Hebrew].
41 Hannes Ludyga, *Philipp Auerbach (1906–1952): Staatskommissar für rassisch, religiös und politisch Verfolgte* (Berlin: Berliner Wissenschafts-Verlag, 2005).
42 ISA, G-3/5564, Philipp Auerbach to the government of Israel, January 20, 1949.
43 HHA, 3–95. 15 (3), Hecht to Ben-Gurion, March 30, 1949.
44 ISA, G-2/8023, Tartakover to various addresses, April 3, 1949.
45 CZA, CC6/415, Shenhavi to Tartakover, April 10, 1949.

government also devote the necessary attention to everything related to the national Holocaust and heroism commemoration enterprise and to our situation today."[46]

A number of months later, Hecht once again appealed to the Prime Minister's Office, when he saw that his proposal of establishing a "grave of the anonymous Jew" had not aroused interest. He mentioned his plan and that "Jerusalem should preserve two temples as one, two martyrs' graves, Herzl's grave and the grave of the unknown Jew who was killed and massacred, one next to the other, both organized and built in dimensions befitting their value and decorated by art and standing for eternity."[47] This time, too, Ben-Gurion chose not to respond.

In the absence of other bodies that could take the organization of the funeral for the Flossenburg ashes under their wing, including Yad Vashem, it was once again Kahana who stepped in and determined that 10 Tevet 1949 would be the day of the ashes' burial in the Chamber of the Holocaust, near David's Tomb. This date obscured a serious political and religious struggle around the day of Holocaust commemoration in the State of Israel. While traditional Judaism saw the General Kaddish Day as the appropriate one for marking the extermination of Jews in the Second World War, the Zionist Left saw things differently, and took action to set 27 Nisan (the day when the Warsaw Ghetto uprising started), as the memorial day.[48]

"The Committee for Holocaust Commemoration" – which was, in essence, "The Committee for Mount Zion" that Kahana headed and through which he acted in David's Tomb and its environs[49] – organized the burial ceremony for the ashes from the Flossenburg concentration camp and ran it exclusively, without the participation of any other official agents.

A number of urns of ashes, draped in black, containing the remains of the "Flossenburg martyrs," were at the center of the burial ceremony. The remains were presented at the Tel Aviv offices of the *Va'ad Hakehila* (Jewish local community) along with other remains,[50] and, after Tel Aviv Chief Rabbi Isser Yehuda Unterman eulogized the dead, the funeral proceeded to Jerusalem. At the event, held

---

[46] HHA, 3–95. 15 (6), Shenhavi to the government secretariat, April 20, 1949.
[47] ISA, G-3/5564, Hecht to Ben-Gurion, October 10, 1949.
[48] "Burial of Martyrs Ashes during 'Holocaust Day,'" *Davar*, December 5, 1949; HHA, 3–95. 15 (6), "Summary of a Discussion between Remez and Kahana," n.d.; Roni Stauber, "The Debate in the 1950s Regarding the Establishment of a Holocaust Remembrance Day," in *A State in the Making: Israeli Society in the First Decades*, ed. Anita Shapira (Jerusalem: The Zalman Shazar Center for Jewish History, 2001), 189–203 [in Hebrew].
[49] Doron Bar, "Between the Chamber of the Holocaust and Yad Vashem: Martyrs' Ashes as a Focus of Sanctity," *Yad Vashem Studies* 38 (2010): 195–227.
[50] "Today Is the Funeral of the Martyrs Ashes in Jerusalem," *Herut*, December 29, 1949.

at the cemetery in Sanhedria and run by the Chief Rabbinate, the remains of ashes and "Jewish soap" were buried there; in a ceremony held on the same day on Mount Zion, the ashes that had been brought from Austria earlier were moved from Sanhedria to Mount Zion and deposited in the Chamber of the Holocaust.[51]

Figure 6: Glass box with thirty vessels of ashes displayed in the Chamber of the Holocaust (private collection, Unknown photographer).

This ceremony and the memorial day events on 10 Tevet gave further validation to the Mount Zion Chamber of the Holocaust's status as a central commemoration site, and to the Ministry of Religions as the heart of Israel's endeavor of collecting the victims' ashes. The burial of the ashes in the Chamber of the Holocaust created a unique fusion of a grave and a commemoration site, a sacred space in which the ashes of those killed in the Holocaust were buried with a symbolic commemoration site that underscored the Jewish traditional side of the Holocaust. From this point on, the Chamber of the Holocaust became the sole legitimate site, at least according to those in the Ministry of Religions and Chief Rabbinate, for the burial of Holocaust remains.

---

51 *Yedioth Ahronoth*, December 29 and 30, 1949.

As long as there was no Yad Vashem, this perception was not problematic; but, as we will see, after Yad Vashem's founding and its firm establishment over the fifties, many conflicts arose between Kahana and the institute's management about the legitimacy of the commemoration site on Mount Zion and whether Yad Vashem had the right to collect and bury martyrs' ashes on the Mount of Remembrance.

The Martyrs' Forest and the JNF

The most prominent body dealing with physical Holocaust commemoration in the State of Israel in the early fifties was the JNF. In 1951, it began to plant the Martyrs' Forest in the barren hills in what was then called the Jerusalem corridor, in an effort to cover the area with six million trees that would serve as a "memorial candle" for the six million Jews who had been murdered in the Holocaust.

The idea of planting a JNF memorial forest first arose after the end of the Second World War. The forest was perceived as part of the JNF's extensive and prolonged activity of making the "wilderness" bloom by planting forests.[52] The Zionist forest was a clear national symbol, part of the State of Israel's desire and need to immortalize the Holocaust victims. But the Martyrs' Forest and the JNF's attempts to make it the central national Zionist endeavor in the State of Israel highlighted the tension that prevailed at that time between the JNF and other bodies that were occupied with Holocaust commemoration, primarily Yad Vashem. This rivalry had begun, of course, before the establishment of the state, when Yad Vashem made its first hesitant steps and its heads struggles to find an internal Zionist political solution that would put the minds of the national foundations at ease. But even after the establishment of the state and with Yad Vashem crumbling in the background, the JNF's enterprise was threatening to Shenhavi. He felt that the Fund was exploiting Yad Vashem's wretched state to replace it as the national body charged with Holocaust commemoration, effectively eliminating all chances that the institution would ever be built.

---

[52] Sigal Barnir, "On Forests as Sites of Commemoration," *Itzuv Zikaron* 1 (1998): 86–97 [in Hebrew]; Nili Lifshitz and Gideon Biger, *Forestry in Eretz Israel: First 100 Years 1850–1950* (Jerusalem: Ariel, 2000) [in Hebrew]; Jacob Markovitzky, *Spirit of the Valleys: The Enterprise of the JNF as Stepping-Stones in the Development of the National Homeland (1920–1936)* (Tel Aviv: Misrad Habitachon, 2007) [in Hebrew].

The Martyrs' Forest was meant to spread across an immense area, more than 8,000 acres (as opposed to Yad Vashem's 350) of the Jerusalem hills.[53] This land was chosen primarily because of its unique geographical and geopolitical features and its national symbolism in particular. Zivia Lubetkin, a Warsaw Ghetto fighter, stated that

> it is no coincidence that the Martyrs' Forest is being planted on the road to Jerusalem. It is not just that the eyes of all of those who were exterminated were raised to Jerusalem, but that this generation, too, which peeked into the abyss of destruction [the Holocaust] and at the joy of Israel's rebirth, must remember that the road to independence leads through the Martyrs' Forest.[54]

The first tree-planting ceremony held in the Martyrs' Forest in March 1951 opened with the raising of the state's flag and the singing of Hatikva, the national anthem, after which Yosef Weitz, a member of the JNF's board of directors (as well as Yad Vashem's) spoke, having also planted the first cypress tree there. Minister of Education Remez (no longer chair of Yad Vashem) noted in his address that

> planting trees, planting memorial trees on the land of the Jewish National Fund, in the sovereign State of Israel, gathering its exiles from the ends of the earth for the ascent of the souls of millions of dead . . . contains not only the establishment of memory; this act also contains the revenge of the Eternity of Israel on the great diabolical destroyer.[55]

The representatives of the "lands of destruction" planted the first trees and, around these, representatives of the parties' central institutions and members of youth movements planted additional seedlings.[56] The sowing of the forest near Ksalon also created a strong impression; the JNF hoped to exploit the public support and encourage donors – community members in Israel and the Diaspora – to contribute to the forest's planting and expansion.[57]

After the ceremony, the JNF began to focus on the question of the forest's structure and the form of commemoration. The forest, it was decided, would include not just trees but also pavilions, boulevards, paths, gardens, and signs. The forest would be split into subdivisions, as many as the number of countries in which communities were eradicated, as well as other forests dedicated to the

---

53 CZA, KKL5/17351, Map of the "Area Dedicated to the Martyrs' Forest," 1:100,000, 1951.
54 Zivia Lubetkin, "We Should Remember and Not Forget," in *A Memorial for the Holocaust and the Revolt*, ed. Yitzhak Mann and Sarel Baruch (Jerusalem: Keren Kayemet Leyisrael, 1953), 72 [in Hebrew].
55 CZA, KKL5/17352, "The Speech of the Minister of Education and Culture during the Planting Ceremony," March 7, 1951.
56 CZA, KKL5/17352, "First Trees Planting Ceremony at the Martyrs' Forest," March 7, 1951.
57 CZA, KKL5/19079, "Expansion of Martyrs' Forest Planting," n.d.

Holocaust's heroes, to the leaders of the Warsaw Ghetto, to the paratroopers who landed in Europe, and others. It was suggested that a "Memorial Committee," an international body made up of seventy people from Israel and the Diaspora, would head the enterprise under the auspices of the State of Israel's president.[58]

The growing success of the Martyrs' Forest, the public response to it, and the news of the wide-ranging and successful fundraising being carried out by the JNF aroused the ire of Shenhavi, who challenged the Fund's right to establish an independent Holocaust memorial site. In the main, he was horrified by the fact that many of the elements that he had proposed integrating in Yad Vashem in the past were found in the Martyrs' Forest. "Registering the names of martyrs in memorial books," Shenhavi protested, "making special pavilions for these memorial books in the Martyrs' Forest, and more were all central foundations in Yad Vashem's action plan. In effect, it means that the JNF is about to execute a small-scale memorial enterprise."[59] Shenhavi claimed that the use of "the remembrance slogan for the six million" overshadowed the national memorial enterprise and the chances of realizing it, and he suggested that the JNF take responsibility for establishing Yad Vashem, saving it from demise. Alternatively, he suggested, the JNF could focus on planting trees only,[60] leaving the opportunity to reestablish Yad Vashem to a different national or official body.

Granot, JNF's director-general, was unequivocal in stating that the JNF would not surrender its right to appeal to different bodies and institutions, to communities and organizations, in order to raise funds for planting the Martyrs' Forest; in his words, "these have always been the JNF's traditional tactics for all of its activities."[61] Shenhavi was disappointed that after so many years of joint effort on the part of the different Zionist bodies "for the great and holy mission," the JNF was working on its own; he asked Granot to refrain from making such a radical move.[62]

The pressure applied by Shenhavi may have been what led to the early-1952 agreement between the JNF and Yad Vashem; alternatively, it may have been the discussion of the Yad Vashem Law in the Knesset and government. The agreement stated that the two bodies, the JNF and Yad Vashem, would cooperate in commemorating those killed in the Holocaust and immortalizing the Jewish fighters in the Second World War. It determined that the registration of the victims would be conducted by the JNF and, after the establishment of Yad

---

58 CZA, KKL5/17352, "Martyrs' Forest Plan," September 14, 1951.
59 CZA, KKL5/19079, Shenhavi to Granot, November 3, 1951.
60 Ibid.
61 Ibid.
62 Ibid.

Vashem, the JNF would serve as the state's agent in its activity. It was further agreed that the income from the memorial enterprise would be split evenly between the two bodies and that "there will be a complete separation between the Martyrs' Forest, which will remain in the hands of the JNF, and Yad Vashem, which will act in all fields of commemoration independently and on its own responsibility." It proudly declared that "this joint activity will contain an eternal response to the Paris agreement [i.e., the commemoration center founded there by Schneersohn]."[63]

In advance of 27 Nisan 1952, the press published notices about a national convention in memory of the Holocaust's victims, to take place in the Martyrs' Forest. At the time, in the absence of an agreed-upon national day of memory, Holocaust memorial ceremonies still took place in different locations around the country and at different times, often being scheduled on days in which different communities in Europe had been annihilated. The memorial ceremony being held in the Martyrs' Forest was an innovation, the beginning of a "tradition" that continued for some years and was later replaced by the ceremony held on the Mount of Remembrance in Jerusalem.

Prior to the planting ceremony, the JNF made great efforts to recruit national leaders and policy-makers to its enterprise, drawing encouragement from the fact that a series of central public figures, headed by Prime Minister David Ben-Gurion, encouraged it to continue its activities. Ben-Gurion saw no conflict between the JNF's vigorous activity and the attempts being made at the time in the Knesset and in Israeli's government to establish a national authority occupied with Holocaust commemoration. Before the ceremony, he wrote that "the single monument, fitting to the memory of European Jewry exterminated by the Nazi beasts of prey, is the State is Israel as a whole," but, nevertheless, "the Jewish National Fund is doing something valuable and praiseworthy in planting the 'Martyrs' Forest.'"[64] Editorials in the country's press also related to the ceremony, promising that "the Yad Vashem enterprise – in memory of the Holocaust and heroism – still awaits the execution of the extensive plans laid out" and that, in the meantime, "the Martyrs' Forest will doubtless be a magnificent part of the general framework of a Jewish and Israeli memorial monument in memory of the martyrs and heroes. Its creation cannot be too early or too late."[65]

---

[63] YVA, AM1 146, Shenhavi to Weiss, March 14, 1952.
[64] BGA, 138180, Ben-Gurion to Granot, April 21, 1952.
[65] "Martyrs' Forest," *Davar*, April 21, 1952.

The ceremony on 27 Nisan was held in a place that would later become the symbolic center of the Martyrs' Forest, close to the channel of the Ksalon Valley, a place where a martyrs' cave would be hewn in the late fifties. Hundreds of people, most of them Holocaust survivors, representatives of communities, and organizations that the JNF had recruited for the event, took part. In the ceremony, the format that would repeat itself in the ceremonies that took place in the subsequent years was shaped; it was comprised of speeches integrated with dramatic artistic elements.[66]

At the end of the ceremony, and throughout 1952, the JNF continued to encourage survivors to take an active role in planting the forest. In order to generate a buzz around it, the Fund invited symbolic figures, politicians, survivors, and others to plant trees. The Martyrs' Forest even had a symbol: a lit candle against the backdrop of a forest, behind which the sun shone. Its posters emphasized the contrast between the devastated Diaspora and the realization of the Zionist dream in the State of Israel.[67] The JNF's publicity department produced a film titled *We Will Remember Them*, showing the horrors of the extermination camps and the destruction of the Jewish centers in Europe. The film ended with the first planting of seedlings in the Martyrs' Forest.[68] It was presented at gatherings held by survivors' organizations and served as a first-rate propaganda tool for fundraising, along with a book published by the JNF.[69] All of these were elements in the efforts to position the Martyrs' Forest as a national enterprise – and underscored the public silence that characterized Yad Vashem's activities.

The initial success of the Martyrs' Forest and the great effects of the commemoration enterprise made it necessary for the JNF to define the content it wished to infuse into the enterprise.[70] Fourteen forests, divided into the countries of destruction, would be planted, made up of community forests and groves. Alongside the national forests, two special forests would be planted: the ghetto fighters' forest and the martyred children's forest, which would be called the "tombstone forest" – one of the first memorial projects dedicated to the memory of the children who had been killed in the war. The concept included a commemoration tower at the center of each forest, serving as a pilgrimage destination for survivors. Leading to each of

---

66 "Memorial Day at the Martyrs' Forest," *Karnenu* 29, no. 5 (June 1952): 2; "Many Make Their Way to Mount Zion to Commemorate the Holocaust," *Yedioth Ahronoth*, April 22, 1952.
67 KKLFA, d1281-031; CZA, KRA 233; CZA, KRA 416; Yael Zerubavel, "The Forest as a National Icon: Literature, Politics, and the Archaeology of Memory," *Israel Studies* 1, no. 1 (1996): 60–99.
68 "We Shall Not Forget Them," *Davar*, September 3, 1952; SSJFA, VT DA0039.3838.
69 David Ben-Gurion, "Martyrs' Forest," in Mann and Baruch, *A Memorial*, 70–71.
70 CZA, KKL5/19081, S. Levi to Hiram, Krakauer, and Klarwein, December 19, 1952.

these foci would be a paved boulevard, and inside the tower, on a special table with an eternal flame, would be the "Martyrs' Book," containing the names of those killed.[71]

The Yad Vashem Law

In the early 1950s, Yad Vashem was in a poor state; it seemed that the curtain would soon fall on the institution, which had not yet achieved even a few of its objectives. But a turning point came with an idea raised by Shenhavi in May 1950: giving symbolic Israeli citizenship to the Jews who had perished in the Holocaust, a proposal that cleverly concealed his plan to keep Yad Vashem "alive."[72] At the core stood Shenhavi's idea that the endeavor of collecting names – defined with Yad Vashem's founding as one of its most crucial goals – must continue at all costs. Shenhavi suggested, therefore, that the collection of names continue, now under the umbrella of a law to be passed in Knesset, which would determine that each of the Holocaust's victims was also an Israeli citizen. In a detailed document that he formulated, "The Israeli Citizenship Law for Those Slain in the Jewish Extermination at the Hands of the Nazis," he wrote that "the State of Israel, as the official expression of the dispersed Jewish nation, will grant those lost [the slain in the Holocaust] its citizenship and in that way salvage their memories and their human dignity, return [them] to the bosom of their homeland, and decry the Nazi villainy for generations to come."[73] Among other things, he suggested that a national institution be founded that would be charged with executing the law and even hinted that the JNF could shoulder the responsibility.[74]

Paradoxically, it was at a meeting of Yad Vashem's management in August 1950 to declare its resignation and the "transfer of keys to an appropriate institution" that Shenhavi's new proposal to give citizenship to the Holocaust victims was presented. Dinur, who one year hence would be appointed minister of education and would later serve as the chairman of Yad Vashem, felt that "it [the proposal] contains a special and important element and it has the power to give new shape to the commemoration enterprise [Yad Vashem]." Dinur was one of the people who

---

71 CZA, KKL5/19081, Martyrs' Forest Structure, no name, n.d.
72 Stauber, *A Lesson*, 61–64.
73 ISA, G-3/5564, Shenhavi, law granting citizenship rights to the victims of the Nazi destruction, May 21, 1950; Ronald W. Zweig, *German Reparation and the Jewish World: A History of the Claims Conference* (Boulder: Westview Press, 1987).
74 CZA, KKL5/17418, Avraham Kamini to Granot, June 13, 1950.

had vehemently opposed the dismantling the institution, claiming that the commitment Yad Vashem had taken upon itself must be realized.[75]

Thus, despite the fact that in early 1951 David Remez (now minister of transportation) tendered his resignation from Yad Vashem to Ben-Gurion and declared the transfer of responsibility for the future of the endeavor to the State of Israel, he left an opening in his words for the renewal of Yad Vashem's activity. He wrote to Ben-Gurion that at the right time all of the institutions that had sent representatives to Yad Vashem's management would be willing to support the government if the execution of Yad Vashem were raised by the government.[76] Despite Ben-Gurion's lack of enthusiasm over the occupation with Holocaust and commemoration,[77] Remez hoped that the prime minister would nonetheless be persuaded to act.

Shenhavi "gambled" on Ben-Gurion, attempting to pressure him so that he and his peers in the government would advance the legislation.[78] He also consulted with public figures in Israel and the Diaspora and attempted to draft them to apply pressure on the prime minister. But the Yad Vashem Law did not see a significant turning point until Shenhavi abandoned the proposal to give the victims citizenship and instead promoted the idea that a national authority be established to act on the subject of Holocaust remembrance. Giving Israeli citizenship to the six million was replaced with honorary citizenship, an idea that was not a legal expression and was therefore easier to execute. Ben-Gurion and Minister of Education Dinur, along with different officials, discussed the opportunity to establish a national state authority for the commemoration of the slain and, in early 1952, a bill was prepared.[79] Shenhavi worked through his own channels and, in parallel to the government and Knesset activity, appealed to many intellectuals, jurists, and academics in Israel and around the world in order to ask for their opinions on the emerging law.[80]

One of the most significant factors driving those toiling to enact the law and establish Yad Vashem, undoubtedly, was the threat of the center for Holocaust documentation and commemoration in Paris. Isaac Schneersohn, a rabbi and industrialist who was devoted to Holocaust documentation, planned to build the Memorial of the Unknown Jewish Martyr, a sort of "museum-pantheon that would contain all of the historical sacred mementos that we were able to collect

---

75 KMHA, S-29, 3, "Yad Vashem Meeting," August 10, 1950.
76 CZA, KKL5/17418, Remez to the prime minister, February 15, 1951.
77 Stauber, *A Lesson*, 64–70.
78 HHA, 3–95. 16 (1), Shenhavi to Ben-Gurion, June 14, 1951.
79 Stauber, *A Lesson*, 74–83.
80 HHA, 3–95. 16 (1), Shenhavi to Hersch Zvi Lauterpacht, July 10, 1951.

after the Nazi Holocaust" near the banks of the Seine and the municipality building.[81] He managed to recruit a series of leaders and renowned figures in France and outside of it, Jewish and non-Jewish, to support the project and convinced them to join the founding committee.

A booklet published in advance of laying the cornerstone for the center stated that "the laying of the cornerstone upon which we will immortalize the memory of the victims is possible only in blood-soaked Europe, that is, Paris. Paris is and will remain the center of the world's spiritual life." This statement illustrated to the State of Israel's actors that they must quicken their pace regarding Yad Vashem, as "only the nation in its land and its state must and has the right to establish a pan-national enterprise to immortalize the memory of the pan-national Holocaust victims."[82] The center in Paris was a tremendous threat to Shenhavi in particular. He was certain that construction in Paris would precede Yad Vashem, rendering its building redundant, and he appealed to Ben-Gurion a number of times to get involved. "With my fingernails, I cling to the internal, cautionary decree that still threatens to make the element of the Holocaust a 'public bomb,'" Shenhavi warned the director-general of the Prime Minister's Office, a bomb "that will stir the winds and add oil to the bonfire of the interpartisan tension that is eating at us."[83] Shenhavi cautioned Ben-Gurion that "in the eyes of the entire world, Jewish and non-Jewish, Paris will acquire for itself the right of precedence in the field of sanctifying the memory of millions of our people. This can be interpreted as a division of roles: Paris commemorates the Holocaust victims and Jerusalem receives the reparations," referring to the funds that were meant to be received from Germany as a result of signing the reparations agreement.[84] "The great enterprise, overlapping almost entirely with the Yad Vashem plan, will be established in Paris and, moreover, with the agreement and support of state figures and the Zionist movement," Shenhavi stated, "I cannot support that."[85] Shenhavi attempted to enlist public opinion; he exploited journalists who could apply pressure on the politicians to approve the law.[86]

---

[81] ISA, G-2/5564, "International Council for the building of a Monument for the Anonymous Jewish Martyr," n.d.
[82] ISA, G-2/5564, Warhaftig to Ben-Gurion, March 23, 1952; "Paris against Jerusalem"? *Ha-Boker*, November 23, 1952.
[83] HHA, 3–95. 16 (1), Shenhavi to Ehud Avriel, March 6, 1952.
[84] ISA, GL-2/1087, Shenhavi to Ben-Gurion, September 2, 1952; the agreement between the State of Israel and Germany was signed on September 2, 1952.
[85] ISA, GL-2/1087, Shenhavi to Ben-Gurion, September 2, 1952.
[86] Theodore Hatalgui, "Will Israeli Citizenship Be Granted to the Nazis' Six Million Victims?," *Yedioth Ahronoth*, January 18, 1952.

After the fact it became clear that the crystallizing reparations agreement with Germany did indeed have an influence on the Yad Vashem Law. Israel's government, which during those months was occupied with the painful and complex subject, saw an advantage in supporting the Yad Vashem Law at the same time, and therefore gave its approval in principle. On June 29, 1952, the government approved the establishment of a Remembrance Authority that would be occupied with Holocaust and heroism commemoration and charged the ministerial committee (whose members included Ben-Gurion, Dinur, and Haim-Moshe Shapira) to formulate the law's articles relating to the subject. A public committee, they decided, would simultaneously be formed to examine the moral and political dimensions of the proposal and to submit a draft of the Holocaust and heroism remembrance law to the Knesset. This committee was later united with another Knesset committee that was occupied with the same subject.

Shenhavi proposed "creating facts on the ground," holding a cornerstone ceremony for the institution on the tenth anniversary of the Warsaw Ghetto Uprising, on 27 Nisan 1953. "I am convinced that the combination of laying a cornerstone and the tenth anniversary of the ghetto uprising," he wrote, "can be a sublime expression on this remembrance day and a substantial expression of our state's decision before the nation and the entire world to undertake the center for Holocaust and war commemoration."[87] He hoped that the ceremony would become "great leverage for introducing the memorial element to the nation and the transfer of the centers of gravity of activity to Jerusalem," and a means to determine the location of the memorial enterprise and its architectural plan.[88] As we will see, Yad Vashem's cornerstone was laid only one year later, at the end of July 1954.

The Yad Vashem Law was once again pushed to the margins while Israel's government was occupied with other subjects; only in early 1953 did the ministers return to the issue. The government assembled an additional ministerial committee on the law and it generated the bill's final formulation, which was approved by the government on March 18, 1953.[89]

At this stage, the question of the memorial enterprise's financing arose. Before the establishment of the state, the heads of Yad Vashem had assumed that funding would come from contributions, primarily from the relatives of victims wanting to immortalize their families. Now Shenhavi raised the possibility that in order to preserve its popular, Jewish, and Israeli character, the

---

87 KMHA, S-29, 3, Shenhavi to Dinaburg (Dinur), October 6, 1952.
88 Ibid.
89 Government Meeting 36/413 (18.3.1953), Records of the fourth government meetings, 4 (1953), 3–5.

funding would be divided between the State of Israel (35 percent); the Jewish Agency (25 percent); and the "masses," in the form loans and bonds (40 percent).[90] It appears that public opinion had also undergone a transformation on the subject, and the press was full of items and opinions about the enterprise's importance: "The memorial enterprise shall be established soon in its full scope, as planned a few years ago, and shall be the one authorized center for **Holocaust research**" [my emphasis].[91]

During those months, a stormy and scathing debate raged in Knesset about the law and its ramifications. Part of it related to questions of physical commemoration and Holocaust remembrance, elements that were new to Israeli society which was, at that time, dealing primarily with questions of immortalizing the casualties of the War of Independence.[92] Dinur's remarks to the Knesset about the importance of establishing Yad Vashem in Jerusalem opened by emphasizing that "This is the heart of the nation. This is the heart of Israel, this is where everything should be focused."[93] Most of the members of Knesset agreed, but differed about the enterprise's image. Rabbi Yitzchak-Meir Levin, representative of Agudat Yisrael, raised the question of whether it should be built monumentally and whether with "halls, [with] monuments of wood and stone we can immortalize the memory of our martyrs. Can we replace the most lofty and holy in the soul of the nation with monuments of wood and stone and empty it from all original Jewish essence and content? And can we say of it 'remove your shoes from your feet'?" Levin stated that it was impossible "to emulate the nations without modifications to Jewish essence," and that "popular holidays and mourning days" could not be created "artificially"; he claimed that Yad Vashem should focus on traditional Jewish commemoration through learning of Mishnah and prayer. MK Yona Kesse of Mapai replied that "there is nothing of the sculptured image," but rather "using all means to commemorate the Holocaust – literature, monuments, documents, symbols, art – all that can form and cultivate and embody the existence of memory."

Zerach Warhaftig, deputy minister of religions, highlighted an additional point of conflict tied to Yad Vashem in the discussion – the question of whether a Remembrance Authority must focus on Holocaust research, as Dinur had hinted in his words at the Knesset, or on commemoration. "If our opinion that Yad Vashem

---

90 HHA, 3–95. 16 (1), Shenhavi to the minister of education, June 17, 1953.
91 "Message [davar] of the Day," Davar, April 12, 1953.
92 Stauber, A Lesson, 84–91.
93 CZA, S5/111351, "Martyrs' and Heroes' Remembrance (Yad Vashem) Law," minister of education and culture speech at the Knesset, May 12, 1953.

need not stand out so much as a result of its size, monuments, and buildings, but rather because of its content and profound research is accepted," he stated,

> we will not need so much money in order to erect this monument. In particular, this Yad Vashem must be with no monuments. "You shall not make for yourself a sculpted image." It is imprinted in our blood, in the blood of Israel. I do not dream so much of that large monument, as one of the members of Knesset has spoken here. I do not know if the large monuments are the great memory. We have a different approach to memory.

Dinur, in his closing remarks to the discussion before the vote, noted that Yad Vashem would be composed of three buildings. He declared that aside from the building dedicated to Holocaust remembrance that would hold everything related to the destruction of European Jewry, the ghetto uprisings, and all forms of Jewish revolts, another building would be devoted to the Diaspora communities, a kind of archive and museum that would present the lives of Jews there and the "world that had been destroyed." The third building would be an archive in which documents and materials related to the Zionist movement and the struggle to establish the State of Israel – settlement, clandestine immigration, and war – would be housed.[94]

On March 25, 1953, the Yad Vashem bill was registered in the Knesset's records; a number of weeks later, on May 18, it was passed on its first reading. Three months later, on August 19, 1953, the Martyrs' and Heroes' Remembrance (Yad Vashem) Law was passed. This law defined the many and varied goals of the authority that was founded and illustrated how serious and complex the task on its shoulders would be. The law determined, among other things, that the role of Yad Vashem

> is to collect in the homeland the vestiges of all of those of the Jewish nation who fell and gave their lives, [who] fought and revolted against the Nazi enemy and its supporters, and to erect a name and remembrance for them, for the communities, for the organizations, and for the institutions that were destroyed for belonging to the Jewish nation.[95]

This broad, rather vague formulation meant that in the years that followed the authority's heads would continue to deliberate what a "name and remembrance" was and how the Mount of Remembrance should be formed so that it would serve as a place of remembrance and inspiration for generations.

---

[94] KMHS, S-29, 3, "Members of the Knesset Propositions and Requests, May 18, 1953"; Arielle Rein, "Historian as a Nation Builder, Ben Zion Dinur's Evolution and Enterprise, 1884–1948" (PhD diss., Hebrew University of Jerusalem, 2000), 178–95 [in Hebrew].

[95] "Martyrs' and Heroes' Remembrance (Yad Vashem) Law, 5713–1953," 132 Book of Laws, August 28, 1953.

Figure 7: The Yad Vashem Law, passed in the Knesset in August 1953 (YVA, Unknown photographer).

Signifying the approaching realization of the dream, a number of days before the bill's approval a Yad Vashem budgetary plan – standing at an estimated 7 million Israeli pounds – was prepared. It included different financial dimensions of the memorial enterprise and a construction plan that was based on Yad Vashem's previous architectural outline. These included, aside from the offices, the library, remembrance hall and heroism hall, synagogue and house of religious study, and a remembrance plaza.[96]

Shenhavi now felt great satisfaction: the idea raised more than a decade earlier was taking shape before his eyes. He celebrated the victory by broadcasting a statement on the "history" of Yad Vashem and the process that had led to the passing of the Yad Vashem Law on Kol Yisrael Radio. Among other things, he mentioned building "a monumental remembrance site as an architectonic frame for these and other activities, an enterprise that will extend on the continuation of the Mount Herzl range."[97]

---

[96] HHA, 3–95. 17 (2), "Yad Vashem Five-Year Budget," August 2, 1953.
[97] Mordechai Shenhavi, "Yad Vashem following the Knesset Approval of the Law," *Yediot Yad Vashem* 1 (1954), 14.

Finding a Site for Yad Vashem

The decision that Yad Vashem would be established on the ridge to the west of Mount Herzl may have been taken only weeks before the passing of the Yad Vashem Law, but it resulted from an extended and intricate process – and, in order to understand it, we must return to 1948 and Yad Vashem's complicated standing at the time.

Despite the grave concerns for the institution's future and the danger of its closing, Shenhavi continued to search for an alternate location for the commemoration site in Jerusalem and its environs. So, for example, the possibility of dedicating the Castel Hill, a symbolic battleground in the breaking of the siege on Jerusalem during the War of Independence, to the project was examined.[98] Shenhavi felt that it would constitute a perfect link between the heroism of the soldiers in the Second World War and the heroism displayed in the War of Independence.

But in late 1948 or early 1949, the idea of establishing Yad Vashem in western Jerusalem, near the Bayit Vegan neighborhood and at a site that was still outside of the city's municipal limits, was raised. The idea was formed before the final decision was made about Theodor Herzl's reburial on the hill, the highest peak in Jerusalem's western section (834 meters above sea level), in January or February of 1949.[99]

It appears that at first, because of the thought that Yad Vashem would need a very large area in which the extensive building plan formed in 1948 could be carried out, the entire territory of the hill, some 250 acres, was meant to be apportioned to the institution.[100] But when the hilltop was chosen for Herzl's burial with the progression of the funerary plans, a decision to focus on other parts of the area was made – and attention shifted to the range that stretched from the western slopes of Mount Herzl in the direction of Khirbet al-Hamama. This area was almost entirely empty and held primarily the remains of agricultural terraces. The suggestion to establish Yad Vashem there was backed by Shenhavi as well as the heads of the governmental planning committee and the JNF's central office.

Despite the fact that the Mount Herzl region seemed fitting to Shenhavi, he still considered the possibility of integrating Yad Vashem within other enterprises being developed at the time in Jerusalem, primarily due to the memorial enterprise's organizational and budgetary straits. For example, he raised the

---

98 HHA, 3–95. 15 (7), Shenhavi to the military governor of Jerusalem, n.d.
99 Doron Bar, *Landscape and Ideology: Reinterment of Renowned Jews in the Land of Israel, 1904–1967* (Berlin: De Gruyter, 2016).
100 HHA, 3–95. 7 (1), Map of "Ein Karim," 1:20,000, 1944.

possibility of combining Yad Vashem with the Defenders' Forest (*ya'ar ha-meginim*). At that time, the JNF initiated the planting of forests in a number of places in the land in memory of the thousands who had fallen in the War of Independence, and on the holiday of Tu B'Shvat 1949 planting began in a number of places around the country.[101] Shenhavi was convinced that the combination of planting the Defenders' Forest next to Yad Vashem, an echo of the Martyrs' Forest that the JNF was planning at the time, would "highlight with even more clarity the continuation of the idea of an enterprise in memory of European Jewry by the connection to the commemoration of Israel's soldiers in our War of Independence."[102] But Yosef Weitz, a JNF man, rejected Shenhavi's proposal out of hand. Aside from his claim that Mount Herzl had already been dedicated to the reburial of the country's visionary, and that the JNF planned to plant a cedar forest in Herzl's memory, he also rebuffed the connection Shenhavi wished to draw between the fallen in the War of Independence and those who had died in the Holocaust: "There is not and there should not be a connection between the Yad Vashem enterprise, which from its inception was created to establish a memorial monument to the Jews exterminated in Europe, and the Defenders' Forest that is being erected for the Jews who fell in the war for the nation and the land's independence."[103]

Another idea raised at the time was to position Yad Vashem near Jerusalem's military cemetery, possibly even connecting the two. In March 1949, people from the unit for soldiers' commemoration in the Ministry of Defense approached Shenhavi, asking him to transfer twelve acres from the thousand he had been allocated in order to erect a cemetery in the northern end of the hilltop earmarked for Herzl's burial.[104] Shenhavi rejected the possibility, claiming that it was in this space that the central halls of Yad Vashem were slated to be built. "It is impossible," he stated, "that a cemetery can be erected so close to our enterprise's central buildings."[105] Ultimately, the space was nonetheless designated as a military burial site.[106]

---

[101] "Defenders' Forest (*Ya'ar HaMeginnim*)," *Davar*, January 11, 1949; Efraim Talmi, "A Memorial," *Davar*, February 15, 1949; S. Zarchi, "Yehiam Convoy," *Davar*, March 18, 1949. Tu B'Shvat is the Jewish-Zionist new year for trees.
[102] CZA, KKL5/16006, Yosef Yizrael to the JNF, February 6, 1949.
[103] CZA, KKL5/16006, Weitz to Yosef Yizrael, March 8, 1949.
[104] YVA, AM1 138, S. Tzemach to Shenhavi, March 16, 1949.
[105] YVA, AM1 138, Shenhavi to Tzemach, March 20, 1949; YVA, AM1 138, Shenhavi, "Building a Military Cemetery in the Area designated to Yad Vashem," March 20, 1949.
[106] Maoz Azaryahu, *In Their Death They Ordered: The Architecture of Military Cemeteries – The First Years* (Tel Aviv: Misrad Habitachon, 2012), 57–64 [in Hebrew].

An additional direction examined at this time was to establish Yad Vashem as part of the new government precinct in the Givat Ram area. Weinraub and Mansfeld, members of the Yad Vashem architectural team, had won a closed competition to establish the national institutes' campus in 1951,[107] and Shenhavi felt that the combination of Yad Vashem and the governmental and state offices was a good idea. Another possibility examined was attaching Yad Vashem to the International Convention Center (Binyanei Ha'uma), an endeavor that began in early 1950.[108] Given that the building's objective was to serve as a public and civic convention center for the State of Israel's residents as well as Diaspora Jewry, the combination was ostensibly a good one.

A further path explored was connecting Yad Vashem to the new Hebrew University campus in western Jerusalem.[109] Shenhavi felt that now, in contrast with the forties, proximity to an academic institution would give Yad Vashem many advantages – not only "a fitting landscape" but also the sense of "one unit" in terms of location.[110] While maintaining that the Hebrew University would swallow Yad Vashem, he now viewed it as a benefit, primarily in terms of budgetary efficiency and architectural and perhaps even academic integration with the institution as well. The idea of uniting Yad Vashem with a central national archive was also raised.[111] As Shenhavi was working at the time on founding the Hibbat Yerushalayim Association, whose goal was to develop the city and initiate the founding of tourist endeavors within it, he wished to tie his two projects together; he felt that they would add "a special element to Jerusalem the capital city both in terms of content and in terms of its monumental scope and image."[112]

---

107 Ingersoll, *Munio Gitai*, 234–35; Anna Minta, "Government Quarter, West-Jerusalem, 1950," in *Munio Weinraub Amos Gitai Atchitektur und Film in Israel*, ed. Winfried Nerdinger (Munchen: Edition Minerva, 2008): 112–17.
108 Kobi Cohen-Hattab, "The Formation of National Identity in West Jerusalem during the First Decade after the Establishment of the State of Israel," Zion 72, no. 2 (2007): 189–217 [in Hebrew].
109 HHA, 3–95. 17 (2), Shenhavi to Heinz Rau, March 2, 1953; Diana Dolev, "An Ivory Tower in the National Precinct: The Architecture Plan for the University Campus in Giva'at Ram," *Zmanim* 96 (2006): 86–93 [in Hebrew].
110 HHA, 3–95. 16 (3), Shenhavi to the minister of education, June 17, 1953; Rau prepared a new architectural plan for Jerusalem in 1949. See: Avyah Hashimshoni, Tsiyon Hashimshoni, and Yosef Shavid, *Jerusalem Master Plan 1968*, II (Jerusalem: Municipality of Jerusalem, 1974), 78–80 [in Hebrew].
111 HHA, 3–95. 17 (2), Shenhavi to Rau, March 2, 1953; "Archives' Law at the Knesset," *HaTzofe*, January 8, 1953.
112 ISA, G-33/2204, Shenhavi to Israel Rokach, March 28, 1953.

The question of the selection of the area for Yad Vashem, becoming ever more urgent given the progress of the government and Knesset's discussion of the law in 1953, was also tied to the question of the size and nature of the desired territory – hilly or plain, in Jerusalem or on its outskirts. A decision about "what we will build within the memorial enterprise" must be made, Shenhavi cautioned, adding that "with time, the feasible plots are dwindling. And the determination of the land, its state, and its size – are very crucial for the enterprise's future." He thus asked Dinur to help him arrive at an agreement about the main components that Yad Vashem would include in its plot and, afterwards, about architectural expressions. "There is no need to emphasize how important and correct it will be when we can, at the passing of the law in Knesset, publicly announce this plot," he wrote him.[113]

The reason for Shenhavi's many efforts to find an alternate location for Yad Vashem, and not only the space close to Mount Herzl that had ostensibly been promised to the institution, was the dogged opposition he faced from his peers on Mount Herzl's board of governors to the establishment of Yad Vashem there. After Herzl's burial in 1949, the Zionist Executive had resolved to appoint a board of governors that would manage the place, composed of a partnership between Israel's government, the JNF, and the World Zionist Organization,[114] a body that held as one of its goals guaranteeing the exclusivity of Herzl's burial there. The primary opponent to Shenhavi's proposal to establish Yad Vashem near Mount Herzl on the board of governors was Arieh Leo Lauterbach, secretary of the Zionist Executive, who claimed that the proximity between the two memorial sites would damage the importance and singularity of the visionary of the state's grave.[115] Dinur, who understood the advantage of positioning Yad Vashem near Mount Herzl, pushed in this direction and hoped that Weitz, a JNF man and a member of the Mount Herzl board of governors as well as a member of Yad Vashem's administrative bodies, could point to a fitting place, a hill that would be distant enough from Mount Herzl and could be dedicated to the building of a memorial site.[116]

In a tour held in the area in early August 1953, just days before the passing of the Yad Vashem Law, Weitz led the participants to a hilly stretch of land to the west of Mount Herzl, an area whose westernmost point had been known as Khirbet al-Hamama prior to 1948. This hilltop, which rose to 806 meters above

---

113 HHA, 3–95. 16 (3), Shenhavi to the minister of education, June 17, 1953.
114 Yosef Weitz, *Mount Herzl* (Jerusalem: Committee for Mount Herzl, 1968) [in Hebrew].
115 HHA, 3–95. 16 (3), Shenhavi to the minister of education, June 17, 1953.
116 CZA, S5/111351, Dinur to Locker, July 9, 1953; CZA, S5/111351, "Note Sent to Lauterbach 'Locating a Mountain for Yad Vashem,'" July 20, 1953.

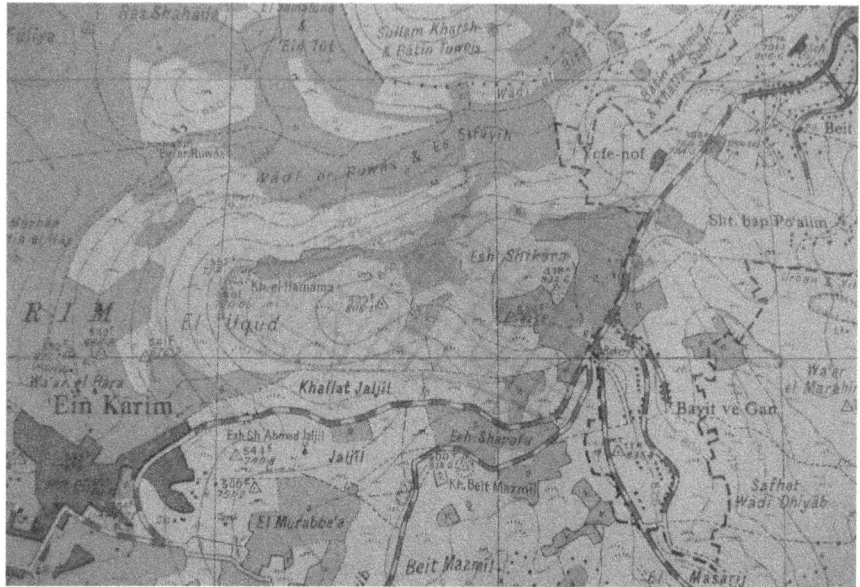

Figure 8: Map of the Jerusalem area, with the area allocated to Yad Vashem outlined, 1949. This area encompasses what would eventually become Mount Herzl, the military cemetery, the Great Leaders of the Nation's Plot, and Yad Vashem. (HHA).

sea level, extended from Herzl's grave westward, bounded on three sides by valleys and steep slopes. During the tour, they examined the question of the location's suitability to Yad Vashem. Dinur was immediately convinced of the site's advantages and resolved to recommend it to the government as the institution's future location.[117] Israel's government promised to symbolically and with no need of recompense transfer a small space of twenty-five acres there to Yad Vashem. This territory, later expanded through the purchase of nearby plots, constituted the foundation for the building of the memorial enterprise on the Mount of Remembrance.

Conclusion

From the very depths to the peaks – thus can we describe the change in Yad Vashem's status in the roughly five years that elapsed from the State of Israel's founding until the passing of the Yad Vashem Law in August 1953. This change

---

117 HHA, 3–95. 16 (6), Shenhavi to the minister of education and culture, September 17, 1953.

was expressed in the move from Yad Vashem's near eradication at the beginning of the period to Israel founding a state authority tasked with collecting and preserving the memories of the Jews who had been massacred by the Nazis as well as those who had fought and revolted against them. The law defined Yad Vashem as responsible for erecting "a name and memory" for individuals, communities, organizations, and institutions that had been destroyed during those years. Despite the many problems involved, the law made it possible for Yad Vashem to return to a path of building and confronting various challenges – defining its content and activity, finding a budget, and preparing architectural plans for building the Mount of Remembrance and shaping commemoration there.

Over this time period, Shenhavi's great significance once again became clear. In 1952, he wrote to Ben-Gurion that "for ten years I have fought for the simple truth that the nation must establish a central memorial enterprise in Israel and in the city of Jerusalem. And can there be any doubt today that the place of commemoration is in Jerusalem, and only in Jerusalem, especially now that the nation has won its state independence?"[118] Shenhavi wrote this when all of the other agents occupied with Yad Vashem had lost hope that the institution would ever be built. In retrospect it became clear that over the years 1948–1953, Shenhavi's role in the institution's defense and success was crucial. The fact that he continued to believe that the institution would be founded – and in Jerusalem, recently made the capital of the State of Israel, no less – was decisive, and the spirit of his vision saved the institution and led to its establishment as an Israeli state institution.

---

118 HHA, 3–95. 16 (1), Shenhavi to Ben-Gurion, September 2, 1952.

Chapter 3
Building the Mount of Remembrance: First Steps

From the end of 1953 until mid-1956, crucial strides were made to establish Yad Vashem, to firmly ground the institution, and to build the Mount of Remembrance. During the years covered in the current chapter, the institution's working budget was defined, the cornerstone for Yad Vashem's administrative and archive buildings was laid, and a new construction plan was prepared for the site following the formalization of a working relationship with a team of five architects. Over the course of this period, the rivalry between Yad Vashem and other bodies working on Holocaust commemoration – the JNF, the Ministry of Religions, Kibbutz Lohamei HaGeta'ot, and the documentation and remembrance institute founded in Paris – grew. Yad Vashem formed a relationship with the Claims Conference, making it possible to raise the funds necessary for the institution's establishment and construction; in June 1954, the Claims Conference's heads signed a commitment to provide financial aid for the establishment of the Jerusalem memorial enterprise.

Much of this work was undertaken by Shenhavi; he had been named director of Yad Vashem, though later on he would become a sparring partner for Prof. Ben-Zion Dinur, the chairman. The internal tension within Yad Vashem's management and the conflict between the directorate and the employees was manifest in the physical planning of the Mount of Remembrance as well, a process that underwent many changes due, in part, to significant pressure exerted on the institution's directorate and on the Mount of Remembrance's architects.

The lack of clarity regarding Yad Vashem's planning led Dinur to initiate two symposia in mid-1956, the goal of which was to define the construction in a more precise fashion. In his opening remarks at the second symposium, Dinur noted that "the name Mount of Remembrance expresses that the mount as a whole must symbolize remembrance – this entire area, with its buildings, and its arrangements, and its content, image, and form."[1] This determination had a great effect on Yad Vashem's appearance in subsequent years. With the symposia drawing to a close and the adoption of some of the conclusions reached, it became possible to begin the process of building the memorial structures, first and foremost the Hall of Remembrance.

---

1 HHA, 3–95. 17 (2), "Protocol of a Symposium Assembled by Yad Vashem," July 15, 1956.

Formalizing the Relationship with Yad Vashem's Architects

In November 1953, following the passing of the Yad Vashem Law, a directorate was appointed for Yad Vashem. Dinur was elected the institution's chairman and three ministers were appointed to work alongside him – Minister of Internal Affairs Israel Rokach, Foreign Minister Moshe Sharett, and Minister of Religions Haim-Moshe Shapira. The directorate also contained representatives of the JNF, the Jewish Agency, survivors' organizations, and underground and ghetto fighters. It was further determined that the Remembrance Authority would be managed by a public council and administration. The state was obligated, by the law, to take part in establishing and maintaining Yad Vashem while permitting the institution to receive allotments, income, and donations from other sources.[2]

Figure 9: Prof. Ben-Zion Dinur, chairman of Yad Vashem, speaks at a memorial ceremony at Yad Vashem (YVA, Unknown photographer).

In early December 1953, the Remembrance Authority's directorate held its first meeting, focusing on executing the newly passed law. Participants debated how

---

[2] "Yad Vashem Organization and Activities," *Yediot Yad Vashem* 1 (1954), 15.

to realize Yad Vashem's two central tasks: Holocaust research and Holocaust commemoration.[3] A more limited directorate was selected, composed of Dinur, Shenhavi, Weitz, Moshe Kol (of the Progressive Party), Mark Dworzecki (a Holocaust survivor and the chair of the International Association of Former Underground Fighters, Survivors, and Camp Inmates), and Shragai. Discussions were then devoted almost exclusively to coordinating the relationship between Yad Vashem and various organizations, for example YIVO, the Jewish scientific institute founded in Vilnius which had been transferred to New York during the Second World War, or Schneersohn's documentation center in Paris. It was more complicated to coordinate Yad Vashem's working relationship with the JNF, given the complex and long-standing ties between the two bodies. Abraham Granot, director general of the JNF and a Yad Vashem directorate member, presented the broad plan of the Martyrs' Forest, which, at the end of 1953, was the central locus of Holocaust commemoration in the State of Israel.

While in his closing remarks during the December meeting Dinur had announced Yad Vashem's full cooperation with the JNF and while it was resolved that the Fund's representatives would take an active role in the "equal execution committee" for the establishment of the Remembrance Authority, it was clear that each body was wary of the other. Dinur was concerned that the JNF's activities would render Yad Vashem unnecessary; Granot worried that Yad Vashem would become firmly established and that the Remembrance Authority would appropriate some of the activity in which the JNF was already engaged.

The Yad Vashem directorate asked itself: How do we proceed from here? How can we now, after the law has been passed, establish the buildings on the Mount of Remembrance? Shenhavi, now administrative director of the institution, cautioned that Yad Vashem had no organized strategy for the planning and construction of the mount. But the fact that he had maintained a close relationship with the veteran team of architects made it possible for him to promote the renewal of ties between them and the institution's directorate behind the scenes, and the latter accepted his proposal that the relationship with them be formalized.[4] The architects were asked to modify their plans to suit the site that had been selected in western Jerusalem.[5]

The team of architects now included five professionals; in mid-1948, with the appointment of Arieh Sharon as the head of the planning unit in the Prime Minister's Office, Benjamin Idelson had become his partner, and he was now

---

[3] "Yad Vashem Management Assembled in the Capital," *Davar*, December 3, 1953; ISA, GL-2/1087, "First Protocol of Yad Vashem Management Meeting," December 2, 1953.
[4] ISA, GL-1/1229, "Protocol of a Meeting of Yad Vashem Limited Directorate," March 16, 1954.
[5] ISA, GL-2/1087, "Protocol of a Meeting of Yad Vashem Limited Directorate," March 2, 1954.

involved in the Yad Vashem project.[6] The architects agreed with the Yad Vashem's assessment that the necessary budget would stand at 7 million Israeli pounds, and suggested stretching construction over a number of years in order to "complete the building on time and in its entirety."[7] Their suggestion was based on the assumption that the plan to be carried out on the Mount of Remembrance was similar to the outline that had been prepared a few years prior, a spacious assembly plaza that would connect a remembrance hall to a heroism hall.

Some members of Yad Vashem's directorate took issue with the decision to formalize ties with the architects. They maintained that an international competition should be announced for planning the Mount of Remembrance, open to architects from Israel and abroad – they felt that they must "establish a monumental building for generations" and that they had "a responsibility toward all of Jewry." Shenhavi opposed the proposal, in part because "the results of a tender are usually a failure, because architects work separately and a jury does not always select the best proposal for execution."[8] Yad Vashem's directorate chose to appeal to the Association of Engineers and Architects to request its assistance in establishing an advisory committee, architects who would cooperate with Yad Vashem's directorate and oversee the work of the veteran architects.[9]

The directorate settled on the procedure for construction on the Mount of Remembrance. First the archive and library would be built, along with the administration building. Later on, the memorial monuments – the remembrance hall and heroism hall – would be undertaken, and, finally, the synagogue.[10] This order reflected the belief that the most urgent task on Yad Vashem's shoulders was collecting historical material about the Holocaust and preserving it appropriately. "It is no coincidence that this building is first in Yad Vashem's construction," stated the magazine that the Remembrance Authority had begun to publish at the time, *Yediot Yad Vashem*, as "we have been charged with carefully preserving each certificate and document, each remnant and book, linked to the period of the Holocaust."[11]

Weinraub and Mansfeld began to plan the first two buildings – the administration, archive, and library.[12] According to the blueprints, the archive building

---

6 HHA, 3-95. 17 (2), "Benjamin Idelson," December 19, 1954.
7 ISA, G-33/2204, Arieh El-Hanani to Shenhavi, March 10, 1954.
8 ISA, GL-1/1229, "Protocol of the Sixth Meeting of Yad Vashem's Extended Administration," March 16, 1954.
9 CZA, S115/506, "Summary of Decisions on Yad Vashem Buildings and Architects," n.d.
10 Ibid.
11 "Yad Vashem's Activities," *Yediot Yad Vashem* 2 (1954), 15.
12 Ingersoll, *Munio Gitai*, 233–34.

would house an archive of documents, microfilm devices, and copying rooms in its basement. The other two floors of the building would hold the library, a research room, and a reading room for the general public. The Remembrance Authority was proud of the fact that these buildings would not stand out against the memorial buildings slated to be built next to them in the future. In contrast with these structures, which would "be seen from afar by all those entering Jerusalem," the archive building, with its "regular, modern architecture," would be absorbed by the ridge between the two hills around it.[13]

Analogous Projects and the Risk of Dividing Holocaust Commemoration

The danger of fragmenting Holocaust commemoration and the fear of the subject being "poached" by others had kept Shenhavi awake at night for years. Now, with the establishment of the national authority and the enactment of the Yad Vashem Law that gave the institution's heads exclusivity over Holocaust memory and immortalization, the institution could demand that other commemoration enterprises – such as The Ghetto Fighters' House, with whom they had held negotiations – be shuttered.[14]

As long as Yad Vashem faltered, and its activities were nearly at a standstill, there had been no problem with Kibbutz Lohamei HaGeta'ot's vigorous activity in Holocaust commemoration, activity that had begun with the its settlement in 1949. But the Yad Vashem Law led the institution's heads to contest the redundancy that now existed in Holocaust commemoration. Dinur initially felt that the Ghetto Fighters' House should merge with Yad Vashem but the kibbutz members were vehemently opposed; they wished to preserve their independence and singularity. The kibbutz suggested resolving the overlap between the two institutions by limiting the Ghetto Fighters' House to "research on the resistance and fighting movement in Europe," a proposal that infuriated Dinur. He claimed that "it is impossible that the Ghetto Fighters' House will take the heroism and leave us only the Holocaust."[15] Yad Vashem's directorate declared that it "opposes any

---

13 "Building, Planting, and Paving on the Mount of Remembrance," *Yediot Yad Vashem* 7 (1957), 22.
14 Stauber, *A Lesson*, 226–33.
15 ISA, G-33/2204, "Protocol of a Meeting of Yad Vashem's Limited Directorate," February 2, 1954.

institution that is occupied with the Holocaust separately and can be an organic part of Yad Vashem," and that the Ghetto Fighters' House must be integrated within Yad Vashem's framework. Only after that integration would it be furnished with tasks by the Remembrance Authority.[16]

Another example of Yad Vashem's sensitivity regarding Holocaust commemoration was tied to efforts to shape a site in Haifa in memory of Jewish fighters in Allied battles during the war. This proposal had been raised in 1947; at that time, Shenhavi wrote resolutely to the Jewish community council in Haifa: "What answer would you have if all Jewish communities followed your path? Would you say that we will establish a central enterprise for the nation in memory of its heroes and fallen – and their names would be engraved in this cemetery or that one?"[17] In 1954, Shenhavi also turned to Abba Hushi, mayor of Haifa, and insisted that he not cooperate with the committee working on establishing the memorial site. "Did the initiators of the site really not know that there is a central national memorial enterprise [Yad Vashem] and that from its very first steps the participation of Jews in Allied armies was one of its primary foundations?"[18]

In Tel Aviv, too, the Association of Warsaw Jews initiated the building of a monument to those who had perished. Yad Vashem replied "generally, we are uncomfortable with this form of commemoration (monument) but because on the Mount of Remembrance a series of memorials will be erected for communities as well, they should turn to us on this subject."[19] Moshe Kol, a member of the Yad Vashem directorate born in Poland, wondered "why it is not possible to erect a fitting monument in an appropriate fashion to the Jews of Warsaw within Yad Vashem on the Mount of Remembrance in Jerusalem. Why is Tel Aviv preferred over Jerusalem for the commemoration of Warsaw Jewry?"[20]

Yad Vashem's efforts to prevent the "division" targeted the Diaspora as well, as Dinur and Shenhavi's view was that the Remembrance Authority has exclusivity over Holocaust commemoration not only in Israel but in the Jewish world as a

---

16 CZA, S115/512, "The Ghetto Fighters' House Suggestions for a Settlement with Yad Vashem."
17 CZA, J1/360 II, Shenhavi to Haifa's Va'ad Hakehila, June 12, 1947.
18 CZA, S115/512, Shenhavi to Abba Hushi, October 21, 1954; ISA, GL-2/1087, Hushi to Shenhavi, October 24, 1954.
19 ISA, HZ-1/151, "Summary of Yad Vashem Directorate Decisions," February 7, 1956.
20 CZA, S115/533, Association of Warsaw Jews in Tel Aviv to Moshe Kol, May 13, 1956; CZA, S115/533, Kol to Association of Warsaw Jews in Tel Aviv, May 23, 1956. The debate about Holocaust commemoration in Tel Aviv lasted until 1975, when Yigal Tamarkin's monument was built in the Kings of Israel Square (today Rabin Square); see Maoz Azaryahu, "Public Controversy and Commemorative Failure: Tel Aviv's Monument to the Holocaust and National Revival," *Israel Studies* 16 (2011): 129–48.

whole. Especially noticeable was the vehement opposition that Schneersohn's documentation and commemoration center in Paris engendered. In late 1953, Dinur and Schneersohn signed an agreement regulating the relationship between the two institutes,[21] but in reality the tension between Yad Vashem and the French center lingered. Shenhavi's fear that the Paris center would overshadow the one in Jerusalem grew when he read Schneersohn's words in its publications: the place would "serve as memorial house of national scope for the Jews of the world. There will rest, to the light of an eternal flame, the ashes of the fallen, burnt in the extermination camps." He discerned ideas that were similar to those that had been raised over the years, such as the burial of the martyrs' ashes or the establishment of a historical museum that would curate "Jewish, religious, and national treasures saved from the Holocaust" along with documents and publications related to the destruction. "At the entrance to the museum," Schneersohn's document read, "a fitting inscription will remind humanity of what the Nazis did to the nation of Israel and all free humans." Aside from the signatures of the president of France, Winston Churchill, and the queens of Belgium and Holland, the enterprise's publications also featured that of Prime Minister David Ben-Gurion.[22] The establishment of the center outside of the State of Israel would be a severe act on both the nation and state levels, Dinur asserted, as it would be "an international display of the exilic sense that nests deep within us." The activity in Paris "satisfies the nations and Jews of a certain type, with the care for the memory of the dead coming for them in place of responsibility for the living. It further satisfies the exilic – and to a great extent the 'Zionist' – inclination, which does not wish to gather everything in Israel."[23]

Yad Vashem Confronts the Ministry of Religions and the JNF

Among the disputes between Dinur and Yad Vashem's directorate and the competing bodies working on Holocaust commemoration in parallel with the Remembrance Authority, the most prominent were with the JNF and with Kahana and his Committee for Mount Zion. Kahana, as noted, had founded the Chamber of the Holocaust on Mount Zion in 1949, a place whose sanctity emanated from

---

[21] ISA, GL-1/1229, "Agreement between Yad Vashem and the Center for Documentation in Paris," December 30, 1953.
[22] ISA, G-2/5564, "International Council for the Building of a Monument for the Anonymous Jewish Martyr in Paris."
[23] ISA, G-2/5564, Dinur to the prime minister, April 3, 1954.

the martyrs' ashes preserved there which, over time, had taken on Jewish traditional communal significance.

In September 1950, before the establishment of the Remembrance Authority, a raging debate developed between Shenhavi and Kahana: Kahana wished to dedicate a Torah scroll to those who had perished in the Holocaust, and to hold the dedication ceremony in the Chamber of the Holocaust. Kahana suggested that the JNF collect the names of the dead and the donations for the writing of the scroll.[24] "The proposal of the Ministry of Religions purports, with no trace of cover-up or camouflage, to inherit the place of Yad Vashem," Shenhavi raged, claiming that "it is the JNF's duty to ask the Ministry of Religions whether this proposal is based on an agreement with Yad Vashem or a government decision to transfer this role to the Ministry of Religions."[25] Kahana had other plans for cooperation with the JNF[26] – for example, a proposal to integrate within the JNF's afforestation activity the engraving of names of victims and communities on the walls of the Chamber of the Holocaust.[27] The Ministry of Foreign Affairs felt that "the government should not give a hand to any plan from which wafts an odor of exploitation of the sentiments and respect that we hold for those who have perished and for their loved ones for financial purposes."[28] Shenhavi also expressed doubts about the way in which the Ministry of Religions was turning Holocaust commemoration "into something from which arises a spirit of the dark and medieval ages, into idol worship," despite the fact that he admitted that Kahana and the Ministry of Religions excelled at "understanding the value of the connection with the masses of loved ones and the use of that connection in the past and even in the present. And all of this the secular State of Israel has forgotten."[29]

And, indeed, during the fifties, a strong bond formed between the *landsmannschaften*, on one hand, and Mount Zion, the Chamber of the Holocaust, and Kahana, on the other. Kahana made available commemorative and sacred elements that could not be found elsewhere in the state. It was first and foremost the ashes buried there that gave the Chamber of the Holocaust the standing of a grave, along with the desecrated holy objects that had been brought

---

[24] CZA, KKL5/17418, S. Z. Kahana to the JNF, September 24, 1950.
[25] KMHA, S-29, 3, Shenhavi to M. HaEzrahi, September 28, 1950.
[26] ISA, G-3/5564, Kahana to the secretary of the government, October 12, 1950; HHA, 3–95. 16 (1), "Proposal for the Commemoration of the Holocaust Victims," October 1950.
[27] ISA, G-3/5564, "Proposal for Holocaust Martyrs Memorials in the Holocaust Cellar (Mount Zion)," n.d.
[28] ISA, G-3/5564, Walter Eytan to the secretary of the government, November 11, 1950.
[29] KMHA, S-29, 3, "Kibbutz Talk about Yad Vashem's New Proposal," December 27, 1950.

from Europe that were displayed there. Kahana convinced many of the community leaders to see the Chamber of the Holocaust as the "general grave of the Holocaust," a place that would immortalize their loved ones.[30] The site gave the survivors a fitting resolution to the question of their loved ones' commemoration, precisely because it was a "small place," personal, local, and with a Jewish-traditional character. The lighting of candles at the place, the prayers, and the community tombstones affixed to the walls gave commemoration on Mount Zion a nature that was nearer to some of the survivors, who had preserved their communal frameworks and Jewish tradition.

The Yad Vashem Law and the gradual formation of the Remembrance Authority shifted the relationship between Yad Vashem on one side and Kahana, with the Ministry of Religions, on the other, generating much tension between the two bodies. The struggle was manifest in the question of the Chamber of the Holocaust's funding and the existential dilemma of a Holocaust commemoration site alongside Yad Vashem. Kahana submitted a survey conducted by the Committee for Mount Zion that he addressed to Dinur, proudly describing the remains held there: "ashes from thirty-two camps; soap (martyrs' fat) buried in the ground, others in a special casket for display. Torah scrolls orange with blood, some tied with facts and revelations of martyrdom."[31] Dinur was hesitant and claimed that "there is the binding Yad Vashem Law and a state institution [the Ministry of Religions] cannot simultaneously do similar things. Yad Vashem aspires to the recognition of the historical truth and therefore the territory of the legend and story are not close to our realm of activity. The Committee for Mount Zion cannot appear as a commemorative body." Dinur distinguished between Yad Vashem, an institute that was scientific in nature, and the Chamber of the Holocaust, part of a "complex" cultivated by Kahana on Mount Zion, associated with David's Tomb and with a series of displays developed there based on traditions, stories, and legends. Warhaftig, deputy minister of religions, defended Kahana, claiming that "today this [the Chamber of the Holocaust] is a living body and therefore one cannot speak of plans but rather of something that is already in existence and active. Tens of thousands of Jews journey there [to Mount Zion] each year and for them this is also a substitute for the Western Wall."[32]

Despite Warhaftig's exaggeration regarding the number of visitors to the Chamber of the Holocaust, it appears that Yad Vashem's directorate was nonetheless concerned about the site's development and the possibility that

---

30 ISA, GL-15/6315, Mordechai Shirshblum to Dinur, September 10, 1954.
31 ISA, GL-2/1299, Kahana to Dinur, March 1, 1954.
32 ISA, GL-3/14913, "Protocol of a Meeting of Yad Vashem's Limited Directorate," June 22, 1954.

it would take up too much volume among the Holocaust survivors. For this reason, many identified with the position expressed by Weitz in the limited directorate forum that "we must declare war on them [the Chamber of the Holocaust]."[33]

Talks between Yad Vashem and Kahana led to an agreement between the two bodies, under which the Committee for Mount Zion agreed to Yad Vashem's oversight of their "traditional commemoration."[34] But the disputes between Yad Vashem and Kahana continued. Alongside the financial question and Yad Vashem's refusal to foot the bill for the Chamber of the Holocaust,[35] the question of whether Yad Vashem was permitted to engage in "traditional commemoration" remained. Kahana felt that the two realms should be separated, leaving the Chamber of the Holocaust as the site in which the religious-traditional side of Holocaust commemoration would be accentuated.[36] This was tied to the religious community's lack of faith in Yad Vashem at the time. In 1955, Rabbi Yonah Sztencl demanded that the institution's religious directorate members, as "representatives of traditional Judaism," leave Yad Vashem's directorate immediately. Yad Vashem "is neither a memorial [*yad*] nor a name [*shem*] and all the more so not a martyrs' memorial. The title of statistics institute is more fitting for it," he stated, adding that "Yad Vashem has no right to take upon itself the name of martyrs' commemoration because it is not that. The religious representatives, in participating in Yad Vashem, give it a religious seal and general approval, when Yad Vashem is a secular research institute."[37]

The dispute between Kahana and Yad Vashem swelled after Schneersohn asked the Ministry of Religions to transfer martyrs' ashes from Mount Zion to him so that he could make a memorial site in Paris, a "grave of the unknown Jew" like the one in the Chamber of the Holocaust. Yad Vashem feared that burying ashes in Paris would lend the monument added legitimacy and sanctity. Yaakov Tzur, Israel's ambassador in France, suggested that Yad Vashem make the monument in Paris into part of the global memorial enterprise that

---

33 ISA, GL-3/1087, "Protocol of a Meeting of Yad Vashem's Limited Directorate," August 19, 1954.
34 ISA, GL-3/14913, "Agreement between the Ministry of Religions and Yad Vashem," February 4, 1955.
35 ISA, GL-3/14913, Series of letters between Dinur and Kahana on the budget of the Chamber of the Holocaust, 1956.
36 *HaDor*, June 6, 1954.
37 ISA, GL-6/14913, Yonah Sztencl to Yad Vashem, February 19, 1955.

would have Jerusalem at its center,[38] but the Remembrance Authority's directorate acted with the minister of religions to prevent the transfer to Paris; the ashes remained in Israel.[39]

The heads of Yad Vashem wrangled not only with Kahana but also with the JNF. When the Yad Vashem Law was passed in the Knesset in August 1953, the JNF began to receive appeals from community leaders in Israel and abroad who had discovered that the memorial enterprise they had supported until that point, the Martyrs' Forest, was now competing with Yad Vashem.[40] As noted, an agreement was signed with the JNF at the first meeting of Yad Vashem's directorate, determining that the Martyrs' Forest would be integrated within the institution.[41] Yad Vashem asked to use the JNF's well-organized mechanism in order to advance the state enterprise; the JNF hoped to exploit the new status of Yad Vashem in order to guarantee the future of the Martyrs' Forest, whose donations and planting had declined over time.[42]

In advance of 27 Nisan 1954, members of Yad Vashem's directorate proposed holding the ceremony for the Holocaust and ghetto uprising day on the Mount of Remembrance. Weitz, as a member of both Yad Vashem's directorate and the JNF, may have agreed that "the nation must recognize that the Mount of Remembrance is a central place for Holocaust and heroism commemoration," but felt that since the site in Jerusalem was still vacant and the Martyrs' Forest already had a "tradition" of the ceremony (though only a one-year tradition), the ceremony should be held there.[43] The state memorial ceremony was indeed held at the Ksalon Valley, with thousands of people in attendance. Speeches and lamentations were heard from a stage positioned atop a huge boulder on which the name "Martyrs' Forest" was inscribed. The innovation was that at the side of the stage a tin sign bore the words "The Yad Vashem Remembrance Authority for Holocaust and Heroism." The sign reminded the audience of the existence of an exclusive Remembrance Authority in the State of Israel.[44] In a letter sent by Yad Vashem before the ceremony "to the house of Israel in Zion and the Diaspora," the fact that one of its goals was "establishing the Yad Vashem halls in Jerusalem" for "pilgrims from the entire world to unite [together] with the memory

---

38 ISA, HZ-5/1623, Yaakov Tzur to Dinur, June 19, 1956.
39 *HaTzofe*, July 1, 1956.
40 "Letter to the Chairman of the Knesset," *Davar*, September 1, 1953.
41 "Yad Vashem Management Was Assembled in the Capital," *Davar*, December 3, 1953.
42 For the agreement between Yad Vashem and the JNF, see *Karnenu* 31, no. 2 (1954): 3–4.
43 HHA, 3–95. 18 (5), "Protocol of a Meeting of Yad Vashem's Limited Directorate," March 16, 1954.
44 "Yad Vashem Enterprise Will Be Declared during Memorial Day," *Davar*, April 26, 1954.

of our holy martyrs and our heroic fighters" was mentioned.⁴⁵ In his speech to those at the ceremony, Dinur stated that "at this national event, we announce the opening of Yad Vashem's activities in accordance with the Yad Vashem Law that was passed in the Knesset," and reported that "first, Yad Vashem will carry out the command 'inscribe this in a document as a reminder' (Ex. 17:14)." He emphasized that "We will also erect 'memorial stones.' We will establish memorial halls for sanctifying God's name and the heroic wars [and] remembrance halls for synagogues."

Figure 10: Israeli Prime Minister Moshe Sharett speaks at a Holocaust Martyrs' and Heroes' Remembrance Day ceremony in 1954 in the Martyrs' Forest. A sign notes the Yad Vashem Holocaust and Heroism Remembrance Authority's involvement in the ceremony. (NPA, Hugo Mendelson).

Shenhavi, on the other hand, was not mollified by the partnership between Yad Vashem and the JNF. He compared the JNF, with its interest only in Yad Vashem's financial income for the Martyrs' Forest, to a body "that must appear toward the nation as giving, as serving something that will speak to the hearts of the masses; as an institution that comes to give sublime expression to this

---

45 HHA, 3–95. 16 (6), Yad Vashem, "To the House of Israel in Zion and the Diaspora," May 23, 1954.

tragic-national-fateful element."[46] He concluded that "the entire issue of the Martyrs' Forest was a knife in the back of Yad Vashem. If it were not for the stubbornness of a few people [in effect, himself], we would be facing a state in which the Martyrs' Forest was the memorial and not Yad Vashem."[47]

Funding for Yad Vashem's Construction

The issue of the institute's funding was thrown into stark relief after the passing of the law in 1953. The estimate was that 7 million Israeli pounds would be needed to build Yad Vashem, but there were those who estimated that the figure would actually be double that. Dinur conducted financial negotiations with Minister of Finance Levi Eshkol and the heads of the Jewish Agency, but the grim financial reality in the country during the first half of the fifties made it hard for them to allocate funds to the project. In order to resolve the problem, a new idea was raised for funding the building of Yad Vashem: contributions from the families of those who had perished, who would register the names of their loved ones at Yad Vashem.[48]

But the solution for the financial problems was ultimately found in New York, when, in late 1953 and early 1954, ties were forged between the Remembrance Authority and the Conference on Jewish Material Claims against Germany. The body, founded in 1951 by more than twenty large Jewish organizations, represented the Holocaust survivors in the Diaspora on the subject of the reparations that Germany had paid.[49] Despite the fact that under the conference's mandate, the resources were not meant to fund activity in the State of Israel,[50] in June 1954, the heads of the organization agreed to a special appeal on behalf of the state and Dinur for financial aid in order to build Yad Vashem.[51] Nahum Goldmann, who,

---

46 ISA, GL-3/1087, "KKL," n.d.
47 ISA, 3–95. 16 (4), "Protocol of a Meeting of Yad Vashem's Limited Directorate," August 11, 1954.
48 ISA, HZ-2/151, Abraham Herman to the Ministry of Foreign Affairs, December 17, 1953.
49 On the "Conference on Jewish Material Claims Against Germany," see Zweig, *German Reparation*; Henry Marily, *Confronting the Perpetrators: A History of the Claims Conference* (London: Vallentine Mitchell, 2007); see also: "The Conference of Jewish Material Claims against Germany," *American Jewish Year Book* 57 (1956): 540–47, with the agreement with Yad Vashem.
50 CZA, Z6/1997, Uveeler to Dinur, February 8, 1957.
51 Cohen, *Holocaust Research*, 87–96.

among other things, served as the head of the Claims Conference,[52] was a prominent proponent of establishing the institution. He was able to overcome the qualms of some members of the Claims Conference regarding Yad Vashem's Zionist and Israeli values, and led to the penning of an agreement for the support of Yad Vashem.[53]

At first, the Claims Conference's board agreed to allocate the funds only for the collection and cataloguing of archival material on the Holocaust as well as the publication of *Pinkas Kehillot* books, volumes that collected historical information on the lost communities.[54] Later in the fifties, the organization's heads agreed to partially fund the construction of the Mount of Remembrance – first the archive and library buildings in which the historical materials would be housed and later the remembrance buildings.

The financial agreement with the Claims Conference also had less convenient dimensions for Yad Vashem's directorate, primarily the oversight and involvement of the organization's heads in the activities and appearance of the Mount of Remembrance.[55] Yad Vashem's directorate at times found itself adapting its plans in order to appease the Claims Conference. So, for example, in advance of a critical discussion with the heads of the organization, Dinur warned that "the impression is that the plans here are for the establishment of a vast enterprise with excessive pretensions" and directed that the scope of building be diminished, and that, in contrast, "the budget for the synagogue and the house of religious study [be] slightly increased, because it is possible that it is this item that will make an impression in the organizations' [Claims Conference's] meetings."[56] The emphasis placed on the synagogue, which had now become one of the first three buildings slated for construction by the directorate, signaled to the Claims Conference that Yad Vashem would blend Jewish and Israeli content – a decision designed to placate them. In the backdrop stood the dispute regarding the place that would be allotted at Yad Vashem for heroism as opposed to extermination. While Israel wished to give much space to the heroism of those who fought the Nazis, to the Jewish fighting in the ghettos and forests, the Claims Conference saw the subject as secondary.

---

52 Nahum Goldmann, *Memories* (Jerusalem: Weidenfeld and Nicolson, 1969), 228–58 [in Hebrew].
53 Zweig, *German Reparation*.
54 ISA, G-33/2204, "Protocol of a Meeting of Yad Vashem's Extended Directorate," February 2, 1954.
55 Ronald W. Zweig, "Politics of Commemoration," *Jewish Social Studies* 44 (1987): 161, 164.
56 HHA, 3–95. 16 (4), "Protocol of a Meeting of Yad Vashem's Extended Directorate," April 21, 1954.

Figure 11: The cornerstone ceremony for Yad Vashem's archive and administration building, July 1954 (YVA, Unknown photographer).

The First Ceremony on the Mount of Remembrance

On July 29, 1954, the cornerstone was laid for the archive and library building on the Mount of Remembrance. This ceremony, in effect, constituted the cornerstone for the commemoration enterprise as a whole. But the preparations for the ceremony exposed a crucial dispute about whom Yad Vashem represented: Was it just the Jews of the State of Israel, or did it represent Diaspora Jewry as well? There were those who felt that a speech on the part of the state's president, Yitzhak Ben-Zvi, "first in the entire Jewish nation, 'uniter of world Jewry,'" would suffice,[57] but it was ultimately decided that Nahum Goldmann, president of the World Jewish Congress and representing Diaspora Jewry, would also speak at the ceremony.[58] *Yediot Yad Vashem* noted:

> Not as guests do the representatives of this organizational framework [the Claims Conference] come to us. . .but as full partners in the founding of the national commemoration enterprise in Jerusalem, as they carry the financial burden of the enterprise equally with

---

57 ISA, GL-1/1229, Shenhavi to Dinur, March 31, 1954.
58 ISA, GL-3/1087, "Protocol of a Meeting of Yad Vashem's Limited Directorate," July 9, 1954.

the state and the national institutions. Thus will the fundamental idea of Yad Vashem be expressed in the ceremony: establishing an enterprise for the nation as a whole.[59]

The space for the festive ceremony, which was designed by Sharon and El-Hanani, was hung with state flags. On an elongated stage, against a black backdrop upon which white letters formed the words "Yad Vashem," sat the dignitaries, state leaders, *landsmannshaften* representatives, Holocaust survivors, and representatives of the Claims Conference before an audience of hundreds of invitees.[60] The ceremony opened with the chanting of the Kaddish prayer and El Malei Rahamim, the Jewish memorial prayer for the dead, and then Dinur and Goldmann spoke. Minister Mordechai Nurock read selections from the declaration of the foundation of Yad Vashem, composed by writer Haim Hazaz:

> May this house be forever and for eternal memory for the bereaved and orphan and widower in Israel when the evil Nazi Germany and its partners stood. . .to preserve in this house together with the memory of the nation's heroes and their memory shall not depart from Israel. May this house be forever and for eternal memory for the supreme heroism of spirit of tens of thousands of Israelites who walked into the inferno.[61]

Israel's president, Yitzhak Ben-Zvi, agreed: "Our legs stand here, in your gates, Jerusalem, to lay a cornerstone for an enterprise whose goals have within them to fill all Jews' hearts with awe." Ben-Zvi related to the archive building that was slated to be built:

> Today we lay a cornerstone for establishing the first of Yad Vashem's buildings. ... This building will be an archive for the Holocaust and the heroism, in which all certificates and documents, all registries and testimonies of the Holocaust and the heroism will be gathered. ... This building will be the foundational building on the road to realizing the great objective of Yad Vashem for the Holocaust and heroism in Israel. And may it be God's will that we may complete this building and establish it from bottom to top and add great buildings that will be worthy of serving as a symbol in memory of our martyrs and heroes.[62]

Shenhavi was honored with lighting the memorial torch, positioned prominently;[63] following that, the ceremony reached its peak with the symbolic laying of the

---

[59] "Cornerstone for Yad Vashem's First Building," *Yediot Yad Vashem* 2 (1954), 1.
[60] Ibid.
[61] HHA, 3–95. 14 (6), "Yad Vashem's Founding Scroll."
[62] KMHA, S-29, 3, "President's Speech."
[63] CZA, PHAL/1650251, "Torch Lighting during Yad Vashem Cornerstone Ceremony."

founding scrolls at the four cornerstones that had been positioned at the foot of the stage before the audience.⁶⁴

Figure 12: Mordechai Shenhavi lights a remembrance torch during the cornerstone ceremony for Yad Vashem's archive and administration building, July 1954 (KMHA, Unknown photographer).

The Claims Conference, Mark Uveeler, and Yad Vashem

In late July 1954, a meeting was held between the heads of Yad Vashem and the representatives of the Claims Conference in which the arrangements of the cooperation between the two was resolved. The Claims Conference approved Dinur's request that construction of the archive building, preserving documents, would be completed by the end of 1955. They agreed to transfer 2 million dollars to Yad Vashem (of a total budget of 7 million dollars) and promised to help in

---

64 "Cornerstone for Yad Vashem was Laid," *Haaretz*, July 30, 1954; for a documentary film of the ceremony see HS, 21020, 20:17.

establishing the remembrance and heroism halls, the synagogue, the memorials, and the monument.⁶⁵ The agreement between Yad Vashem and the Claims Conference was signed in New York in October 1954. Dinur represented Yad Vashem and Goldmann signed for the Claims Conference.⁶⁶

At the end of 1954, Mark Uveeler, executive director of YIVO, the Institute for Jewish Research in New York, was selected as the representative of the Claims Conference on the Yad Vashem directorate. Other representatives of the Claims Conference were members of Yad Vashem's various administrative bodies.⁶⁷ The transfer of funds to Yad Vashem was conditioned on strict oversight of Yad Vashem's work and decisions.⁶⁸

Uveeler critiqued, for example, Yad Vashem's choice regarding the size of the archive and library building and objected to Dinur's wish to collect historical and academic material that related not only to the Holocaust but also more specifically to the chronicles of Jewish communities in Europe. Uveeler claimed that Yad Vashem's decision to build an archive that would house eight million pages of documents, books, and eyewitness pages was misguided; he estimated that the scope of material that Yad Vashem would receive would be more limited. He also "reminded" Dinur that the National Library, located in Jerusalem, rendered a large and independent library at Yad Vashem unnecessary. "An American gives money for building an archive and he wants to see the building as it was described and not to have partners," Uveeler stated, rejecting the directorate's proposal to unite the administration building and the archive.⁶⁹

Uveeler also protested the directorate's priorities in construction on the Mount of Remembrance – the emphasis placed on gathering historical material and the delay of building commemoration. "People who come to Jerusalem from Europe and America go through Paris and the result will be that in Paris they will see the great monument in memory of the martyrs [Schneersohn's center] and in Jerusalem research on the martyrs." Uveeler pleaded with Yad Vashem not to forget "the importance of the psychological element. It will not be good if a Jew sheds a tear at the monument in Paris and in Jerusalem hears only statistics."⁷⁰ This was tied to the Claims Conference's critique of the plan to establish two remembrance

---

65 HHA, 3-95. 16 (6), "Summary of a Joint Meeting in New York between Yad Vashem and Various Jewish Organizations," July 30, 1954.
66 KMHA, S-29, 3, "Agreement between the Claims Conference and Yad Vashem," October 6, 1954.
67 "YIVO's Representative in Yad Vashem Head Office," *Yediot Yad Vashem* 3 (1956), 11.
68 Cohen, *Holocaust Research*, 87–96.
69 HHA, 3-95. 17 (2), "Summary of a Meeting with Mark Uveeler," October 14, 1954.
70 ISA, HZ-3/151, Uveeler to Dinur, October 30, 1954.

buildings on the Mount of Remembrance, a remembrance hall and a heroism hall. Aside from the heavy and ostensibly unnecessary financial burden involved, the Claims Conference did not look kindly on the monumentality that the architects and the directorate aspired to or the emphasis placed on immortalizing Jewish heroism during the war. Uveeler asked that Yad Vashem build one building with various wings dedicated to "all of the areas of our war against Hitler. One such monumental building will symbolize the ties between the martyrs who perished in the concentration camps and ghettoes and the heroes from among the partisans and from the Israeli groups of the Haganah, the [Jewish] Brigade, etc."[71]

Discussions about the Architectural Image of the Mount of Remembrance

The founding of Yad Vashem and the laying of the cornerstone made it possible for the five architects to create a construction plan for the Mount of Remembrance.[72] While in 1946 and 1948 the architects had created outlines whose purpose was to impress donors and interest people in Yad Vashem, the series of plans made beginning in early 1954 and into 1955 had a practical goal: they were based on the topography of the Mount of Remembrance and included the locations of the memorial buildings and their architectural form. "The Yad Vashem memorial enterprise is singular, and some say unprecedented, in history," *Yediot Yad Vashem* wrote, and therefore "it is clear that the architecture must find fitting expression, unique buildings meant for the remembrance of millions of victims, magnificent for the living generations."[73]

The five versions of blueprints for the Mount of Remembrance prepared in those years reflect the changes that took place in the architectural team's concepts as a result of the work in the field and the ties with Yad Vashem's directorate.[74] The plans show a process of gradual disconnection from the Mandate-era plans and a transition to independent ones. In these plans, it is clear that the division between the archive, library, and administrative buildings and the remembrance

---

71 Ibid.
72 The official name of the site as the "Mount of Remembrance" was determined during 1954. See: CZA, S6/6759, Ben-Zion Eshel to Yad Vashem, July 7, 1954.
73 "Plans for Yad Vashem Buildings Approved," *Yediot Yad Vashem* 4–5 (1956), 4.
74 Order of plans: 1. HHA, 3–95 7 (1), booklet titled "Yad Vashem," August 1954; 2. HHA, 3–95 7 (1), plan with no title and date; 3. HHA, 3–95 7 (1), plan of "Yad Vashem. 12–444," n.d.; 4. HHA, 3–95 7 (1), a photo of a plan with no details; see also air photo (KMHA, S-29, 3) where this plan is drawn over; 5. HHA, 3–95 7 (1), photos of a model of Yad Vashem.

compound on the western part of the ridge is preserved. A wide boulevard (which later became the Avenue of the Righteous among the Nations) leads visitors to the elevated compound. The large dome that appeared on earlier plans in now gone, and the Holocaust hall is designed as a rounded structure of impressive dimensions, with an inner space that is open to the sky; only the perimeter is built. Across from it, on the west side of the plaza, is the long, narrow heroism hall.

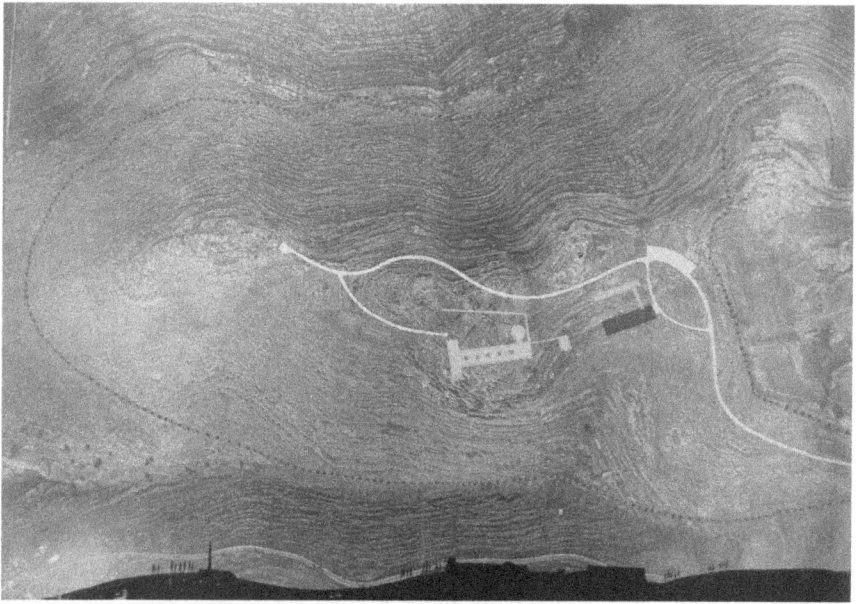

Figure 13: Construction plan for Yad Vashem, 1954 (HHA).

At the end of October 1954, Yad Vashem's directorate reapproved the construction plan. It was decided that the archive, library, and offices of Yad Vashem would be built in 1955; the remembrance hall and synagogue would be built in 1956; and the museum, an innovation that had not appeared in earlier plans, would be built in 1956.[75] In parallel, an agreement was signed between the five architects and the Remembrance Authority directorate. The general planning of the Mount of Remembrance and the preparation of plans for all of the buildings would now be their responsibility.[76]

---

[75] ISA, HZ-3/151, "Protocol of a Meeting of Yad Vashem Limited Administration," October 31, 1954.
[76] ISA, GL-10/13362, "Problems with the Tenders," March 24, 1957.

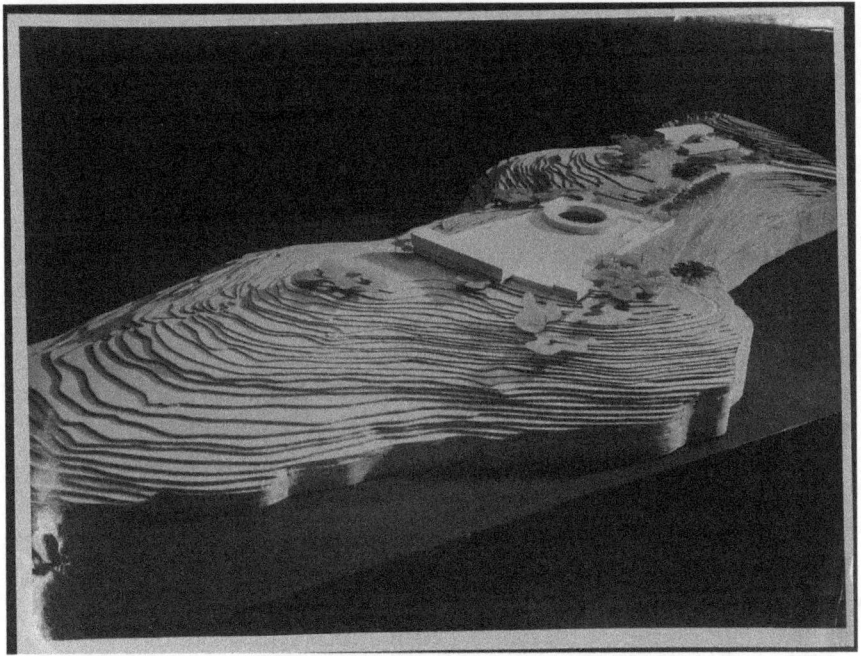

Figure 14: Model of Yad Vashem, late 1954 (HHA, Unknown photographer).

Shenhavi, as director of Yad Vashem, met with the architects to once again present his concept for the institution's construction plan. He reminded them of the eleven years that had elapsed since he had first presented his first plan and how "throughout all of the years I stood earnestly against attempts at partial solutions." They agreed that the first monumental building that visitors to Yad Vashem would encounter would be the remembrance hall. Thus, Shenhavi determined, planning the hall would be "one of the most critical tasks that architecture has confronted. It must find support in the form of its construction, its size, its scope, its heights, the decorative elements." The remembrance hall, Shenhavi requested, should be built of cells dedicated to the countries of destruction. "The cells are equal – as their fates were equal," he explained, and suggested that each contain "the last outline from the historical existence of the collective" or "a number of monuments of natural size, some of which carry the names of Jewish persons from that land." In order to the resolve the question of immortalizing millions of dead "while preserving the name of each and every victim," he suggested using an innovative method, projecting the names of the victims on tombstones positioned in the remembrance rooms dedicated to the communities. In the center of the hall, he proposed, would be an eternal flame, the type whose "blaze will rise day and night from the hall." He asked the architects not to cast the atmosphere of a cemetery in the remembrance hall but rather "a sacred corner in an essential-historical array."

Shenhavi warned the architects that little thought had thus far been devoted to the heroism hall, as "a subconscious understanding has arisen here that this element is 'easier' than its associate, the 'remembrance hall.'" In contrast with the remembrance hall, where Shenhavi suggested avoiding presenting the means of extermination and mass murder, in the heroism hall he felt that the weapons of the Jewish fighters in armies, forests, and ghettoes should be displayed. These, to his mind, would be "permanent exhibitions, realistic displays, certificates, photographs, and lists of names of Jewish fighters in the Second World War and their chronicles – all of these and other similar ones will hold a central place of honor in the hall's space."[77]

But in December 1954, less than a month after he met with the architectural team and at the height of momentum at Yad Vashem, when he could see the first buds of his vision for Holocaust commemoration, Shenhavi announced his resignation as director of Yad Vashem and the severing of ties with the institution. His complicated personality and his bitter disagreements with Dinur and others on the directorate led him to take the decision.[78] From then on, he became an observer in opposition, a member of Yad Vashem's advisory council who voiced harsh criticism of the goings-on.

Shenhavi's resignation actually had a positive effect on the planning and building of Yad Vashem. While Idelson wrote him that "in your absence, professional creativity alone will not suffice to advance the enterprise and delineate its path,"[79] Shenhavi's departure from his role freed the architects from their earlier pledges, from their commitment to him, and from his dated outlooks. This independence made it possible for them to express more modern architectural approaches with regard to the Mount of Remembrance.

In early 1955 – now sans Shenhavi – Yad Vashem's Building Committee, a body that had been established in order to supervise the planning and building of the site, held an important discussion about the image and form of commemoration at Yad Vashem, against the backdrop of the need to submit blueprints for the municipality's approval.[80] The months that elapsed were used by the architects to develop and update their plans. The architects spoke first at the meeting.

---

77 CZA, S115/506, "Planning Fundamentals for Yad Vashem," November 17, 1954.
78 ISA, GL-2/1087, Shenhavi to Dinur, December 10, 1954; "Shenhavi Is Leaving," *Yedioth Ahronoth*, December 18, 1954.
79 HHA, 3–95. 17 (2), Idelson to Shenhavi, December 19, 1954.
80 HHA, 3–95. 17 (2), "Protocol of the Planning and Building Committee," January 3, 1955.

Sharon, who was now, informally, the lead architect on the team, presented the committee with the updated plan for the Mount of Remembrance. A path would lead visitors from the mount's entrance to a sunken courtyard, an atrium in which antiquities of the land of Israel would be positioned. From this courtyard, visitors would pass through a staircase and a dark passageway to the internal, underground plaza of the remembrance hall, Yad Vashem's central building. This two-story building was of large dimensions, round, and open to the skies. The bottom floor of the remembrance hall was dedicated to describing the extermination of the Jewish communities in the European lands; the upper floor would be devoted to immortalizing individuals. The communities would be commemorated using wall murals and mosaics that would illustrate the horrors of the Holocaust. There was almost no reference to the heroism hall; it was suggested that building a museum of "the heroism of Israel in the past, present, and future" later on be examined. With that, Sharon hinted at the immense change that had taken place in the architects' consciousness vis-à-vis the building and the commemoration of heroism on the Mount of Remembrance, which they were inclined to reject. Mansfeld also presented the materials that would be used for the memorial buildings – stone, marble, and basalt – out of a desire to use local stone, black and primitive, and to integrate concrete as well, a material that symbolized the momentum of Israeli innovation and construction.

The presentation led to a heated debate about the construction plan and the symbolism of the buildings on the Mount of Remembrance. So, for example, an argument arose about the space that the architects proposed building in the center of the Holocaust hall. "A pit surely symbolizes the Holocaust," Dinur said, and is "a sacral sentiment, a sense of fate," but he asked the architects to find a more fitting architectural expression that would prevent the entry of too much light, which might "eliminate the sense of awe." Architect Dov Karmi asked to accentuate and raise the heroism building, as it "must be a fitting expression of triumph. A tall building with its highs and lows. A sort of citadel in which the height supplants the length."

Another part of the discussion touched on the synagogue and the question of its essence and function. In earlier plans, the synagogue had had a secondary function, and it was situated in the educational part of Yad Vashem, meant for the use of observant visitors. But now, after the passing of the Yad Vashem Law and the solidification of the relationship between Yad Vashem and the Claims Conference, the synagogue's importance increased, and it became one of the three central buildings slated for construction on the Mount of Remembrance. Dinur resolved that the synagogue must portray the "singular architecture that was destroyed" and serve as a type of living museum for Jewish construction in Europe. He asked that the synagogue depict Jewish art and Jewish life and be a "monument to the Judaism that was destroyed." There were those who warned of transforming the synagogue into a museum that must "lead to uniting with the memory of the past, creating feelings of respect and uniqueness, and not an atmosphere of a museum for the synagogues that were destroyed." El-Hanani clarified that the "architecture of synagogues in Poland and Russia would be alien to the landscape of our land because it is in Baroque style or wooden architecture," and proposed that the synagogue be built in a style similar to the rest of the Mount of Remembrance buildings, but with an internal arrangement that was comparable to that of the destroyed synagogues.[81]

The Dispute about the Construction Plan

As no large and significant archive existed in the State of Israel, in early 1955 Weinraub and Moshe Wind, the foreman at Yad Vashem, as well as Sharon and El-Hanani, conducted visits to Europe to observe how documents and books were preserved in libraries and archives. One prominent impression El-Hanani came away with was of the use of cast concrete,[82] the material with which the Hall of Remembrance would later be built.

The Building Committee began to work on the storage methods and forms of construction that had been recommended by Wind and the architects. The archive building, they decided, would house the archive, the library, the exhibition hall, and the research room that would serve the scholars and visitors to Yad Vashem; space would be prepared for the millions of documents that the heads of the institution expected would soon arrive in Israel.[83]

Uveeler, who in June 1955 began to participate in the meetings of Yad Vashem's limited directorate, disagreed.[84] He objected to Dinur's plan to build so many different archives on the Mount of Remembrance – "Archive of Jewish (including Diaspora) History," "Archive of the Zionist Movement," "State of Israel Archive," and the Yad Vashem Archive – because he did not believe that millions of documents would be collected.[85] "We know that there are no longer

---

[81] Ibid.
[82] CZA, S6/6760, "Report of El-Hanani and Moshe Wind to Yad Vashem."
[83] HHA, 3–95. 17 (2), HHA, 3–95. 17 (2), "Protocol of the Planning and Building Committee," February 11, 1955; "Plans for Yad Vashem Buildings Were Approved," *Yediot Yad Vashem* 4–5 (1956), 4.
[84] CAHJP, CC18557, "Protocol of a Meeting of Yad Vashem's Limited Directorate," June 7, 1955.
[85] MGWAA, "Report of a Meeting Held in Yad Vashem," August 22–24, 1954.

many archives that belong to the period of the Holocaust that do not have a resting place," he stated. "These archives are in the hands of government or public institutions and the maximum that Yad Vashem can get from these archives is microfilm and this demands little space." Uveeler warned of "this inclination," building a large archive in order to transfer other archives that were not an integral part of Yad Vashem.[86] He feared that in the future Yad Vashem's founders (including himself and the Claims Conference) would find themselves under fire for "building without accounting and without recognizing the existing situation and allowing themselves to be generous at the expense of the public."[87] This critique, as well as the severe financial shortage, led Yad Vashem's directorate to unite the archive building with the administrative building and to limit its size.

Uveeler also demanded a discussion on the question of "what . . . we want to find in the 'hall of martyrs'"; to his mind, it was the directorate's duty to decide about the building's appearance and content (and not the architects').[88] "A hall for the sake of a hall does not correspond with Jewish tradition," Uveeler stated. "According to Jewish tradition a hall as a monument must include appropriate content. Our forefathers did not build halls for splendor. They built yeshivas, hospitals, and in our generation school and library buildings, community centers, and so on." He demanded that the memorial buildings at Yad Vashem have an educational objective and not "the purpose of glory, which is the architects' inclination."[89] Uveeler's advice was "to minimize the financial demands for the synagogue and for the hall and in this way receive the necessary funds for both buildings."[90]

An additional issue that generated conflict with the Claims Conference was the "lighthouse" (*migdal-or*), a monument that appeared on Yad Vashem's plans which now became a memorial tower. Uveeler felt that its construction should come first, first and foremost because of Yad Vashem's public relations. "The expense for building the lighthouse is not great, but the impression this sort of eternal flame will make will be great," he claimed, tying the tower to the claims voiced against Yad Vashem's problematic public image and dedication of excessive resources to Holocaust research and documentation. "I am disturbed by the fact that the research building and administration building will be the only ones on the Mount of Remembrance for a long time," Uveeler wrote to Dinur, and "visitors will have the sense that it is a research institute and has nothing of the monument to

---

86 CAHJP, CC18557, Uveeler to Dinur, August 21, 1955.
87 CAHJP, CC18557, Uveeler to Dinur, June 26, 1955.
88 HHA, 3–95. 17 (2), Uveeler to Dinur, August 19, 1955.
89 Ibid.
90 CAHJP, CC18557, Uveeler to Goldmann, August 4, 1955.

Holocaust victims." He further felt that "it is undesirable that Jews from abroad who come through Paris to Jerusalem will find in Paris a hall for the memory of the martyrs and in Jerusalem only a research building." Uveeler emphasized how important it was that "there will be the 'eternal flame' on the Mount of Remembrance from day one, and people in Jerusalem, in the [Jerusalem] corridor, on the kibbutzim and in moshavim, many kilometers from Jerusalem, will answer their children's question about the light that is seen from afar, an eternal flame for the memory of the six million."[91]

Holocaust and Heroism in the Future Construction of Yad Vashem

The need to make decisions about construction on the Mount of Remembrance compelled Yad Vashem's directorate to delve into key questions tied to the Remembrance Authority's relationship to memory and commemoration. "The Yad Vashem Law charges us with establishing remembrance enterprises for the displays of Jewish heroism," Dinur opened the directorate meeting on the subject. "The problem is how memorial enterprises are erected. Is it only in books, or only in building? Perhaps in a museum exhibition, and so on?" According to the architectural plan, a "remembrance hall for the Holocaust and heroism and a synagogue" were to be built on the Mount of Remembrance but "the problem is what will be there. Will the building itself be the memorial? Will all the names be written in the heroism hall, will there be a museum there? There is a decision to build a synagogue. What will its character and function be?"

Throughout Yad Vashem's planning process from the forties and until the mid-fifties, the perception was that two memorial buildings would be erected at Yad Vashem – a heroism hall, dedicated to Jewish fighting against the Nazis, and a remembrance hall devoted to those who had perished. Now, in the final third of 1955, the idea that crystallized among the architects was that one memorial building – "the Holocaust building" – should be built, constituting a single architectural-commemorative unit.

This suggestion aroused great debate about the relationship between Holocaust and heroism among the heads of Yad Vashem; most were opposed to the division between the two terms, as "division can only distort."[92] Dinur felt that

---

91 CZA, S6/6761, Uveeler to Dinur, August 23, 1955.
92 Neima Barzel, "The Concept of Heroism Between Collective Memory and Privatized National Memory," *Dapim – Studies on the Holocaust* 16 (2000): 86–124 [in Hebrew]; Roni Stauber, "Confronting the Jewish Response to the Holocaust: Yad Vashem – A Commemorative and a Research Institute in the 1950s," *Modern Judaism* 20 (2000): 277–98; Idit Gil, "The Shoah in

Yad Vashem should contain three buildings – the Holocaust hall, the heroism hall, and the synagogue – which should become one architectural unit.[93] Many were also put off by the architects' inclination to give greater weight to the Holocaust, and felt that remembrance buildings should be given a uniform form which would make the Holocaust and heroism equal architecturally. Others even felt that the Holocaust and heroism could be united in one building, with one built next to the other, or to devote one floor of the building to the Holocaust and another to heroism. Dinur brought the discussions to a close with his proposal that the two remembrance buildings stand on either side of Yad Vashem's synagogue. "If the Holocaust hall is on one side of the synagogue and the heroism hall is on the other, the wholeness and unity will be expressed in the fact that on both sides of the synagogue there will be the same architectonic shape. This will be a series divided into three buildings," he determined.[94]

The architects submitted Yad Vashem's general urban plan to the regional committee in September 1955. The map accompanying the blueprint shows the area at Yad Vashem's disposal as some 190 acres; the five buildings slated for construction are marked, including the rounded Holocaust hall and the elongated heroism hall.[95]

But the Remembrance Authority's dire financial straits made it clear to Yad Vashem's directorate that it would be impossible to execute the plan. The funds that had been promised by the State of Israel's Ministry of Finance were not transferred and the directorate knew that an emergency plan must be formed, reworking the architectural blueprints and minimizing the scope of the building.[96] "The entire dispute is taking place with no security regarding budgetary realization," asserted Avraham Harman, until recently Israel's consul-general in New York and now deputy director of the Ministry of Foreign Affairs. He noted that everything that had been accomplished at Yad Vashem until that point had been done "stealthily," and asked "From where shall we take 50 percent of the money to supplement the Claims Conference funds? From where will

---

Israeli Collective Memory: Changes in Meanings and Protagonists," *Modern Judaism* 32 (2012): 76–101.
93 Zvi Zameret, "Between Palestino-centrism and Judeo-centrism: Benzion Dinaburg (Dinur) and the Holocaust of European Jewry," in *When Disaster Comes from Far: Leading Personalities in the Land of Israel Confront Nazism and the Holocaust, 1933–1948*, ed. Dina Porat (Jerusalem: Yad Izhak Ben-Zvi, 2009): 263–95 and especially pages 280–81, 284–85, 290–92 [in Hebrew].
94 HHA, 3–95. 17 (2), "Protocol of Building Committee," September 4, 1955.
95 HHA, 3–95. 7 (1), "Jerusalem Planning Area: Detailed Plan."
96 CAHJP, CC18557, "Protocol of Management Meeting," September 6, 1955.

we take money for buildings, with Jerusalem already sown with unfinished buildings [hinting at the International Conference Center]?"[97]

As noted, Dinur greatly stressed the place and importance of the synagogue in Yad Vashem's future plans before the Claims Conference people; at the same time, he deliberately blurred the fact that this building was only a small part of the architectural complex. It was Uveeler who suggested that "on this issue we [Yad Vashem] will go a little surreptitiously. We will propose a complex of small buildings or one large building with two small buildings. That is to say, there will be a synagogue, and in it there will be halls and a museum, to the Holocaust and to heroism." "The building must be one," Dinur confirmed, "but we must be clever and build it so that it supplies all of our needs. That is, in this building will be the Holocaust hall and the heroism hall and the synagogue. That is to say, in the legal, official sense the building must suit them [the Claims Conference] and conceptually – it must suit us."

This idea provoked many opponents, who reminded Dinur and Uveeler that the composition and the order of construction of the buildings on the Mount of Remembrance had already been approved – first the archive and library, then the Holocaust and heroism buildings, and finally the synagogue. "If the Claims Conference does not understand us now, it will understand us in a few years, when the buildings [the Holocaust hall and the heroism hall] are erected," Weitz stated. He compared Yad Vashem's synagogue, which must, in his opinion, be the smallest of the buildings – "this house of worship where all who want and have a spiritual need . . . will be able to come" – to the Holocaust and heroism buildings that must "give expression and not supplement anything else." Many on the directorate felt that because "every Jew must pass through the Holocaust and heroism building, because not everyone suffices with documents [referring to the archive]," the building should be the most prominent and attractive in Yad Vashem and not the synagogue.

One month later, in December 1955, Uveeler reported to Goldmann on the internal dispute now taking place within Yad Vashem and on the differences of opinion between the directorate's members. He criticized the directorate for inflating the institution's budget in order to bargain with the Claims Conference. "All of Israel's ministries and bodies inflate their budgets and hope that the Ministry of Finance will give them some of the money," he stated. Yad Vashem's people, he determined, preferred that the monumental building be established; moreover, Dinur saw the Mount of Remembrance "as the seat of the archive of the Historical Society of Israel" as well as of other archives. Uveeler cautioned

---

97 HHA, 3–95. 18 (3), "Protocol of Yad Vashem Management Meeting," November 1, 1955.

that the architects, who had worked on their plans for many years and been influenced by Shenhavi's megalomaniacal ideas, were now unable to trim their building plans and bring them to a "realistic place." The issue of payment to the architects seemed problematic to him as well. "As dedicated and honest as they may be, they [the architects] are no more than human," and would try to cut building expenses because it would affect the payment due to them.[98] Goldmann warned Yad Vashem's heads that construction should not under any circumstances commence on other buildings before an agreement on the subject was signed with the heads of the Claims Conference. "We understand that a hall is necessary here," Goldmann added, "but not two buildings. Not a Holocaust hall and a heroism hall separately. They should be one building, even if it contains both."[99]

The First Global Yad Vashem Council

The 1956 ceremony for Holocaust and Heroism Remembrance Day was held for the first time on the Mount of Remembrance. The ceremony generated concern and anticipation among Yad Vashem's directorate, which made efforts to publicize it in newspapers, on notice boards, and on the radio. The Mount of Remembrance still had almost nothing built; nonetheless, competition with the JNF ceremony in the Martyrs' Forest and parallel ceremonies at Kibbutz Lohamei HaGeta'ot and Kibbutz Yad Mordechai and other places in Israel stood in the background. A tour held for journalists in advance of the occasion presented the archive building, with construction still in progress, and the innovative methods that Yad Vashem would use to preserve historical materials.[100]

The ceremony was held toward the close of Holocaust and Heroism Remembrance Day and was attended by over eight thousand people, the state's president, and many ministers. It included Berl Katznelson's Yizkor conducted by Joel Engel and an elegy to the missing by Ephraim Ben Haim, both accompanied by the Israel Broadcasting Authority's orchestra. Towards dark, six torches were lit in the background by six pairs of children who had survived the Holocaust,

---

98 CAHJP, CC18557, Uveeler to Goldmann, December 8, 1955.
99 ISA, P-27/1976, "Yad Vashem Management Meeting," February 1, 1956.
100 "Yad Vashem Archive and Library are Being Built on the Mount of Remembrance," *HaTzofe*, April 6, 1956.

while Habima Theater actor Shimon Finkel read Ezekiel chapter 37, with its description of the vision of the dry bones.[101]

Ten days later, the First World Council of Yad Vashem opened, another significant milestone for the Remembrance Authority.[102] Dinur attributed much importance to this assembly, and held extensive discussions in the directorate prior to it. He asked "to come to the council with a clear proposal. We want the Mount of Remembrance to be all remembrance and not only research, therefore a remembrance hall, synagogue, and monument to heroism [as well as the archive building] should be built."[103] Indeed, among the subjects the council discussed was the future of construction. The participants approved the architectural plan headed by Dinur and resolved that the remembrance building, synagogue, and monument – "a symbol of the six million and the war of the nation against the enemy" – would be built as one unit.[104] This decision made it possible for Yad Vashem's chairman to embark on building the structures that had been decided upon.

The establishment of Yad Vashem – the founding of the Remembrance Authority institutions, the ceremonies on the Mount of Remembrance, and the decisions about the construction plans – all helped Dinur present a firm stance before the Claims Conference and Uveeler.[105] Aside from the complaints about the quality of the Solel Boneh company's work and pace in the construction of the archive building, most of Uveeler's claims related to Yad Vashem's financial conduct. "All they do is travel to meetings at the Ministry of Finance and write requests," but "if Yad Vashem does not receive the balance due to it from the Ministry of Finance soon . . . Yad Vashem will face chaos in the construction," he warned.[106] Aside from the fact that "there is no definition of the domain of Yad Vashem's plans and work, a prerequisite for building any type of budget," the Remembrance Authority must know now what its plans were for the future. "There is a need [to know] in what direction Yad Vashem will go in the future in terms of income – if it only depends on funds received from the Ministry of Finance and the

---

101 CAHJP, CC18557, "Ceremony on the Mount of Remembrance," April 8, 1956; for a documentary film of the event see: HS, 4569, 16:44.
102 "Enterprises for Commemorating Holocaust Victims Will Be Built on the Mount of Remembrance," *Davar*, April 20, 1956.
103 CZA, KKL5/22479, "Protocol of Yad Vashem Directorate Meeting," April 13, 1956.
104 CZA, KKL5/22479, "Summary of Results of Yad Vashem First International Council," April 19, 1956.
105 CAHJP, CC18569, Uveeler to Goldmann, April 9, 1956.
106 Ibid.

Jewish Agency or if it will go the route of receiving amounts from abroad in place of what it now receives from the Claims Conference."[107]

Goldmann warned Dinur of the Claims Conference's negativity toward the Remembrance Authority because "they do not see that you are doing anything" and because the enthusiasm that had abounded when the transfer of funds to Yad Vashem was approved was waning. He cautioned that "if during this year there is no progress in administration, [community memorial] books do not appear, and the impression that you are functioning is not created – then I am unsure what next year will hold."[108] Dinur tried to soften and balance Goldmann's words, replying that Yad Vashem was working in full cooperation with the Claims Conference. "We know that only by joining forces with the government of Israel, the Zionist movement, and the Claims Conference will we realize Yad Vashem and our plans," but he refused to assent to "general oversight" over Yad Vashem on the part of the Claims Conference. "We understand the desire of the Claims Conference to be a partner not only in allocations but also in execution, but I do not understand how it is possible to suggest that an agent of the Claims Conference would be in the role of 'supervisor' over Yad Vashem."[109]

The Symposium for Planning the Mount of Remembrance

At the end of May 1956, Yad Vashem's directorate elected to convene a symposium with prominent public figures – artists, writers, architects, and academics – people who held "Yad Vashem's problems close, for exchanging ideas about the buildings' plans and about the architectonic expression that should be given to the buildings."[110]

In the months that led up to the decision, the directorate's sense that it and its architects were missing a fuller understanding of the future appearance of the Mount of Remembrance grew. Aside from the archive and administration building, whose planning progressed relatively quickly,[111] there was a lack of clarity about the rest of Yad Vashem's buildings – primarily the remembrance hall and the heroism hall. Uveeler protested the fact that Yad Vashem's directorate did

---
107 CAHJP, CC18566, Uveeler to Herman, May 10, 1956.
108 ISA, P-27/1976, "Yad Vashem Directorate Meeting," February 1, 1956.
109 CAHJP, CC18533, Dinur to Goldmann, April 10, 1956.
110 CZA, S80/3441, "Decisions of Yad Vashem's Directorate," May 29, 1956.
111 ISA, GL-8/13362, "Tender Committee Meeting," July 25, 1955. This building would eventually become today's Administration and Research building, but at the time it was known by its two central functions.

not discuss the character, function, and shape of the building in depth. "A hall for the purpose of a monument must include within it proper content," he stated, and asked Dinur to support his position that the "martyrs' hall" that would be built on the Mount of Remembrance must be dedicated for an educational purpose. "I would be happy," Uveeler said, "if, for example, space could be found for a museum for the chronicles of Israel-Europe. So schoolchildren, youth from kibbutzim, and so on would come to this hall each year. What I ask is a hall with life content."[112] This critique, along with a sense of responsibility and a recognition that the directorate needed broader public support, led Dinur to the decision to convene a symposium that would be occupied with the future of building at Yad Vashem and bring the "fundaments of commemoration to architectonic expression" in a fitting way.[113]

Prior to the symposium, Dinur composed a document meant to present the dilemmas tied to planning the Mount of Remembrance. Under "Fundamental Problems in the Design of Yad Vashem's Buildings on the Mount of Remembrance," he related to the question of the desired and necessary integration of the Remembrance Authority's different functions – collecting and studying archival material on the Holocaust and physical commemoration of the Holocaust and heroism. "How can we build remembrance structures that are both very efficient, meant to serve their purpose," he asked, "while also being remembrance structures that have within them to uplift a person, to infuse in him the sense of 'Remove your shoes from your feet, for this ground is holy'?"[114]

Dinur noted that the Yad Vashem Law stated that the institution was authorized "to establish memorial enterprises at its initiative and under its management." He explained that the directorate felt that the commemoration buildings should be tied to these memorial enterprises in a creative way and added that they should constitute one unit architectonically, organizationally, and financially. "Everything that the law imposes on the Yad Vashem Remembrance Authority should find architectonic expression in these buildings," he stated, and detailed: the six million Jewish brethren who had been named "sacred martyrs to the slaughter," "Jewish households" that were destroyed, communities, and synagogues. Dinur emphasized the commemoration of "the martyrs' self-sacrifice," the heroism of the fighters and rebels, and "the sublime struggle," ever present, of the masses and the righteous among the nations. This complex and onerous task made it necessary, Dinur stated, "to work diligently on the entirety of

---

112 CAHJP, CC18567, Uveeler to Dinur, May 6, 1956.
113 YVA, AM1 448, "Summary of Decisions of Building Committee," July 17, 1955.
114 HHA, 3–95. 17 (2), Dinur, "Fundamental Problems in the Design of Yad Vashem's Buildings on the Mount of Remembrance," n.d.

the plan. So that each corner, each stake, and each detail and detail will have some expression of commemoration." The building style should be "of the sublime, in the sense of lofty and exalted, but not necessarily in terms of dimensions. The size of the pain and the depth of the grief must find suitable architectonic expression."

Dinur highlighted a number of fundamental problems that the symposium's participants should consider. First came "the utilitarian and the sublime," that is, the deliberation of how to build commemoration structures that would be efficient and useful but at the same time give Yad Vashem's visitors the feeling that they were visiting a holy site. Second was "the concrete and the abstract," the question of how to give architectural expression in Yad Vashem's memorial buildings to the concrete, to the Holocaust victims, and to the abstract, to the spiritual means – "the sanctification of God's name, the boldness of spirit, the fraternity, that were in the hearts of the people and their spirit, and shaped their character in the days of horror." The third question was "the one and the many," how to give the individual the opportunity to unite with his or her grief and agony in the memorial building, and to express the "individual's sorrow" architecturally but at the same time give national and general expression "to the Holocaust of the nation and the girding of the general public, to the image of the nation as a whole in this dire time." Fourth came "the Holocaust and heroism," the question of how these two "united" terms could be commemorated. "There was heroism in the self-sacrifice, and there was a Holocaust with Jewish rebellion" and the problem was therefore "how to unite the two [Holocaust and heroism] and also individualize them." The challenge, Dinur concluded, was that in the absence of "dimensions with which we can express the depth of our tragedy and the strength of our grief there is a need to find a symbolic expression" for the Holocaust and heroism that Yad Vashem wished to immortalize.

The First Symposium

It was with these questions that Dinur stood before the participants of the symposium that met on June 10, 1956. Aside from Yad Vashem's directorate, the Building Committee, and the five architects, a number of others were invited: architects Dov Karmi and Yehoshua Steinbock (Shani), representatives of the architects' association, as well as different public figures such as Jerusalem Mayor Gershon Agron, Uri Zvi Greenberg, Haim Hazaz, Leah Goldberg, sculptor Moshe Ziffer, artist Mordecai Ardon, archaeologist Jacob Pinkerfeld, and professors Benjamin Mazar and Yigael Yadin. Also invited were Abba Kovner and Sholem

Asch.[115] Of these, only a few came to the meeting – representatives of those intellectuals whom Dinur hoped would help in his undertaking.[116]

The sparse attendance did not deter Dinur, who opened the meeting by recounting Yad Vashem's long history, the thirteen years that had elapsed since Shenhavi first raised the idea, and the fact that the Mount of Remembrance was the third location (actually, it was the fourth) that had been selected. "Many incarnations passed before we were privileged to attain this space. And this space and its nature constitute the basis of the plan, and [are] even a valuable component of it," he said, relating to the architectural plans that had been presented to those who had been at an earlier tour held at the Mount of Remembrance. He mentioned the remembrance hall, the heroism hall, and the synagogue as well as the decision to build them as one structure that would be practical and commemorative as one, "both functional and also serving as a symbol and an immortalization of all that we have been charged with immortalizing." He posed the question of how this could be accomplished and opened the floor to the architects.

Arieh Sharon began by explaining the way in which he and his colleagues viewed the task they'd been given. "Our primary role," he said, "is to take over the territory. [To answer the question of] how to raise the group of buildings . . . to a level where they will indeed symbolize what they were meant to symbolize." He spoke about how the Mount of Remembrance's unique topography had led him and his colleagues to plan the space and its Holocaust hall. This hall would be built as a circle and would be comprised of two stories, a ground floor and an upper floor that would connect to Yad Vashem's central assembly plaza. He explained that the architects' decision to choose a circle for the Holocaust hall stemmed from their desire to commemorate all lands of destruction equally. He also briefly mentioned the "museum," the "heroism" or "combat hall," the other building to be founded at Yad Vashem, dedicated to commemorating heroism.

El-Hanani also focused on the Holocaust hall and mentioned that space and light, the most prominent tools and fundaments in the architects' work, were what influenced the planning of the hall. He described the dramatic lighting in the building, the natural light that would come from the large circular opening that would remain at the center, and the eternal flame that would stand in the center of the circular building. On the bottom floor would be the museum; the upper floor, which would be divided into twenty equal parts, would be dedicated to the communities that had perished in the Holocaust. The

---

115 CZA, S80/3441, "Decisions of Yad Vashem Management," May 29, 1956.
116 HHA, 3–95. 17 (2), "Protocol of Yad Vashem Symposium," June 10, 1956.

image of Jewry in the different lands would be accentuated using mosaics. Czech Jewry would be represented by the synagogue of the Maharal (Rabbi Judah Loew) of Prague while the Krakow ghetto would be the symbol of Polish Jewry. He reported that his colleagues planned on etching beneath each of these paintings, on marble panels, inscriptions that would note the number of Jews before and after the destruction in each land. The Holocaust hall, El-Hanani said, would be built with "basalt stones and at the entrance there would be large boulders that would give the impression of something very ancient."

The architects' descriptions of the building plan on the Mount of Remembrance stirred a lively debate on a variety of subjects, some financial and some architectural. Abraham Herman, Israel's general consul in New York, was one of the first to speak. After cautioning of the possibility that Yad Vashem would begin building the remembrance buildings without having financial cover, he asked the architects about their ability to continue building Yad Vashem if they only had a small amount of the sum necessary at their disposal. Weinraub replied that the directorate must define for the architects what the minimal and the maximal construction plan would be, and Herman half-warned, half-asked whether a budget cut could lead to only one of the planned floors in the Holocaust building being built, "and in place of commemoration it would be a certificate of shame for the Jewish nation who began a holy enterprise and did not complete it?"

Rishon LeZion's former mayor Aryeh Sheftel separated the financial dilemma from the deliberation about the Mount of Remembrance's physical image. He warned that Yad Vashem could be established in "miniature" fashion, and in the future it would defiantly be stated, "See what the state established in 'Yad Vashem' in memory and immortalization of its martyrs." He emphasized that "We are doing something here for the world as a whole, to which tourists will come – Jews and non-Jews. They will come to see the great enterprise and we will not be able to explain to them that we only had a budget of 1 million Israeli pounds." Sheftel noted and warned that Jewry and the State of Israel had no tradition of commemorative building and no experience designing cemeteries. "We have no tradition like this in stone," he said, noting the Scriptural prohibition against making statues and images, which, in his opinion, had limited the Jews' occupation with the subject for generations. "We cannot show the character and beauty of the land – that can mislead us and will not leave the desired impression," he noted. "The image of the Maharal or the Krakow Ghetto will not make the necessary impression," he felt, but rather the intensity of the destruction and the methods of destruction in each land must be shown. Sheftel related to the question of commemorating heroism as well, rejecting integrating the War of Independence within the Mount of Remembrance. His central claim was that "we will trivialize the War of Independence if it is included in this." He did suggest including the clandestine immigration nonetheless, "because it is part of the Holocaust – the ships that sank."

Baruch Zwi Ophir was also of the opinion that the question of whether Yad Vashem would be able to build a "monument for generations" on the Mount of Remembrance should be considered, and posited that it was better not to embark on the enterprise than to be stopped "mid-way and to give it a wretched look." He warned of the possibility that Yad Vashem's directorate and architects would have a hard time completing the task as long as the way in which "our idea" would be expressed on the Mount of Remembrance was unclear. He also criticized the decision to allocate equal space to each of the lands and communities. "Is it possible that we will allot Yugoslavian Jewry, with all due respect, the same space as, for example, Polish Jewry?" He suggested planning the Yad Vashem building in such a way that it could be adjusted for future change and "dynamic development," and emphasized that the Yad Vashem enterprise should be viewed as a mission for Diaspora Jewry and as "a memorial center for Diaspora Jewry," making the Mount of Remembrance a "lodestone, a place of pilgrimage for the coming generations."

The two external architects who participated in the meeting, Karmi and Jacob Pinkerfeld, related in the main to the architectural and design dimension of the Mount of Remembrance. Karmi stated that "it would be good if they simplified it [the internal planning of the Holocaust hall] slightly and there were less prose and inscriptions." He also suggested erecting "something central about the situation" in the middle of the remembrance building, so that visitors could walk around it, giving the building a monumental feel. Pinkerfeld summed up the two planning outlooks proposed by the architects: one was to create a central building containing all remembrance elements; the other was to make a central plaza on the Mount of Remembrance around which and in which the remembrance buildings would be constructed. Pinkerfeld supported the second approach.

Shenhavi, who was present at the meeting, also joined the debate, speaking out decisively and angrily against the decisions made by Yad Vashem's directorate. He cried out,

> How can we turn the idea of six million individuals to something that speaks, to six million!!! And not a vague statement that means nothing when we say six million people. When we speak of thirty thousand communities!!!. . . How will we show a person who comes there and wants to remember, who has a stake in it, that he will receive the necessary connection within in? We will not give him this on a lifeless card.

Shenhavi compared Yad Vashem to other places in Israel in which remembrance sites had recently been built, wishing, of course, to emphasize how deficient the architectural planning of Yad Vashem was and how misguided was the path the directorate had outlined. He mentioned "Yad Chaim Weizmann," the "monument" that had been established in those days to immortalize Chaim Weizmann, and the burial site of the Baron Benjamin de Rothschild in Zichron Yaakov, asking "Do we know how many Weizmanns were lost among these six million?"[117] Even if the work extended for many years – five or ten – the two halls, the remembrance hall and the combat hall, should be insisted upon, he demanded. This despite the fact that, in his opinion, the fitting scale for the scope and size of the Holocaust's tragedy had become lost to those involved in the work.

Weitz, like Shenhavi, had accompanied the process of establishing Yad Vashem almost from its very beginning; he placed the ideal of Yad Vashem and its architectural expression on the Mount of Remembrance at the center of his words. He asked: How can the intensity of the destruction be expressed? "This all begins with an idea and afterwards it must materialize," he stated, emphasizing the symbolic importance of the construction, the "evocation of feeling," which would lead to a visitor entering a remembrance space "and the great awe [that] will seize him." He mentioned that this could be "simple, total simplicity, without décor," and tied this simplicity with the idea of bringing martyrs' ashes into the remembrance building. "That can stir the sense of grief that eats the entire body . . . in effect, whatever else you add – you will diminish." "You must position the man in front of this simple thing, so that he cannot escape thinking about its implications" – Weitz in effect foresaw the appearance of the Hall of Remembrance that would be built at Yad Vashem in the early sixties.

Many of the participants identified with the minimalist experience that Weitz wished to convey at Yad Vashem, but others felt that it would not suffice. "Thinking an unconventional thought" was necessary, it was claimed, because this was the first time that the State of Israel would immortalize in stone and edifice and there was a need to create a special atmosphere and spirit. One participant contrasted his experience visiting Yad Vashem with that of his daughter: "What association would she have if she entered an empty building?" An additional element, then, should be added to the building, the participants recommended, in order to

---

117 Doron Bar, "Zionist Pantheons? The Design and Development of the Tombs of Herzl, Weizmann and Rothschild during the Early Years of the State of Israel," *Israel Studies* 25, no. 2 (2020): 72–94.

stir unique feelings amongst the visitors who had not experienced the Holocaust, perhaps names of the communities engraved on the building's walls or entrance.

Sharon spoke again before those present, giving a sort of summary. He made note of the architects' desire to complete the construction on the Mount of Remembrance. "But in order to complete it we must first begin," he said, and asked for a pragmatic approach, such as defining the amount of money at their disposal or being given "a more practical program for a number of spaces." In any event, he emphasized the need to dominate the space. "This area stirs some feeling and association, and it can be dominated only by a group of buildings, because a group of buildings around a plaza will have a much greater effect than one building, whether of small or large scale."

Dinur noted that the question that had been presented was how practicality could be merged with symbolism and admitted that the response he had received from the participants differed from the direction in which he had wished to lead the meeting. The participants, in contrast, expressed satisfaction with the division and declared that "remembrance should be on its own and the museum on its own." He noted again the idea of bringing martyrs' ashes to Yad Vashem and added that he imagined "that the monument's remembrance hall would be a building and that the martyrs' ashes would be there and there would be a list of the lands and communities and their people."

The Second Symposium

Yad Vashem's directorate approved the symposium's conclusions;[118] nonetheless, one month later, in mid-July, Dinur called for another meeting.[119] It appeared that there was dissatisfaction due to the lackluster participation in the first symposium, particularly with regard to its conclusions, which remained too vague. The discussion there had been heated and fruitful but it had contributed next to nothing to clarifying the questions with which the directorate contended regarding construction on the Mount of Remembrance.

This time, participation was somewhat broader than it had been at the first symposium. Aside from Yad Vashem's people, members of academia, writers, and officials from government ministries and the Jerusalem municipality attended. Shenhavi did not take part.

---

118 CZA, S115/533, "Decisions of Yad Vashem's Directorate," June 12, 1956.
119 HHA, 3–95. 17 (2), "Protocol of Yad Vashem Symposium," July 15, 1956.

Dinur opened the meeting and moved to discuss the central questions on the agenda. "The issue we are speaking of is so vast and important and of great responsibility that we thought it would be fitting to involve the wider public in the discussion and deliberations," Dinur stated, presenting the dilemmas that he wished to place center stage. "We want the remembrance building to be symbolic and, in its form, like a remembrance tent." He stated that "There must be a special idea for the remembrance tent," and referred to the idea of burying martyrs' ashes. "We receive requests from overseas about bringing ashes – some ashes – of Jews from the camps instead of them becoming trampled," ashes that could be buried there. "The problem," according to Dinur, was that "the mount in its entirety must be a remembrance in its shape. [It] must combine all of the buildings" and tie its utilitarian practical components, the archive, library, museum, and synagogue, to the "remembrance tent." "How can we arrange this? What form can be given to the expression of the greatness of the catastrophe? And how will the individual have a place to unite with his sorrow, so that we can give the entire nation this remembrance?"

Sharon presented the updated blueprints and described how he and his colleagues "went along the ridge and tried to adapt the buildings [on the Mount of Remembrance] to the topography and the hills" and to state-public building in other parts of the city. He noted the quarried courtyard on the hill that would constitute the entrance space to the Holocaust hall, a courtyard that "must set the mood before entering the Holocaust hall." This courtyard led to the circular Holocaust hall, the center of Yad Vashem. "The building is rounded," Sharon explained, "because we wished to express the identical fate of all those who were killed by the Nazi enemy – the same fate for all the communities, for all the lands. Inside we did not differentiate between a land that lost many and a land that lost few." The assembly plaza was "a forum for the entire memorial enterprise," he emphasized, looking out in all directions; around it stood three buildings, the rounded one to the east and the museum, the heroism building, to the west. Despite the fact that he admitted that there was still no clear plan for this final structure, he reported that it was meant to rise two or three stories and its goal was to "commemorate and collect the remains of the Diaspora and the Holocaust and give expression to the Diaspora."

Sharon confessed that he and his colleagues were aware of their inability to express the intensity of the Holocaust and heroism through "immense and representative" buildings but noted the "milestones that we have set for ourselves [which] will keep us from overconfidence." "Our first goal is to take care and not to scale the hills," Sharon said, "as one of the biggest faults of our architecture is that we always surpass the height of the hill." Therefore, he said, even Yad Vashem's central remembrance building would not rise too high. Sharon also added details about the future design of the building. "We want to mark the circular building only using very strong expressions, using stones that indicate the lands, some engravings, fire, and ash," he determined.

El-Hanani added to Sharon's words; he reported on how visitors would walk

> in a tunnel, in dark and in deep [and then] see the grave [of ashes] by the eternal flame whose light will draw the visitor's eye. All in a basalt structure. A person seeing the light from afar and drawing closer to it will be accompanied throughout by the light. And he will rise to the territory of the plaza which contains an eternal list of the communities that were destroyed.

"The same basalt walls . . . will envelop the place of this grave," El-Hanani added, "the same mystical light . . . will come from above. These will certainly be noticeable and affect the religious and secular person as one," he noted, contrasting it to the exit to sunlight and the landscape seen from the assembly plaza, a landscape "that again creates a transition and liberation from the overpowering impression."

Once the statements were over, the participants began to discuss. Dinur noted that in the earlier symposium, a decision had been made to separate the functional building, with the museum and space for exhibits, from the symbolic, commemorative structure. "The problem is with the remembrance," he noted. "We agreed that a mark of remembrance should not be erected without ashes," but the problem was "what the symbol should be." He also reminded the group of their duty to commemorate heroism, that is, "a feature tent" in which the names of the "platoons, partisan regiments, and brigades" would be listed. He further contemplated the visitors' route on the Mount of Remembrance – the archive building, the museum, the tent, the heroism memorial monument, and the synagogue – "from the concrete to the abstract."

"Can we illuminate the Holocaust that has descended upon our nation and the heroism as well in one building? Can we give it expression?" Moshe Kol asked. "We, who lived during the period of the Holocaust and were hurt by the Holocaust and have seen the heroism and the establishment of the state," Kol claimed, can be shaken in structures with a "different expression." But the buildings at Yad Vashem, Kol noted, were being established for the coming generations. "We must think at least about the second generation." He demanded that they seek a fitting expression that could stir "the awe and silence and respect and some expression that can move the coming generation." For this reason, he rejected the suggestion that mosaics, reliefs, and stained glass reflecting the devastated communities in artistic fashion and the scope of the tragedy be used. "This type of expression will say nothing and will not affect the second generation nor those who lived through the Holocaust and forgot it." He thus added his weight to the proposal that building an anonymous tomb in the remembrance hall (containing ashes) was "an unparalleled idea." He suggested that the walls be entirely bare without paintings or sculptures and the building be a symbol; "all who enter it will be shocked and stand in silence and awe." Finally, he suggested finding a different name for the Holocaust remembrance building, as "when we put the word *heikhal* [hall] with the word *Shoah* [Holocaust, destruction]" it elicits a sense of discomfort.

Prof. Efraim Elimelech Urbach also agreed that a Holocaust building must be minimalistic, "and the less there is in it – the more it will contain." If nothing absurd were done in the building but rather it used the "impression of what is missing in it," then the building, in his opinion, would create an immense impression, rendering the need for a list of those who perished unnecessary; the El Malei Rahamim prayer would suffice. He stated, then, that "the building must make a statement with the structure itself, without any additions," and rejected the need to establish a monument to heroism at Yad Vashem, as Dinur had suggested. Urbach felt that the feature tent would serve as a remembrance "to all those who fell, with no difference as to how they fell, during the Holocaust." He explained that Jewish cemeteries buried all Jews without taking into account the way they had died, which made the need to allocate heroism its own space in Yad Vashem unnecessary. Most of all, he warned of the architects' desire to create a mystical sense while building the Holocaust building. "Mysticism is bound up in a little danger," he said. Mysticism in Judaism, he claimed, "has not succeeded for the most part when it is built on external things."

Prof. Nathan Feinberg took the discussion in a different direction – the fact that the planning had been conducted by a team of architects and was never an architectural challenge posed to the more general Jewish world. He asked whether the Jewish world knew of the building of Yad Vashem at all and whether artists had been asked to express their opinions on the subject and propose ideas for planning the space. He suggested receiving aid from various people in the Jewish world "who have the same spark of the artist who can perhaps contribute to the idea of the form of commemoration." Feinberg stated that for the commemoration of the Holocaust of "the entire nation," they must appeal to Jewish architects of repute around the world in order to use their ideas.

"One thing is crystallizing here and both symposia have been very helpful," Kol said. The central building should symbolize the Holocaust and must be a complete abstraction, containing nothing but the symbolic grave that holds "the anonymous Jew who was killed or fell." This building must "shock" and "overtake" the visitors and the rest of the "items" must sit in the museum building, which would be the place to establish a model of an extermination camp. "This thing must be illustrated and around it must be photographs of the places in which these camps were, because people will once again say that this type of thing never existed."

Dinur could now sum up what had been discussed by the participants in the two symposia – the first and central building on the Mount of Remembrance would be the remembrance tent, and it would be tied to the ashes and the grave of the anonymous Jew.[120] This building was meant to stand out in its simplicity and symbolism and the central figurative component that would constitute the heart of the remembrance was the El Malei Rahamim la-Aratzot (the mourning prayer for the lands). Following the construction of this building, the remembrance hall would be built, containing the museum, in which the names of the communities would be displayed in one form or another, "and then place must be found for the brigades of fighters," where exhibits and the museum of the Holocaust, the "museum of Jewish life," would also be. Finally, Dinur mentioned the synagogue, a building that would always be open, whose construction would serve to commemorate the synagogues that had been annihilated.[121]

Conclusion

> The place on which we stand is holy ground – the ground of the Mount of Remembrance, near the mount that carries the name of the visionary of *The Jewish State*. And the Mount of Remembrance is fitting for this juxtaposition, as it will serve as a symbol of eternal remembrance – a hand and a name [*yad va-shem*] – that we are coming to establish to the Holocaust and heroism in our nation, within the Jewish state.[122]

These were the words of Israeli president Yitzhak Ben-Zvi, when he spoke at the end of July 1954 at the cornerstone ceremony for the archive and administrative buildings of Yad Vashem. And, indeed, the first year after the passing of the Yad Vashem Law in Knesset proved to be a very significant one. In this period, the foundations were laid for funding Yad Vashem's activity and construction, the institution grounded itself organizationally, and, for the first time, architectural plans that were suited to the Mount of Remembrance were prepared. These blueprints created by the team of architects changed a number of times, primarily due to the deliberations of the architects and the directorate about the architectural character of Yad Vashem. It was precisely this extensive and complicated

---

[120] Saul Friedlander and Adam B. Seligman, "The Israeli Memory of the Shoah: On Symbols, Rituals, and Ideological Polarization," in *Now Here: Space, Time and Modernity*, ed. Roger Friedland and Deirdre Boden (Berkley: University of California Press, 1994), 363–64.
[121] HHA, 3–95. 17 (2), "Summary of Yad Vashem's Two Symposia."
[122] KMHA, S-29, 3, "President's Speech."

process that made it possible for them and the heads of Yad Vashem to create so significant an architectural construction in the form of the Hall of Remembrance and the other buildings that were inaugurated in the early sixties.

During this time, a complicated relationship developed with the Claims Conference, whose representative, Uveeler, became more and more involved in events at Yad Vashem. In exchange for the transfer of funds for the institution's activities and the construction of the Mount of Remembrance, the Claims Conference now had the right to take part in the directorate's discussions and to supervise it. After the preliminary agreement between Yad Vashem and the Claims Conference was signed in October 1954, the funds may have been transferred, but the disagreements between the two bodies grew. These were tied, inter alia, to the lack of consensus about the institution's objectives and whether it should focus on research and collecting names of the victims or, rather, commemorate heroism and the Holocaust physically. One question mark related to the need to build a synagogue on the Mount of Remembrance and to defining its goal. Earlier plans for Yad Vashem had a synagogue as a place of prayer for visitors to the memorial site, but later the house of worship became one of the three prominent memorial components on the Mount of Remembrance.

The conflict about the synagogue was not the only one that Yad Vashem's directorate faced during this period; other issues tied to building the memorial also arose. Central was the discussion about the place of heroism on the Mount of Remembrance. From the very early planning of Yad Vashem it was clear that the institution would commemorate heroism alongside Holocaust. But in the first half of the fifties, heroism's place as central faded, and a greater emphasis was placed on the Holocaust in the emerging plans for the mount.

The period of time discussed in this chapter closed with the convening of two symposia at the initiative of Yad Vashem's directorate. This was a bold move on the part of Dinur, who felt that he needed public support in the process of building the Mount of Remembrance. At the end of the two meetings, after he had succeeded in directing the discussions as desired, it was decided that the Hall of Remembrance, *Ohel Yizkor*, would stand at the center of the Mount of Remembrance, a structure that would be dedicated to the memory of the Holocaust and in which martyrs' ashes would be buried. This building would stand out in its simplicity and its symbolism would be conceptual. In addition to the Hall of Remembrance, a museum would also be built at Yad Vashem, displaying the lives of the Jews before the destruction, the names of the communities that had perished, and the role of those who combatted the Nazis. Finally, a synagogue would serve as a memorial for the synagogues that had been destroyed.

Chapter 4
The Path to the Hall of Remembrance's Construction

The present chapter explores the period that extended from July 1956 to April 1961. It began with the end of Dinur's second symposium, after which the goals of memorial building at Yad Vashem were defined; it closed in April 1961, with the Hall of Remembrance's inauguration on the mount, a pinnacle in Israeli architecture. Over these six years, many crises arose; the institute's directorate was forced to deal with a string of hardships, primarily financial and organizational. The relationship with the Claims Conference ran aground a number of times, though it was restored later on. Ultimately, this period can be seen as one of significant achievements, with the erection of Yad Vashem at the heart of the State of Israel's symbolic memorial landscape.

A central issue at the time was the burial of the martyrs' ashes on the Mount of Remembrance. In Yad Vashem's earlier stages of activity, in the forties, the idea of transferring martyrs' ashes to Israel – and thereby sanctifying the remembrance site – had been raised. In the second half of the fifties, with the crystallization of the building plans, Yad Vashem made noticeable efforts to attain ashes, which were buried in the Hall of Remembrance's floor in 1961. But the Remembrance Authority's vigorous activity stirred up opposition on the part of religious circles, who objected to the burial. This further heightened the conflict that surrounded the Ministry of Religions' involvement in Holocaust commemoration on Mount Zion. And, in a similar vein, questions were raised about the role and function of the Mount of Remembrance's synagogue.

Between 1956 and 1961, Yad Vashem's architectural outline became clearer and the plan for construction on the mount was finalized. A spatial division between the archive and administration building and the remembrance compound, in the Mount of Remembrance's western area, was created: a plaza would rise above its surroundings, with the Hall of Remembrance – originally planned as circular but later becoming a square – to its east. In the plaza, a thirty-meter-high tower would be dedicated to immortalizing heroism and combat against the Nazis. With this, a bitter dispute around the immortalization of heroism erupted both among Yad Vashem's directorate and between it and other groups in the Israeli public. Despite the conflicts and missteps, however, Yad Vashem emerged from this period with its dream well on its way: the Hall of Remembrance had finally been built and visitors began to arrive at a new kind of memorial space.

Financial Hurdles and Changes to the Building Plan

The discussions held in the two 1956 symposia gave Yad Vashem's directorate and the architects a basis on which they could advance the Mount of Remembrance's construction plan.[1] After Dinur summarized the different proposals and opinions that had been raised for the directorate – primarily the desire to highlight the Hall of Remembrance, which it was decided should be "modest, effective, and shocking" – the symposia approved the conclusions that had been reached.[2] Dinur asked the architects to submit a detailed outline for the Hall of Remembrance and the synagogue and to plan more generally "different museum-like buildings," such as the heroism museum and the museum of "Jewish Diasporas." He further requested that the different monuments stand between the Hall of Remembrance and the memorial hall containing the museums.[3]

At the end of 1956, five or six months later, Yad Vashem's architects submitted their updated plans for Yad Vashem, having adopted many of the directorate's recommendations. The team emphasized the entry courtyard into the remembrance compound, which would lead to the Hall of Remembrance using a subterranean passageway. The building was planned as circular, with a sloping stairway connecting it to the remembrance plaza. As a result of notes they had been given, the architects emphasized that the building's roof would not be open to the sky, but rather covered with a shallow dome resting on six buttresses. The synagogue was planned as a rectangular building, bordering the entry plaza to the south and thus complementing the other buildings "that appear as one perfect spatial unit to the public entering the courtyard."[4]

But the painful financial reality now became clear to Yad Vashem's directorate. In December 1956, the Claims Conference announced that Yad Vashem's budget would be cut by half. This was due to the budgetary straits in which the Claims Conference found itself, both from having come to the rescue of Jews emigrating from Hungary as a result of the revolt that had erupted and from its plan to help the Jews of Tunisia and Morocco who were in crisis with the end of French rule. These shifts made it necessary for the Claims Conference to halt the flow of funds to Yad Vashem.[5] The budget cut meant that Yad Vashem would need to cancel plans for the memorial buildings' construction or at least postpone the work.

---

1 CZA, KKL5/22479, Yad Vashem Architects to Yad Vashem, August 1, 1956.
2 ISA, HZ-1/151, "Decisions of Yad Vashem's Directorate," August 7, 1956.
3 MGWAA, Dinur to architects, September 10, 1956.
4 CZA, S115/537, Yad Vashem architects to Yad Vashem, December 23, 1956.
5 CZA, Z6/1997, Uveeler to Dinur, December 7, 1956.

The news was received with alarm by Yad Vashem's directorate. Dinur addressed a complaint to Goldmann and Uveeler, the two channels through which he hoped to influence the decision-makers in New York and bring about a change. "I have the impression that the decision was also taken out of a lack of appreciation for Yad Vashem's work," he wrote, insulted, to Uveeler. "This lack of appreciation is founded in the main on an insufficient knowledge of the goings-on and a lack of consideration of all of the difficulties that faced us until we were able to create a suitable, talented, and dedicated team of people for this work." To Goldmann, he expressed his frustration that "the Claims Conference decided things that determine the form of Yad Vashem without even asking us. And we are, at the very least, agents of the other side of the government."

In particular, there was great anger that at Goldmann's suggestion, one year earlier, Yad Vashem's directorate had changed the budget proposal submitted to the Claims Conference so that it could build the remembrance buildings over the 1957–1958 fiscal year. Now, Dinur stated, "There is no recourse from the plan after we reached an agreement about its execution with the heads of the Jewry from the lands of the Holocaust." Dinur was referring to the campaign to bring martyrs' ashes from Europe that Yad Vashem's directorate had begun. "I see no moral or practical possibility to not begin building the Hall of Remembrance. We will not place a wooden plank over the burial site of the martyrs," Dinur stated, claiming that the ashes must be buried in fitting fashion, as already determined, in the Hall of Remembrance. The "delay of all building until next year," he stated, "I think is an insult not only to Yad Vashem but also to the memory of the dead."[6]

Dinur's grievances relating to the Claims Conference and Uveeler were tied to a feeling that had been brewing within him. Uveeler had long "harassed" him and the rest of the directorate's members with requests and demands regarding the Remembrance Authority's activity. Uveeler's comments related to a variety of subjects – from the width of the too-narrow road leading to Yad Vashem, through the too-grandiose entry doors for the archive and library, to his suggestion that the building be named the "Research Building."[7] He inserted himself in the relationship between Yad Vashem's directorate and the architectural team and claimed that they had too great an influence on the construction and that "the taste of the simple man coming to the place must also be taken

---

6 ISA, GL-4/1299, Dinur to Goldmann, January 1, 1957.
7 ISA, GL-3/1299, Uveeler to Dinur, August 16, 1956; ISA, GL-3/1299, Uveeler to Weitz, August 21, 1956.

into account."[8] He even warned Dinur against festively marking the end of the archive building's construction and inviting delegations of Jews from abroad to the event, as Yad Vashem's guests "will pass through Paris and without a doubt stop there and visit the hall for Holocaust victims. There they will see not only a research building but also and foremost the hall [that Schneersohn built]. Under this tremendous impression they will come to Jerusalem and here they will see one more house, not really large or spacious or picturesque."[9] More than anything, Uveeler was occupied with financial matters generally and Yad Vashem's construction budget in particular. He sent Dinur dozens of letters dealing with various dimensions of the building process and its financial ramifications.[10] Dinur tied these issues to the drastic restriction of the Claims Conference's budget for Yad Vashem and felt that Uveeler had had a hand in it.

Figure 15: The archive and administration building, February 1957 (CAHJP, Unknown photographer).

---

8 CZA, KKL5/22478, "Report of the Building Committee," September 5, 1956; ISA, GL-3/1299, Uveeler to Dinur, August 29, 1956.
9 CZA, S115/532, Uveeler to Dinur, September 3, 1956.
10 ISA, GL-3/1299, Uveeler to Weitz, August 21, 1956.

As a pragmatist, Dinur suggested a resolution to the problem, preferring to "sacrifice" the synagogue's construction and delay its completion in exchange for finishing the Hall of Remembrance. "Let us not fool ourselves," he wrote to Uveeler and Goldmann, as "postponing construction is not brief . . . many are the needs of your nation." He, too, brandished the comparison to the documentation center in France as a weapon, claiming that it would be highly irregular "not to build the Hall of Remembrance over the ashes of the Holocaust victims, and to leave their memorial monument only in Paris."[11]

In order to intensify the pressure on New York, the directorate's members met for an emergency discussion and made an unequivocal resolution.

> The directorate unanimously rejects the proposals to cut the budget and delay the construction of the Hall of Remembrance to next year. The directorate does not forgo the construction plan because it sees in that a great danger to the enterprise and harm to all of Yad Vashem's plans. Yad Vashem committed before world Jewry to bring the martyrs' ashes and it is not authorized to rescind its plans. The construction plans are already prepared and the government and Jewish Agency approved the budget.[12]

Despite the directorate's resolute position, the Claims Conference's board did not alter its rejection of Yad Vashem's proposed delay in building the synagogue. Uveeler defined it as a "bad idea," and explained that this was likely to lead to "unnecessary protests of the religious circles" and opposition on the part of the Claims Conference's board of directors, which was most interested in establishing a synagogue on the Mount of Remembrance. The resolution he proposed was to spread construction on the mount over three years and to postpone completing the buildings.[13] With no other choice, Yad Vashem accepted; the plan was now to complete construction by the end of 1960.[14]

Yad Vashem's Building Committee set a new timetable for the remembrance buildings. The excavation and development of the Mount of Remembrance would begin shortly, it was decided, and the planning would soon be completed by the architects. They would be accompanied by a professional committee.[15] The architects, who emphasized their dedication to the quick and successful construction of the commemoration buildings, committed to the challenge and estimated that they would need roughly eight months to complete the planning, after which the

---

11 CAHJP, CC18551b, Dinur to Uveeler, January 1, 1957.
12 CZA, KKL5/22478, "Decisions of Yad Vashem's Directorate," January 7, 1957.
13 AHJP, CC appl. 1957/331, Uveeler to Shaul Kagan, January 11, 1957.
14 HHA, 3–95. 19 (1), "Decisions of Yad Vashem's Directorate," February 5, 1957.
15 CZA, KKL5/22478, "Decisions of Building and Planning Committee," February 12, 1957.

building's frames could begin to be built; their construction would be completed in 1958, in under two years.[16]

The Martyrs' Ashes and the Mount of Remembrance

The idea that martyrs' ashes, brought from the sites of annihilation in Europe, should be buried in Yad Vashem had been raised in the forties. Now, with the advancing construction plan, Yad Vashem's directorate discussed it again. In mid-1956, Dinur reported on a proposal from Avraham Haim Shag, a member of Knesset and a representative of the Public Council for Commemorating the Soldier at Yad Vashem; it recommended bringing the martyrs' ashes from Europe and burying them on the Mount of Remembrance. He noted that President Yitzhak Ben-Zvi supported Shag's idea, as did "religious circles that complain about Mount Zion [the activity of the Chamber of the Holocaust]." He also described discussions he had held on the subject with Rabbi Yitzhak-Meir Levin, the leader of Agudat Yisrael, who "did not rule it out."[17]

These words stirred a lively debate in the directorate about the burial of the ashes on the Mount of Remembrance. Dworzecki claimed that using the ashes as a foundation for remembrance was legitimate and that this was a "strong movement in Judaism"; he also noted that Schneersohn had "established such a grave in Paris and attracted the masses." Mordechai Shatner added that the combination of the ashes and the Mount of Remembrance would make the place "in the coming generations, a central locus for the Jewish nation no less than the Western Wall." Among the members of the directorate there were some who had reservations about burying the ashes in the remembrance building, such as Weitz, who worried that "idolatry" would harm Yad Vashem.[18]

The question of the ashes was discussed in the second symposium convened by Dinur. Shag asserted that "martyrs' ashes which first symbolize the great tragedy, the Holocaust in the fullest sense of the world . . . these ashes require burial as per the halakha, a real burial. These ashes must be buried in the right place [on the Mount of Remembrance]." It was the State of Israel and Yad Vashem's duty "in the national sense" to collect all of the ashes, he claimed, "and to transfer [them] for burial and add [them] to this holy land," the place that masses were

---

16 CAHJP, P28/6/150, Arieh Sharon to Yad Vashem, February 14, 1957.
17 ISA, HZ-1/151, "Decisions of Yad Vashem's Directorate," June 26, 1956.
18 Ibid.

streaming to "because they know that the bones of the great visionary Herzl were brought here for burial."[19]

With these statements in the background, Yad Vashem's directorate resolved to establish a committee to examine the subject and the methods of transferring the ashes from the extermination camps to the Mount of Remembrance.[20] The directorate elected to accept the recommendation that the mount contain a plot in which "some of the martyrs' ashes will be brought to burial from all of the camps to the extent that this is possible." It was further decided that Yad Vashem would execute this via the Ministry of Foreign Affairs, which would ask its representatives to clarify, using a list of camps and places that Yad Vashem would supply, if it was possible to find ashes and bring them to Israel. The directorate hoped to bury ashes on the Mount of Remembrance on Holocaust and Heroism Remembrance Day, 27 Nisan 5716 (1955/56).[21] Subsequent to this decision, the Ministry of Foreign Affairs appealed to a number of Israeli delegates in Europe, who began to work on the issue.

Ashes began to arrive at Yad Vashem a number of months later. Meir Tuval, Israel's attaché in Bucharest, transferred a bag of ashes from Auschwitz to Israel. He stressed that the credibility of the bag's contents had been approved and signed off on by one of Hungary's rabbis.[22] William Karl, director of the Jewish community office in Vienna, gave the general consul of Israel there an urn with ashes of Mauthausen's martyrs. The urn was accompanied by a confirmation produced by the Jewish community in Vienna that the ashes were of Jewish prisoners who had perished there.[23] The legateship in Warsaw located "soap and powder made from the bodies of exterminated Jews."[24] The efforts to locate ashes at times made use of Israel's unofficial delegates acting in different areas in the Soviet Bloc to whom ashes and other remains were transferred.[25]

Yad Vashem's activity regarding the martyrs' ashes quickly became a subject of conflict after it aroused Kahana's ire. He wrote to Walter Eytan, director general of the Ministry of Foreign Affairs, protesting the involvement of the ministry in the transfer of ashes to Israel. "As the question of burial is not under

---

19 HHA, 3–95. 17 (2), "Protocol of Yad Vashem Symposium," July 15, 1956.
20 ISA, GL-6/14913, Arieh Bauminger to the minister of religions, August 2, 1956.
21 ISA, GL-6/14913, "Yad Vashem Directorate Meeting," August 7, 1956.
22 ISA, HZ-6/3108, Meir Tuval to East Europe Department in the Ministry of Foreign Affairs, February 12, 1957.
23 ISA, HZ-7/3108, Bauminger to William Karl, April 25, 1957.
24 ISA, HZ-7/3108, S. Leibovich to Yad Vashem, January 22, 1958.
25 ISA, HZ-6/3108, Dov Matat to Moshe Carmil, February 14, 1957; ISA, HZ-6/3108, Matat to Bauminger, February 24, 1957.

the auspices of Yad Vashem and the Chief Rabbinate of Israel has ruled that the ashes should be buried according to halakha on Mount Zion and not the Mount of Remembrance, there is to my mind no reason to involve the delegates of Israel in the subject." Kahana warned that those sending the ashes believed it was being done with the blessing of Israel's government and the Chief Rabbinate and with no dissent while the opposite was true.[26] Eytan, in response, explained that "the Ministry of Foreign Affairs supports this appeal and has asked the delegates to take care of Yad Vashem's directorate's request, with the knowledge or assumption that Yad Vashem is indeed the official institution authorized to treat this subject." He added that "it is not the Ministry of Foreign Affairs' interest to express an opinion or take a position about the disagreements between Yad Vashem and the Chief Rabbinate, if there are such disagreements."[27]

On the other side, Kahana's words stirred much anger on the part of Yad Vashem's people, especially when it became clear that in parallel with his efforts to prevent the transfer of ashes to Yad Vashem he was involved in transferring ashes from Mount Zion to Paris. In mid-June 1956, Schneersohn, whose documentation and commemoration center in Paris had reached the final stages of construction, asked him to send martyrs' ashes.[28] Initially, Kahana replied that the Committee for Mount Zion's members "see this [the transfer of ashes to Paris] as a necessary and important subject in relation to ties with the Diaspora."[29] This agreement aroused great anger among the members of Yad Vashem's directorate, who had struggled against the opening of the Paris center. Dinur met with the minister of religions and objected to the fact that Kahana, who stood at the head of an Israeli ministry, was helping to ground the commemoration site in Paris.[30] Kahana was forced to back down; he withdrew his earlier decision to help Schneersohn.[31]

The rising tones between Kahana and Dinur and between the Committee for Mount Zion and the Ministry of Religions and Yad Vashem drew the attention of journalists, who attacked Kahana over the "Holocaust monument" that he had established next to David's Tomb.[32] "The mixing of the domains between Mount Zion and the monument in memory of the Holocaust is unacceptable," *HaDor* wrote. "The Yad Vashem enterprise must also gather within the monument that

---

26 ISA, HZ-8/3108, Kahana to Walter Eytan, June 22, 1956.
27 ISA, HZ-8/3108, Eytan to Kahana, June 26, 1956.
28 ISA, G-2/5564, Isaac Schneersohn to Kahana, June 13, 1956.
29 ISA, G-2/5564, Kahana to Ze'ev Scharf, June 17, 1956.
30 ISA, HZ-1/151, "Decisions of Yad Vashem's Directorate," June 26, 1956.
31 *HaTzofe*, July 1, 1956.
32 *Yedioth Ahronoth*, February 24, 1957.

will be established the values that are focused on Mount Zion and in this respect it appears to us that a place near the cemetery for the fallen in the War of Independence better suits the mausoleum for the Holocaust victims than does Mount Zion."[33]

The tension between Yad Vashem and the Ministry of Religions reached a peak in early 1957, when the institution invited Berl Mark, head of the Jewish Historical Institute in Warsaw, to visit the State of Israel. Mark brought with him seven small bags holding the ashes of Jews who had been murdered in Poland. Yad Vashem's directorate wished to exploit the opportunity to bury the ashes in a public ceremony.[34]

But now the question of where to preserve or bury the ashes on the Mount of Remembrance arose. First, the directorate felt that the ashes should be buried at the site designated for the construction of the remembrance hall.[35] Then the decision changed, and it was suggested that the remains be buried elsewhere, and that the possibility of moving them later to the Hall of Remembrance be examined. The directorate asked for the architects' advice in finding a temporary location for the ashes' burial.[36] The place selected was north of the construction site slated for the Hall of Remembrance, on the mount's sloping incline to the north.[37] Kahana and other religious circles, however, continued to throw their weight around in order to safeguard the Chamber of the Holocaust's monopoly as the sole space where these ashes would be buried and to thwart Yad Vashem's plans. Kahana warned the minister of religions that Yad Vashem was acting in too independent a fashion on religious questions and subjects of traditional commemoration; the decisions they made regarding building the Hall of Remembrance and the synagogue on the Mount of Remembrance were not taken with sufficient consideration. "It is fitting that we guard these buildings, the form and content, so that we do not falter on the facts post factum," he wrote to Haim Moshe Shapira.[38] The chief rabbis also heatedly demanded that Yad Vashem abstain from acting with relation to the ashes before a discussion could be held in the rabbinical council,[39] and later even passed a resolution forbidding their burial on the Mount of Remembrance.

---

33 Yaakov Kiper, "Mount Zion's Atmosphere – For and Against," *HaDor*, June 6, 1956.
34 ISA, HZ-6/3108, "Decisions of Administrative Committee," February 12, 1957.
35 ISA, HZ-6/3108, "Decisions of Yad Vashem's Directorate," January 22, 1957.
36 YVA, AM1 448, Wind to Bauminger, February 14, 1957.
37 HHA, 3–95. 7 (1), "Yad Vashem," Change in the location of the synagogue, 1:200, April 29, 1958.
38 ISA, GL-6/14913, Kahana to the minister of religions, January 14, 1957.
39 CZA, S115/536, Elimelech Yerachmiel Wolgelernter to Yad Vashem, February 4, 1957.

Yad Vashem's people were not deterred by the opposition and sent invitations to a ceremony dedicating the temporary burial site.[40] The invitations raised the tension among religious circles; growing criticism was voiced against Yad Vashem's actions, out of a "fear for the disgrace of the martyrs' ashes."[41] Kahana again warned Dinur that "establishing a special cemetery for this purpose nonetheless requires the consent of Israel's chief rabbis," and wondered why Yad Vashem was acting "to separate ashes from ashes . . . why not bury the ashes on Mount Zion alongside the traditional grave of King David." He also hinted that it was possible that the ashes Mark had brought were not those of Jews. "It must be examined in any event," he wrote, "whence come now, thirteen years after the Holocaust, the martyrs' ashes and whether they are ashes of Jews at all."[42]

The pressure from the chief rabbis, the minister of religions, and Kahana made its mark, leading Yad Vashem's directorate to postpone the burial ceremony on the Mount of Remembrance and find a temporary solution in the form of transferring the remains to a representative of the Hevra Kadisha.[43] The ashes were stored in a special coffin placed in the cemetery in Sanhedria, most likely in the Martyrs' Square, the plot where the ashes brought from Austria in 1949 had been buried.[44]

Journalists reported on the clash between Dinur, who wanted to bury the ashes on "his hill," the Mount of Remembrance, and Kahana, who wanted to bury the ashes on "his" hill, Mount Zion. "Let him [Dinur] take for himself the papers and documentation for the Mount of Remembrance but the religious side, the burial of the ashes, should be left for me for Mount Zion," Kahana said to reporters.[45] "Two are holding an urn of ashes," *Yedioth Ahronoth* wrote, concluding that "the conflict that has ignited over the ashes of martyrs who were burned in the furnaces of Auschwitz is not for the honor of the martyrs' memory nor is it for the memory of the institutions whose job it is to establish a memorial for the Holocaust's martyrs."[46]

The controversy led to the involvement of Rabbi Yehuda Leib Maimon; during his tenure as the first minister of religions, Mount Zion had been named the

---

40 CZA, S61/326, Dinur to Shazar, February 14, 1957.
41 ISA, HZ-6/3108, Mordechai Fogelman to the chief rabbis, February 25, 1957.
42 ISA, GL-9/4738, Kahana to Dinur, February 25, 1957.
43 CAHJP, P28/6/125, Bauminger to Israel Bar-Zacai, March 22, 1957.
44 ISA, HZ-7/3108, Bauminger to Israel Bar-Zacai, April 25, 1957.
45 *Yedioth Ahronoth*, March 4, 1957.
46 Alexander Zauber, "Martyrs' Ashes from Poland Have Become a Bone of Contention," *Yedioth Ahronoth*, March 14, 1957. Zauber was clearly referring to the renowned issue (*sugiya*) found in Mishnah Bava Metzia, which relates to two people holding a *tallit* (prayer shawl), each claiming that he found it.

place of burial for the ashes brought from Austria. He turned to the chief rabbis and Yad Vashem's directorate and even published his letter in the media, demanding that the ashes not be buried on the Mount of Remembrance but rather in the Chamber of the Holocaust. He protested against Yad Vashem, which

> wants to change the accepted custom and now establish a second burial site, in a place that is not a cemetery and has no special tradition and to divide ashes from ashes and martyrs from martyrs, something that cannot be both in terms of humanity and in terms of tradition, and will only bring disgrace upon us in the eyes of the martyrs' relatives and many visitors.

Maimon added that "Yad Vashem is a secular scientific institution and has no relationship to issues of sanctity and burial and it also cannot be known if Prof. Mark can be trusted regarding the identification of the ashes, whether they are of Jewish martyrs."[47] But *Yedioth Ahronoth* leaked that Rabbi Maimon's objection was tied to the fact that "Prof. Mark was a member of the Bund movement in the past and today is a Communist, and he is not, therefore, taken as an authority on issues tied to tradition."[48]

Yad Vashem viewed things differently. Dinur claimed that the Mount of Remembrance was already recognized as a significant, central place of Holocaust commemoration for many in the Jewish nation. As "word of it has spread between the communities in the holy lands," the "martyrs' ashes" were sent to the Mount of Remembrance; Yad Vashem should therefore bring it to burial there in accordance with law and custom. Dinur stressed that Yad Vashem's directorate had decided that the plot of land dedicated to burying the ashes would be placed next to "the Hall of Remembrance and the 'synagogue' in memory of the martyrs" that would be established there "because only in this way can we bring commemoration into the framework of Jewish tradition, which is our duty." He added that "Yad Vashem is not a solely scientific institution; it is also an institution for the immortalization of the Holocaust's victims. It is for this reason that we are doing it" – that is, burying the ashes.[49]

In early April 1957, the question of the ashes reached the Knesset. Deputy Speaker of the Knesset Aharon-Ya'akov Greenberg, a representative of Hapoel Hamizrachi, raised a parliamentary question about Yad Vashem's decision to bury martyrs' ashes on the Mount of Remembrance. He asked whether Yad Vashem – a "secular institution with no authority in matters of burial

---

[47] ISA, GL-12/6261, Yehuda Leib Maimon to the chief rabbis, March 4, 1957.
[48] Alexander Zauber, "Martyrs' Ashes from Poland Have Become a Bone of Contention,' *Yedioth Ahronoth*, March 14, 1957.
[49] ISA, GL-8/14913, Dinur to Warhaftig, March 18, 1957.

and sanctity – is authorized to decide and determine on this matter." He further wondered: Was it not "more appropriate to bury these ashes, too, on Mount Zion, and to expand and renovate and improve this burial site as the sole and exceptional place in order that it be fitting for the memory of the martyrs?"[50]

Dinur directed his answer to the religious public in Israel and its representatives. He denied that the ashes brought to Yad Vashem came only from Poland; they were sent from many communities, with the express directive that they be buried on the Mount of Remembrance. The decision to bury martyrs' ashes on the mount had been discussed "by various circles in the land and overseas, including famous rabbis and Torah scholars," Dinur stated, countering Kahana and the Ministry of Religions' activity on Mount Zion. He mentioned Yad Vashem's agreement with the Hevra Kadisha regarding the lawful sanctification of the grave on the Mount of Remembrance and concluded that it was "against the law and custom to not fulfill the desire of the communities that wish for the martyrs' ashes from their communities to be buried next to the Hall of Remembrance and the 'synagogue' for their memory that will be established on the Mount of Remembrance."[51]

In order to manage the rabbinic pressure, the Remembrance Authority's directorate appointed an additional committee, charged with confronting the question of the ashes' burial. The committee was comprised of Dinur, Weitz, and Yehuda Bialer, a member of Yad Vashem's directorate who also worked in the Ministry of Religions.[52] This committee approved the preparation of a plot that was chosen for the ashes' burial on the Mount of Remembrance and recommended furthering ties with Jerusalem's Hevra Kadisha so that it would take the site's oversight upon itself.[53]

The agreement between Yad Vashem and the Hevra Kadisha stated that they would indeed take charge of the burial site, but their supervision came with two conditions – the Hevra Kadisha would have sole, absolute, and unchanging rights of oversight over the plot, and the plot would be used exclusively for the burial of martyrs' ashes and for no other burial. Yad Vashem approved the agreement and acted to establish a "halakhic" committee; it would include the head of the Hevra Kadisha, Israel Bardaky, as well as Bialer on behalf of Yad Vashem.[54]

---

50 CAHJP, P28/6/125, "Knesset Parliamentary Question 966, Yaakov Greenberg to Dinur," April 10, 1957.
51 CAHJP, P28/6/134-135, Dinur, "Answer Letter," n.d.
52 ISA, HZ-7-3108, "Decisions Made during Yad Vashem Meeting," June 11, 1957.
53 ISA, GL-8/14913, "Yad Vashem Directorate Meeting," June 25, 1957.
54 ISA, GL-9/1639, "Decisions of Yad Vashem's Directorate," December 24, 1957.

But the agreement did not appease all of Israel's religious community, and Yad Vashem's rapid progress in making the Mount of Remembrance the place of the ashes' burial raised the ire of some. They protested Yad Vashem's founding of its "mausoleum" and the "disgracing" of the ashes. "There is a great concern that the institution caring for them will bring the ashes to burial not in a cemetery and not according to the tradition," stated Rabbi Isaac Jacob Wachtfogel, the head of the Meah Shearim Yeshiva and one of the heads of the Mizrachi movement in Jerusalem.

> Is it possible that this will be the fate of the ashes of our nation's martyrs, our brothers and sisters who were as ashes of the *akeda* [binding; a reference to the sacrificial binding of Isaac], their good deeds should protect us? Should they also not have a fitting burial? And should they not be brought to Jewish burial in a sanctified, public cemetery, as per the tradition of the holy nation from time immemorial?[55]

Wachtfogel may have emphasized the question of the ashes' burial on the Mount of Remembrance, but there were other bones of contention between Yad Vashem's directorate and Kahana. One was the budgeting of the Chamber of the Holocaust, a subject tied to the question of the place of traditional commemoration on the Mount of Remembrance. Immediately after the establishment of the Remembrance Authority, Kahana had begun to assert that Yad Vashem, as the institution responsible for Holocaust commemoration in the State of Israel, must transfer some of its funds for the maintenance of the Holocaust memorial site on Mount Zion and take ownership over its development. Dinur, in contrast, was willing to consider a one-time transfer of funds if, in exchange, Kahana would hand over all of the displays and materials collected over the years on Mount Zion to Yad Vashem "because the State of Israel has chosen that there will be only one place authorized for commemoration and it is Yad Vashem."[56]

In order to gain a fuller picture of the goings-on on Mount Zion, Dinur sent Avraham Palmon, secretary of Yad Vashem's scientific department and, later, general secretary of the Remembrance Authority, there. The report he submitted was particularly bleak. "Anyone who has not entirely lost all sense of beauty and the sublime, anyone who still searches for a trace of inspiration in a place meant to immortalize millions who are no longer," he stated, "could certainly not be overcome by the most depressing form in the place chosen by whoever chose for this purpose. Dark, walls that are not the cleanest, tasteless crowding of displays, candlelight. Is this a fitting way to commemorate the millions and does tradition dictate that this is the fitting form of 'traditional commemoration'?

---

55 ISA, GL-6/14913, Isaac Jacob Wachtfogel to Kahana, May 3, 1957.
56 CZA, S115/533, "Decisions of Yad Vashem's Directorate," June 26, 1956.

I am doubtful!" Palmon reported on the fixed memorial plaques for the communities found on the walls of the Chamber of the Holocaust and on the various displays such as desecrated Torah scrolls or the Zyklon gas that the Nazis had used for extermination. He recommended that some of the displays be moved to Yad Vashem, including the martyrs' ashes buried there. He also related to the memorial days for the communities and the Mishnah learning held at Mount Zion and recommended that in the future the Mount of Remembrance adopt fixed patterns of traditional commemoration, which he suggested be given to "people who observe traditions . . . true to the majority of the religious public in Israel."[57]

Yad Vashem's directorate, however, had no consensus regarding the approach toward Kahana and the Chamber of the Holocaust. In contrast with Dinur, who rejected any ties with the site, Bialer represented a compromise, hoping that Yad Vashem would contain Mount Zion. He felt that as a significant public – "which does not distinguish between commemoration and commemoration and does not appreciate the difference between the 'palace' of Yad Vashem and the wretched site of Mount Zion" – flocked to Mount Zion, the problem should be resolved by agreement, especially because Yad Vashem was not taking care of the "traditional and spiritual [side] of commemoration."

Dinur vehemently opposed this approach. Aside from the fact that he had committed to Yad Vashem making efforts to bring the material preserved at Mount Zion to the Mount of Remembrance, he felt that the "problem" of traditional commemoration would be resolved when the synagogue was established on the Mount of Remembrance; then the ceremonies that had initially been held on Mount Zion could be held there. Uveeler insisted, claiming that "Mount Zion is part of Yad Vashem. There the traditional remembrance occurs and it should be preserved. There will always remain two centers and it will be like the two remembrance days [27 Nisan and 10 Tevet]." He requested that there be unity, as "here [regarding the Holocaust] there is no secular and religious because there are not two nations but one nation."

The decision made by Yad Vashem's directorate accorded with the line held by Dinur, determining that Kahana and the Committee for Mount Zion must "agree in advance that with the establishment of the synagogue they will stop the Holocaust worship and transfer it all to us."[58] Kahana may have accepted these conditions "with the agreement of the rabbis,"[59] but the relationship between the two bodies deteriorated. Josef Melkman, director of Yad Vashem's

---

57 CAHJP, P28/6/134-135, Avraham Palmon to Dinur, May 21, 1957.
58 CZA, KKL5/24136, "Protocol of Yad Vashem Directorate Meeting," August 21, 1957.
59 ISF, GL-8/14913, Kahana to Dinur, September 1, 1957.

scientific wing (he later changed his name to Michman and also served as general director of Yad Vashem), noted that as a result of the visit he had held at Mount Zion and after he heard Kahana's explanations the site had made a particularly bad impression on him. "Creating fables, determining dates that have no hold in history, the distortion of facts for purposes of worship seem to be a desecration of the Holocaust and not its sanctification." It was decided that all ties should be cut with the Committee for Mount Zion in order to prevent the public's identifying Yad Vashem with it.[60]

Yad Vashem's Construction Plan

The series of decisions made by Yad Vashem's directorate made it possible for Dinur, standing before the participants at Yad Vashem's Second World Council, which convened on the Mount of Remembrance on Holocaust and Heroism Remembrance Day in 1957, to speak with more confidence than ever before about the architectural future of the Mount of Remembrance. He reminded the participants that Yad Vashem's mission was not limited to research alone, a subject with which many members of the council identified, and that the Remembrance Authority still faced many other important tasks. He stated that "the very name of Yad Vashem is establishing a memory. What is called 'immortalization.'" This was one of the Remembrance Authority's fundamental tasks – to establish "a hand and a name (*yad va-shem*), a name and a memory for the past, not in order to commemorate it but rather in order for the past to be immortalized for generations." Dinur added that at this point the Mount of Remembrance was already recognized within the Israeli public as a place whose entirety was destined for "an eternal remembrance" to the Holocaust, a site "meant to infuse the memory of the Holocaust and heroism as an organic part of Jerusalem." To illustrate this, he noted that ashes had been sent from various communities to Yad Vashem, as "a first concrete pattern for remembrance . . . one of the first conditions for establishing remembrance is the gathering of all foundations of remembrance in this place, on the Mount of Remembrance."[61] The council's participants unanimously agreed to ask Yad Vashem's directorate to "accelerate" the pace of establishing the mount and to speedily complete the construction of the Hall of Remembrance and the synagogue.[62] The architects

---

60 CZA, KKL5/24136, "Decisions of Yad Vashem's Directorate," April 29, 1958.
61 CZA, S60/5491, "Yad Vashem Second World Council," April, 29, 1957.
62 CZA, S6/6680, "Summary of Yad Vashem Second World Council Decisions," April 29, 1957.

were asked, based on this resolution, to prepare the architectural plans quickly so that construction could begin.[63]

The reality was more complicated, and the blueprints' preparation was delayed. One central reason behind the delay was the professional tension between the two veteran architects, Weinraub and Mansfeld, which affected the work of the entire team. When Weitz and Dinur reported on the Remembrance Authority's activity to participants in Yad Vashem's Third World Council in August 1957, they promised to publish a tender for the construction of the Mount of Remembrance – without knowing when it would take place.[64]

Dinur and Weitz may have taken pride in the decision made at the council and the progress taking place in building the Mount of Remembrance, but others were more cautious. Minister of Development Dov Yosef wondered about the "division of labor" that had been decided upon between the "Diaspora" and Israel, referring to the division between the Claims Conference, on one hand, and Israel's government and the Jewish Agency, the Israeli bodies funding the construction, on the other. Yosef raised a crucial claim that this equal division between the two sides was unjustified, as the remembrance buildings "are not meant to serve or satisfy the feelings of Israel's Jews alone; the opposite is the case. They are being established to be available to all of the world's Jews, and Diaspora communities are interested in the founding of Yad Vashem no less than are Israel's Jews." "The fact that Jerusalem, for intrinsic reasons, is considered the most fitting city in the world to establish this memorial in," he protested,

> does not mean that the burden of its establishment must fall on the residents of Jerusalem or Israel. If we were making determinations based on the figures of Jewish population in the different countries, it is clear that in Israel there are 1.75 million Jews as opposed to 11.25 million in the other countries of the world – that is, less than 14 percent of all of the world's Jews.[65]

It was only at the end of 1957, after a months-long delay, that the five architects completed their work and submitted the updated plan to Yad Vashem. The plan included the plaza, the Hall of Remembrance, and the synagogue. It may have been based on elements suggested and developed by the architects in 1948, but it was a new creation, the result of a multiyear process.[66]

---

63 HHA, 3–95. 17 (2), Bauminger to Sharon and Idelson, June 12, 1957.
64 CZA, KKL5/24136, "Protocol of Yad Vashem World Council," n.d.; CZA, KKL5/22482, "Protocol of Yad Vashem Third World Council," August 26, 1957.
65 CAHJP, P28/6/150, Dov Yosef to Dinur, September 9, 1957.
66 CAHJP, CC appl. 1957/331, Josef Melkman to Uveeler, April 12, 1957; HHA, 3–95. 7 (1), "Yad Vashem," 1:200, with the signature of the five architects, n.d.

The most prominent element in the plan was the raised plaza, which served to architecturally unite all of the site's commemorative components. The excavation and flattening of part of the hill would make it possible to change the surface of the Mount of Remembrance and construct a rectangular plaza measuring ninety-three meters in length by sixty meters width (5,580 square meters).[67] This raised temenos would be built on an east–west axis and would rise, according to the plan, a number of meters above its surroundings. The square was planned to be suitable for the gathering of thousands of people and underlined the separation between the archive and administration building at the Mount of Remembrance's entrance and the remembrance compound standing at its west. The architects decided that the underground space created with the building of the raised plaza would be used for storage and service rooms and that the synagogue would be placed there as well, with its roof part of the assembly plaza.

The plaza itself and the buildings in it were also planned anew. The courtyard that had in the past been meant to lead visitors to the Mount of Remembrance's underground entrance was done away with, exchanged for a relatively broad and long staircase leading up to the plaza and the Hall of Remembrance, the sole and prominent building within it, rising to a height of eight meters above it. The plan to build the Hall of Remembrance as a rounded structure was altered and it became a square, with each side stretching some twenty-seven meters. The architects decided that the internal side of one of the building's walls, built of basalt stones, would contain the engraved words of the El Malei Rahamim prayer, and next to it would be a plaque with the names of the lands of destruction and the number of Jews who had perished.

Another innovation in the blueprint was the remembrance tower that would be built in the southwest corner of the plaza. The tower, ascending thirty meters above the square, had been intended in earlier versions of the plans to replace the "monuments," the remembrance structures of the earlier blueprints that were dedicated to the underground fighters, ghetto warriors, righteous among the nations, and others. It was decided that this tower would replace the heroism hall, now entirely absent from the plans. The tower would have the word *Yizkor* – Remember – engraved on it a number of times and, it was suggested, could have a torch lit atop it, devoted to displays of fighting and heroism.

At the end of 1957, Yad Vashem's directorate approved the suggested building plan and the necessary budget (roughly 1 million Israeli pounds), after the architects submitted their plan and a detailed quantities list.[68] One month later,

---

67 JMA, 1959/715, "Areas Calculation," November 23, 1959.
68 ISA, GL-9/1639, "Decisions of Yad Vashem's Directorate," December 24, 1957.

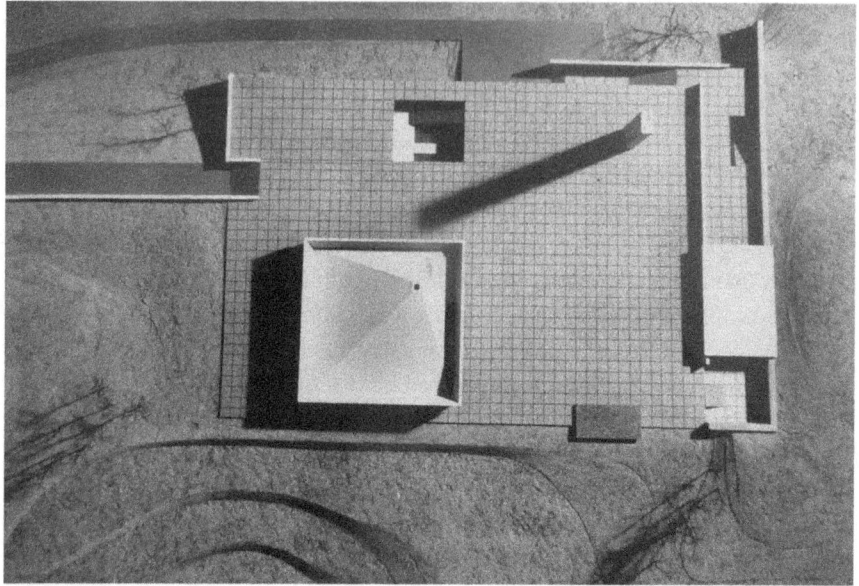

Figure 16: Model of Yad Vashem containing the Hall of Remembrance, Pillar of Heroism, and synagogue (CAHJP).

the Claims Conference approved its aid.⁶⁹ These steps seemingly attested to the nearing onset of construction, but in reality the building was overshadowed by the murky relationship within the architectural partnership. The architects had trouble completing their part, due, among other things, to the many changes that had been introduced into the plans. El-Hanani, who had become the team's lead architect, was busy with other projects – for example, overseeing the State of Israel's *First Decade* exhibition, whose opening was scheduled for June 1958.⁷⁰ These delays greatly frustrated Dinur and the directorate, and the public pressure on them grew; accusations were voiced regarding the prolonged construction process. Some of the directorate's members were inclined to blame the Remembrance Authority's previous administration for these failures. "We have an inheritance from the past that overshadows the present and that is highlighted in the conclusions published in the press as well."⁷¹ But this explanation did not diminish the problem the directorate faced – the harsh public criticism lobbed at it. "I

---

69 "Towards New Construction," *Yediot Yad Vashem* 15–16 (1958), 32.
70 CAHJP, CC appl. 1958/291a, Letter with no author to Uveeler, April 30, 1958.
71 Ibid.

cannot understand the slow tempo of constructing buildings at Yad Vashem," complained Edward Elisha Gelber, as "public opinion is that we have done nothing in commemoration." Others admitted that "our weak point is that the Hall of Remembrance does not yet exist. The Mount of Remembrance will contain sanctity [only] when this hall is built."[72]

Deliberations Regarding Yad Vashem's Synagogue

In early March 1958, Yad Vashem's directorate once again discussed the planning of the synagogue, after the architects and members of the Building Committee raised doubts about the building's appearance, location, and – most importantly – symbolic and practical essence and function.

The architects had positioned the synagogue under the assembly plaza. A staircase would lead visitors from the height of the plaza down to its entrance. But the location of the house of worship felt to some of the Building Committee's members like "desecration of the sacred." The fact that the synagogue's roof was also part of the plaza detracted from its sanctity. "It is known to all that a synagogue is by its very nature higher than all of the houses," it was claimed, relating to the halakhic directive that houses of worship must be built "at the height of the city"; and thus Yad Vashem's synagogue could not be "concealed in the slope of the hill." The fact that visitors to the mount, on their way to the Hall of Remembrance, would in effect be stepping on the roof of the synagogue felt problematic. "It is possible that what the architects have suggested is very successful architecturally speaking," Bialer said, "but this is not the accepted concept of a synagogue."[73]

El-Hanani, trying to "save" the synagogue that he and his partners had planned, explained the logic behind the unique position of the synagogue to the directorate, tying it primarily to the budgetary constraints imposed on his colleagues, which made it necessary for them to focus on the Hall of Remembrance. He claimed that there was no precedent here; many synagogues in Jerusalem were actually dug into a slope and built "in the depths," and they would be able to create an "atmosphere for prayer" that would not be determined by the building's location but rather by its internal substance.[74]

---

[72] CZA, KKL5/24136, "Protocol of Yad Vashem Directorate Meeting," May 13, 1958.
[73] CZA, KKL5/24136, "Yad Vashem Directorate Meeting," March 2, 1958.
[74] Ibid.

"We are not building a synagogue here for the individual to say the Kaddish prayer. This is not the place for building a synagogue for a minyan [quorum] to come and pray. We are building a synagogue in order to create a memorial for the synagogues that were destroyed," Bialer stated, adding that the synagogue itself must serve as memorial and symbol. "The architect's words affect the heart of the matter and we must not approach such a holy thing in this manner." "There has been a noticeable misunderstanding between the architects on the subject," Yaacov Matrikin joined the protest. "When we speak of a synagogue dominating the buildings this is indeed an accepted thing. The synagogue is found in the midst of the neighborhood and also at the highest place and so it stands out." But, he felt, the synagogue that would be built on the Mount of Remembrance must be part of the overall remembrance space; it must be integrated within it and not overshadow it. "We must return to the architects' ground plan that is entirely prepared and entirely balanced except for the place and form of the synagogue."[75]

The preoccupation with the synagogue's location among the heads of Yad Vashem raised a far more fundamental question: What was the purpose and mission of the synagogue at Yad Vashem? "This synagogue will not serve Jews who come to pray on a daily basis," Bialer noted, joining forces with some directorate members who felt that there was no need to design a synagogue that was "comfortable" for worshippers; it should, rather, be a commemorative space. Moshe Kol noted that the intent had been that the synagogue would serve as a place in which community members could hold their gatherings and prayers and claimed that "if we take this purpose into account, it is clear that the synagogue cannot be too concealed." The architects were asked to seek a more fitting place for the synagogue on the Mount of Remembrance, and to fit it into the general architectural plans in a more appropriate way.[76]

One month later, Yad Vashem's architects submitted an updated plan that included a crucial change in the synagogue's location: the building had been moved to the western side of the remembrance plaza, west of the Hall of Remembrance. Now the synagogue's structure was an integral part of the assembly plaza but also disconnected from it. The roof of the synagogue rose above the plaza to a height of a few meters and visitors would descend a number of stairs to its entrance. A stone wall would separate the synagogue from the assembly plaza, and its ark would be positioned on the southeastern wall, a wall of black brick. Aside from a symbolic women's section and a small, raised square

---

75 Ibid.
76 Ibid.

positioned next to the building's entrance, there would also be a symbolic bima (prayer platform).[77]

The question of building the synagogue was also tied to Yad Vashem's aspiration to have space for traditional commemoration on the Mount of Remembrance. This subject touched on the complicated relationship with Kahana and the Chamber of the Holocaust. After a period of calm, the fraught relationship with Yad Vashem began afresh after Kahana renewed his demand that Yad Vashem provide financial support for activity on Mount Zion. Yad Vashem's people – Bialer and Uveeler – were in favor of Yad Vashem funding activities on Mount Zion in part, and the minister of religions, Ya'akov Moshe Toledano, sent a written request on the subject to Yad Vashem's directorate.

Dinur was vehemently opposed, and asserted that the only place for Holocaust commemoration in the State of Israel was the Mount of Remembrance. His belief was that as long as the Hall of Remembrance and synagogue were not inaugurated and Yad Vashem could not yet hold traditional commemoration, the activities on Mount Zion could continue.[78] Kahana had trouble accepting the decision; he hoped that with Dinur's resignation and the appointment of Arieh Leon Kubovy as chairman of Yad Vashem in March 1959, the Remembrance Authority's attitude toward his enterprise on Mount Zion would change. A number of weeks later he met with Kubovy but, much to his chagrin, the new chairman stuck to his predecessor's stance – the solitary nature of the Mount of Remembrance must be preserved and no other parallel memorial enterprises would be allowed.[79]

Figure 17: Arieh Kubovy, chairman of Yad Vashem, 1959–1966 (YVA, Unknown photographer).

---

77 CZA, KKL5/24136, "Minutes of Building Committee Meeting," April 1958.
78 ISA, GL-2/1230, "Decisions of Yad Vashem's Directorate," January 20, 1959.
79 CZA, S115/242, "Decisions of Yad Vashem's Directorate," April 14, 1959.

Later on in 1959, Kubovy visited Mount Zion with Bialer and Daniel Auster, the former mayor of Jerusalem who had joined Yad Vashem's directorate. Auster reported how surprised he and his colleagues were by the progress, order, and cleanliness found there. He reiterated the suggested division of labor between Yad Vashem and Mount Zion: "Anything touching on the traditional side will be on Mount Zion and anything relating to research will be coordinated by us." Bialer suggested exploiting the "folkloristic side" and the abundance of material gathered on Mount Zion for Yad Vashem's purposes.[80] Yad Vashem would be the umbrella institution, he proposed, and activity at Mount Zion would take place under its auspices.

There were many detractors to this approach, especially the idea of dividing functions between Yad Vashem and the Chamber of the Holocaust – research here and worship there. "Until now I thought that Yad Vashem was the central authority established for the commemoration of the Holocaust," Shatner said, noting that "we are establishing a synagogue and a cemetery [the ashes' grave] in consideration of the nation's religious component." Zvi Lurie stated that "we cannot agree to Yad Vashem not [also] representing the part of the nation that went to its death to sanctify God's name."

Kubovy took people by surprise when he reported on the visit to Mount Zion, where he went "in order to make peace." "When I was there," he stated, "I was embarrassed by our excessive arrogance. There is tastelessness and confusion there but on the other hand there is a great popular traditional movement and it is not in our hands to change it. Great things have been done there." He reminded those present that the Yad Vashem Law noted that the Remembrance Authority was authorized to approve and guide enterprises that acted to commemorate the Holocaust's victims. He therefore believed that this clause could be used to establish a partnership with Kahana. His reasoning was unexpected. He felt, in contrast with Dinur, that Yad Vashem must not take upon itself the traditional commemoration. "I am not an advocate of establishing a synagogue on the Mount of Remembrance because I fear that *gabbaim* [beadles] will appear here and so forth." "We do not want this commemoration nor all of its positive phenomena and it is good that there is a place where there is traditional commemoration," that is, Mount Zion. "The past can be seen as over, and we will open a new page," he concluded.

In light of these words, Josef Melkman added that "the most important thing about cooperation [with Kahana] is that it will grant us contact with the

---

80 CAHJP, CC appl. 1959/293d, "Cooperation between Yad Vashem and Committee for Mount Zion," October 22, 1959.

tens of thousands who come there and not only the material collected there in the past. . . . We will be able to benefit in the future from their ties with the immigrant associations." He related to the many memorial services that Kahana led there in cooperation with the *landsmannschaften*. "To there [Mount Zion] the public is drawn: the emotion, the religion, the memories," Auster claimed, "while here [on the Mount of Remembrance] it is all foreign to the public and to here they will never come." The directorate's decision was to allocate 6,000 Israeli pounds to Mount Zion for a trial period of one year and to "draw a line through the past accounts."[81]

The Question of Heroism on the Mount of Remembrance

In all of Yad Vashem's previous plans, Holocaust and heroism had taken equal space; independent, impressive halls were designated for each. But the plan presented by the architects in late 1957 eliminated the heroism hall and the question of the place of commemoration for the ghetto fighters, partisans, and soldiers who fought in Allied armies was left unanswered.

In 1958, the tension regarding heroism at Yad Vashem reached its peak. Not coincidentally, it was Shenhavi who exposed the disagreements and conflicts between Yad Vashem's directorate and the Remembrance Authority's council. During the Fourth World Council, he fiercely protested the disappearance of heroism from the Mount of Remembrance. The council was the public body supporting the Remembrance Authority's activity; its members represented different sectors of Israeli society and the Diaspora.[82] The public critique of the institution and the state comptroller's report that had censured the institute's conduct constantly hovered in the background.[83]

Shenhavi joined the protest of Natan Eck, a Holocaust survivor and scholar of the era who claimed that Yad Vashem was misrepresenting one of its two central functions, Holocaust commemoration. Eck, who spoke before the council's participants, bemoaned the directorate's lack of success in instilling an understanding within the public that the "Hall of Remembrance – [was] instead of the Jewish grave that they were not granted, that the Mount of Remembrance is

---

[81] HHA, 3–95. 19 (1), "Protocol of Yad Vashem Directorate Meeting," July 13, 1959.
[82] Cohen, *Holocaust Research*, 247–59.
[83] "Yad Vashem – For and Against," *Maariv*, June 18, 1958.

a place of pilgrimage and uniting with the memory of the martyrs, a place of sighs and tears."[84] These words expressed some of the criticism voiced both within the Israeli public and within a group of Yad Vashem's employees, who protested the directorate's development of the institute under Dinur's leadership.[85] The accusations united with objections to Yad Vashem's omission of the Jewish struggle and heroism displayed in the Holocaust.[86]

The critique voiced by Shenhavi at the Yad Vashem council was put forth, then, on well-trodden ground. He railed against the fusion of Holocaust and heroism and against the changes made in the site, changes that were far-removed from the plans prepared fifteen years earlier. "There was once a basic assumption," he claimed, "that Yad Vashem was grounded in two foundations: Holocaust and heroism. No one said what was preferable to what and what was greater than what. It is history that will decide and raise this." It was only after the "hint from above" – that is, from Dinur, from the rest of the directorate, and primarily from the Claims Conference – that "the territory was limited, the element of heroism was removed entirely from the enterprise's plan, the monuments in memory of the partisans, paratroopers, ghetto fighters, and righteous among the nations were removed." Shenhavi asked the council participants how the present reality had come to be, a reality in which it was decided that

> in the Hall of Remembrance there will be nothing more than an eternal flame in the center and El Malei Rahamim and something else on the walls. . . .. Why divide this from the synagogue? Why can the eternal flame not stand in the synagogue? And the heroism hall – is vanished and gone. In the fundamental plans there was an element called a *gal-ed* (monument). And here the scholars of science and architecture have sat and changed it into a tower.[87]

Dinur, along with the rest of the directorate, could not ignore the criticism – from Shenhavi as well as the media, the Yad Vashem council, and the Israeli public. Dinur was forced to admit that "Yad Vashem's directorate has taken many important steps in both fields [commemoration and gathering historical material about the Holocaust] but its most noticeable success and achievements are in the second field." He agreed that Yad Vashem had not yet been able to

---

84 CZA, S115/242, "Protocol of the Fifth Meeting of the Fourth World Council," July 16, 1958.
85 CZA, S115/242, "Yad Vashem Devotees" to members of Yad Vashem Council, conveyed June 17, 1958.
86 CZA, S23/1017, Melkman to Herman, June 8, 1958.
87 CZA, S115/243, "Protocol of the Fourth World Council," June 17, 1958.

create broad interest around the institution and provoke the public to uphold the commandment of "Remember what Amalek did to you" (Deut. 25:17).[88]

How could the problem – the muting of the commemoration of heroism – be solved? Dinur once again suggested to the directorate that the Holocaust and heroism both be commemorated in the Hall of Remembrance. Perhaps Rapoport's monument to the Warsaw Ghetto Uprising (at this stage in storage at Yad Vashem; see chapter 5) could be placed in the building or perhaps its walls could be devoted to immortalizing heroism. Another proposal discussed was to focus the commemoration of heroism as planned in the tower, which was originally meant to fill the role of the "monuments" which had been removed from the building plans. Now Dinur proposed that this would be the "element of heroism" at Yad Vashem. The conclusion reached by the directorate was that the Hall of Remembrance would contain Holocaust and heroism together and that "the hall will contain 'El Malei Rahamim' on one side and the partisans' song on the other side, thus expressing both the Holocaust and heroism."[89]

The Fourth World Council met on the Mount of Remembrance in November of 1958; one of the main speakers was El-Hanani, who presented the construction plan.[90] He spoke proudly about the blueprints that he and his colleagues had prepared. But instead of his words inspiring support of the plans the directorate had created, they led to a stormy debate. The discussion, rather than advancing the architectural development of the Mount of Remembrance, highlighted the debate and the many problems – inter alia, the question of the place of heroism in constructing remembrance.

El-Hanani stood before a small model of the remembrance buildings and explained how Yad Vashem would look in the future.[91] "The fundamental decisions were in the spirit that the great architects are now teaching us. Less is more." He explained that "the foundation of the model is the simplicity, and perhaps the cruelty of simplicity. The basis is the one building: 'the Hall of Remembrance.'" He reported that the building would be made of basalt and concrete, "two materials that give the association of black and grey, with all of the variations between them." He also detailed what visits to the Hall of Remembrance would look like – visitors would walk over a bridge that was built over a "deepened" floor in which the eternal flame would stand. The internal walls would be made of polished basalt, so that engravings and "symbols that speak

---

[88] HHA, 3–95. 19 (1), "Protocol of Yad Vashem Directorate Meeting," September 26, 1958.
[89] HHA, 3–95. 19 (1), "Protocol of Yad Vashem Directorate Meeting," October 21, 1958.
[90] CZA, S61/326, "Protocol of the Third Session of Yad Vashem Fourth World Council," November 9, 1958.
[91] Photo of the model: CAHJP, CC appl. 1959/293a.

about the extermination, about those who were destroyed and fell" could be etched on the walls. He estimated that the building would be able to hold approximately one thousand people.

El-Hanani did not mention heroism or its commemoration at Yad Vashem at all, and this immediately set Shenhavi off. He interrupted El-Hanani to ask why he and his colleagues had removed it from the Mount of Remembrance's plans. "For eleven years it was one of the clear foundations of Yad Vashem's plan, the polar, shared, or parallel foundation of Holocaust and heroism. This was one of the foundations of the perception of what we are speaking of and what we want to show generations." He continued: "Where is the heroism?"

"What we said to the architects they did not do," he hurled accusations at Yad Vashem's directorate. "Certainly he has architectonic reasons that a tent is something more than a sanctuary, and a tent is more fitting for the memory of six million than a sanctuary," Shenhavi added in response to El-Hanani's satisfaction with the change of the name from *Heikhal Yizkor*, Sanctuary of Remembrance, to *Ohel Yizkor*, Tent of Remembrance.[92] But "Must we already bow our heads before this reality and sneak in elements of commemoration at Yad Vashem? Why was the remembrance structure changed to the insignificant and small tent, which is not much larger than the one that stands in Paris and which contains no expression other than what exists in Paris?"

Gad Rosenblatt, a central member of the Organization of Underground Partisans and Ghetto Fighters, echoed Shenhavi's criticism and described how "the two issues of Holocaust and heroism have descended from heaven bound together. At every opportunity, on every matter, and in every place the two things are bound together, and the one swallows the other." His claim was that the heroism should be highlighted and given a far more significant and broad place. "A monument to fighters must be something special that expresses and symbolizes the devotion of the heritage of the power, rebellion, and heroism of the youth and the Jewish nation in the days of the Holocaust and revolt."

Weitz turned to Shenhavi:

> Here sit the architects. These are your architects, Shenhavi. Better ones you could not have selected. Better than them architecturally, in terms of thought and idea, better in terms of planning power and executive skill I do not know of in the land. These architects

---

[92] The decision to call the main memorial monument at Yad Vashem *Ohel Yizkor* (literally the tent of remembrance) was reached at a relatively late stage in the process. This name reflected the aspiration of the leaders and architects of Yad Vashem to link the memorial site with the ancient history of the Jewish people and *ohel mo'ed*, the tabernacle through which they worshiped God during their years in the desert.

lived on the idea of Yad Vashem from its inception. They were with it even before the establishment of the law and after it.

Weitz continued: "These architects first proposed one plan, then a second plan and a third plan. And recently brought us a plan that must be placed in everyday life – in reality." The hall could be fitting for Holocaust as well as for heroism, he asserted. "The buildings will come," he concluded, "and then we will fill them with substance. We will hold onto the small bird we have today."

El-Hanani pleaded with the participants to reexamine the model of Yad Vashem and approve the plan. "We have been working for years and years and you, out of your own designs, allow yourselves to speak this way," he protested. Had changes not been made to Yad Vashem's plan, it would already have been possible to execute it. The framework "will honor everyone," he maintained. "No one felt that the heroism could be eliminated here," he added, as "for us – and you will not take this from us – each Jew that died is equal. Those who died in the Holocaust and those who died in heroism. All are equal in our eyes." He demanded: "Let us work."

Weitz and Dinur succeeded in passing a resolution:

> Recognizing that the building plan must be of an image, essence, and scope that befits the sacred and special mission of Holocaust and heroism as one – the council resolves to approve the plan of the hall and the synagogue and recommends that the directorate check the plan in a special committee including members of the council – the plan of the tower and the execution of the commemoration.

It was further decided that "in the construction that will be carried out, the heroism and rebellion as well as the fighting of Jewry against the Nazis in the ghettoes, forests, camps, and Allied forces should be commemorated in a more prominent fashion."

Shenhavi could not conceal his offense at the council's resolution and at their disrespect for his views. As he had done often before, he chose not to remain silent; he communicated his anger in a sharp letter to the architects.[93]

A few days later, the five architects met for a discussion with Shenhavi.[94] After he tendered his indictments at them once again, they opened up about the many difficulties they had encountered during their work planning the Mount of Remembrance. Though they may have had the choice to "get up and go," El-Hanani said, it was "hard to stand before the inclination to reduce and reduce . . . [none] of us kicked you, Shenhavi. We fought. [And] thanks to that fight we achieved what we

---

93 HHA, 3–95. 18 (7), Shenhavi to architects, November 29, 1958.
94 HHA, 3–95. 18 (7), "Shenhavi's Meeting with the Five Architects," December 8, 1958.

present to you today." Sharon, who admitted that he had at first been pessimistic about Yad Vashem's architectural future, added his perspective and claimed that "unfortunately, what we are doing is not abstract"; Yad Vashem's planning team was dependent on a budget that had shrunk over the years. Aside from the fact that the directorate had repeatedly changed its decisions and delayed the end of building, "we are experiencing physical and financial exhaustion," he explained. He added that "Perhaps we should have resigned. We even spoke about it between us more than once . . . we are not opportunists." He claimed that he did not think that anyone could really find "people who would fight until the last drop of blood were they in our place." Weinraub and Mansfeld tried to calm the discussion, to balance the bleak picture and lead the team not to "throw away the keys" and abandon the project. Weinraub suggested that they continue the planning and construction of Yad Vashem but also felt that the directorate should be cautioned time and again about not executing the plans and diverging from the content.

Shenhavi, aware of the way in which Yad Vashem's establishment would be perceived in the future and his place within that perception, documented his perspective on it and preserved it in his own "archive" for "history to judge." He sent a bitter summary, expressing his thoughts about his involvement in the Yad Vashem project, to the team of architects.[95] "If indeed you were so far as a collective from all that was proposed and discussed for sixteen years about Yad Vashem," he cried out in his letter, "Why were you silent? How did you take upon yourselves to plan something that you were distanced from in spirit? And why did you not raise your own suggestions?" He had cutting questions. His primary claim was that

> while the element of heroism was entirely eliminated, you have raised the synagogue as a polar axis in the plan. Only the Hall of Remembrance with El Malei Rahamim and the synagogue across from it. Is this all? And this is being realized by people who "thought for eleven years." What about the tower that led the monument to its death, whose primary function was to serve as a symbolic element of the remembrance enterprise?

He determined that "even when what you propose is built, you will not be distanced from the judgment of generations . . . the public will know . . . what should have been established and what you said to establish – and what ultimately was established."

---

[95] HHA, 3–95. 18 (7), Shenhavi to the five architects, December 10, 1958.

A Return to the Issue of Martyrs' Ashes

In 1956–1957, Yad Vashem's people made a noticeable effort to attain martyrs' ashes. These were primarily sent by Israel's representatives in Europe, but they also came from other sources. In April 1958, with the building plan progressing, a seven-member committee was founded; five were representatives of the Hevra Kadisha and two were representatives of Yad Vashem. Its goal was to reach decisions – primarily halakhic – about the ashes. Its members, all halakhically observant people, included Prof. Kalman Jacob Mann, director general of the Hadassah Medical Organization, Israel Bar-Zacai (Bardakey) from the Hevra Kadisha, and Bialer. Heading the committee was Rabbi Shag, mentioned above, who had been one of the first to raise the suggestion of bringing martyrs' ashes to burial in Israel. Shag felt that the primary role of the Martyrs' Ashes Committee was to look into ways to collect more ashes from Europe. He suggested that the gravesite for the ashes be prepared in such a way that identified ashes, from specific places, could be separated from general ashes. The idea of also preparing a "place for burying the martyrs whose names are known" was raised as well.[96]

The committee further dealt with the question of a temporary place for the ashes. It was resolved that they would be buried on the slope near the location of the planned Hall of Remembrance; Yad Vashem performed preparatory work there. Opinions were divided on whether the ashes would later be brought into the Hall of Remembrance or whether it would remain an exposed grave, surrounded by a garden and places for sitting and communion. The architects noted that if this solution were adopted, access to the grave from the Hall of Remembrance would be necessary as well.[97]

In July 1958, Yad Vashem's directorate discussed bringing ashes and other human remains to burial on the Mount of Remembrance. Some members of the committee felt that the ashes that had arrived at Yad Vashem until that point would not suffice and that it was imperative that the Remembrance Authority itself collect other remains. Shag suggested that a special emissary be dispatched to Europe to coordinate the transfer of ashes that might be discovered in the places of extermination and work camps to the State of Israel.[98] But not everyone on Yad Vashem's directorate supported a widespread campaign for collecting and bringing remains from Europe. The primary critique related to what some felt was an expansive and unnecessary preoccupation with the victims' remains, which could turn

---

[96] ISA, GL-6/14913, "Meeting of the Joint Committee of Hevra Kadisha and Yad Vashem on the Problem of Martyrs' Ashes," May 25, 1958.
[97] CZA, KKL5/24136, "Memorandum of Building Committee Meeting," April 1, 1958.
[98] CZA, S115/239, Israel Bar-Zacai to Yad Vashem, July 8, 1958.

the Mount of Remembrance into a cemetery. A disagreement arose between the committee members and the directorate about the way in which the ashes would be buried. While Yad Vashem wished to make the ashes' burial a ceremony and give it great public weight, Shag and others felt that they should suffice with a modest burial, without publicity.[99] Dinur emphasized that collecting the ashes may be symbolic "but if we send a dedicated person with relatives who were killed there and he is tied to the subject then this will be a great enterprise." However, Weitz opposed those who supported active collection of ashes, warning that the Remembrance Authority could be involved in "unpleasant subjects." He added that they must "avoid trading in dust and ash." There was no need, he felt, to initiate a search in camps in Europe; rather, "Jews can send ashes much as they transfer documents." The disagreement concluded with a decision that the ashes' collection would not be symbolic; ashes would be brought from all places possible. It was further decided that the ashes would be brought to Israel only if they were undeniably those of Jews and that this activity would continue to be executed in cooperation with the Ministry of Foreign Affairs and under its guidance.[100]

Toward the Building of the Hall of Remembrance and Another Financial Crisis

The new building plan on the Mount of Remembrance was approved and it appeared that construction would soon begin. At the end of 1958, the directorate chose to transfer the execution of construction of the Hall of Remembrance, synagogue, tower, assembly plaza, and museum to a construction company. The construction was meant to adhere to a budget of 900,000 Israeli pounds.[101] The decision was preceded by feverish discussions about the complex budgetary issues and a fear that the Claims Conference would refuse to fund the new, expanded building plan, which had added a museum to the other remembrance buildings (see chapter 5). Additional budget, some claimed, should be demanded from the Claims Conference for the museum's construction, as Yad Vashem could not be established without it. The directorate decided to suffice with building the museum's frame under the assembly plaza.[102]

---

99 Hevra Kadisha, *Hevra Kadisha, Jerusalem: Jubilee Book 1939–1999* (Jerusalem: Hevra Kadisha Jerusalem, 1992), 149 [in Hebrew].
100 HHA, 3–95. 19 (1), "Protocol of Yad Vashem Directorate Meeting," July 21, 1958.
101 ISA, GL-2/1230, "Decisions of Yad Vashem's Directorate," January 13, 1958.
102 CAHJP, P28/6/150, "Protocol of Building Committee," December 30, 1958.

The building plan may have been approved by Yad Vashem's directorate, but it became clear that its many changes had led to a significant breach in the budget. The price of construction had increased and the change of the synagogue's location led to a noticeable expansion of the building's scope. Dinur was now forced to write to Uveeler and Goldmann to explain the depth of the problem: "Our directions to the architects were clear and unequivocal," but when the discussions on the directorate and especially in the council about the building's scope and form began, "the architects were carried away by their great imagination and carried us away with them, without informing us of the financial results that would derive from this."

Dinur therefore asked the Claims Conference to help with the financial straits that had been created, and to cover the difference. "The great difficulties we confront are clear to the directorate members, as it has become clear that the buildings cannot be completed with the amount we have at our disposal," Dinur announced to the Claims Conference, and reported that the directorate had

> almost entire unanimity that Yad Vashem's buildings must befit the sacred goal for which they are being established and that it is our duty, the directorate and all those who have acted and will continue to act to realize the mission, to ensure that the buildings suit the purpose for which they were intended and that the funds necessary can be attained sooner or later.

Dinur focused his request on the need to complete the museum.[103]

Uveeler, in response, removed the responsibility from the Claims Conference's shoulders, stating that the solution could only come from an appeal to Israeli authorities for an additional allocation of budget.[104] He suggested one other solution – scrapping the construction of the Hall of Remembrance, a structure that to his mind was devoid of all content, and building the museum in its stead. He explained the Claims Conference's budgetary considerations, that "with the current state of new immigration and in the face of the difficult problems that confront the entire state and Jewry as a whole in relation to the new immigration and its settling in the land, it is impossible to consider increasing the budget for construction and development, even if these plans are related to the Holocaust." He added that even Yad Vashem's most devoted friends (Goldmann?) felt that at the present time it would be impossible to demand additional funds for a new construction plan.[105]

Yad Vashem's directorate, then, faced a problematic situation: it could not execute the building plan it had prepared. It was clear to all that the Remembrance

---

103 CAHJP, CC appl. 1959/293a, Dinur to Uveeler, January 1, 1959.
104 CAHJP, CC appl. 1959/293a, Uveeler to Melkman, January 5, 1959.
105 CAHJP, CC appl. 1959/293a, Uveeler to Dinur, January 21, 1959.

Authority would have great difficulty raising hundreds of thousands of additional pounds in order to complete construction.

Al HaMishmar journalist Ferenc-Iosef Jámbor described the situation well, having received information about events at Yad Vashem from Shenhavi; he represented a staunch oppositional line against Yad Vashem's directorate in general and Dinur in particular. He claimed that Yad Vashem had been "sold" to the Claims Conference in exchange for its participation in construction and that, after this "sale," "all search for financial sources among the nation ceased, sources that were prepared ... to lend a hand in the commemoration enterprise." He suggested – channeling Shenhavi – that "it is possible that we can still return to the original plan and prepare the 'national pantheon,' rife with honor, majesty, and splendor, as it was originally planned, instead of the cold monument, I would say bureaucratic monument, which is pictured in the imaginations of Yad Vashem's directors at present."[106]

Despite these problems, Yad Vashem's directorate signed an agreement with a contracting company, stating that the Hall of Remembrance, synagogue, monument, and frame of the museum would be built within a year.[107] This decision made it possible for Dinur to announce at the final meeting that he ran as chairman of Yad Vashem, on the eve of his resignation from the role, the onset of construction of the Mount of Remembrance. "We have set a special place, the Mount of Remembrance, a place distinguished from the city in which all of the institutions, archive, library, reading rooms, etc. will be concentrated," he reminded his replacement, Kubovy. He added that "pilgrimage here should be tied to communion, and the uniqueness of this place is an issue of first-rate importance, uniqueness [that is] on its own and for its own sake and not incidental." He cautioned the directorate against the temptation "to forgo any matter for reasons of convenience, [even if] it is easier to be in the center of town. We must not give up. Yad Vashem in its entirety must be here." Dinur also related to the completion of the construction, "a combination of elements of remembrance from the Holocaust and heroism in structures," the establishment of the remembrance tower, the arrangement of the burial site for the martyrs' ashes, and the erection of a monument above it. He felt that with the end of the construction there would be a need to deal with the question of developing the museum, which would only be a frame. He expressed confidence that at the end of the two years allotted for

---

106 Ferenc-Iosef Jámbor, "Yad Vashem – How Small You Became," *Al HaMishmar*, January 23, 1959.
107 ISA, GL-2/1230, "Decisions of Yad Vashem's Directorate," February 17, 1959.

construction "the Mount of Remembrance will be a central focus in Jerusalem for all of Jewry in its land and in the Diaspora."[108]

The "keys" were transferred to Kubovy and he was now forced to confront the budgetary problems which, it emerged, were severe. When the assembly plaza's construction began it became clear that more than 1,250,000 Israeli pounds needed to complete it were missing. Sharon believed that this figure was too low and additional funds would be necessary to complete the construction. "The buildings are not regular"; therefore, the sum set aside for unforeseen expenses was too low, he claimed. He further noted that he expected construction materials to become significantly more expensive, deepening the financial hole.[109]

Kubovy decided to nonetheless submit a budget proposal to the Claims Conference that included the missing sum and to travel to New York to meet with the organization's heads.[110] His primary claim was that Yad Vashem's requested addition was not tied to the expansion of the construction plan (except for the museum and the Hall of Names; see chapter 5), but rather was a necessary outcome of the process of executing the original plan that had already been approved by them. Kubovy warned the organization's heads that not approving the budget's increase meant "destroying buildings or leaving new ruins" and claimed that with the completion of construction the Mount of Remembrance would bestow "honor" on the Claims Conference.

After a sharp exchange between Kubovy and the heads of the Claims Conference the latter agreed to examine supplying the additional financial aid in order to complete construction. Their demand was that a committee be formed including three external architects who would represent the bodies funding Yad Vashem – Israel's government, the Jewish Agency, and the Claims Conference – that could examine Yad Vashem's budgetary demands.[111] At the end of 1959, two architects, Werner Joseph Wittkower and Gad Asher, together with the engineer Jacob Reiser (representing the Jewish Agency), submitted a report on events at Yad Vashem and their evaluation of the possibility for completing the building there. They approved Yad Vashem's building plan and estimated that it could be completed by the spring of 1961.[112]

In early 1960, Kubovy stood before participants in Yad Vashem's Fifth World Council. In contrast with the previous council, which had convened in 1958 and whose debates about the future of Yad Vashem had been stormy, this time the

---

108 CZA, S115/242, "Protocol of Yad Vashem Directorate Meeting," March 11, 1959.
109 ISA, GL-3/1638, "Building Committee Meeting," November 17, 1959.
110 CAHJP, CC appl. 1959/293a, Uveeler to Goldmann, August 27, 1959.
111 YVA, AM1 360, "Protocol of Yad Vashem Directorate Meeting," December 15, 1959.
112 YVA, AM1 360, "Report on Yad Vashem's Development," December 31, 1959.

discussions were held in a far more pleasant atmosphere, due, among other things, to the new chairman of the Remembrance Authority who, it was felt, brought a new spirit to the institution. This fact made it possible for Kubovy to announce that the Hall of Remembrance, along with the other buildings, would be inaugurated on Holocaust Martyrs' and Heroes' Remembrance Day, 1961, and that "already now it is possible to see that the four buildings will honor the martyrs and heroes as well as the people sitting in Zion and the nation as a whole." He reported that alongside the Hall of Remembrance, the synagogue "that will symbolize the synagogues and the houses of religious study that were destroyed," a hall for the holy books which would contain "in the form of a line written in trembling and affection the tombstone for each Jew who was not privileged to receive a Jewish burial," a museum would also be founded in which a permanent exhibit of the image of the Jewish world that had declined would be displayed. "Already now the Mount of Remembrance is becoming a place of pilgrimage for thousands," he stated, and expected that with the completion of construction tens of thousands would stream to "this holy place," a place in which annual memorial services would be held for community members. "Yad Vashem will become the global center for commemoration and at the same time will grow in the importance and supremacy of research on Jews and non-Jews of the time." Shatner took pride in the Mount of Remembrance's proximity to Mount Herzl and the military cemetery and noted that "in this way the site will contain a concentration of a number of remembrance enterprises of the state and of the nation as a whole."[113]

The Heroism Hall Becomes a Heroism Tower

The road to completing construction on the Mount of Remembrance was still a long one, and bound up with no small number of questions and problems that remained open. Kubovy had a sense of dissatisfaction as a result of the gaping holes in the Mount of Remembrance's development plan, the most prominent of which was the heroism tower. "The time has come to know clearly how the architects describe the visitors' route," Kubovy stated, based on his assessment that Yad Vashem would host masses of "pilgrims" and out of a fear that the current plan would not facilitate a comfortable visit for large numbers of visitors.[114]

---

[113] ISA, GL-1/13346, "Yad Vashem Directorate Report during the First Session of the Fifth Council," January 17, 1960.
[114] ISA, GL-3/13346, "Building Committee Meeting," May 5, 1960.

The deliberations regarding integrating the monument – later a tower – in Yad Vashem's memorial landscape had begun in the early stages of planning the compound and became ever more complex as the architects' work progressed. Standing before the participants at the Yad Vashem council in November 1958, El-Hanani reported on the difficulty that the architectural team encountered and focused on the monument, which he and his colleagues were meant to integrate within the building plan. "What is a monument?" he asked. "One can pile stones on one another and say that it is a monument. An artist can also create a dubious work and it will be called a monument."[115] He suggested that, as he and his colleagues had not been able to find a fitting architectural expression – "a monument is something that is not given to expression in a clear fashion" – an artists' competition be declared to determine the monument's appearance.[116]

Yad Vashem's Building Committee discussed the necessity of the tower. While some felt it superfluous, the architects managed to convince the committee that integrating a tower in the landscape of Yad Vashem was highly important, as it was "the most radical element of the remembrance structures." The Building Committee tackled the tower's shape and symbolism. Yaakov Zerubavel, for example, had his reservations about the tower's interim shape – with its straight sides, facing heavenward – and suggested that "if a sculptor creates some work of art in this tower that speaks to the heart, then it will be possible to accept this building." Bialer cautioned that the tower "is [too] similar to the chimney that emerges from a factory" and suggested shortening it "because height does not determine the expression but rather the strong expression, the scream."

In July 1959, it was suggested that twelve artists and architects be approached to take part in a "limited open tender" for the tower which would be "a beacon for Jerusalem's environs" and would symbolize Jewish heroism during the war.[117] The directorate decided that the competition would be open to Jewish artists living in the Diaspora and that the monument would not include images of people.[118] Kubovy asked that the tower's construction be complete by Holocaust Martyrs' and Heroes' Remembrance Day, 27 Nisan 1960, and that it be the first building standing in the assembly plaza, preceding the Hall of Remembrance. The official name it was given was the Monument of Remembrance to Heroism.[119]

---

115 HHA, 3–95. 7 (1), *Yad Vashem* (booklet), August 1954.
116 CZA, S61/326, "Protocol of the Third Session of the Fourth Yad Vashem World Council," November 9, 1958.
117 CAHJP, CC 18540, "Protocol of the Building Committee," July 16, 1959.
118 ISA, GL-3/1638, "Protocol of the Building Committee," November 17, 1959.
119 HHA, 3–95. 19 (1), "Protocol of Yad Vashem Directorate Meeting," July 28, 1959.

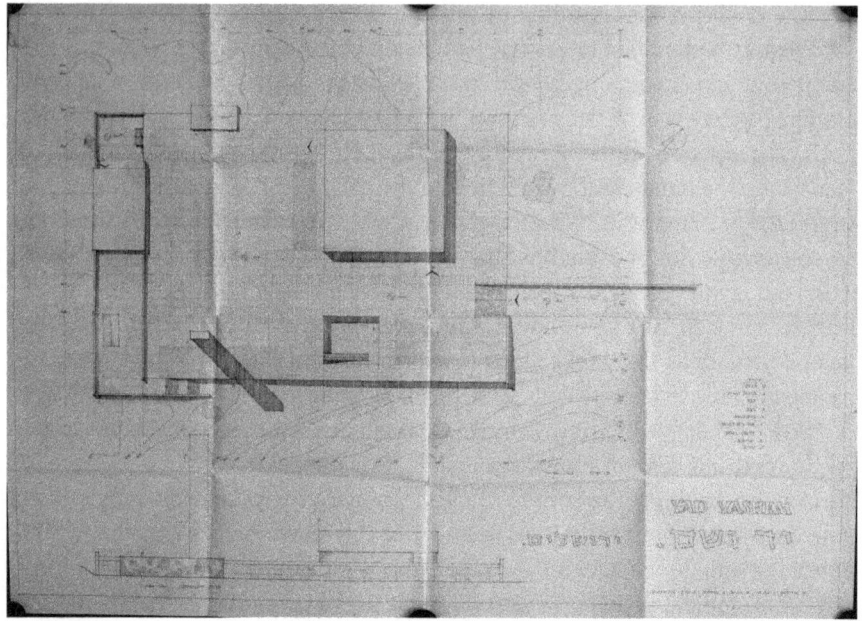

Figure 18: Construction plan for Yad Vashem, late 1950s (HHA).

The architects met with representatives of the Israel Painters and Sculptors Association and came up with a list of ten notable Israeli plastic artists who were invited to compete. They included Kosso Eloul, Naftali Bezem, Daniel "Dani" Karavan, Yitzhak Danziger, Batya Lishanski, Moshe Ziffer, and Yechiel Shemi. At the same time, a judges' committee was formed.[120]

The location of the tower, it was determined, would be the southwestern section of the assembly plaza, but many had concerns. Bialer claimed that erecting the monument in the plaza would be a mistake, as "if it [the pillar] will stand against the backdrop of the synagogue and the martyrs' hall – it will cause congestion in the structures" and "inefficient and unaesthetic density." Shatner worried that the monument would become a secular place, that the visitors would pass by but not visit it. He explained that "our deliberation must be based on the function of the monument, which is communion with heroism." Others claimed that the monument built in the assembly plaza "will appear to those who come from afar like a chimney rising above the roof of the Hall of Remembrance," perhaps a hint to the crematoria's chimneys in the extermination camps.

---

120 ISA, GL-3/13346, "Protocol of Building Committee," January 6, 1960.

In contrast, placing the tower atop the hill, many felt, would mean that visitors to the Hall of Remembrance would not pass the monument but would rather have to go to it, which would emphasize its singularity. They contrasted the masses who would "suffice with assembly and speeches" heard at the plaza with the lone visitor, who would reach the monument "without becoming involved in a crowd assembled for a specific ceremony," preferring to visit the monument in its discrete place.[121]

Sharon ruled that the monument should remain part of the remembrance plaza and claimed that it would stand "in the center of traffic of the large crowd" that would come to Yad Vashem, much like the Arc de Triomphe in Paris. "The fire in Atuel is also in the center of traffic and it does not diminish," he explained. "The plaza should not be left exposed and breached," especially when, after it was paved, he claimed, it would appear far larger than it currently looked. Most of all, Sharon cautioned that moving the monument out of the plaza would create a "new complex" there, an alternate "pilgrimage" destination, competing with the Hall of Remembrance.[122] As we will see, the process of establishing the monument would extend for many more years.

The Inauguration of the Hall of Remembrance

Discussions about the Hall of Remembrance's visage and its interior's design continued during the entire process of planning the mount. At the end of 1959 and throughout 1960, when the walls of the building were going up and the roof was cast above them, Yad Vashem's directorate was compelled to make a decision about its internal appearance.[123]

One of the primary points of contention was the question of the names in the Hall of Remembrance. In earlier plans of Yad Vashem, it had been decided that the Holocaust hall – in its later incarnation, the Hall of Remembrance – would have the names of the thousands of destroyed communities immortalized on its walls. And while in the past the idea had been that these inscriptions would be engraved on the walls of the building, now, in 1959, the concept of names marked on its floor crystallized. The reason for this was the architects' decision to leave the basalt stones from which the building's walls had been

---

[121] ISA, GL-3/13346, "Protocol of Building Committee," May 5, 1960.
[122] ISA, GL-3/13346, "Protocol of Building Committee," May 17, 1960.
[123] On the building of the Hall of Remembrance see: Doron Bar, "The Hall of Remembrance at Yad Vashem: Israel's Holocaust Commemoration Monument," *The Journal of Holocaust Research* 34, no. 1 (2020): 24–48.

built in their natural state – unchiseled, dramatic, and imposing. The grave of the martyrs' ashes was fixed in the floor, and the eternal flame was meant to stand there as well. The floor of the Hall of Remembrance now became the architectural-commemorative center of the building.

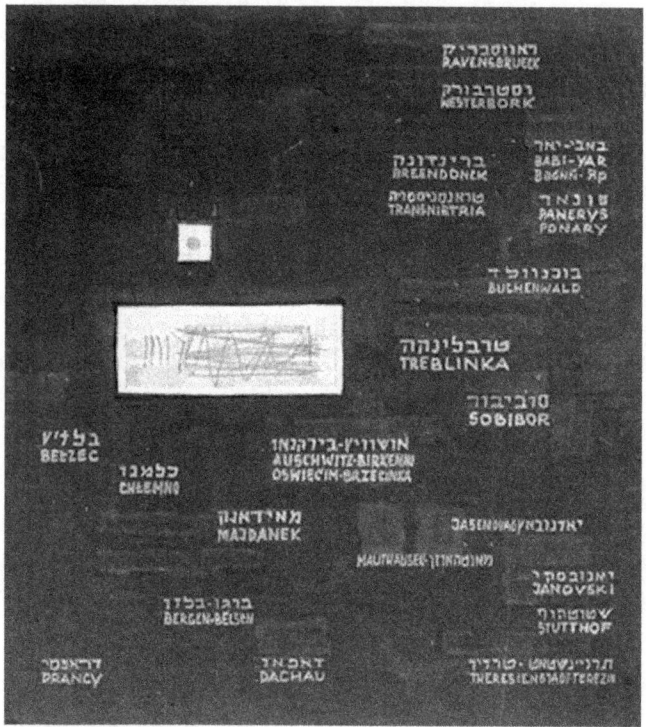

Figure 19: Suggestion for placement of the names of twenty-one extermination camps, concentration camps, and sites of murder and transport within the floor of the Hall of Remembrance (YVA, Unknown photographer).

Now the question of which names would be set in the Hall of Remembrance's floor arose. Would these be the names of the communities that had been destroyed, the cities and villages in which the Jews had lived? Would they be the names of the countries of destruction or the names of the places in which the Jews had been concentrated and exterminated? How could the great numbers of names be limited to a list small enough that it could be displayed on the floor of the Hall of Remembrance in a manner and scale that visitors would be able to read? And, if the location of extermination – the concentration and death camps – were the focus, would these camps then be immortalized on the floor?

Would the dozens and hundreds of places in which the Nazis had assembled Jews be named or only the prominent ones? Would the names be written in Hebrew or in other languages?

In the early stages of discussions, a decision was made to focus on the names of the death camps. Zerubavel compared this to the issue of the martyrs' ashes, stating that just as one container of ashes, "representing everything," was enough to sanctify the Hall of Remembrance, there should not be too many names of death camps. "We want '*Yizkor*' and there are only dozens of names at the very most that are notorious and only they should be written as they serve as a symbol," he stated. This was indeed the decision of the Building Committee, which resolved that on the floor of the Hall of Remembrance, in front of the grave of ashes, approximately ten to twenty names of extermination camps would be written – names "that will be decided upon as the names that have been engraved in the conscience of the world as a whole that will symbolize all."[124] The recommendation was to engrave these names in Hebrew and to add a symbol next to each (for example, the gates of the Auschwitz death camp, with the inscription "Arbeit Macht Frei").[125] Later on in 1960, it was decided that in addition to the names being given in Hebrew, they would be given in the European languages.[126] The list was completed in October 1960; it included twenty-one extermination and concentration camps, places of massacre and deportation.[127] The recommendation was that among these names the six significant extermination camps, "in which millions of Jews met their deaths" would be highlighted. These were Auschwitz-Birkenau, Belzec, Chełmno, Majdanek, Sobibor, and Treblinka.[128]

Yad Vashem asked artist Aharon Kahana to create the inscriptions of the extermination camps,[129] while their typography was developed by Yerachmiel Schechter, head of the Bezalel school.[130] The Hall of Remembrance's two artistic metal gates were ordered from David Palombo and Bezalel Schatz, and

---

[124] ISA, GL-3/1638, "Protocol of Building Committee," November 17, 1959.
[125] ISA, GL-3/13346, "Protocol of Building Committee," May 17, 1960.
[126] YVA, AM1 360, "Protocol of Building Committee," June 14, 1960.
[127] YVA, AM1 345, List of places that will be set into the floor of the Hall of Remembrance, Hebrew and foreign languages. Ultimately, the names of twenty-two places were written on the floor: six death camps, ten concentration camps, three sites of massacre, one place that was used to transport people to death camps, a notorious fortress, a ghetto, and a death camp.
[128] YVA, AM1 345, Arieh Kubovy to Aharon Kahana, October 3, 1960.
[129] YVA, AM1 345, Aharon Kahana to Yad Vashem, September 19, 1960.
[130] YVA, AM1 345, "Technical Description of the Preparation of Ceramic Inscriptions and Their Installation in the Floor of Hall of Remembrance"; this work is documented in: YVA, film number 10004432.

Figure 20: General appearance of the Hall of Remembrance (NPA, Moshe Milner).

included a composition of metal parts and rods that lent the gates a wild, rough appearance.[131]

The inclusion of the symbolic memorial candle in the Hall of Remembrance was a relatively new idea. As noted, earlier plans of Yad Vashem had included a fire element in the remembrance tower; symbolic flames were meant to emerge from its top. With the changes that had taken place in the tower – in its location and appearance as well as the fire element – a need to find a place for a symbolic memorial candle arose. It was suggested that a memorial candle be erected in the Hall of Remembrance and serve as the focus in future ceremonies.

At first, it was felt at Yad Vashem that the eternal flame would be in the form of the "memorial candle" designed by Zahara Schatz, which had recently been selected in the competition Yad Vashem had declared for the Holocaust lamp.[132] But Sharon felt that this candle and the eternal flame should not be connected, as an "enlarged memorial candle" would not be fitting in the Hall of Remembrance.[133]

---

131 YVA, AM1 344, David Palombo and Bezalel Schatz to Yad Vashem, October 3, 1960.
132 "Memorial Candle," *Yediot Yad Vashem* 25–26 (1961), 44.
133 YVA, AM1 360, "Protocol of Building Committee," June 14, 1960.

Figure 21: Gateway to the Hall of Remembrance, designed by David Palombo (NPA, Moshe Pridan).

The directorate thus decided to appeal to the artist Kosso Eloul, and he presented his "eternal flame" at the end of 1960. The bronze sculpture was over three meters in height and a meter and a half wide, its face was textured, and its colors were those of fire – reddish brown, green, and black, with "droplets of gold and silver resembling tears" on them. The candle conceptualized how "from a horizontal body, a sort of torn and open heart, many flames of fire rise upwards and create a sense of a general burning, a 'burnt offering.'"[134]

In the Building Committee and on Yad Vashem's directorate instinctive opposition was voiced to the candle's abstract-artistic form, which felt to many like a sculpture and not like a traditional memorial candle. They also raised doubts about its extraordinary height, not customary in Jewish tradition; the flame would be the vertical element in the eternal candle rather than the sculpture itself. El-Hanani noted that the eternal flame was tailored to the dimensions of the

---

134 YVA, AM1 347, "Description of Works," n.d.; YVA, AM1 347, Photo of the proposal for the eternal flame.

Figure 22: Eternal flame designed by Kosso Eloul for the Hall of Remembrance (YVA, Unknown photographer).

Hall of Remembrance, which satisfied the directorate members, who signed a contract with Eloul.[135]

Another central issue tied to the Hall of Remembrance was the question of the ashes' integration within it. The Hevra Kadisha had prepared a temporary place for the ashes to the north of the hall's planned construction site. But as the remembrance building took shape, Yad Vashem's directorate and the members of the Building Committee had trouble deciding whether to leave the burial site there and make it permanent, perhaps with a dedicated building, or to return to the original plan and move the ashes into the Hall of Remembrance.

The architects pressured Kubovy to bring the ashes into the Hall of Remembrance, but a halakhic question arose regarding the entry of kohanim – priests – there. The ashes' burial would make the building a grave, a place kohanim could not enter. Bialer looked for a halakhic resolution to the problem. He met with Rabbi Shlomo Yosef Zevin, of the Habad Hasidic movement and the editor of the *Encyclopedia Talmudit* (talmudic encyclopedia) and asked for his help. He also spoke with Israeli Chief Rabbi Yitzhak Nissim. They both felt that the problem was not tied to the ashes (which were not ritually impure halakhically), but with the concern that bones or remains of bones might be buried

---

[135] YVA, AM1 347, Contract signed between Kosso Eloul and Yad Vashem, January 11, 1961.

there as well. Bialer suggested that if there were a fear that the martyrs' ashes contained ritual impurity, the Remembrance Authority would resolve the problem within the boundaries of halakha, for example, by building a curvature over the ashes, "a sort of catacomb within the hall, so that the ritual impurity would not emerge."[136] At Yad Vashem's request, Rabbi Zevin sent a responsum letter in which he determined that the agreement of the rabbis should be accepted, relying, inter alia, on rulings of Maimonides and of Rabbi Jacob Emden (Ya'avetz), who had stated that a kohen cannot become impure from ashes.[137] Yad Vashem's directorate resolved that the ashes would be buried inside the Hall of Remembrance.[138]

Now the deliberations about whether to build a special structure for the burial of the ashes in the Hall of Remembrance's floor or to suffice with a burial shaft arose. Should one "coffin" be built to hold all of the ashes, or should space be left for separate vessels in which ashes "from places that had become a symbol" could be buried?[139] Bialer suggested that the niche be divided into spaces in which vessels with identified ashes and a larger vessel dedicated to ashes that would be brought from various places would stand. Ultimately, it was decided that the ashes would be buried in one container, would constitute a mass grave, and would be built in a way that would prevent people stepping on it, with no access for the visitors. Near the end of 1960, the ashes' "sarcophagus" was presented – a subterranean box covered with a massive moveable stone lid.[140] A committee with Kubovy, Bialer, and Kahana was selected to oversee the ashes' site on the Mount of Remembrance, which was defined as a "symbol grave." Chief Rabbi Yitzhak Nissim approved the agreement.[141]

On 27 Nisan 1961, the Hall of Remembrance was inaugurated in the presence of the state's president and many other dignitaries; a central assembly marking Holocaust Martyrs' and Heroes' Remembrance Day took place, for the first time, in the new assembly plaza.[142] In the morning, a ceremony was held in which the martyrs' ashes were removed from their temporary grave. Soldiers from the Military Rabbinate carried the coffin of ashes to the grave within the Hall of Remembrance while other soldiers served as an honor guard. The ashes

---

136 HHA, 3–95. 19 (1), "Protocol of Yad Vashem Directorate Meeting," July 28, 1959.
137 CAHJP, CC 18551a, Shlomo Yosef Zevin to Kubovy, July 30, 1959.
138 HHA, 3–95. 19 (1), "Protocol of Yad Vashem Directorate Meeting," July 28, 1959.
139 ISA, GL-3/1638, HHA, 3–95. 19 (1), "Protocol of Yad Vashem Directorate Meeting," October 27, 1959.
140 YVA, AM1 346, Plan of the sarcophagus to be built in the floor of the Hall of Remembrance.
141 ISA, GL-2/6362, "Minutes," April 11, 1961.
142 ISA, GL-9/1639, "Yad Vashem Activities during 1961."

Figure 23: The Hall of Remembrance, with the Pillar of Heroism in the background (YVA, Unknown photographer).

were placed in the designated vessels. Bialer and Minister Mordechai Nurock gave a eulogy and then the eternal flame was kindled.[143]

The many participants who accompanied the ashes into the Hall of Remembrance were struck by the power of the building, so different from the other memorial structures that had been built in the State of Israel until that time. It was a square space with no internal walls. Its external walls, outside and inside, were built of unprocessed basalt stones that had been brought from the Bet Shean valley and the eastern Galilee. The face of the stone was intentionally left protruding from the lines of the foundational concrete walls, adding to the impact and hinting at antiquity and at the small stones that are traditionally laid atop graves in haphazard piles.

The concrete roof of the building was designed in the form of a tent. From the outside, the roof looked like the continuation of the basalt stone wall, riding atop it, but from inside it "rested" atop iron pillars, which created a minimal

---

143 "Israelis Commemorated the Memory of Holocaust Victims," *Davar*, April 14, 1961. For a photo of the coffin carried into the Hall of Remembrance, see: "Martyrs' Ashes Reburied: Memorial Day Ceremony," *The Jewish Herald*, April 21, 1961. The ceremony is documented in the film "Tent of Remembrance," kept in YVA, 10004432.

space that brought in a little bit of light from the outside and gave a sense of a lack of connection between the roof and the cement ceiling. The exposed ceiling was like a pyramid; however, its peak was not positioned at the center but rather above the eternal flame, which was to the side. At that point, an approximately one-meter-squared opening tore through, making it possible for symbolic light to enter the building and for smoke to rise to the sky.[144]

The building's internal space was intentionally designed to be dark. At the height of about one meter, along two of the building's sides, was a sort of gallery or bridge upon which visitors could walk. This structure was meant for the kohanim, in order to avoid the concern of contact with impurity – but it also intensified the general impact.

The floor of the building was composed of dark grey mosaic pieces, two centimeters squared, which integrated the names of the concentration and death camps and other sites of murder. Most of the inscriptions were distributed with no order or hierarchy, except for the names of the six extermination camps that had been set close to the niche in which the martyrs' ashes were buried. All of these became a type of symbolic map of Europe. The grave of ashes was located next to the eternal flame and, despite the fact that there was no inscription there, it was clear to the visitors what was buried there – the entire memorial structure's raison d'être.

In the evening, the Holocaust Martyrs' and Heroes' Remembrance Day ceremony began. Thousands of participants sat in straight rows in the new assembly plaza. Minister of Education Abba Eban gave the main address. On the dais sat Gideon Hausner, the prosecutor from the Eichmann trial, which was in progress at the time. At the end of the ceremony, a military unit opened the gates of the Hall of Remembrance and marched in, and the participants followed it into the hall and viewed the building's interior. As night fell, the youth battalions lit torches on the nearby hill and held a torch march while in the background the vision of the dry bones (Ezek. 37) was heard. The assembly closed with the singing of Hatikva.

One month later, the president's wife, Rahel Yanait Ben-Zvi, lit the eternal flame and the Hall of Remembrance was opened to the general public. Kubovy thanked Shatner for his work as chairman of the Building Committee and Bialer for succeeding in overcoming the many difficulties that were tied to the collection and transfer of the ashes to the Hall of Remembrance.[145] Standing before

---

[144] CZA, S30/4189, *Yad Vashem* (booklet), December 15, 1960; Yosef Lishinsky, "Yad Vashem as Art," *Ariel* 55 (1983): 14–25 [in Hebrew].
[145] CZA, C6/420, Protocol of directorate meeting, May 2, 1961.

the participants at Yad Vashem's Fifth World Council, he also thanked the three architects who had taken part in building the Hall of Remembrance, Arieh El-Hanani, thought to be the head architect on the project, as well as Arieh Sharon and Benjamin Idelson, who had helped him. Weinraub and Mansfeld were not mentioned at all, their place in the enterprise entirely forgotten. "The fusion of the rough basalt stone with the simple concrete above, the entrances made of powerful iron protrusions," Kubovy said, made the Hall of Remembrance "a sublime expression of our nation's mourning, and of the choice to remember that beats within it."[146] He did not relate to the building as a "holy place," but the combination of the grave of martyrs' ashes, the eternal flame, the names of the extermination camps, and the dark lighting there made a fitting atmosphere for holiness. Already at this stage it was determined that those entering the Hall of Remembrance should cover their heads, like in a cemetery.

Prof. Alexander Dushkin reported on the very positive sense that the Hall of Remembrance aroused, "a masterpiece of Israeli architecture," and on the huge impression that the building made. He suggested nominating the building for the Israel Prize.[147] Indeed, Edwin Samuel, eldest son of early-Mandate-era High Commissioner Herbert Samuel, was the person who best expressed the stir that the Hall of Remembrance created among its visitors. The Remembrance Authority published a small booklet in a number of languages, which included the notes from his visit to Yad Vashem. He described the experience of walking from Mount Herzl and the surprising revelation of the mount, "full of glory, standing on the extension of a mountain – the Mount of Remembrance, surrounded by deep and divided gorges . . . you feel that your feet are treading some ancient Hebrew stage," he added, "but here, it is not animals that are the sacrifices, but rather human beings." Samuel expressed the feelings of visitors to the remembrance building well. "A person feels as if he is trapped in a huge fortress. It is completely impossible to escape from here. There are no windows and no distracting pictures, no wall openings." Rather a person "now stands face to face with a cruel reality, entirely isolated from the rest of humanity." His conclusion

---

146 Arieh Leon Kubovy, "Opening Remarks during the Fourth Session of the Fifth Council," *Yediot Yad Vashem* 28 (1962), 76–77.
147 ISA, GL-3/13346, "Yad Vashem Directorate Meeting," August 8, 1961; the quotation about the Hall of Remembrance as a work of art (*melekhet mahshevet*) is taken from: ISA, GL-9/1639, "Yad Vashem Activities during 1961." In 1972, Yad Vashem's directorate decided to put forward the Hall of Remembrance as a candidate for the Israel Prize: YVA, Protocols of Yad Vashem Directorate Meetings, Protocol of the Board of Directors, November 13, 1972; Arieh El-Hanani won the Israel Prize for architecture in 1973: "Israel Prizes Awarded in Jerusalem," *Davar*, May 8, 1973. It seems that his direct involvement in the design of the Hall of Remembrance was one of the main reasons to grant him the prize.

was that there was no doubt that the building was an ingenious creation, an exceptional site of assembly, to which Jews from the entire earth would journey for generations.[148]

A routine formed: Each day at eleven o'clock a memorial ceremony was held at the Hall of Remembrance. Verses from Psalms were read, the Yizkor prayer was said, and then Avraham Shlonsky's poem, "Oath," was read aloud. The Remembrance Authority tried to make the Hall of Remembrance into a place of assembly for the *landsmannschaften*, offering them the option to hold assemblies on the day of their community's demise on the Mount of Remembrance. When organized groups came to the site, sometimes groups of survivors, they were honored with the lighting of the candle after they had approached the grave of ashes.[149]

Conclusion

The inauguration of the Hall of Remembrance on 27 Nisan 1961 was the culmination of a process that had begun in the 1940s. Yad Vashem's planning and building knew ups and downs and saw despair mixed with hope. But now, in mid-1961, many on the directorate and in the Israeli public had a sense of spiritual elevation and pride. Kubovy crowned the Hall of Remembrance "a masterpiece of Israeli architecture."[150] A visit to the site demonstrated how Yad Vashem's architects, led by El-Hanani, had managed to distill the idea of Holocaust commemoration into one inspirational building, a monument containing nothing but the names of the concentration and death camps, an eternal flame, and a grave of martyrs' ashes. The difference between Yad Vashem's architects' complex ideas in the forties and the modern building, shaped in concrete and basalt, that now stood at the heart of the Mount of Remembrance was noticeable, and demonstrated that they had come a long way in their understanding of the subject.

The road to the building of the memorial compound was a long and complex one. The architectural plans were changed a number of times, a result of pressure exerted on the architects and the directorate from a variety of agents.

---

148 Edwin Samuel, *Tent of Remembrance at Yad Vashem* (Jerusalem: Yad Vashem, 1975), 3–4 [in Hebrew].
149 "Tent of Remembrance," *Yediot Yad Vashem* 28 (1962), 24; Yad Vashem, *Yad Vashem: Memorial Candle at the Tent of Remembrance* (Jerusalem: Yad Vashem, n.d.).
150 ISA, GL-1/1424, "Kubovy's Words during the Opening Session of the Discussions of the Public Committee Examining Yad Vashem's Activities," October 4, 1964.

The Claims Conference and its representative in Israel, Uveeler, greatly influenced the design of the Mount of Remembrance, and the noticeable financial difficulties were tied to this. The pressure that the Claims Conference applied on Yad Vashem's directorate and on Dinur made it necessary for them to compromise and change parts of the plan – the synagogue, whose location was moved a number of times, and the heroism monument, which at this point still had no agreed-upon location or form. A central issue in the directorate's discussions was the question of the place of heroism in the memorial landscape. All of Yad Vashem's plans until the mid-fifties had given it a central place, but during the period discussed in this chapter the status of heroism waned. This change was the result of external pressure from the Claims Conference, among others, as well as the difficulty of expressing the concept architecturally.

One of the most striking and symbolic components on the Mount of Remembrance was the grave of martyrs' ashes inside the Hall of Remembrance. Yad Vashem's legitimacy in receiving the ashes and burying them on the Mount of Remembrance had occupied the heads of the Remembrance Authority throughout the years. In this period, the struggle between the authority and various religious bodies – the Ministry of Religions, the chief rabbis, and other rabbis – reached its peak. The latter's demand that Yad Vashem be barred from burying the ashes and that the Chamber of the Holocaust on Mount Zion be the sole place in the state in which ashes could be buried was rejected out of hand. Yad Vashem continued to work decisively to collect ashes and bury them in the floor of the Hall of Remembrance, giving the impressive building specifically, and the Mount of Remembrance more generally, the status of a sacred Jewish and Israeli space.

Chapter 5
The Mount of Remembrance: A New Look

The Hall of Remembrance's inauguration in April 1961 was a significant turning point for Yad Vashem. It was then that the memorial building became a symbolic center of commemoration, a status it maintained for many years – until 2005, when it was replaced by the new historical museum. The Mount of Remembrance now attracted many more visitors; in 1964, for example, nearly one hundred thousand people visited Yad Vashem, roughly half of them tourists.[1] These number continued to rise throughout the sixties and seventies.

Yad Vashem's desire to highlight the centrality and significance of the site within the Israeli and Jewish public began to be realized, shifting it from its previous position on the margins of Israeli society. It became the central state venue for Holocaust remembrance. Each year, initially on the evening that closed Holocaust Martyrs' and Heroes' Remembrance Day and, later on, on the evening that opened the day, a state ceremony was held; the country's leaders, heads of survivors' organizations, and others were invited. The assembly plaza in front of the Hall of Remembrance was at times too small to hold the abundant crowds. The Mount of Remembrance and the Hall of Remembrance were now part of heads of states' official visits to Israel; when they arrived at Yad Vashem after Mount Herzl, they kindled the eternal flame and signed a special document.[2]

But the shaping of the Mount of Remembrance did not end with the Hall of Remembrance; many elements were yet to be built, and questions remained. These related to the function and place of the synagogue at Yad Vashem; the place that would be given to the commemoration of heroism, after the plan to build a dedicated hall was abandoned; the institution's desire to build a fitting space in which exhibits and displays could be presented; and, finally, the need for a building where the pages of names of Holocaust victims, collected over the years by the institution, could be preserved and shown.[3] But completing construction of the memorial elements now became problematic: in late March 1965, the Claims Conference ceased to transfer funds to Yad Vashem and the Remembrance Authority was forced to seek alternate sources.[4] This financial hurdle was

---

[1] Yad Vashem, *Summary of Meetings*, 10.
[2] CZA, S62/1031, "Protocol of the Limited Public Oversight Committee Adjunct to Yad Vashem," April 14, 1965.
[3] CZA, S64/354/1, "Reports of Visits to Yad Vashem," April 1962.
[4] CZA, S62/1031, "First Session to the Public Committee for Examining Yad Vashem Activities," October 4, 1965.

further compounded by other issues – internal disagreements within the directorate and conflicts between the directorate and external bodies regarding a variety of concepts that were tied to the Holocaust and its commemoration.

The current chapter focuses on the end of construction in the 1960s and 1970s, and details the building of the significant memorial features in Yad Vashem's memorial landscape: the Pillar of Heroism, the Hall of Names, the synagogue, the Avenue of the Righteous among the Nations, the historical museum, and Nathan Rapoport's monument to Holocaust and heroism.

The Heroism Monument

The debate about the future of the heroism monument at Yad Vashem had ceased in mid-1960 due to the disagreement within the directorate and the Building Committee. The dispute was about the place of the memorial monument – whether it should be in the remembrance plaza, as suggested by the architects, or outside of it. The architects attempted to push the directorate to announce a competition for the monument, warning that a delay in its erection was preventing the completion of the assembly plaza's construction.[5] Meanwhile, iron piles that the contractors had left behind, intended to serve as a foundation for the overdue monument, began to rust. These stood as a sort of abstract sculpture at the southwest side of the plaza, signaling to all that the monument to heroism might be built there.[6]

In mid-1961, after the inauguration of the Hall of Remembrance, the directorate was once again free to discuss the subject. In order to infuse "content" into the monument – which many felt was too "naked" and devoid of symbolic meaning – Kubovy suggested that a number of rooms be built next to it. Here the heroism and combat of the Second World War could be depicted in a museal manner, infusing the site with content. But the suggestion was dismissed out of hand by the architects and the members of the Building Committee, who felt that "heroism and Holocaust should not be divided";[7] the "content," they said, would be presented in a different place at Yad Vashem.

---

5 YVA, AM1. 450, Architects to Kubovy, April 4, 1960.
6 "Proposals for the Monument for Heroism to Be Built in the Mount of Remembrance," *Yediot Yad Vashem* 30 (1963), 17.
7 ISA, HZ-4/151, "Protocol of Yad Vashem Directorate Meeting," December 26, 1961.

The directorate announced a competition, and listed its conditions:

> The monument must symbolize the courage of the Jews during the Holocaust, who gave their lives for their nation in holiness and purity, and their displays of heroism and steadfast honor in the ghettos, in the camps, underground, in the forests, and in the armies of the nations in their fight against the Nazis and their helpers, without detailing the different ways in which the heroism was expressed.

The instructions emphasized that the monument must be designed vertically, "rising to great heights" – twenty-five or thirty meters – so that it could be seen from afar.[8]

At the end of 1962, forty-one artists submitted their proposals for a heroism monument. A committee selected for the task met and judged the proposals, which were presented anonymously. After determining that the monument must appeal "to the entire nation, to all of Israel," the committee chose to filter out unsuitable proposals, including ones that used figures or figurative art.[9]

The judges' panel chose three standout proposals. On number 34, they noted the nice sculptural idea that expressed power and heroism; the proposed tower's "transparency" was very effective. Proposal 35 reached second place; it was "an original and impressive idea that is tied to the history of the Jewish nation. A fine sculptural solution [that has] a successful interplay of light and shadow," but at the same time, a concern was voiced that "the [proposed] structure will overshadow the existing buildings with its power." On proposal 12, chosen with a small majority, it was stated: "The monument expresses the subject of heroism well. The concrete wall expresses stability. The tower blends well with the landscape. A good selection of materials."[10]

When the envelopes were opened and the names of the artists connected to their creations, it emerged that first-rate Israeli artists had taken part in the contest and not won. Third place went to David Palombo, the sculptor who had created the entry gate to the Hall of Remembrance;[11] second place was awarded to Nathan Rapoport; and in first place was Naomi Henrik,[12] who at the time was involved in the Memorial for the Pioneers of the Road to Jerusalem.

---

8 ISA, GL-3/1786, "Protocol of Yad Vashem Directorate Meeting," July 17, 1962; YVA, AM1 348, "Exhibition of the Proposals for the Monument for Heroism to Be Built on the Mount of Remembrance," January 16–February 15, 1963.
9 YVA, Protocols of Yad Vashem Directorate Meetings, Protocol of the Board of Directors, January 8, 1963.
10 ISA, GL-3/1299, "Public Competition for the Design of a Monument for Heroism on the Mount of Remembrance," n.d.
11 David Palombo, *David Palombo* (Jerusalem: David Palombo Museum, 1991) [in Hebrew].
12 For photos of the three selected proposals, see: ISA, GL-3/1299.

Figure 24: The winners of the first three places in the competition to design the heroism monument at Yad Vashem. David Palombo and Nathan Rapoport's proposals were rejected and that of Naomi Henrik (right), winner of the competition, was accepted. (ISA, Unknown photographer).

The tower proposed by Henrik was divided in two lengthwise using a cement wall. This wall rose between the two parallel narrow walls, dividing them so that on either side only the section of one wall could be seen. Between the light-colored pillars, a kind of "wild" metal lattice with metal bands twisted together was planned. These bands also filled the plaza at the foot of the tower. Their symbolic purpose was to "hinder" easy access for the visitors to the tower itself and to increase a sense of unease, a feeling that made people "symbolic partners in the desperate struggle they represent."

The dark rails symbolized the Holocaust; the light-colored concrete tower rising to a height of more than thirty meters above them represented heroism. "In contrast with heroism that contains some of the hope for triumph, the monument comes to express heroism that contains the spiritual elevation of withstanding pain," she wrote,[13] explaining that what had accompanied her in preparing the monument, split and cut through in its entirety, was the memory of the biblical description of the war against the Amalekites. "In a tower that is surrounded by struggling bodies and that rises and opens to above I visualized seeing the raised hands [of Moses] which turned the scales in the campaign," she explained, and added that the borders of the "narrow and very tall" remembrance tower that she proposed were "[intentionally] refined to express restraint."

---

[13] YVA, AM1 348, "Exhibition of the Proposals for the Monument for Heroism to Be Built on the Mount of Remembrance," January 16–February 15, 1963.

These attributes and the fact that it was "in effect enclosed with straight lines meant to inspire the feeling that the pain expressed by the slashes in the body of the tower remains concentrated and stifled within it with no outlet" drew the attention of the judges,[14] who noted that the first-place winner was distinguished by "a lack of immensity, a leap upwards from a thicket of barbed wire, 'heroism in adversity,' while giving expression to the idea using a broken tower."[15]

The process of selecting an artist to establish the heroism monument at Yad Vashem had thus come to its close. Recommending a number of changes to the proposed monument, the judges' panel gave Henrik its blessing. However, it became clear that the monument that had been chosen aroused doubts and question marks within Yad Vashem's directorate. In one meeting, some asked that Henrik's explanatory words, which had accompanied her proposal, be read so that they could understand her artistic intention. A sense of dissatisfaction from the selection led some to ask whether Yad Vashem had committed to accepting the proposal. "I am full of fear," said Yaakov Sarid, as "this monument must symbolize the Holocaust [like so] to the entire world and millions of people will come to this [Henrik's] monument to whom this monument will not say anything without the words of explanation we have just heard." "Is there another court?" he asked; he hinted that perhaps it would be possible to abandon the choice, suggesting that "a specialist in Holocaust subjects" be invited to give an opinion about the monument and to ask about whether it was fit to express the idea of heroism at all. In order to escape discomfiture, Kubovy suggested that the question of the monument's suitability be checked by presenting it to the populace, to see whether it could capture the hearts of the public.[16]

Models of the monuments, including Henrik's, were in fact presented at an exhibit held on the Mount of Remembrance that was seen by many,[17] but the directorate had a hard time drawing conclusions. Kubovy ruled that "we [Yad Vashem's directorate] must surround it [Henrik's monument] with interpretation and explanation, and our understanding will infect the public."

---

14 ISA, GL-3/1299, "Public Competition for the Design of a Monument for Heroism on the Mount of Remembrance."
15 YVA, Protocols of Yad Vashem Directorate Meetings, Protocol of the Board of Directors, January 8, 1963.
16 Ibid.
17 YVA, AM1 348, "Exhibition of the Proposals for the Monument for Heroism to Be Built on the Mount of Remembrance," January 16–February 15, 1963; "Exhibition of the Models for the Monument of Heroism Opened in Jerusalem," *Davar*, February 7, 1963.

Indeed, in mid-February 1963, when Yad Vashem's Fifth World Council convened, Kubovy announced Henrik's triumph in the competition and his confidence that the tower she had proposed would become "a symbol of the capital [Jerusalem] that has been reestablished by the remnants of the prisoners of Zion of various kinds." Kubovy permitted himself to ask those present a kind of rhetorical question: Might they "see the erection of the monument and the completion of the existing buildings as the end of our work?" He wished to indicate that an important and significant phase of the process had been realized. In reality, the road to building the monument would still be a long and complicated one in many respects.[18]

Many of the directorate's members felt that Yad Vashem had erred and that Henrik's artistic-sculptural memorial pillar should not be built. In the blueprints, the architects had placed a simple vertical pillar in the central plaza, representing to the decision-makers the architecturally simple shape of the memorial monument. In reality, the pillar that was chosen was more of a sculpture and work of art than an architectural unit. The rounded lines of the monument, the materials it was meant to be built of, and primarily the artistic complexity – none of them accorded with the right-angled architectural line of the assembly plaza and the Hall of Remembrance. This only served to reinforce the opinion that had already been voiced: Henrik's monument should be moved rather than being built within the square. The new location discussed was the hill to the east of the Hall of Remembrance, in the area between the assembly plaza and the archive and administration building – a place where Moshe Safdie's Children's Memorial would later be built.[19] But now a problem arose with Henrik, who insisted that the tower she had planned stand in its intended space, in the assembly plaza.

It seemed that the only solution was another competition, but Kubovy warned the directorate against doing Henrik an injustice. "If we cancel the competition, it is not only an issue of a public storm," he stated, but also a personal slight to the artist. He pointed out the absurdity that had been created: "An artist was crowned by the judges and afterwards by Yad Vashem's directorate and suddenly we will come with a second competition in which none of the prize-winners [Palombo, Rapoport, or Henrik] can submit proposals."

At the end of 1963, Yad Vashem's directorate resolved to establish another committee, which would rule on the heroism monument's location: Should it

---

[18] CZA, S62/1031, "Protocol of the Sixth Session, Fifth Council Meeting," February 19, 1963.
[19] Moshe Safdie, *Jerusalem: The Future of the Past* (Montreal: Optimum Pub. International, 1989), 195–97.

be built in the assembly plaza, on the hill suggested by Kubovy, or perhaps elsewhere on the Mount of Remembrance?[20] The committee members toured the mount, met with some of the directorate members, and examined the different proposals that had been raised for the monument's location. The possibility of erecting it in the assembly plaza was dismissed, as was the proposal that it be positioned on the hill between the plaza and the archive and administration building. The possibility of setting it on the hill to the west of the plaza was also rejected; it would, it was feared, create a "new focus" on the Mount of Remembrance. The committee decided that the monument should be built outside of the plaza, beyond the synagogue. In order that the monument not rise too high above the assembly plaza and Hall of Remembrance, they suggested that its foundations be lower than the plaza.[21]

But Yad Vashem's directorate ultimately chose to build the monument to the east of the assembly plaza in any event, atop the mount's highest peak,[22] and on 27 Nisan 1964 a cornerstone ceremony was held. The founding scroll that was buried there was signed by Abba Eban, Kubovy, Jerusalem mayor Mordechai Ish-Shalom, and representatives of partisans' organizations.[23] In his speech, Kubovy emphasized that the ceremony and the monument constituted "an additional tier in the framework of bestowing the Holocaust's lessons and the binding work of the memorial buildings on the Mount of Remembrance." He mentioned the delay in building the monument, but felt that "there was no escaping the fundamental internal disagreement over the meaning of the concept of heroism in our consciousness in general, and in the days of horror in particular. It was necessary for us to arrive at today's occasion mentally prepared to give the concept general instruction as far as possible."[24] Miriam Kubovy, his wife, published a poem, "The Tower of Heroism," describing how Holocaust survivors who display "the remains of heroism, the remains of hope, and tattered faith" collect these fragments "and solder them, and unite them into one wave: surely it is the heroism tower. And this sign shall wave over the Judean mountains; so that a child as one of

---

20 ISA, GL-6/1423, "Directorate Meeting Held in Beit Hillel," December 3, 1963.
21 ISA, GL-6/1423, "Committee for Locating a Site for the Monument of Heroism on the Mount of Remembrance," n.d.
22 ISA, GL-7/1423, "Directorate Meeting," February 11, 1964.
23 "People of Israel Commemorate the Holocaust," *Davar*, April 10, 1964; for photos of the ceremony, see: YVA, 5330/295.
24 YVA, AM1 433, "'Meaningful and Multicolored Heroism,' Kubovy's Speech during Ceremony in Yad Vashem," April 9, 1964.

little faith should know, so that the city shall watch it, over the valley light will spread – until forever, from the sanctum of forgetting."²⁵

At the end of 1964, with construction on the monument still not underway, Yad Vashem's directorate chose to sever ties with Henrik, using various pretenses in order to rescind her victory.²⁶ Negotiations with Henrik began in 1966, with the directorate attempting to convince her to withdraw her proposal. The pretext given was that it exceeded the expected budget. Her demand that she be compensated for the plan not being executed was rejected.²⁷

In parallel, Yad Vashem's directorate turned to El-Hanani and asked that he and his partner, Nissan Cnaan, take on the task of designing the monument. But as El-Hanani and Cnaan had no experience in plastic arts, they asked young artist Buky Schwartz to work with them. Schwartz had competed to plan the memorial tower in the early sixties and had not won.

In early January 1967, El-Hanani and his partners presented a model of the monument based on Schwartz's creation. They suggested erecting a triangular pillar, built of three concave, stainless steel surfaces, at the highest point on the Mount of Remembrance. A path would lead visitors from the Hall of Remembrance to the monument, which would be their final destination before leaving Yad Vashem. It was suggested that the pillar be positioned in the center of a plaza hewn in an opening in the hill, where memorial ceremonies in honor of fighters and heroes could be held. It was further proposed that on either side of the pillar, which would rise more than twenty meters in height, concrete walls would be built, dedicated symbolically to the two types of forces that had battled the Nazis: those who had fought in the Allied armies and those Jews who had combated the Nazis clandestinely.²⁸

The architects proposed writing "To the nation's volunteers" in the languages of the nations in whose armies Jews had fought on the concrete walls around the pillar, a proposal that stirred much opposition. No less fraught was the argument about the word "Remember" (*Zakhor*), which El-Hanani suggested be written at the pillar's top. Some members of the directorate claimed that this word was tied specifically to extermination and not heroism. Instead of "Remember what Amalek did to you" (Deut. 25:17), some suggested writing atop the pillar "To Israel's heroism" (*li-gvurat Yisrael*), and even asked to consult with Masada excavator Yigael Yadin, to ask him for help finding a fitting expression that would tie Yad

---

25 Miriam Kubovy, "Tower of Heroism," *Davar*, April 5, 1967.
26 ISA, GL-7/13387, I. Semet to Y. Gal-Ezer, April 5, 1967.
27 YVA, AM3 868 V, Chaim Krongold to Yad Vashem, October 27, 1966; YVA, AM3 868 V, Aharon Paritzki to Erwin Shaul Shimron, February 7, 1969.
28 YVA, photo number 71830.

Vashem to the fortitude of Masada's warriors.[29] Ultimately, Shmuel Spector's suggestion to write nothing at the top of the pillar was adopted. "Our generation is being raised on art that expresses itself with no words . . . no word can encompass everything and any verse will entangle us with interpretation. Any inscription on the façade in different languages will only lead to complications."[30]

Later, a decision was made to note on the lower part of the pillar that the monument was dedicated in memory of "those who rebelled in the camps and ghettos, fought in the woods, in the underground and with the Allied forces; braved their way to *Eretz Israel*; and those who died sanctifying the name of God." Further added, in slightly bigger letters, was the inscription "For eternal life (*le-hayei olamim*)." This formulation attests to the disagreement that erupted between the directorate's members, some of whom claimed that those who perished in the Holocaust should have a part in the monument and not just the fighters. The decision made was that the inscriptions should relate primarily to active displays of bravery but that nonetheless they would also make mention of "the sanctifiers of the name (*mekadshei ha-shem*)," referring to the victims. Parallel metal inscriptions were made in English, French, and Yiddish and placed at the foot of the monument.[31]

The Pillar of Heroism was officially inaugurated on March 8, 1970, when the first global conference of Jewish fighters in the Second World War was held on the Mount of Remembrance.[32] At the ceremony, a call to revolt originally composed in the Vilna Ghetto was read aloud and Chief Education Officer Colonel Yitzhak Arad (who also served on Yad Vashem's directorate and would later be appointed the institution's chairman) noted in his speech how "this pillar will symbolize Jewish bravery in all generations and in our day."[33] There were those who suggested that Arad's words and the completion of the monument should be tied to the atmosphere at the time in the State of Israel, after Israel's victory in the Six-Day War.[34] But, as is clear, the monument's erection in 1970

---

29 Zerubavel, "The Death."
30 YVA, Protocols of Yad Vashem Directorate Meetings, Protocol of the Board of Directors, January 3, 1967.
31 YVA, Protocols of Yad Vashem Directorate Meetings, Protocol of the Board of Directors, January 26, 1968; Photo of the monument: YVA, photo number 28723.
32 Buky Schwartz, "Monument of Bravery," *KAV* 8 (1968): 59–60 [in Hebrew].
33 "Inauguration Ceremony of the Pillar of Heroism," *Yediot Yad Vashem: Events, Activities, and Publications* 2 (1970), 2.
34 Mooli Brog, "Besieged within Walls of Memory," *Alpayim* 14 (1997), 149 [in Hebrew].

Figure 25: The Pillar of Heroism and the memorial plaza at its base (YVA, Unknown photographer).

on the Mount of Remembrance was really the completion of a bureaucratic process that had taken many years, a process that had begun in 1942.

While it was true that heroism had now found its place in the landscape of the Mount of Remembrance, its architectural expression was very different from what Shenhavi had envisioned. The heroism "compound" at Yad Vashem stood out in its marginality relative to the Hall of Remembrance. It was built outside of the "sanctified" temenos and distanced from the hall, which was seen by many as one of Israeli architectural feats. The Pillar of Heroism was perceived by visitors as nothing more than a "chimney-like concrete pillar,"[35] whose symbolism many had a hard time accepting.

---

35 KMHA, S-29, 5, no writer, n.d.

Yad Vashem's Synagogue

The survey prepared in advance of the World Council assembly in late 1958 proudly laid out the plan for the construction and development of Yad Vashem; its synagogue was mentioned in the same breath as the Hall of the Remembrance and remembrance tower.[36] But in the council's discussions, crucial differences of opinion surfaced between the participants and the institution's directorate as to the objective of the Remembrance Authority in general and regarding the building plan in particular. Shenhavi, one of the directorate's most prominent opponents, called the architects' plan "a disgrace."[37]

Yad Vashem's directorate and the architects viewed the synagogue as an important component in the mount's development plan. Its construction was planned for the northwestern side of the assembly plaza, with a staircase leading to the sunken courtyard before it. Its black southern-eastern wall, a shrine to the synagogues that had been destroyed in Europe, would symbolize the horrors of the Holocaust; the ark and eternal flame would also be located there. A raised symbolic bima (prayer platform) would stand in the center of the hall; a women's gallery would be positioned near the entrance.[38]

But the emerging look of the synagogue, both inside and out, troubled the directorate's members. Aside from a memorial to the destroyed synagogues in Europe, they hoped that Yad Vashem's synagogue would also serve as a place of remembrance for the cemeteries that had been destroyed, for the yeshivot and houses of religious study "with their internal shape and the vestiges of the ritual articles that were desecrated." Some suggested using the Ministry of Foreign Affairs to seek furniture from Italy or other European locations that could be integrated in the synagogue.[39] Others felt that the synagogue "must be of our time because it is meant for the coming years, for the coming generations."[40]

In August 1963, Kubovy surprised Yad Vashem's directorate when he wondered why a synagogue was necessary on the Mount of Remembrance to begin with. The simple hall that was being built as a synagogue, he asserted, was far from serving as a real symbol of the destroyed synagogues. If the original intent

---

36 CZA, S60/5491, "Summary of Yad Vashem Activities Submitted to Yad Vashem World Council," June 1, 1958; on Yad Vashem's synagogue see: Doron Bar, "A Prayer House or a Memorial for the Holocaust? The Debate Over Yad Vashem's Synagogue, 1945–1964," *Yad Vashem Studies* 43 (2015): 179–209.
37 HHA, 3–95. 19 (1), "Protocol of Yad Vashem Directorate Meeting," September 26, 1958.
38 YVA, AM1 343, "Protocol of Building Committee Meeting," December 23, 1958.
39 ISA, HZ-4/151, "Protocol of Directorate Meeting," December 26, 1961.
40 ISA, GL-3/13346, "Building Committee Meeting," May 17, 1960.

had been that the synagogue would express "religious life and religious sentiment," the Hall of Remembrance already filled those functions.[41] When the planning and construction of the synagogue had begun, "the Hall of Remembrance did not yet have the character that it now has and there was no existing Hall of Remembrance when traditional memorial services were discussed." But, now, he asked, when the hall had become a place in which this type of activity took place, what was the purpose of another building whose entire function was commemorating and immortalizing Jewish communities?[42] Kubovy suggested using the structure meant for the synagogue to display exhibits.

Kubovy's proposal was met with fierce opposition by the directorate. "The complex of buildings on the Mount of Remembrance constitutes one composition which is completed by one building," warned Shatner, and determined that if the synagogue were not built, the Hall of Remembrance would need to contain the "idea" of the synagogue. Bialer noted that the idea of a synagogue at Yad Vashem had predated the idea of establishing a museum, and thus had "precedence" and greater importance. He added that the synagogue was a monument to destroyed synagogues "and it is impossible to not establish it." Some directorate members were convinced that part of the visiting public really needed a synagogue in which they could express their emotions. Ultimately, Kubovy's suggestion of tabling its construction was removed from the agenda. Nonetheless, the question of the synagogue's content remained. The architects, it was decided, would attempt to recreate the image of European synagogues; it would serve both as an active synagogue and as a monument to the synagogues that had been destroyed in Europe.

The decision was only partially executed. In advance of the synagogue's inauguration on the Hebrew anniversary of Kristallnacht, 15 Heshvan 1964, the construction was completed and the furniture brought in – but it did not evoke Europe at all. More than anything, the simple building projected Israeliness and localness. Like the Hall of Remembrance across from it, the synagogue made use of a concrete ceiling, brutalist in architectural style, which adorned the building both inside and out. A thin belt of windows separated the building's walls from its concrete ceiling. Like the nearby Hall of Remembrance, the synagogue was also characterized by architectural abstraction; it contained no memorial components or hints to the past. The synagogue's walls were intentionally left exposed, with the ceiling floating above them. The bima was erected at the

---

41 YVA, Protocols of Yad Vashem Directorate Meetings, Protocol of the Board of Directors, August 13, 1963.
42 ISA, GL-7/1423, "Directorate Meeting," February 11, 1964.

center of the building, like in Eastern synagogues, while the prayer leader's stand was near the ark, in Ashkenazic tradition. Simple benches lay across the long building and the symbolic and slightly raised women's gallery was placed near the building's entrance.[43]

Figure 26: Yad Vashem's synagogue (YVA, Unknown photographer).

The synagogue's inauguration ceremony was modest. It opened with a prayer in the Hall of Remembrance, from which a procession of Torah scrolls left for the new synagogue, where a Torah scroll that had been brought from the Łódź Ghetto was deposited in the ark. Kubovy, who spoke at the ceremony, noted that "We are inaugurating here today a small sanctuary (*mikdash me'at*) which, even though it was not built of the stones and dirt of synagogues and houses of religious study that were destroyed, will be illuminated by the hidden light of tens of thousands of tabernacles that our nation built to its God in the European Diaspora." He explained that the synagogue was built modestly, as

> we wished to provide in it a shelter for the weary soul and a place for man to commune with himself. The Mount of Remembrance is a stormy, noisy place and its experiences are

---

[43] YVA, photo number 5432/24.

experiences of pain, tempest, and rage, such that at times the person who comes on a pilgrimage here is filled with anxiety lest his faith should fail and the need to be alone and commune with himself arises in him. In this sanctuary he will sit. Here he will contemplate the whys and wherefores of the great destruction that befell us and the personal catastrophe that befell him.[44]

Despite the festivity, Yad Vashem's heads had difficulty infusing the synagogue with meaning in the months that followed, and it stood rather neglected. The hopes that the synagogue would become a place in which survivors could remember their relatives in a personal and traditional manner were dashed. Later, too, during the years of Yad Vashem's activity, the synagogue was not able to take on a significant role in the memorial landscape. The survivors' memorial ceremonies were generally held in the Hall of Remembrance and the expectations that the synagogue would attract many visitors were never realized. In contrast with the Chamber of the Holocaust, which gave the *landsmannschaften* an experience of traditional Jewish remembrance, the synagogue at Yad Vashem was never able to fulfill their religious needs. Mount Zion had a place where candles could be lit, where prayers and Mishnah learning could be held individually or communally; the synagogue did not suit this need, and the hall gradually became a space of assembly, lectures, and other ceremonies.

In the mid-nineties, another synagogue was established at Yad Vashem, one that primarily served the employees. The original synagogue became a workshop and warehouse. In 2005, a third synagogue was inaugurated at Yad Vashem, and it serves as both a memorial site and a place of worship.

The Avenue of the Righteous among the Nations

Afforestation, planting, and gardens had always held a central place in Yad Vashem's designs. Forests were mentioned in each stage of planning before the decision to establish the institution in Jerusalem, and constituted an important part of the perception of remembrance. The forests were slated to be planted by the JNF within its partnership with Yad Vashem.

Even after the Mount of Remembrance was selected as Yad Vashem's location, afforestation and planting still played a vital role. "What more than the tree and greenery, than flora and making areas of stone into flourishing gardens and fresh forests, can serve this type of purpose?" Shenhavi asked when speaking to the

---

[44] YVA, AM1 433, Kubovy's speech during inauguration ceremony of Yad Vashem's synagogue at the Mount of Remembrance, October 21, 1964.

architects in 1954. Shenhavi wished to surround the buildings, the gardens, and the parks with a forest that would cover the Mount of Remembrance's slopes.[45]

In 1954, at the recommendation of the architects and with Weitz's encouragement, Lipa Yahalom was selected as the gardener responsible for Yad Vashem's landscaping; he was later joined by Dan Tzur.[46] In late 1954, the two prepared a plan for planting that included dozens of types of trees and bushes.[47] The JNF also intended to sow tens of thousands of trees on the slopes of the mount.[48]

In reality, the Mount of Remembrance remained bare, entirely devoid of greenery. It was that way at the cornerstone ceremony in 1954 and it was still empty when the Hall of Remembrance was inaugurated in 1961; the rocky fields were noticeably stark around the assembly plaza.

The issue of afforestation and the beautification of Yad Vashem was tied to a decision to plant trees on the mount that would be dedicated to the righteous among the nations. In the initial plans for Yad Vashem, both in the Ramat Rachel version and in the earlier blueprints for the Mount of Remembrance, a monument had been dedicated to the righteous among the nations.[49] But the idea that one of the structures on the mount would be devoted to those who had saved Jews faded over time and when the Hall of Remembrance was inaugurated in 1961 there was no trace of it.

The solution found – which tidily united the desire to immortalize those who had rescued Jews, the task of the Mount of Remembrance's beautification, and the Zionist-Israeli ethos of "making the desert bloom" – was the planting of a boulevard of trees in honor and memory of those who had rescued Jews. At first, Yad Vashem's heads hoped to cooperate with the JNF, which had planned to plant the "Righteous among the Nations Forest" on the slopes of the Mount of Remembrance.[50] But as planting this forest was meant to take many years,

---

45 HHA, 3–95. 15 (6), Sharon to Shenhavi, December 10, 1954.
46 ISA, GL-10/13362, Sharon to Yad Vashem, October 31, 1954. The contract between Lipa Yahalom and Dan Tzur and Yad Vashem was signed in 1955. The two were later selected by Yad Vashem to plan the Valley of the (Destroyed) Communities, a monument that was inaugurated in 1992 in the western part of the Mount of Remembrance. On their vast activity in designing Israel's landscape, see: Nurit Lissovsky and Diana Dolev, eds., *Arcadia: The Gardens of Lipa Yahalom and Dan Zur* (Tel Aviv: Babel, 2012) [in Hebrew].
47 HHA, 3–95. 17 (2), "Protocol of Building and Planning Committee," February 11, 1955; Lissovsky and Dolev, *Arcadia*, 512–13.
48 YVA, AM1 448, "Summary of Building Committee Decisions," July 17, 1955.
49 YVA, AM1 36, Shenhavi's words during a conference for teachers sent to teach in the Diaspora, May 7, 1947.
50 ISA, GL-3/1786, "Protocol of Yad Vashem Directorate Meeting," May 15, 1962.

Yad Vashem decided to begin with a more modest activity, and to plant single trees.

A small inauguration ceremony for the Avenue of the Righteous among the Nations was held on 27 Nisan 1962 with Foreign Minister Golda Meir in attendance,[51] and the plan was to plant trees gradually along the main path leading to the memorial compound. During the ceremony, the avenue's founding scroll was buried and twelve symbolic trees planted, eleven of them by rescuers from different places in Europe and from Israel.

This ceremony constituted the beginning of a tradition that extended for many years. From mid-1962, planting ceremonies were held at Yad Vashem in the presence of rescuers; signs were affixed at the foot of the trees, noting their names and the countries in which they had acted.[52]

Figure 27: Johannes Bogaard, a Dutch farmer who hid Jews on his farm during the Second World War, plants a tree on the Avenue of the Righteous among the Nations, 1964 (YVA, Unknown photographer).

---

51 ISA, GL-3/1786, "Protocol of Yad Vashem Directorate Meeting," July 17, 1962.
52 CZA, S61/327, "Protocol of Directorate Meeting," May 15, 1962; "Oscar Schindler Plants a Tree in the Avenue of the Righteous among the Nations," *Davar*, May 10, 1962.

In early 1963, a commission for the righteous among the nations was formed at Yad Vashem; it was tasked with determining which rescuers were worthy of note.[53] Over the sixties, between ten and fifteen planting ceremonies were held annually and thus an impressive band of trees – primarily carob – formed, becoming a boulevard.[54] In the mid-seventies, an additional path was laid out; it led visitors to the entrance to the new museum and later to the Warsaw Ghetto Square. This change made it possible to redefine the planting areas, and the trees now blossomed along both paved pathways.[55]

The Hall of Names

The Hall of Names, in which Yad Vashem preserved and displayed pages of testimony, was a central component added to the memorial landscape in the mid-sixties. Until that point, a fitting place had not been found for the witness pages and martyrs' books. The goal of the pages was to turn the huge collective mass of millions into individuals and names and, in that way, to immortalize them. But it was only in this period that a solution was found: the Hall of Names, in which the pages were curated.

Efforts to record the names of those who had died – to document and preserve – had begun in the forties. In the plan that Shenhavi submitted to the JNF heads in 1943, he proposed that the "memorial books," with the names of those who had perished, be deposited in a "pavilion of the missing" built at Yad Vashem.[56] This idea was expressed in other architectural blueprints throughout the years as well, where a place was set aside for the "martyrs' books." The Ramat Rachel plan and early ideas for the Mount of Remembrance contained a "card room" at the entrance to the memorial compound, where visitors would be able to add the names of their loved ones to immortalize them.[57]

The gathering of names began immediately with the end of the Second World War. Despite many hurdles, Yad Vashem's people were able to advance; they collected many lists and names of those who had perished. It was only

---

53 Kobi Kabalek, "The Commemoration before the Commemoration: Yad Vashem and the Righteous among the Nations, 1945–1963," *Yad Vashem Studies* 39, no. 1 (2011): 169–211.
54 CAHJP, CC 18536, "Yad Vashem – Activities during 1963/1964;" "Planting Trees in the Avenue of the Righteous Among the Nations," *Yediot Yad Vashem* 34 (1964), 61.
55 KMHA, S-29, 4, M. Gavrieli, n.d.
56 HHA, 3–95. 14 (2), Shenhavi, "Proposal," January 18, 1943.
57 CZA, S62/1031, "Protocol of the Public Committee adjunct to Yad Vashem Headed by Aryeh Pincus," May 24, 1965.

natural that after the Yad Vashem Law was passed and with the founding of the Remembrance Authority the institution's heads would focus on the subject. In early 1954, Yad Vashem's directorate decided that the "year of recording the Holocaust's victims and fighters" would begin on 27 Nisan. Supreme Court Judge Moshe Zilberg helmed the national committee founded for this purpose; it also contained people such as Abba Kovner, Izaak Grünbaum, and Marc Dworzecki.

Pages of testimony were available at Yad Vashem's offices in Jerusalem, Tel Aviv, and Haifa, and they were distributed in Israel and the Diaspora. Notices in newspapers encouraged relatives of victims to complete pages and agents made home visits to help. The Remembrance Authority joined forces with the Chief Rabbinate, the IDF, regional council heads, the Ministry of Education, and the Israel Postal Company and encouraged the Israeli public to register the names of its loved ones. By the end of 1955, more than 700,000 pages of testimony had been distributed – though the success was partial: only 150,000 completed pages were returned to the Remembrance Authority.[58]

The collection and storage of the pages of testimony, it soon emerged, were problematic. While in previous plans a place of honor had been dedicated for the storage and display of the pages, the current blueprints for the Mount of Remembrance no longer held such a building. One of the rooms on the second floor of the archive and administration building was converted to a "Hall of Names" and the pages of testimony were preserved there in special boxes. This form of storage was challenging both for Yad Vashem's team and for visitors searching for the names of their loved ones.[59]

The change in the building plan was tied to the opposition of the Claims Conference's heads to funding the collection of the names. They objected to the assertion that the State of Israel had a moral and practical responsibility to all Jews who had perished in the Holocaust, whose names Yad Vashem wished to immortalize on the Mount of Remembrance.[60] The institution may have been authorized by the Knesset in 1953 to grant the victims honorary citizenship, but the Conference's people, primarily the non-Zionists, firmly opposed it and conditioned the signing of the contract with the Remembrance Authority on their money not funding the collection of victims' names – a task that, for Yad Vashem, was one of the authority's most important objectives.[61] To this was added a fear that the number of names Yad Vashem would succeed in collecting

---

58 "Registration Enterprise," *Yediot Yad Vashem* 7 (1956), 19.
59 The Hall of Names appears in a 1969 film, *Kaddisch nach Einem Lebenden*, YVA, film archive, 58639.
60 Zweig, "Politics of Commemoration," 162–64.
61 Ibid., 128–46.

would be low, further casting doubt on the legitimacy of stipulating that six million Jews had been killed in the Holocaust.[62]

No small number of visitors to the Mount of Remembrance made note of the perceptible difference between the investment that had been made in collecting names and the undignified way in which they were preserved. "It makes no sense," Natan Eck stated, "to continue registering pages of testimony for the tens and hundreds of thousands if they remain buried in storage spaces in the future as well." He proposed setting aside a space on the Mount of Remembrance, perhaps a pavilion, and temporarily housing the prepared pages of testimony there. "Jews shall come and see with their own eyes the corners that were allotted for the lands and communities of their origin. The visitors will see not only what is there but also what is not there – and there is no more efficient form of educational publicity and influence than this view," he felt.[63]

In 1959, Yad Vashem's directorate found time to discuss the pages of testimony, after some hundreds of thousands of them had accumulated in storage. The discussion dealt with a variety of questions – preparing a fitting format for the pages of testimony; whether the card catalogue should be ordered by community, country, or alphabet; the problem of double pages; and the connection between these pages and the martyrs' books.[64] Most of the attention was devoted to the question of mechanizing the registry in a card catalogue, computer, or manual form. Kubovy warned that "We must not do a job that does not stand the test of history," and determined that "the question of the six million will not leave the agenda for many generations."[65]

Despite the progress on the subject, the question of a place for preserving and displaying the pages of testimony on the Mount of Remembrance had not yet been resolved. Some of the directorate members felt that they could be preserved in a special cupboard in the Hall of Remembrance, where visitors could examine the names.[66] This issue further underscored the sense that the planning of the Hall of Remembrance was monumental and "too cold." This "vacuum," some thought, could be filled using the martyrs' books, which would add "warmth to the building's interior." "The Hall of Remembrance must be universal

---

[62] Yad Vashem Administrative Archive, "Summary of Meetings of the Public Committee for Examining Yad Vashem's Activities," Jerusalem, 1966, 7.
[63] CAHJP, CC 18547, Natan Eck to various addressees, August 2, 1955; "Yad Vashem Has Registered Names of 750,000 Holocaust Victims," *Davar*, January 1, 1957.
[64] HHA, 3–95. 19 (1), "Protocol of Yad Vashem Directorate Meeting," July 7, 1959.
[65] HHA, 3–95. 19 (1), "Protocol of Yad Vashem Directorate Meeting," July 28, 1959.
[66] HHA, 3–95. 19 (1), "Protocol of Yad Vashem Directorate Meeting," June 23, 1959.

and monumental," other directorate members responded; "there is no value to a symbol within the symbol." El-Hanani dismissed the possibility that an "intimate spirit and place for communion" could be created within the Hall of Remembrance. He further noted that if the martyrs' books were put there for the public to read, there would be a need to bring in chairs and tables. "In the Hall of Remembrance people [only] pass through," he stated.[67]

This discussion led to a decision, made in July 1959, to dedicate a special building to preserving the pages of testimony and memorial books.[68] The place selected for the purpose was at the western side of the assembly plaza, just south of the planned synagogue. The transfer of the synagogue to this part of the Mount of Remembrance created a building addition on the western side of the plaza, only part of which had been filled with construction. The directorate therefore decided that an area of seven hundred square meters would be covered and the place would be dedicated to displaying the martyrs' books.[69] But some members of the directorate disagreed with the location selected; they felt that the space set aside was too small and it would look like no more than a hallway. A dispute about the storage of the card catalogue with the names of the victims arose: Should it be in the hall with the martyrs' books or close to the entrance to the Mount of Remembrance?[70]

The discussion about this issue was bound up with the expected visitors' route on the Mount of Remembrance and where the martyrs' books' hall would be located. Would it belong to the "historical" and educational part of Yad Vashem or to the commemorative area? The directorate felt that there were two trends among visitors to the Mount of Remembrance that should be distinguished – those who were interested in "the history about the Holocaust and its commemoration," that is, the museum and the archive, and those who wished to visit the remembrance buildings. The commonly accepted idea at the time was that "most visitors will come for purposes of communion (commemoration) and not for historical research." El-Hanani felt the same way, claiming that only some people would come to the planned museum, as a visit there "will take much time for the tourist whose goal is different." But Kubovy felt that "two planes in the commemorative area" had been formed on the Mount of Remembrance already, "the plane of quiet and communion, the plane of 'remove your shoes'" in which the Hall of Remembrance, synagogue, and hall of martyrs'

---

67 HHA, 3–95. 17 (2), "Building Committee Protocol," July 16, 1959.
68 HHA, 3–95. 19 (1), "Protocol of Building Committee Meeting," July 28, 1959.
69 Ibid.
70 ISA, GL-3/13346, "Building Committee Meeting," May 5, 1960.

books would be found, and, across from it, the museum with its exhibits, where it would be impossible "to prevent loud responses and running."[71]

In June 1960, Sharon reported on the emerging internal arrangement of the martyrs' books hall. The elongated hall would be divided into two unequal spaces. The first would be a sort of entryway, its walls designed as two gates and containing large pictures of Auschwitz or the Warsaw Ghetto. In the central hall there would be a long, broad table and, around it, chairs available for visitors who wished to peruse the pages of testimony. Along one wall would be a "stained glass that opens," behind which the martyrs' books would stand.[72]

But much like in other cases discussed in this book, the execution was greatly delayed, primarily due to financial obstacles. Kubovy, reporting to Yad Vashem's public oversight committee in 1964, beat his breast that "we have not yet completed the registry of our dead, we have not yet arranged the pages of testimony we collected, we have not yet begun to edit the martyrs' books." He noted that the room devoted to this purpose was currently being used as an exhibit hall because there were no books of names to display; tens of thousands of Jewish families did not have "the minimal comfort that they can hang on the walls of their apartments," a certificate attesting to the fact that the state had granted their loved ones memorial citizenship.[73]

Meanwhile, the Israeli public grew skeptical about the utility of continuing to collect pages of testimony and names of victims. They defined it as a "sentimental" problem, as "the educational-historical element in pages of testimony is minimal." In 1965, the public oversight committee heard claims that while the pages of testimony are "the sole connection between the individual and those who are no long among the living," the "honorary citizenship has lost its value. It has been more than twenty years. The entire issue is questionable."[74] This spurred the directorate to try to improve the appearance of the Hall of Names, a task that was assigned to architect and exhibit designer Rivka Bar Yehuda Idelson. Bar Yehuda Idelson was asked to determine the proper form for storing the 2,500 boxes in which the pages of testimony would be preserved.[75] At that time, she was busy designing exhibits at Yad Vashem, such as the *Heroism and Rebellion* exhibit that had opened in advance of Holocaust Martyrs' and

---

71 Ibid.
72 YVA, AM1 360, "Building Committee Meeting," June 14, 1960.
73 CZA, S62/1031, "First Meeting of the Public Committee for Examining Yad Vashem Activities," October 4, 1964.
74 Yad Vashem, *Summary of Meetings*, 7.
75 YVA, Protocols of Yad Vashem Directorate Meetings, Protocol of the Board of Directors, November 21, 1967; YVA, November 6, 1968.

Heroes' Remembrance Day in 1969.[76] In order to complete the room's renovation, Yad Vashem solicited a donation from New York philanthropist Leon Jolson. In April 1968, the new Hall of Names was festively inaugurated, and Yad Vashem's employees transferred the pages of testimony that had previously been housed in the administration building. The transfer was exploited to better preserve the pages and reorganize them in phonetic order.[77]

But it soon became clear that the dedicated hall was far from being a true solution to the problem of preserving and presenting the martyrs' books. Not only were claims voiced about the fact that the hall had no "soul"; its location, which had at first seemed fitting to the directorate, was now felt to be terribly problematic. While a number of suggestions to improve the dreary appearance of the hall – a change of lighting, integrating Palombo and Rapoport's artwork there – were raised, these did not bring about the desired change.

The directorate chose to move the hall to the second floor above the synagogue and the old Hall of Names,[78] and at the end of 1973 a tender was published for its construction.[79] The Remembrance Authority's directorate turned to businessmen Ya'akov Meridor and Mila Brenner, who agreed to fund the construction of the new Hall of Names.[80] The construction was completed in June 1975 and the hall was officially inaugurated at the end of 1977.[81]

Black boxes with *Yizkor* written on them, containing the alphabetically ordered pages of testimony, were placed on shelves in cupboards leaning against the hall's elongated eastern wall. Above the cabinets and along the length of the hall were an inscription from the vision of the dry bones, an artistic creation by Zvi Aldubi based on the verses: "I will cause breath to enter you and you shall live again" (Ezek. 37:4); "I will take you . . . and gather you from all the countries, and I will bring you back to your own land" (Ezek. 36:24); "I will people your settlements, and the ruined places shall be rebuilt" (Ezek. 36:33).[82] Three raised stands served visitors seeking the names of victims. Between these stands and the bookcases stood six lamps, shaped as torches or hands raised to the sky.

---

76 "Heroism and Rebellion," *Yediot Yad Vashem: Events, Activities, and Publications* 1 (1969), 5.
77 "'Hall of Names' Inaugurated at Yad Vashem," *Maariv*, April 23, 1968. See also Geva Films, 143, 1968.
78 YVA, Protocols of Yad Vashem Directorate Meetings, Protocol of the Board of Directors, September 17, 1968.
79 ISA, HZ-16/5248, "Hall of Names," December 28, 1973.
80 YVA, AM1 420, Shmuel Bazak to Avraham Yafe, March 3, 1974; Daniela Ran, *Mila Brenner* (Daliyya: Maarechet, 2003) [in Hebrew].
81 Hall of Names photo: YVA, 5432/23; film: *Yad Vashem*, SSJFA, F00098.
82 Miriam Tal, "Sculptor Zvi Aldubi," *TAVI* 11 (1972): 71–75 [in Hebrew].

Figure 28: The Hall of Names (YVA, Unknown photographer).

These threw light on the black ceiling, partially illuminating the dark hall and serving as another element of tribute to the six million who had perished.[83]

The decision to add a story to the existing building and place the Hall of Names there created an aesthetic problem for the assembly plaza, as the "seam" between the building's two floors was noticeable. El-Hanani proposed that the seam be concealed by "pasting" an external inscription that would run the length of the building's eastern façade, facing the plaza. He suggested inviting artist Gdula Ogen, known for her wall reliefs, to "sculpt" it. The inscription was prepared from metal plates on which the verse that held the name of the institution was carried: "I will give them in My house and within My walls a monument (*yad*) and a name (*va-shem*) . . . which shall not perish" (Isa. 56:5).[84] But visitors to the Mount of Remembrance complained about the difficulty of reading the inscription, which, with Jerusalem's challenging climate conditions, was beginning

---

83 YVA, Protocols of Yad Vashem Directorate Meetings, Protocol of the Board of Directors, November 25, 1974.
84 YVA, Protocols of Yad Vashem Directorate Meetings, Protocol of the Board of Directors, July 10, 1972; Photo of the building before adding the second floor and Gdula Ogen's sculpture: CZA, PHO/1365945.

to crumble.[85] In 1978, graphic designer Dan Reisinger was asked to redesign the inscription, which would now be made of a combination of concrete and cast metal. He "stretched" the words along the side of the synagogue and Hall of Names building to create a new sculpture, an inscription whose letters were clear from a distance and which became, in time, one of Yad Vashem's most recognizable trademarks.[86]

The Yad Vashem Museum

Much like the other memorial elements at Yad Vashem, the idea of establishing a museum on the Mount of Remembrance had first been raised in the forties. When Shenhavi published his plan for the memorial enterprise in 1945, he included an exhibition hall whose function was to curate displays related to Jewish history in general and the fate of the Jews in Europe in particular.[87] In order that the visitor to Yad Vashem spend longer there than the time that elapses "between one bus and another," he suggested building a "general exhibition hall" or a "library for the history of the Diaspora – archive and museum," a building that would focus on the period "from the founding of the first Jewish settlement [in the Diaspora] until the day of total destruction."[88]

After the Yad Vashem Law was passed in 1953, the institution's heads returned to the suggestion of building a museum. It was, among other things, a result of the Claims Conference's pressure on Yad Vashem's directorate. Uveeler's stinging criticism of the emerging building plan on the Mount of Remembrance, its noticeable size, and what he viewed as the unnecessary integration of the too-large archive and library were accompanied by his suggestion that Yad Vashem abandon the plan of building two halls and focus on building a museum that could serve as the focus of the visitor's experience. Preferring a conventional plan and practical structures, Uveeler expressed confidence that the Claims Conference would agree to

---

85 ISA, HZ-20/5847, "Protocol of Yad Vashem Board of Trustees Meeting," April 13, 1975.
86 YVA, Protocols of Yad Vashem Directorate Meetings, Protocol of the Board of Directors, March 5, 1978; on Dan Reisinger, see: Adi Englman and Dan Handel, *Dan Reisinger* (Jerusalem: Israel Museum, 2017), 89–190.
87 YVA, AM1 287, Shenhavi, "Yad Vashem for the Diaspora," May 2, 1945; on the development of the museum in Yad Vashem, see: Cohen, *Horror*.
88 KMHA, S-29, 1, Shenhavi, "Presumptions and Numbers Concerning Yad Vashem Plan," February 16, 1947.

fund the establishment of a museum more readily than the building of the abstract and needless halls.[89]

The directorate resolved that a museum would be built only after construction of the archive and administration building, the Hall of Remembrance, and the synagogue was complete – but its function and goals were not defined.[90] "The Yad Vashem Law charges us with establishing memorial enterprises to Jewish displays of bravery," Dinur stated when he spoke before the Remembrance Authority's directorate in 1956, and emphasized that the great dilemma was how to establish these memorial enterprises. "Is it only in books, or only in building? Perhaps in an exhibit and museum?"[91] He did declare that, among the other "institutions and units" on the Mount of Remembrance, a museum would be built in the future; in its initial stages it would be "the museum of the Jewish communities in the period of their struggle and destruction," which would later be expanded to relate to periods before the Holocaust and the rise of Nazism.[92] It was easy for Uveeler to agree: "A hall for the sake of a monument must include within it appropriate content," he stressed, asking that construction be accompanied by an educational goal. His demand was that a museum of the history of "Israel-Europe" be built on the Mount of Remembrance, "a hall with living content" that schoolchildren and youth "from kibbutzim" could visit.[93]

At the opening of the first symposium for planning Yad Vashem that convened in 1956, Dinur noted that the structure on the Mount of Remembrance must be both functional and commemorative. "Our idea," he added, "is that the buildings must be built in such a way that there will be a museum and there will be place for a ledger in which all of the communities will be listed as well as a place that will symbolize them." Most participants in the meeting were actually inclined to separate the different remembrance components and dedicate a discrete building and clear purpose for each. El-Hanani voiced this view when he stated that while the remembrance building must "give form to the disaster and envelop the visitor with the atmosphere of thirty thousand communities and six million or the entire nation of Israel," a second building must have a museal function. "Is it possible to establish it immediately as a museum?" he asked, and stated that it must contain one integral and central element in any event: a list of the victims and communities that had perished. Dinur, disappointed that the participants in the symposium agreed with this tack, was forced

---

89 ISA, HZ-3/151, Uveeler to Dinur, October 30, 1954.
90 ISA, HZ-3/151, "Protocol of Yad Vashem Directorate Meeting," October 31, 1954.
91 ISA, P-27/1976, "Yad Vashem Directorate Meeting," February 1, 1956.
92 CZA, KKL5/22479, "Yad Vashem First World Council," April 19, 1956.
93 CAHJP, CC 18567, Uveeler to Dinur, May 6, 1956.

to conclude the discussion with the fact that "there is a desire to differentiate and say – the memory must be distinct and the museum distinct."[94]

The second symposium also related to the place and importance of the museum. Dinur insisted that the central building, "whose very construction will be remembrance," would be the museum hall, where the visitors to the Mount of Remembrance would begin their visit. El-Hanani thought the route should be the reverse. "Not the museum and then afterwards the remembrance hall," but the opposite. "First should be the great, powerful impression. Afterwards, if I want, I will go into the museum. First I will go into the remembrance hall and only afterwards to the museum and the synagogue." An interesting discussion about the future exhibit developed. Some suggested that the museum display "authentic" objects and exhibits brought from Europe, including a model of an extermination camp. It was decided that should the Remembrance Authority collect enough historical material, the museum would hold a permanent exhibit. Alternatively, some of the permanent displays would be able to be pulled out and others put in their place.[95] At the end of the second symposium, an order was determined: the first building on the Mount of Remembrance would be the Hall of Remembrance and the second would contain a museum in which the lands of extermination would be presented. This conclusion was communicated to the architects, who were asked to plan the construction based on these directives.[96]

It was now possible for the directorate to respond to the many appeals that had come in over the years from people and institutions who wished to transfer material and objects to Yad Vashem; their place would now be in the museum on the Mount of Remembrance.[97] In the interim, some of the items were preserved and displayed in the archive and administration building. In 1956, an exhibit called *From the Collections of Yad Vashem*[98] opened on the building's second floor, and in April 1958 the institution's first permanent exhibit opened, curated by interior architect Nahum Maron. Accompanied by a detailed catalogue, the exhibitincluded

---

[94] HHA, 3–95. 17 (2), "Protocol of Yad Vashem Symposium," June 10, 1956.
[95] HHA, 3–95. 17 (2), "Protocol of Yad Vashem Symposium," July 15, 1956.
[96] HHA, 3–95. 17 (2), Dinur to architects, August 15, 1956.
[97] CZA, KKKL5/22478, "Yad Vashem Directorate Meeting," November 11, 1956.
[98] M. Shenhavi, "Towards the Opening of the Exhibition *From the Collections of Yad Vashem*," *Yediot Yad Vashem* 8–9 (1957), 11.

over 150 displays that were divided into thirteen different thematic sections.[99] By the end of 1965, fifteen exhibits had been held in the various exhibition spaces on the Mount of Remembrance, and it was clear that a permanent space must be found for the museum.[100]

Figure 29: The *A World Which Was and Is No More* exhibit, the opening portion of the *Warning and Witness* exhibition (CAHJP, Unknown photographer).

When Dinur spoke before Yad Vashem's Third World Council in August 1957, he noted that the Hall of Remembrance "will be, essentially, a museum to Holocaust and heroism, a series of museums to the lives of Jews and the form of these lives in the Diasporic lands."[101] With these words, Dinur hinted at the extensive plan that the directorate was working on: the establishment of three museums whose goal would be "conferring" remembrance and commemoration

---
99 Yad Vashem, *Yad Vashem Exhibitions* (Jerusalem: Yad Vashem, 1960) [in Hebrew]; Catalogue of the first permanent exhibition, Jerusalem, 1958.
100 ISA, GL-4/1423, "Summary of Meetings of the Public Committee for Examining Yad Vashem's Activities," December 1965.
101 CZA, KKL5/22482, "Protocol of Yad Vashem's Third World Council," August 26, 1957.

of the Holocaust and heroism. Aside from the Holocaust and heroism museum, which would display "real remains of these events and their reflection in Jewish art" as well as art by artists "who depicted things in the ghettos and camps," Yad Vashem wished to situate a communities museum in the remembrance building, in which "the appearance of the life of Israel in the lands of the Diaspora" would be presented. A third element of the museum would be a "national gallery of the great scholars of Israel to mark their lives' achievements and their contributions to the culture of the world and the nation." The plan was to build the museum as separate pavilions, in accordance with the lands of extermination and the different subjects tied to the Holocaust and heroism; each such building would carry the name of the philanthropist who had raised the funds necessary for its establishment.[102]

But at the end of 1957, when Yad Vashem's architects presented their plans for construction on the Mount of Remembrance, many components that had appeared in previous blueprints, including the museum, had been removed. The Hall of Remembrance stood at the center of the plan, and next to it was the synagogue. The heroism hall, in which the Yad Vashem museum was meant to stand, had been removed entirely and there was no longer a suitable place for the historical exhibit.

The directorate and Building Committee now asked themselves where to find a fitting space for the Yad Vashem museum. The solution was found in the space underneath the assembly plaza. As noted, in earlier plans the synagogue had been positioned at the southeastern end of the space under the plaza, but widespread opposition to the idea that the synagogue's roof would be part of the entry plaza to the Hall of Remembrance led the architects to move the synagogue to its western edge. This change meant that part of the subterranean space was now empty and could be used and even expanded for the museum.[103]

When Sharon stood before the participants at Yad Vashem's Fourth World Council in late 1958, he explained how a museum to the Holocaust and heroism, with an area of 4,500 square meters, could be arranged "thanks to the ground's topography," a space that "by all accounts is certainly sufficient for the shortest term."[104] The directorate resolved that immediately after a tender was published for the construction of the Hall of Remembrance, synagogue, and monument, the entryway to the future museum would also be built. If Yad Vashem had extra funds at the end of the building process, the museum itself could be

---

102 HHA, 3–95. 17 (2), "Yad Vashem Building Plan," no author, n.d.
103 HHA, 3–95. 19 (1), "Protocol of Yad Vashem Directorate Meeting," September 26, 1958.
104 CZA, S61/326, "Protocol of the Third Session of Yad Vashem's Fourth World Council," November 9, 1958.

built as well. With no other choice, and with insufficient funding, the directorate resolved that only the space of the museum would be built but nothing would be done with its interior for the time being.[105]

When Kubovy took the reins in early 1959, he wondered about the museum's role in the construction plan. "The directorate chose to exploit the change with the move of the synagogue in order to build a frame for the museum," Shatner informed him, "knowing full well that there was no possibility of building the museum at the present time." Kubovy asked to discuss the intended content of the museum and the "way of changing the existing frame into the museum that we need."[106] "The construction planning processes have led to the fact that, with no prior intent, we will have two planes in the commemorative area," he claimed. He related to the Hall of Remembrance and synagogue, on one hand, and the museum and its exhibits, on the other. In the museum, the silence and reverence of the Hall of Remembrance and the synagogue would not be possible, and "it is good, in retrospect, that this difference exists." Some members of the Building Committee felt that most of the visitors would arrive at Yad Vashem for communion and not for the purpose of "historical research" and only a small number would continue from the Hall of Remembrance to the museum; moreover, a stop there would make unnecessary demands on the time of those who might not be interested.[107] "What was thought when we spoke about the 'museum' in the past?" Kubovy asked in 1963 in a directorate meeting. "Did they mean that the hall should contain displays on the Holocaust?" Voicing his concern that Yad Vashem would not have enough items to justify the establishment of a real museum, he suggested using pictures made in the camps and integrating them with archival displays.[108]

Meanwhile, two halls were prepared in the space beneath the assembly plaza, on either side of the staircase that led up to the square. New exhibits – such as the *Bravery and Resistance* exhibit that opened in 1969 – were presented there.[109] It was clear to the directorate that the display halls did not suit Yad Vashem's growing needs. The antiquated exhibit in the administration building, which was devoid of a chronological "spine," required a comprehensive change. In the backdrop stood the reopening of the Ghetto Fighters' House at Kibbutz Lohamei HaGeta'ot in 1959, and the display established at

---

105 HHA, 3–95. 19 (1), "Yad Vashem Directorate Meeting," December 30, 1958.
106 ISA, GL-3/13346, "Building Committee Meeting," May 5, 1960.
107 Ibid.
108 YVA, Protocols of Yad Vashem Directorate Meetings, Protocol of the Board of Directors, August 13, 1966.
109 CAHJP, CC 18536, "Yad Vashem, 1962/1963 Activities."

Kibbutz Yad Mordechai, both of which constituted a threat and competition to the not particularly impressive exhibit at Yad Vashem.

Figure 30: Yad Vashem's historical museum. The tunnel that symbolized the burrows in which rebels fought against the Nazis led to the third and central wing of the museum, which was dedicated to the Jews' uprising against the Nazis. (NPA, Moshe Milner).

The directorate chose, therefore, to expand the space under the assembly plaza and build the new historical museum there. The entrance was in the southern wall of the plaza; later on, Naftali Bezem's artistic relief, "The Wall of Holocaust and Heroism," was positioned there, ultimately becoming one of the Mount of Remembrance's hallmarks.[110]

The museum's festive opening was held in July 1973 in the presence of the state's president; it constituted the peak of the activities commemorating thirty years since the outbreak of the Warsaw Ghetto Uprising.[111] The interior of the museum had been conceived by architect and designer Samuel Grundman as

---

110 "Yad Vashem Wall of Memory," *Yediot Yad Vashem: Events, Activities, and Publications* 3 (1973), 24; Neomi Ben Zur, *Naftali Bezem: Holocaust and Heroism* (Jerusalem: Yad Vashem: n.d.) [in Hebrew].
111 "New Museum Inaugurated at Yad Vashem," *Yad Vashem News*, 1973, 2.

well as David Gafni; it boasted a route that illustrated the historical development from the rise of Nazism in Germany until the end of the Second World War. The display relied on large explanatory plaques with black and white photographs of documents, displays, and historical pictures. Captions for the displays were in Hebrew, English, and Yiddish.

The museum was comprised of four central sections in two lengthwise halls. The first focused on the rise of Nazism until the outbreak of the Second World War. The second was occupied with the Final Solution and the extermination of the Jews. A tunnel symbolized the burrows in which fighters acted against the Nazis and led to the third, central unit, dedicated to the Jewish resistance against the Nazis.[112] The museum's fourth area contained displays about the camps' liberation at the end of the war and the efforts at clandestine immigration to the land of Israel, and included, among other things, the story of the ship *Exodus*. Near the staircase that led to the Hall of Names, plaques on the walls contained the names of the lands of extermination and the number of Jews that had been killed. Later on, these plaques were replaced with symbolic tombstones upon which the size of the population before and after the war were recorded.[113]

Now the route at Yad Vashem clearly led visitors from the Avenue of the Righteous among the Nations to the museum. After spending time there, people ascended an internal staircase to the Hall of Names, visited the Hall of Remembrance, and finished at the Pillar of Heroism.[114]

The *Warsaw Ghetto Uprising* Monument

One of the most impressive monuments at Yad Vashem is Nathan Rapoport's *In Thy Blood, Live* (Ezek. 16:6) monument, also known as the *Warsaw Ghetto Uprising* monument. Sculpted in heroic style, it has two components. The first, made of bronze, depicts the uprising that erupted in Warsaw in 1943 and the Jews' fortitude in their struggle against the Nazis. Next to this tall, impressive, prominent sculpture stands the second, smaller part of the creation, which depicts Jews being led, bent over, to their deaths, while over them stand Nazi soldiers.

Many people think that Yad Vashem's sculpture is a "copy" of Nathan Rapoport's original, inaugurated in Warsaw in 1948, on the fifth anniversary of

---

112 Photo of the tunnel: NPA, D746-062.
113 "Development Plans for Yad Vashem," *Yediot Yad Vashem: Events, Activities, and Publications* 4 (1973), 4; CZA, NZO/2652163.
114 "Route for Visitors," *Yad Vashem News*, 1973, 8.

the uprising's outbreak.[115] But, in fact, both parts of the Jerusalem sculpture were cast in the seventies from plaster copies prepared by Rapoport in the forties and sent to Yad Vashem in 1956.[116] The protracted process in the assembly of these two sculptures at Yad Vashem (they were inaugurated in 1975 and 1976) was tied to various pitfalls over the years – halakhic questions, ideological issues, and financial complications tied to Rapoport's work. The sculpture's erection on the Mount of Remembrance was also related to a broader question that I have addressed, the place of heroism in Yad Vashem's memorial landscape and the institute's years of deliberation on the subject.

Initial Ties with Yad Vashem

Rapoport's bonds with Shenhavi and Yad Vashem were formed immediately with the end of the Second World War. This was based on a prior acquaintance between them: Rapoport had been Shenhavi's trainee in Warsaw's branch of HaShomer HaTzair.

In 1947, when Rapoport was working on a memorial monument to the Warsaw Ghetto Uprising, he approached Shenhavi to ask for details about the Holocaust "mausoleum" (Yad Vashem) that would be founded in the land of Israel.[117] Rapoport felt that his piece could be integrated within the future memorial enterprise and asked Shenhavi about the site's location and topography. He debated the monumentality that Shenhavi wished to lend the site and the use of figurative sculptures for Holocaust commemoration, an issue that preoccupied him more broadly at the time. "Should the face be covered," he asked, as "You shall not make for yourself a sculptured image or any likeness" (Exod. 20:4)? And "How [can one deal] with the problem of monumental sculpture in open space [and its] ties to the religious prohibition against erecting sculptures?" After Yad Vashem reported that negotiations were taking place with the Chief Rabbinate of the land of Israel, which demanded that no sculptures be erected on the memorial enterprise's premises,[118] he suggested solving the problem by using "monumental symbols

---

[115] On the Warsaw monument: James E. Young, "The Biography of a Memorial Icon: Nathan Rapoport's Warsaw Ghetto Monument," *Representations* 26 (1989): 69–106; Young, *The Texture*, 155–84; Brog, "Besieged Within"; Batia Donner, *Nathan Rapoport: A Jewish Artist* (Jerusalem: Yad Izhak Ben-Zvi and Yad Yaari, Givat Haviva, 2014), 73–168 [in Hebrew].
[116] Richard Yaffe, *Nathan Rapoport Sculptures and Monuments* (New York: Shengold, 1980).
[117] YVA, AM1 15, Rapoport to Shenhavi, September 2, 1947.
[118] YVA, AM1 16, B. Ben-Aharon to Rapoport, February 17, 1948.

that can emphasize and revive the entire program both in terms of content and in a formal way."[119]

In the backdrop of the emerging relationship was the nearing inauguration of the Monument to the Ghetto Heroes in Warsaw, an event that provoked tension within Yad Vashem's directorate. Like many in the land of Israel's leadership, Shenhavi felt that commemorating the uprising in Poland was highly important, but nonetheless he was concerned that the monument there would render the establishment of Yad Vashem unnecessary and support for it would diminish. A public relations line was now settled on: the establishment and existence of the monument in Poland was legitimate but the center of Holocaust remembrance must be in the land of Israel. "An eternal hand and name (*yad va-shem*) . . . .. Remembrance will be for generations – not in Poland, the land of the furnaces and Jewish cemeteries. Their place is here, within our nation," that is, at Yad Vashem.[120]

Nevertheless, in order to symbolize the ties between Warsaw and the land of Israel, it was decided that local earth would be brought and spread at the monument's inauguration. A vessel holding bags of soil from around the land of Israel read: "The Yishuv in the land of Israel bows its head before the heroes, the fighters of the Warsaw ghetto, and lays on their tombstone clods of earth from the redeemed homeland."[121] Efforts were made to emphasize the importance of the fatherland and the imminent founding of Yad Vashem. "On the day of the unveiling of the *Warsaw Ghetto Uprising* monument, we must turn the eyes of the entire Jewish world . . . to Jerusalem, the center of the nation in which the central national memorial will be founded for the entire revelation of the Holocaust and heroism period that our generation underwent," it was decided.[122]

The Monument (or a Copy) to Yad Vashem?

The *Warsaw Ghetto Uprising* monument, with its two components, was erected in Poland in 1948, rising above the ruins of the Warsaw Ghetto. The plaster model and the molds for casting bronze for the sculpture remained in Paris, where Rapoport had made the original.

---

119 YVA, AM1 16, Rapoport to Shenhavi, November 6, 1947.
120 CZA, J1/6442/1, "Warsaw Monument for the Uprising," broadcast on Jerusalem Radio, April 7, 1947.
121 CZA, S46/394, JNF management to JNF General Council, March 1, 1948; Moshe Zilbertal, "Bridge over Great Depths," *Al HaMishmar*, April 20, 1948.
122 YVA, AM1 308, no title and no author, April 19, 1948.

In 1953, Rapoport approached Marc Jarblum, head of the Zionist Organization in France, and offered to give them to the Jewish Agency so that they could be transferred to the State of Israel.[123] He suggested situating the sculpture at the International Conference Center (Binyanei Ha'uma), an assembly hall at Jerusalem's entrance that was being built at the time, which was meant to become the most prominent symbolic building in the capital city.[124]

It appears that Rapoport's offer raised interest in Jerusalem, and he began to correspond on the subject with different agents. The artist's plan was to prepare both parts of the sculpture in the State of Israel, the bronze relief and the "uprising" that he would sculpt from stone; he believed that there would not be particular opposition on the part of the "religious institutions" to its erection in Israel because it would be a relief rather than a statue. Its production in Jerusalem, he felt, would realize his dream that "this eternal monument will be returned from the orphaned and foreign Diaspora to the renewing homeland and I know that my modest contribution will add a layer to the great memorial enterprise of Yad Vashem."[125] Berl Locker, chairman of the Jewish Agency's board of directors and one of the people with whom Rapoport had been in contact, recommended to Dinur that he consider the possibility of the Remembrance Authority purchasing the monument.[126] Representatives of the Ministry of Foreign Affairs in France, who were in on the events and in contact with Rapoport, viewed the transfer of the sculpture's plaster copies to the State of Israel as "a political national act of the highest order."[127]

In mid-1954, Yad Vashem's directorate discussed the monument. Shenhavi reported on the sculpture, which had now, in his words, become a "document," similar to other historical displays that Yad Vashem had begun to collect. He presented different options for the sculptures' permanent home – on the Mount of Remembrance or in Haifa. The possibility of positioning them in the Martyrs' Forest, as part of the JNF's commemoration project there, was also raised.[128] In June 1954, Yad Vashem's directorate announced that it felt it was its duty to

---

123 CZA, S41/468, Marc Jarblum to Berl Locker, July 29, 1953.
124 Cohen-Hattab, "The Formation".
125 CZA, S41/468, Rapoport to Locker, September 20, 1953.
126 CZA, S41/468, Locker to Dinur, September 28, 1953.
127 ISA, GL-3/1087, "Arazi-Reshef," May 26–27, 1954.
128 CZA, S/115/509, "Protocol of Yad Vashem Directorate Meeting," June 23, 1954.

cover the expenses of moving Nathan Rapoport's artwork to Israel, an undertaking that would cost some $25,000.[129]

In effect, the Remembrance Authority had some trouble deciding how it would fund the transfer and where the monument would stand. Dinur cautioned that placing the monument in Jerusalem would "raise a great ruckus" on the part of the religious population, which would oppose a figurative statue in the city.[130] Much as in other cases, this time, too, it was decided that a committee would be formed to discuss the issues. The committee included, among others, artist Mordecai Ardon, the Ministry of Education's art advisor and supervisor, and art researcher and director of the Bezalel Museum Mordechai Narkiss. Along with Yad Vashem's people, they decided on the payment that would be transferred to Rapoport; they also defined the Remembrance Authority's responsibility for casting the monument and packing it for transfer to Israel.[131] The question of the monument's location remained open, including the question of whether it would be possible to position sculptures on the mount.

Critiques of Erecting Sculptures on the Mount of Remembrance

Not everyone was happy with the decision to purchase Rapoport's monument. The most prominent of its critics was Uveeler, the Claims Conference's representative, who was vehemently opposed. He claimed that "a monument for the sake of a monument does not accord with the Jewish tradition, let alone religious tradition." He also wondered why a copy of a creation that constituted a symbol for Warsaw and Polish Jewry but not necessarily for other survivors and visitors to Yad Vashem was being erected on the Mount of Remembrance. On the mount, he felt, the "Jew from Bulgaria, Hungary, Romania, Germany, and France" would want "to see something that is a symbol of Europe. When he reads that the monument is a copy of the one in the Warsaw Ghetto he will feel that it belongs only to Polish Jews." He wondered, then, why Yad Vashem's directorate had not requisitioned a universal creation that would represent the horrors of the Holocaust more generally, and raised the concern that the bodies funding Yad Vashem – the Knesset, the Jewish Agency, and the Claims Conference – would find the monument unnecessary and view its purchase as a mistake, damaging Yad Vashem's

---

[129] ISA, GL-1/1229, Yad Vashem to the Ministry of Education, August 17, 1954.
[130] ISA, GL-1/1229, "Protocol of Yad Vashem Directorate Meeting," August 19, 1954.
[131] ISA, GL-2/1229, Chaim Barlas to Mordechi Ardon, February 20, 1955.

ability to raise the necessary funds for the remembrance buildings' construction. He demanded that the contract that had been signed with Rapoport be annulled.[132]

Yad Vashem now found itself in a bind. Influenced by Uveeler's opinion and, it would seem, concern regarding the religious bodies' opposition to erecting a monument in Jerusalem, the directorate suggested that the JNF fund the preparations for the monument and place it in the Martyrs' Forest.[133] The Fund's heads rejected the suggestion.

Shenhavi now proposed that Yad Vashem take care of transferring the monument's molds to the Mount of Remembrance, but not yet cast them. "We will tell Rapoport that there was never an explicit decision about the erection of the monument," Weitz agreed.[134] And so, in January 1956, the molds arrived in Israel and a number of weeks later, on February 20, 1956, an agreement was signed between Yad Vashem and Rapoport in which their ownership was transferred to the institution.[135] The copyright remained with the artist.

On the Mount of Remembrance, a cabin was built; the monument's pieces – which the directorate had no idea what to do with – were placed there. The molds were stored there until the seventies, and then the monuments were cast.[136] This reality, the purchase and transfer of the monument to Jerusalem, and the storage on the Mount of Remembrance with no inkling of what would be done with them, caught the attention of State Comptroller Siegfried Moses, who related to the events in a sharp indictment of Yad Vashem published in March 1958.[137] The investigation emphasized the decision to purchase the monument without checking the question of its erection in Jerusalem; it was felt that Yad Vashem should have first examined the opinions of rabbis and religious figures regarding the positioning of the monument on the Mount of Remembrance.[138] "This is a typical case of human error," Palmon added during a directorate discussion held regarding the comptroller's report. "They knew that the monument could be cast only in Paris and nonetheless decided to bring it to Israel at a time when they knew that there was nothing to do with it in Israel," he said, and wondered, "Why was a decision made to bring a plaster monument here?"[139] Shenhavi,

---

132 CZA, S115/504, Uveeler to Dinur, August 23, 1955.
133 CZA, S115/503, "Protocol of Yad Vashem Directorate Meeting," August 28, 1955.
134 ISA, P-27/1976, "Protocol of Yad Vashem Directorate Meeting," September 20, 1955.
135 CAHJP, CC18563, Bauminger to Uveeler, January 23, 1957.
136 ISA, HZ-4/151, "Summary of Yad Vashem Directorate Decisions," December 27, 1955.
137 "State Comptroller Publishes Report about Yad Vashem," *Davar*, April 30, 1958.
138 CZA, S115/238, State Comptroller, "Report on Yad Vashem," March 1958; Menachem Barash, "Yad Vashem's Weakness," *Yedioth Ahronoth*, June 24, 1958.
139 YVA, Protocols of Yad Vashem Directorate Meetings, Protocol of the Board of Directors, May 13, 1958.

outside of Yad Vashem's circle, was quick to clarify that "It is not at all true that it was due to the religious opposition that the monument remained closed in a crate. It is true that the proposal was brought to the directorate after discussions were held under its auspices with religious figures who found no fault in it."[140]

Rapoport also added his voice to the censure. When he discovered that parts of his monument were sitting useless in storage, "in a state of negligence, with a chance that over time it will be entirely damaged," he demanded that they be brought to his studio in Ramat Gan.[141] It is likely that it was this appeal that led Yad Vashem's directorate to attempt to examine the possibility of nonetheless erecting the monument on the Mount of Remembrance and to resolve the halakhic problem of situating a sculpture on the Mount of Remembrance. Bialer turned to Israel's chief rabbis, asking for their opinion about the possibility of building it on the Mount of Remembrance, where the monument would be a "historical document," with a special room built for the purpose.[142] Within his attempts to convince them to agree to the erection of a monument, he reported on the inauguration of the monument in Warsaw in 1948, and the fact that a religious ceremony had been held with the approval and in the presence of dozens of rabbis. "I, too, was among the organizers of the ceremony and I saw in it a sanctification of God's name," Bialer stated, adding that "in Jerusalem's conditions, everything receives a different form."[143] The rabbis decided that in order to make a determination on the issue, they needed to see the monument.[144] They were willing to suffice with examining "the prominent parts and the ones that constitute a question according to halakha,"[145] but due to the fragility of the monument's plaster pieces, Rapoport demanded that he be allowed to oversee their removal from their place. Ultimately, the monument's pieces remained in storage.

A number of years passed, and at the beginning of 1963, speaking before Yad Vashem's Fifth World Council, Kubovy hinted at a change of some sort in relation to the monument. He announced that within Yad Vashem's other development and construction work, "we will erect a replica of the *Warsaw Ghetto Uprising*

---

140 CZA, S115/238, Shenhavi to Melkman, May 28, 1958.
141 YVA, AM1 363, Rapoport to Dinur, April 21, 1958.
142 CZA, KKL5/24136, "Yad Vashem Directorate Meeting," April 29, 1958.
143 HHA, 94. 116 (2), Yehuda Bialer to Rapoport, July 10, 1958.
144 YVA, Protocols of Yad Vashem Directorate Meetings, Protocol of the Board of Directors, May 13, 1958.
145 It seems that Bialer was trying to guide the rabbis to permitting the erection of sculptures at Yad Vashem on the basis of the fact that it was, in his words, a relief. Halakhically speaking, a relief in which the full body is not visible is at times permissible. On this see Efraim E. Urbach, "The Laws of Idolatry in the light of Historical and Archaeological Facts in the Second and Third Centuries," *Eretz Israel* 5 (1958), 153–54 [in Hebrew].

monument which has become a national treasure," and that one of the Warsaw community organizations had promised to raise the lion's share of the funds necessary for its establishment. He hinted at the monument's placement on the Mount of Remembrance, within the niche of a large stone wall that would be positioned near the entrance to the future museum. The sculpture would be a museal display, serving as a great monument to the Jewish communities that had been destroyed.[146]

Rapoport, having learned from experience, was not content with these statements, and acted to have the sculpture transferred to Ramat Gan, where his studio was located. He chose to do so when he discovered, much to his disappointment, that he had come in second in the competition to design the monument to heroism at Yad Vashem. Now he tried to convince the Remembrance Authority's directorate to allow him to "withdraw" the *Warsaw Ghetto Uprising* monument and reported that Ramat Gan Mayor Avraham Krinitzi had suggested that the monument be erected in his city. "Time passes, it has been nearly ten years and the plaster monument of Warsaw sits in a cellar in Yad Vashem . . . we had an agreement that if Yad Vashem does not erect the monument I will have permission to take it to my workshop in Ramat Gan," he claimed.[147]

But it was only in 1968 that Shmuel Spector, Yad Vashem's new secretary general, wrote to Rapoport and reported that Yad Vashem's directorate was seeking "approaches on the question of the Warsaw monument's positioning, [and] not in the most modest and simple way." He was referring to a suggestion that the monument not be cast but rather that the plaster pieces be placed in the niche, with a glass wall protecting them to solve the question of maintaining the plaster in the open air of Jerusalem.[148] In the middle of that year, Rapoport's statue, Job, arrived at Yad Vashem and was positioned near the entrance to the Hall of Names.[149] This cemented the ties between Rapoport and the Remembrance Authority to a certain extent and increased the sense that a solution must be found for the lingering question of the monument.

---

146 CZA, S62/1031, "Protocol of Yad Vashem Sixth Session, Fifth Council," February 19, 1963.
147 ISA, GL-4/1786, Rapoport to Shmuel Spector, September 23, 1963.
148 HHA, 94. 116 (2), Spector to Rapoport, January 8, 1968.
149 The sculpture was purchased by the Forman family from New York and donated to Yad Vashem. The sculpture was originally prepared for the United Nations building in New York. See YVA, Protocols of Yad Vashem Directorate Meetings, Protocol of the Board of Directors, May 20, 1968; "Job at Yad Vashem," *Yedioth Ahronoth*, April 15, 1969; for a picture of the statue, see National Photo Collection, D812/044 as well as CZA, PHKH/1307459. The statue currently stands near the Holocaust Art Museum's entrance.

A Solution

The financial quandary of Rapoport's monument was resolved in the early seventies. Negotiations were held between Yad Vashem and the Warsaw Ghetto Resistance Organization (WAGRO) regarding financing the monument on the Mount of Remembrance.[150] The organization, whose activities took place in the United States, had been founded in 1963; its goal was to increase awareness about opposition to the Nazis during the Second World War in general and during the Warsaw Ghetto Uprising in particular.[151] Jack P. Eisner, a philanthropist and Holocaust survivor, was behind the communications with Yad Vashem. He promised that the money transferred from the United States would facilitate the preparation of the ground at Yad Vashem and the casting of the monument, which would be unveiled no later than April 1973.[152] The monument, it was decided, would stand at the center of a new square that would be developed by Yad Vashem's architects near the entrance to the new museum.[153] Yad Vashem hurried to sign a contract with Rapoport. The artist committed to finishing preparation of the monument on time and Yad Vashem committed to forming ties and signing a contract with a foundry that would cast the sculpture.[154]

Fervor was high but the connection with Eisner and WAGRO became problematic. In early 1972, it was reported that ties had been cut with New York and funds for the monument were still a problem.[155] Yad Vashem's directorate once again sought sources of financing and it was only in early 1973 that the solution was found in the form of a different philanthropist, Leon Jolson from New York, a Warsaw native and Holocaust survivor who was willing to underwrite the erection of Rapoport's sculptures at Yad Vashem. It is unclear whether Rapoport approached him directly, or whether it was his ties to Yad Vashem and the fact that he had been involved in funding the Hall of Names on the Mount of Remembrance that led him to the partnership. Jolson even suggested that Rapoport add a third

---

150 YVA, Protocols of Yad Vashem Directorate Meetings, Protocol of the Board of Directors, March 14, 1971.
151 "Warsaw Ghetto Resistance Organization Formed in U.S. by Ex-members," *Jewish Telegraphic Agency*, February 19, 1963.
152 YVA, AM3 868 V, "Contract Signed between Yad Vashem and WAGRO," March 23, 1971; on Eisner: "Jack P. Eisner," *The New York Times*, August 31, 2003; autobiographical book: Jack Eisner, *The Survivor*, ed. Irving A. Leitner (New York: W. Morrow, 1980).
153 YVA, AM1 368, "Protocol of the Board of Governors Meeting," May 23, 1971.
154 HHA, 94. 116 (2), "Contract Signed between Yad Vashem and Rapoport," 1971.
155 HHA, 94. 116 (2), "Report of Aharon Paritzki," July 9, 1971.

sculpture to the original two, whose subject would be purely Zionist-Israeli, "On Resurrection."[156]

Figure 31: Nathan Rapoport's *Warsaw Ghetto Uprising* monument is erected, 1975 (YVA, Unknown photographer).

Rapoport now sculpted the central part of the monument, the uprising, in a New York foundry, and it was sent to Jerusalem and inaugurated on January 7, 1975. The bronze statue was placed on a podium, raised above the plaza, with a few stairs leading up to it. Behind it a wall of red brick was built, evoking the wall that surrounded the Warsaw Ghetto. In contrast with Warsaw, where the second part of the monument, "The Last March," was on the reverse side, on the Mount of Remembrance the work was placed to the right of the uprising

---

156 YVA, Protocols of Yad Vashem Directorate Meetings, Protocol of the Board of Directors, January 25, 1973.

Figure 32: Nathan Rapoport's monument in memory of the ghetto heroes (YVA, Unknown photographer).

monument. It contained a number of differences from the original sculpture. The second part of Rapoport's sculpture was inaugurated on April 26, 1976,[157] and its completion further underscored its importance. Near the monument, there was an inscription – *bi-damayikh hayi*, "in thy blood, live," from Ezekiel, a sort of commandment that life must continue[158] – and next to the sculptures writing in Hebrew, English, and Yiddish noted that the monument had been donated by Leon and Anya Jolson, survivors of the Warsaw Ghetto, in memory of the six million people from the Jewish nation who had been killed in the Holocaust.[159] The two sculptures stood at the western side of Warsaw Ghetto Square, which today serves as a place of assembly for national Holocaust Martyrs' and Heroes' Remembrance Day.

---

157 ISA, HZ, 20/5847, "Protocol of Board of Governors Meeting," September 1, 1975.
158 Batya Brutin, *Living with the Memory: Monuments in Israel Commemorating the Holocaust* (Lohamei Hageta'ot: Lohamei Hageta'ot, 2005), 33–43 [in Hebrew].
159 ISA, HZ-19/5847, "Protocol of Board of Governors Meeting," May 20, 1974.

Figure 33: The *In Thy Blood, Live* monument, the second element in Nathan Rapoport's monument in memory of the Warsaw Ghetto Uprising, 1976 (YVA, Unknown photographer).

Conclusion

Exactly fifteen years elapsed between the inauguration of the Hall of Remembrance on Holocaust Martyrs' and Heroes' Remembrance Day in 1961 and the inauguration of Nathan Rapoport's monument on the same day in 1976. This time period, we now know, was a most significant one in the chronicles of the institution. Over these years, research at Yad Vashem developed greatly, and various publications were issued by the institution; moreover, the Mount of Remembrance became firmly entrenched in Israeli public consciousness as the central commemoration site – both in Israel and abroad – for Holocaust and heroism, and state memorial ceremonies held there reflected this dominance.

At the beginning of the period discussed in this chapter, in 1961, all that could be seen at Yad Vashem was the archive and administration building and the Hall of Remembrance, standing high above an exposed square. In 1976, in contrast, Yad Vashem already had an entire remembrance complex and a clear visiting route that provoked an emotional response among visitors. Those arriving at Yad Vashem walked the Avenue of the Righteous among the Nations, continued to

Figure 34: Nathan Rapoport's *In Thy Blood, Live* monument is inaugurated on Holocaust Martyrs' and Heroes' Remembrance Day ceremony, 27 Nisan 1976 (NPA, Ya'akov Sa'ar).

the memorial plaza, and saw the Hall of Remembrance. At the end of the visit there, they descended to the museum to view its different halls and then ascended to the Hall of Names, where the pages of testimony were kept. In 1975, Rapoport's monument was added to visits alongside the heroism monument that had been inaugurated earlier, found at the end of the route. The impressive commemorative complex gave people a profound and meaningful experience, with its historical-documentary dimension (in the museum) as well as its memorial dimension, with commemoration in the Hall of Remembrance and the Hall of Names.

The entirety of the memorial landscape may have been impressive, but the road to building these Holocaust symbols – the synagogue, the monuments, and the museum on the Mount of Remembrance – was a long and complicated one. It seems that none of Yad Vashem's directorate members expected that so many years would elapse before the museum was built or that the "problem" of immortalizing heroism would find its expression in such a minimal way, with the erection of a Pillar of Heroism. The reason for the prolonged process and its complexity was tied to essential disagreements, both internal and external, about the appearance of Yad Vashem and the meaning of these remembrance elements. The many changes that took place with regard to the heroism monument, whose planning Henrik won, but which ultimately was built by Schwartz and El-

Hanani; the delays that took place in erecting Rapoport's *Warsaw Ghetto Uprising* monument; the planned synagogue's move from one side of the plaza to the other; the transfer of the Hall of Names to its new location – all of these reflected the directorate and architects' very real inability to agree on a vision of Yad Vashem and its expression both architecturally and symbolically. Nonetheless, ultimately, with the close of the extensive process, Yad Vashem – a tragic symbol, fusing many national and state memorial elements – became the clear symbol of Holocaust and heroism commemoration in Israel.

Conclusion The Road to Remembrance

A smooth, concrete entry gate with the engraved inscription "I will put My breath into you and you shall live again, and I will set you upon your own soil" (Ezek. 37:14) leads to a round plaza.[1] Beyond it stands a large, square, glass building that serves as Yad Vashem's Visitors' Center. The Holocaust History Museum, a prism-shaped structure in which visitors walk from one side of the Mount of Remembrance to the other, is nearby. Those who choose not to visit the museum continue along the Avenue of the Righteous among the Nations to Warsaw Ghetto Square, at whose edge stands Nathan Rapoport's sculpture. From there, a staircase leads people up to an additional plaza, where the Hall of Remembrance stands. Facing it, on a long wall, is the inscription "I will give them, in My House and within My walls, a monument (*yad*) and a name (*va-shem*) . . . which shall not perish" (Isa. 56:5). Across from the Hall of Remembrance, those leaving Rapoport's monument may encounter groups that have finished their tours of the historical museum and the Hall of Names. This is also the place where visitors can choose whether to extend their stay and walk to the Cattle Car – Memorial to the Deportees, the Valley of the Communities, and other monuments dispersed throughout the Mount of Remembrance's area or make their way directly to the Pillar of Heroism and end their trip to Yad Vashem with a visit to the Children's Memorial.

In this complex and saturated memorial landscape, those coming to Yad Vashem can see that many elements, all dedicated to commemorating Holocaust and heroism, are intertwined – structures, signs, trees, sculptures, and monuments. What may be harder for the visitors to comprehend is that the Mount of Remembrance is made up of a great number of "historical layers"; the place is, in effect, a sort of archaeological "tell" that has bloomed and been built gradually from the fifties until today in a protracted, involved process, one that was rife with value dilemmas and an abundance of bureaucratic and financial hardships.

The present book examined that process, primarily the historical layers of the establishment of the Mount of Remembrance. It revealed how the earliest physical remembrance at Yad Vashem was built and designed, from the first architectural plans and the beginning of the first structure there until the mid-

---

[1] This verse is taken from the vision of the dry bones in the book of Ezekiel. The gate is dedicated to survivors, those who "carry memory in their lives." Nonetheless, it is important to note that in Zionist and Israeli perception the vision and the specific sentence taken from it had a specific interpretation, as if the dry bones of the Holocaust victims had taken shape and come to life on the Zionist holy land.

seventies, when Rapoport's *Warsaw Ghetto Uprising* monument was inaugurated and the first stage of the site's physical shaping drew to a close. This complex of remembrance, which at first might appear grey and meager relative to the new modern construction added to the Mount of Remembrance in recent decades, has, in reality, no small amount of architectural and cultural richness and includes many memorial elements. Some still constitute an important part of the route taken on the mount; others no longer exist or are not in use. Yad Vashem's original historical museum was replaced by its Holocaust History Museum. The Hall of Names, initially located in the elongated building on the western side of the remembrance plaza, was hewn into the rock not long after the year 2000 and today still stands on the northern side of the Mount of Remembrance. The original synagogue became a warehouse; in its stead, another house of worship was built.

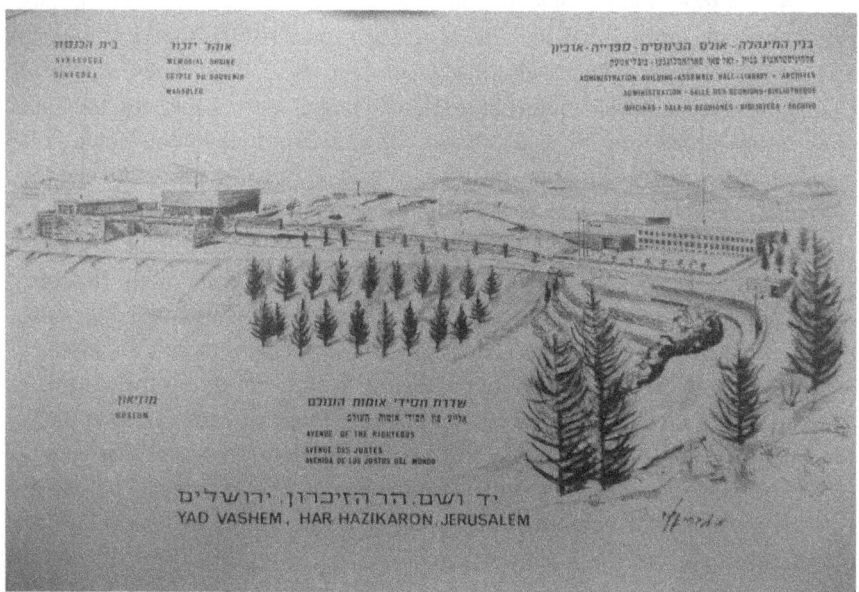

Figure 35: General appearance of Yad Vashem in the mid-seventies (HHA).

Two prominent historical buildings have maintained their original place and meaning – the Hall of Remembrance, which continues to serve as Yad Vashem's focus of tribute, even if in reality few of the groups that visit the mount stay there long; and the administration building, standing near the Visitors' Center, which has functioned as the archive, preserving documents and certificates about the Holocaust, as well as the center from which the Remembrance Authority's activity has been run since the fifties. In addition to these, Warsaw Ghetto Square continues to serve as a hub for ceremonies on the Mount of Remembrance.

The book examined the construction of buildings and monuments, demonstrating how the State of Israel's largest, most complex, and most significant memorial site was created and gradually grew. This characterization is no platitude; a comparison of the mount to other remembrance sites in the State of Israel – those commemorating Zionist thinkers and state leaders or dedicated to the memory of those who fell in Israel's military campaigns or the Holocaust – indicates that none of them comes close to the richness, depth, and intricacy of Yad Vashem. None has the historical, physical, conceptual-commemorative layers that the Mount of Remembrance holds. The power of remembrance at Yad Vashem is not only tied to the mission of commemorating the Holocaust, which seems to be more complex than any other remembrance, nor is it tied to the site's scale, spreading as it does across dozens of acres, nor to the extensive financial investment, nor to the impressive architecture – but primarily to the many layers of memory it holds.

In contrast with other such sites around the country – Herzl's tomb, the Roaring Lion Monument at the Kfar Giladi cemetery, the Monument to the Negev Brigade – in which remembrance and the visiting experience are very focused, in Yad Vashem, over time, the memorial compound has developed as a multifaceted, impressive, profound space, one that facilitates an experience of commemorating the Holocaust in a variety of ways: visiting the museum or standing before the monuments dedicated to rebellion, heroism, extermination, and more. Yad Vashem allows visitors to experience various faces and the complexity of the Holocaust and heroism, and to undergo a profound cultural, historical, and meditative experience. This was in large part the intent of Yad Vashem's architects when they planned the site in general and its memorial focus – the Hall of Remembrance – in particular. The building, containing nothing but the names of the concentration and extermination camps, an eternal flame, and the tomb of the victims' ashes, makes the experience especially complex and rich.

As we have seen, Yad Vashem's planning and construction were not the product of a precise and immediate process; the opposite is the case. The process was rife with difficulties, disagreements, a dearth of funds, and a lack of consensus about the fitting way to approach the complicated issue. Some of the problems tied to building a memorial compound stemmed from the fact that the seminal years in the establishment of Yad Vashem, of shaping the identity of the Remembrance Authority and developing the Mount of Remembrance, were also the first and formative years of the State of Israel. These transitional periods were characterized generally as ones of conflicts, of complex and unsettling processes, of a heightened need for symbols with which meaning could be infused in the new, crystallizing reality.[2] As I demonstrated above, the fusing of the Holocaust and heroism with the memorial landscape in the State of Israel's narrative emerged as problematic and intricate, and the deliberations about how the devastating demise of millions of Jews could be commemorated accompanied the heads of Yad Vashem for a long period of time, engendering endless debates and influencing the image of remembrance that was ultimately formed there.[3]

Mordechai Shenhavi: Visionary and Adversary

History is full of visionaries whose views and ideas led to the founding of states, organizations, and institutions. History typically "loves" to remember those visionaries who managed, with their vision, to break new ground and lead to various conceptual and practical revolutions. But how do we relate to those visionaries whose dreams failed, or, at the very least, were realized but not in ways that they had hoped? What happens when the dream is taken from your hands and reshaped in a different way than you had imagined?

This is the case of Mordechai Shenhavi, the visionary of Yad Vashem, who ultimately saw his concept of establishing a Holocaust memorial institution in the land of Israel transformed and redesigned. He may have managed to bring about the establishment of an Israeli state authority charged with the subject, but Yad Vashem continued to move further from the path that he had defined in the forties and fifties, with others leading it in a different direction.

Shenhavi was a man of vision, not only in the context of Yad Vashem but also with regard to the many different projects in which he was involved – he was part of the establishment of the HaShomer HaTzair movement in Poland and in the land of Israel; industry in the kibbutz movement; an association for Jerusalem's development; the Tanach House in the capital city (though it was never realized); and more. Examining these efforts, the fact that during his

---

[2] Azaryahu, *State Cults*, 12.
[3] Young, *The Texture*, 2, lists five central motivations behind the establishment of Holocaust monuments: the desire to educate; the Jewish directive to remember; the need of European governments to explain themselves to the public; atonement; and the hope of attracting tourism. But in the pre-state period an additional, important dimension also existed: the sense of a pan-Jewish mission and the sense that Zionists and the State of Israel were responsible for all of the world's Jews, including those who had perished in the Holocaust, and that their immortalization must take place on Zionist land.

activities he often conflicted with those who worked with him – sometimes so much so that he was not a part of the ultimate building and inauguration of a number of the projects – is noticeable. And this was the case with Yad Vashem.

Shenhavi is mentioned many times in the present book's first section. In the first and second chapter, his name appears on nearly every page. But mentions of his name become sparser as the process of building the institution progressed, reflecting the tragedy of his connection to Yad Vashem. It is impossible to speak of the process of the institution's founding, from 1942 until the Yad Vashem Law was passed in 1953, without noting his tremendous, crucial contribution. Shenhavi has a place of honor at Yad Vashem, both because he initially raised the idea of establishing a Holocaust remembrance site in the land of Israel and because of his efforts to find it not only sufficient funding but also a fitting location. Shenhavi was the one who "saved" Yad Vashem during the years of decline after the founding of the state, when there was no body in the State of Israel that was interested in its fate. It was he who pushed decisively for the Yad Vashem Law that led to its becoming an Israeli state entity and it was he who organized the enterprise in the early years of its existence as an Israeli institution.

But later on, when Ben-Zion Dinur was appointed chairman and other bodies were added to the directorate, he was gradually pushed out of the institution and became a voice of opposition, clashing with those in charge. Protocols from Yad Vashem councils show his repeated grievances against them and the architects for their departure from the "correct path," from the plans that they had agreed to in the forties. When in 1961 the Hall of Remembrance already stood and the hearts of many were full of pride over Yad Vashem's architectural and symbolic achievement, Shenhavi had mostly words of criticism about what was so praised by many. He had trouble showing enthusiasm for the modern building, made of concrete and basalt, standing in the center of the remembrance plaza; time and again, he asserted that the structure did not suit its original goal: a memorial site for the Holocaust of six million people and the heroism of many fighters against the Nazis.

Today Shenhavi is commemorated at Yad Vashem in quite a trivial fashion. The board rooms for the institution's management are dedicated to him, as is a statue that stands in the sculpture garden. It is an abstract figure holding a Torah scroll that was created by his niece, Miriam Alfenbein Shwergold. In retrospect, more than seventy years after he began to undertake the Yad Vashem enterprise, it is possible to say that without Shenhavi's tenacity about the founding of the institution and the raising of funds, without his stubborn war with various people and bodies for the future of the institution, there would be no Yad Vashem. The present book, with its emphasis on his tremendous contribution to the enterprise, can be seen as a memorial candle to the man and his work.

Dueling Dualities and the Architecture of Remembrance

In 1956, prior to speaking before the assembly meant to determine the future image of the Mount of Remembrance, Dinur related to the challenge of commemoration at Yad Vashem. He asked "How [we can] build memorial structures that will both be highly effective, intended for their roles in terms of utility" but, "at the same time, be remembrance buildings with the ability to lift a person, to infuse him with a sense of 'Remove your shoes from your feet, for this ground is holy?"[4] In his words, he emphasized the dilemma of the pursuit of the "concrete and abstract," that is, the deliberations on how to give expression in the remembrance buildings both to the millions of Holocaust victims and to the abstract, the mental resources – "the sanctification of God's name, the courage, fraternity, that were in the hearts of people and their spirit, and shaped their image in the days of horror." He also asked for the advice of participants in the symposium regarding the fitting way to express the "individual's grief" architecturally, allowing one person to commune in the remembrance structure with his or her mourning and sadness but at the same time giving national and general expression "to the Holocaust of the nation and the girding of the public, to the image of the entire nation in such a horrific time." Despite the lack of "dimensions with which we can express the immensity of our catastrophe and power of our grief, there [was] a need to find a symbolic expression" for Holocaust and heroism, which Yad Vashem's chairman wished to immortalize.

In contrast with the sites of extermination in Europe, covered with the ashes of the victims and with a landscape full of conspicuous shacks, crematoria, and fences, Jerusalem was empty of such articles. And unlike the neighboring Mount Herzl, where the bones of the visionary of the state were buried, and the military cemetery, with the graves of those who fell in Israel's military campaigns, the Mount of Remembrance's terrain contained no traces of the six million who had perished. This was the central deliberation that occupied Yad Vashem's heads and the other people and bodies that took part in the planning and construction of the memorial site: how the frightful events that had taken place in Europe could be commemorated there. How would it be possible to establish a Holocaust

---

4 HHA, 3-95. 17 (2), Dinur, "Fundamental Problems in the Design of Yad Vashem's Buildings on the Mount of Remembrance," n.d.

memorial site in Jerusalem, when the events being remembered took place not there, but rather far away? How would it be possible to establish in the Jezreel Valley, Ma'ale HaHamisha, or the Mount of Remembrance in western Jerusalem a memorial site when Israel's soil contained no trace of what had occurred?

In his recollections, Shenhavi mentioned a number of times that his vision for establishing Yad Vashem was based on a part-dream, part-apocalyptic vision that he experienced in the early forties, when he worked in the fields of Kibbutz Beit Alpha.[5] It was a dream in which masses of people passed before him; each carried a gravestone on his or her back and fixed him with a demanding look, gazing straight into his eyes. Some of those who passed before him in the dream were familiar – family and friends from Poland who, as they disappeared into the distance, lowered the tombstones from their backs so that a massive boulder made of all of the tombstones grew on the horizon. Confronting the vision and the increasing news coming in from occupied Europe became an obsession for Shenhavi; he wanted to establish a monument to the millions who had perished in the Holocaust and, at the same time, preserve the singularity of remembrance for each one of them. Shenhavi persistently worked on the question of commemorating the millions. He saw in it the great mission of his life, contemplating how they could be remembered and immortalized in a way that would honor them as individuals but also be significant for the State of Israel.

This became the key question not only for Shenhavi but also for the rest of those who took part in shaping remembrance at Yad Vashem – how the scope of the inconceivable mass murder and tragedy that the Jewish nation was dealing with could be expressed in a physical and architectural way. This was an intricate issue that had been dealt with continuously in different places around the world and at different times since the end of the Second World War. In physical commemoration, efforts are usually made to tie space to time, place to the event being commemorated. A monument – usually a building, sculpture, grove, or sign – indicates the time and place of the events being commemorated and provides visitors with a sacred space for the act of remembrance.[6] But how could a genocide that took place in Europe – a historical event "filtered" through Zionist and local Israeli politics – be translated to spatial terms, to shapes and architectural images that would precisely express the memory and commemoration of the Holocaust and heroism?

---

5 HHA, 3-95. 2 (6), "Shenhavi's Memories."
6 Eran Neumann, "Monumental Holocaust Landscapes at Yad Vashem," *Dapim – Studies on the Holocaust* 21 (2007): 35–54 [in Hebrew]; Eran Neumann, "Physical Presence of the Holocaust," *Massuah Yearbook* 35 (2007), 27 [in Hebrew]; Neumann, *Shoah Presence*.

The solution found by Shenhavi and his colleagues to these problems – Europe's distance from the land of Israel and the inability to grasp the catastrophe in Europe – was at first quantitative and monumental. Their attempts to confront the difficult questions involved in immortalizing millions used a world of relatively recognizable and explicit symbols. As a result, the size of the site they wished to establish was also immense. Much like in Europe after the end of the Second World War, where Holocaust remembrance sites often used statues, obelisks, and figurative monuments to commemorate victory over the Nazis as well as the extermination of the Jews,[7] Shenhavi and the architects initially attempted to "import" Europe, the Second World War, and the extermination to the reality of the Israeli landscape. They felt that the only way to present and reflect the depths of the disaster would be through large-scale construction – an immense memorial plaza that would be suited for thousands and, around it, halls and monumental structures. Remembrance was perceived by them in the form of colossal monuments, symbolic forests, and museums that could display the horrors of Europe.

But the gradual rejection of the legitimacy of using most of the symbols – a result of internal and external pressure on Yad Vashem's directorate, financial hardships, and the process of conceptual-architectural "refining" – meant that the true difficulty of commemorating the Holocaust in the State of Israel and concretizing such abstract concepts as Holocaust and heroism in three-dimensional-architectural form remained.

The heads of the institution and its architects underwent a profound, gradual, internal process that led to a shift in the initially planned immensity and power, and this change led to the crystallizing idea of building Yad Vashem differently. This book depicted the institution's architects and heads adapting a far more independent line, one that was removed from the "problem" of Europe and Shenhavi's ideas. The memorial landscape at Yad Vashem included more and more independent motifs that the architects and heads managed to skillfully develop. The scope of building on the Mount of Remembrance and its monumentality were reduced and the large, romantic architectural "statues" of the forties, the spacious halls, plazas, and forests, were ultimately replaced with one central remembrance structure, the Hall of Remembrance.

This building, a "total abstraction,"[8] "modest, effective, and shocking,"[9] was built of concrete and basalt and stood at the center of a raised plaza that was

---

7 Marcuse, "Holocaust Memorials."
8 HHA, 3–95. 17 (2), "Summary of Yad Vashem's Two Symposia."
9 CZA, S23/1014, "Decisions of Yad Vashem's Directorate," August 7, 1956.

devoid of all symbols. The inbuilt and continuous tension between the desire to form an abstract creation with an artistic bent that would provoke thought and encourage one to remember the victims and heroes and the wish that remembrance nonetheless be concrete, making it possible to remember and commemorate the names of millions of victims, or at least the places in which they were concentrated or exterminated, was expressed. In a prolonged and purifying move, those involved understood that the immensity and power could be replaced with minimalism and that the aesthetically exposed, slight path of building remembrance, which would not force itself on the visitor but rather provoke thought and increase his or her sensitivity, was more fitting. Visitors to the Mount of Remembrance were led in "manipulative" fashion to the minimalistic Hall of Remembrance, naked of extraneous ornamentation, where they underwent a deep, personal experience pondering the Holocaust and its lessons. They were led from there, if they so choose, to other memorial structures – the museum, monuments, and sculptures – which complemented the experience.[10]

From nearly the very onset of the idea of building Yad Vashem, it was clear that commemoration would take place inside buildings, halls that ultimately became a "tent." This was not commemoration that was open to a view, using it, but remembrance that was "trapped" in a building, and the experience was entirely severed from the landscape. In contrast with Yad Vashem's new museum, where architect Moshe Safdie burrowed into the topography of the Mount of Remembrance and made it a central and significant element in the visiting experience, historical Yad Vashem made almost no reference to the surroundings or the location. The architects planning the original Yad Vashem refrained from relating to the topography and landscape, in contrast with the openly acknowledged intent of the "new" Yad Vashem's planner, who had his visitors finish their trip symbolically by going from darkness to light, to the striking hilly Jerusalem vistas, imparting a Zionist message and a sense of comfort in the rebirth of the State of Israel. The Hall of Remembrance did not grow out of an intricate sense of place developed by the architects in relation to western Jerusalem, nor did it come from a special bond with the Mount of Remembrance (see below). The place was intentionally designed as a universal remembrance structure, a kind of box "riding" on the hilltop, almost entirely cut off from its surroundings intentionally – a structure that could have been built in any place in the State of Israel or in the world.[11]

---

10 Lishinsky, "Yad Vashem."
11 Handelman and Shamgar-Handelman, "The Presence."

This is not to say that the architects did not address the surroundings or modify the building to its topography. The Building Committee and directorate discussions that we saw earlier indicate that they appreciated the space where the Mount of Remembrance was built and the unique ridge in western Jerusalem. But despite all of this, no real attempt was made to integrate the Holocaust within the local landscape that the building sat upon and, consciously, there was no Zionist or Israeli "lesson" in the building. All of those involved were aware that the Mount of Remembrance had no uniqueness tied to the Holocaust and its commemoration or the State of Israel; its selection, after other sites were considered time and again, came with no special felicity.

Not only did the Mount of Remembrance contain no component of Israeli identity; it also contained almost nothing of Jerusalem. The Hall of Remembrance was intentionally not built of local stone but rather basalt brought from the north of the country and concrete, a universal material with no local identity. Whether consciously or unconsciously, the ground of the memorial plaza was covered with nondescript granolithic flooring. In contrast with the plans from the forties, in which many local architectural elements – arches, domes, even a forest in the form of a map of the land of Israel indicating the pioneering settlements founded by the Zionist movement – were integrated, all of these were gradually erased from the plans of the Mount of Remembrance, leaving a commemoration building with a mixture of global and local characteristics, and no lines that related to Israel or Jerusalem. Unlike the commemoration of the fallen fighters, the expressions of which grew in the State of Israel after 1948, in the institution, the essence was based on absence, translating the unfathomable number of millions of victims and the thousands of Jewish communities that had been exterminated to a present that was devoid of local singularity. The authenticity was ingeniously achieved, with the awareness that the space had no remains of victims nor the places of extermination but rather only their memory. The Mount of Remembrance contained nothing more than the names of the victims (without their remains) collected in the Hall of Names, mentions of faraway places in which they were killed written on the floor of the Hall of Remembrance, and a symbolic grave of ashes buried nearby in a sarcophagus.[12]

Despite the fact that Holocaust commemoration was not explicit but rather hinted at, it was possible to make the Hall of Remembrance in particular and the Mount of Remembrance more generally into the most prominent commemorative space in the State of Israel. The Mount of Remembrance managed to

---

[12] Don Handelmam, *Nationalism and the Israeli State: Bureaucratic Logic in Public Events* (Oxford, UK; New York, NY: Berg, 2004), 161.

skillfully express the ties between Israel and Europe, between the years of extermination and the years of the institution's founding, and between Holocaust and rebirth. The Hall of Remembrance, Rapoport's monument, the Pillar of Heroism, and other symbolic structures at Yad Vashem resolved the problem of tying the landscape and location to the myth and narrative of the Holocaust and its commemoration in the State of Israel. All of this was accomplished in a prolonged process that ultimately resolved the social, political, and psychological needs of many and various agents from Yad Vashem's directorate, the State of Israel, and overseas. The opening of the Hall of Remembrance in 1961 "removed the wrappings" from Yad Vashem and exposed it to the Israeli, Jewish and International public, and from that point on the Remembrance Authority's true test began, with its attempts – and success – to bring Yad Vashem into the heart of Israeli public life in a process that extended for many years.

Holocaust Remembrance Meets State Commemoration

Yad Vashem stands next to Mount Herzl, the Great Leaders of the Nation's Plot, and the military cemetery, all of which are focuses of state remembrance that have maintained a complicated relationship for decades. To some, Yad Vashem is considered the most important part of the "Mount of Remembrance" and as such also the most important commemoration site in the State of Israel.[13]

It was with good reason that I opened the book's introduction by asking why Yad Vashem today teems with people while the nearby sites of remembrance suffer from a shortage of visitors throughout most of the year. It seems that the answer is tied to current social and political processes, ones that typify twenty-first-century Israeli society. It is important to bear in mind that, historically speaking, the fifties and sixties saw a picture that was the opposite of the current situation. Mount Herzl and Herzl's tomb at its peak were what served as a clear destination of civil-Israeli pilgrimage. Noteworthy visitors arrived there on official trips to the state, and many ceremonies were held there. In contrast, at that time Yad Vashem was hard-pressed to draw Israelis, who were not particularly interested in Holocaust commemoration. In the first years after Israeli sovereignty, the occupation with those who had fallen in Israel's campaigns and their commemoration was far more crucial and significant to Israelis than

---

[13] Formally, the "Mount of Remembrance" refers only to Yad Vashem. But within the Israeli public, the terms have become blended and at times it refers to Mount Herzl, the military cemetery, and the Great Leaders of the Nation's Plot.

dealing with the wound of the Holocaust. Holocaust commemoration had a relatively limited space in Israeli public space and the extermination did not take a central role in the broad process that characterized the mythmaking period.

Geography also had an influence on the intricate relationship between remembrance elements in the Zionist-Israeli memorial pantheon. While Herzl's tomb was consciously hewn into the highest mountain in western Jerusalem and the military cemetery was established on the slope facing the city, Yad Vashem was located at the rear, not visible from other parts of the city. Much as in the fifties, today there is still no road that leads to the place; a special path primarily serves the employees of Yad Vashem and its visitors, and no regular bus line goes there.

Why was a geographically and topographically peripheral hilltop chosen for the establishment of a Holocaust commemoration site that emerged as the most important and prominent memorial in the State of Israel? Was it an informed decision, hoping to exploit the proximity to Herzl's tomb and integrate Holocaust and heroism commemoration with the prominent national memorial compound? Or does the hilltop location reflect its inconsequence and the desire to suppress preoccupation with the subject, pushing it to the margins of the city and away from public attention?[14] Was there a guiding hand that wished to conceal Yad Vashem and perhaps even to divert it symbolically to Europe?[15]

It is impossible to reject the explanation that the location of Yad Vashem reflected a certain marginalizing approach in the early fifties, when the location was finally selected. Nonetheless, the decision to locate Yad Vashem there should be viewed against the backdrop of the protracted and grueling search for a memorial site in the years that preceded the founding of the State of Israel, a process that continued in the subsequent years. Before the state's founding, there was a serious problem locating a fitting area for this purpose; this was even more pronounced after Jerusalem was divided in 1948, when the territory included in the Israeli part of the city was so limited. While it may be true that more prominent locations had been considered for Yad Vashem – the space inside the national precinct which was being planned at that time or other areas in Jerusalem – given the institution's low public profile and the many difficulties that Shenhavi and other faced while looking for a suitable place, Yad Vashem's heads were happy with the space allotted to them and agreed with almost no hesitation.

---

14 Handelman and Shamgar-Handelman, "The Presence," 122; Friedlander and Seligman, "The Israeli," 363–64.
15 Handelman, *Nationalism*, 162.

Moreover, the decision to situate Yad Vashem in western Jerusalem created a spatial and symbolic relationship between the memorial components in this area – Mount Herzl, the military ceremony, and the Holocaust commemoration site. The institution's heads, led by Shenhavi, well understood that there was great value in the proximity of the Holocaust commemoration site to the visionary of the state's grave. Journalists were also in favor. *Davar*, relating to the news of martyrs' ashes being brought from Europe, wrote that other gravesites should not be sought.

> We will add to them the bones of our fighters and the liberators of our country and assemble them all on the Mount of Remembrance and thus lay the foundation for realizing the vast monument of generations. The Knesset – the nation's chosen people in its homeland and those laying the foundation for our state – should ascend to the Mount of Remembrance in Jerusalem, pay respect to the ashes of our martyrs and heroes and visionaries, and announce in the ears of all of Israel the beginning of the realization of the great memorial enterprise, the Yad Vashem enterprise.[16]

Thus the perception that Yad Vashem was built next to the military cemetery so that it would "ennoble" the Mount of Remembrance[17] is anachronistic; it does not reflect the reality when decisions were being made. The architectural team felt that Yad Vashem's proximity to Mount Herzl "adds to both enterprises as one emotional and architectonic elements without depriving each of the two of its uniqueness."[18] The reality was that for many years Yad Vashem was developed with no connection or relation at all to Mount Herzl and the military cemetery. Throughout this period, there was also no physical connection between the various parts of the memorial compound; in fact, it was impossible to go from Mount Herzl to Yad Vashem and vice versa. In 1963, Shatner, chairman of Yad Vashem's Building Committee, mentioned "the connection with the military cemetery, Mount Herzl, and Yad Vashem," noting that "at the time, efforts were made in this direction but I saw no result to my appeals."[19]

Many years elapsed after Shatner's efforts; it was only in 2003 that the "connecting path" was inaugurated, facilitating physical passage between the

---

16 I. Shuchman, "We will build *Yad va-Shem* [a Monument and Name] to Martyrs and Heroes," *Davar*, March 11, 1949.
17 Jackie Feldman, "Now There's a Bridge Between Them: The Linking Path between Yad Vashem and Mount Herzl," in *Memory, Forgetting and the Construction of Space*, ed. Haim Yakobi and Tobi Fenster (Jerusalem: Van Leer, 2012), 59 [in Hebrew].
18 MGWAA, Weinraub and Mansfeld to Shenhavi, July 19, 1953.
19 YVA, Protocols of Yad Vashem Directorate Meetings, Protocol of the Board of Directors, August 18, 1963.

two memorial sites for the first time.[20] Practically speaking, there is almost no connection between the different sections of the memorial compound at present. From time to time, tour groups, primarily youth, integrate both memorial spaces into one tour. These groups usually begin at the Valley of the Communities, go through the Hall of Remembrance, and end at Herzl's tomb and the military cemetery. The national-didactic symbolism here is clear – an attempt to tie Holocaust to the founding of the state and a walk along a symbolic path that leads from the bustling lives of the Jews in the Diaspora who were annihilated in the Holocaust to the vision of the establishment of the State of Israel.

Holocaust, Heroism, and Yad Vashem

Sacrifice for worthy goals has pride of place in any national movement. The bravery of the soldiers on the battlefield and the use of force to achieve a just national goal are considered an ultimate value.[21] The heroes are not only the soldiers who, in their lives and in their deaths, in victory and sometimes in defeat, serve as archetypes and symbols, but also gods, prophets, poets, religious figures, intellectuals, and rulers who become national symbols.[22]

In Jewish and Israeli society, heroism has been expressed in a variety of ways. Those willing to die for God's name and their faith; the pioneer working the soil who guards his land with his very life; Israel's soldier fighting to establish and protect his state – all are heroes.[23] But the Holocaust, as we saw throughout this book, constituted a special challenge in this sense. The annihilation of six million Jews demanded that the heads of the Yishuv in the land of Israel – and, after 1948, the heads of state – confront the definition of what Jewish heroism was.

In the forties, when Shenhavi began his efforts and contemplated the establishment of Yad Vashem, he placed great emphasis on heroism, and this was tied primarily to the Jewish soldiers in the lines of the armies that fought the Nazis, the ghetto fighters, and the partisans. The symbiotic connection that existed at

---

[20] Feldman, "Bridge"; Moshe Oren, *Linking Trail* (Jerusalem: Yad Izhak Ben-Zvi, 2014) [in Hebrew].
[21] Yael Zerubavel, "Between History and Legend: The Incarnations of Tel-Hai in Popular Memory," in *The Shaping of Israeli Identity: Myth, Memory and Trauma*, ed. Robert S. Wistrich and David Ohana (Jerusalem: Van Leer, 1997): 198–202 [in Hebrew].
[22] Thomas Carlyle, *On Heroes, Hero-Worship, and the Heroic in History* (London: Chapman and Hall, 1852).
[23] Judith Tydor Baumel, *Perfect Heroes: The Parachutists from Palestine during the Second World War and the Making of Israeli Collective Memory* (Sde Boqer: Sde Boqer and Ben-Gurion University Press, 2004), 7–8 [in Hebrew].

that time between Holocaust and heroism led the heads of Yad Vashem to guide the planners to a design in which Holocaust and heroism would stand opposite one another on equal footing, with a "remembrance hall" and a "heroism hall" symbolizing the essence of Holocaust and heroism remembrance.

But during the fifties and sixties, as we saw, the commitment to commemorating the combat and resistance against the Nazis waned amongst Yad Vashem's heads, and the emphasis placed on immortalizing the six million murdered increased. This change, reflecting a broader shift that had begun in Israeli society in relation to Holocaust in general and heroism in particular,[24] was tied not only to the bureaucratic and financial hardships that were growing as the years passed. Heroism commemoration lost its sheen in part because of the half-hearted attitude of the heads of the Claims Conference – the primary funder of Yad Vashem – who were opposed to monumental remembrance on the Mount of Remembrance and the initial emphasis that had been placed on heroism. But this was not the only cause; the process described in the book reflects a deep and significant shift that took place at the time in Israel's understanding of Holocaust and heroism and their forms of commemoration, a process that Yad Vashem both influenced and was influenced by. The narrative of heroism during the Holocaust, which in the forties seemed just and clear, included not only soldiers and partisans in the fifties and sixties; more and more, survivors and victims were included.[25] The dichotomous, distinct division between Holocaust and heroism, between victims and heroes, between losers and winners, which, in the first decade after the war, seemed relatively obvious and straightforward, became a multidimensional, multifaceted issue that ultimately had an impact on the Mount of Remembrance's form.

This change seemed even more significant against the backdrop of contrary processes that took place in other Holocaust commemoration sites that were established in Israel. From the establishment of Kibbutz Lohamei HaGeta'ot, as part of its founders' ethos, its commemoration focused on the heroism of the ghetto fighters. Kibbutz Yad Mordechai placed a sculpture of Rapoport's at the center of its commemoration – the image of the commander of the Ghetto Warsaw Uprising, Mordechai Anielewicz.[26] Yad Vashem, on the other hand, being a state Remembrance Authority whose mandate was determined based on the law

---

[24] Dalia Ofer, "We Israelis Remember, but How? The Memory of the Holocaust and the Israeli Experience," *Israel Studies* 18, no. 2 (2013): 70–85.
[25] Hanna Yablonka, "Survivor Meets the New Jew: Consciousness of Holocaust in Israel," in *The Age of Zionism*, ed. Anita Shapira, Jehuda Reinhart, and Jay Harris (Jerusalem: The Zalman Shazar Center for Jewish History, 2000), 297–319 [in Hebrew].
[26] Azaryahu and Donner, *Beit Lohamei HaGeta'ot*; Donner, *Nathan Rapaport*.

passed in 1953, was obligated to balance Holocaust and heroism and give both equal weight.

Nonetheless, this was not what transpired. As the planning and establishment of Yad Vashem proceeded, the heroism remembrance grew indistinct; ultimately, it was expressed in the erection of the Pillar of Heroism. The Kibbutz Mishmar HaEmek Archive holds a document with no clear identifying marks which, in my opinion, was composed by Mordechai Shenhavi (in third person) in the late sixties.

> With the establishment of the enterprise [Yad Vashem] itself, those holding the purse strings. . .arose and demanded that half of the enterprise be removed – that which was dedicated to Jewish fighters, because they said "Let our Judaism not be an obstacle. We are first Americans, Englishmen, Frenchmen, South Africans" (take your pick). Those with differences of opinion in whose hands the execution was left gave in to the pressure and thus the unity and essence of the idea of Mordechai's Holocaust and heroism commemoration idea was marred. Here, when he did not find sufficient support for his struggle, Mordechai left the directorate of Yad Vashem when all of his plans were in their hands. And there is much doubt if the executors understood what they gave up. Instead of the heroism wing they erected a lone, chimney-like concrete pillar.[27]

It appears that it was Shenhavi who related to the decision of Yad Vashem's directorate to exchange the heroism hall for a heroism monument, which ultimately became the Pillar of Heroism. As demonstrated above, the delay in founding the monument was not only a result of the bureaucratic difficulty in finding a place and funding for the monument, but primarily due to a lack of clarity about the symbolism of the pillar and its meaning. The inscription that was installed on the monument in the late sixties to a great extent illustrates this. After a disagreement on Yad Vashem's directorate, seen above, it was decided that the pillar would be dedicated to "those who rebelled in the camps and ghettos, fought in the woods, in the underground and with the Allied forces; braved their way to *Eretz Israel*; and those who died sanctifying the name of God."[28] The addition of the words "those who died sanctifying the name of God" was highly significant, and illustrates the change that took place at that time in the consciousness of the heads of Yad Vashem, who, while immortalizing heroism, also gave pride of place to those who had perished in the Holocaust.

---

[27] KMHA, S-29, 5, no writer's name, n.d. Handwriting on the other side of the document notes: "This section was removed at Mordechai Shenhavi's request."
[28] YVA, Protocols of Yad Vashem Directorate Meetings, Protocol of the Board of Directors, January 3, 1967; YVA, Protocols of Yad Vashem Directorate Meetings, protocol of January 26, 1968.

National Holocaust Commemoration: A Dream Realized

Anyone occupied with history recognizes that speculation is strictly forbidden. Historians well know not to guess what would have happened if the cornerstone for Yad Vashem had been laid on Mount Scopus, Ma'ale HaHamisha, or Ramat Rachel in the forties. What if the Zionist bodies had been able to agree about the best way to establish Yad Vashem and to raise the necessary funds for building the enterprise prior to the founding of the state? What would have become of Yad Vashem if Shenhavi had failed in his efforts to enlist Israeli politicians' approval for the Yad Vashem Law in the early fifties? And what would have happened if architects Weinraub and Mansfeld, Sharon and El-Hanani, had accompanied the execution of their large-scale plans in one of these sites and the remembrance hall and heroism hall had been built there? None of this, of course, transpired; the way in which Yad Vashem developed and became the memorial candle for six million people was entirely different, far lengthier and more complicated, rife with dilemmas, hardships, and achievements.

Commemoration is a complicated process – politically, bureaucratically, and physically – of social, cultural, and political contention with the challenge of integrating the narrative of the past in the present. During the process, power struggles and power structures related to groups and cultures dealing with the task of commemoration are evident.[29] In all places and times, occupation with remembrance constitutes a real challenge, but occupation with Holocaust commemoration and the question of its presence in the local landscape was particularly prolonged, intricate, and profound. The terrible calamity that befell Jewry may have aroused deep and sharp feelings of pain and rage but these feelings, with all of their intensity, were not initially sufficient to serve as a foundation for a Holocaust commemoration site. Strong conceptual motivation (initially primarily on Shenhavi's part) was necessary, tied to political recognition of the importance of remembering the events in Europe and cultivating the national feelings that were related to them.[30] This recognition gradually grew in a process that only reached fruition in the fifties, when the Israeli political establishment adopted Yad Vashem and made the Holocaust one of the state's sources of legitimacy. Holocaust documentation, its remembrance and commemoration (inter alia at Yad Vashem), became more important,

---

29 Matityahu Mayzel, "Introduction and A Few Remarks on Commemoration," in *Patterns of Commemoration*, ed. Matityahu Mayzel and Ilana Shamir (Tel Aviv: Misrad Habitachon Press, 2000), 7 [in Hebrew]; Azaryahu, "Memory in the Landscape."
30 Don-Yehiya, "Statehood and Holocaust"; Eliezer Don-Yehiya, "Memory and Political Culture: Israeli Society and The Holocaust," *Studies in Contemporary Jewry* 9 (1993): 139–62.

and occupation with the Holocaust took a growing place in the accepted and constitutive national tradition.

As I demonstrated above, the Holocaust, its memory and commemoration, and its evolution into a national "tradition,"[31] posed a unique challenge. There was a tremendous drive to forget and suppress the memory of such a terrible event, to leave what had happened behind, without relating to it. But at the same time there was commitment and desire to remember the murder of Jews and the heroism of fighters against the Nazis – not only through prayer, research, or collecting names, as preferred by many and dictated by Jewish tradition, but also by building remembrance and commemoration in the landscape. Different Zionist bodies – Keren Hayesod and the JNF, for example – and different political forces wished to keep the subject off of the public agenda. Shenhavi and others, stubbornly, refused to give up on his vision and insisted that the Holocaust would be commemorated in the land of Israel. But it is hard to believe that those who helped develop the Mount of Remembrance knew that the process would take so much time and require so many human and financial resources.

In 1964, the newspaper *Herut* decried Yad Vashem: "There [on the Mount of Remembrance] an immense building, like a vast, abstract lump of concrete, with no trace of the nation's sacred symbols, the holy ark, the Ten Commandments, Torah scroll, menorah, or (yellow) Star of David flying above, will commemorate, will tremble . . . here everything is planned and settled."[32] The writer protested the heads of the authority and what he viewed as their meager achievements. He also related to the claim voiced publicly at the time against Yad Vashem that, in contrast with other Holocaust memorial sites (in this case, the Chamber of the Holocaust on Mount Zion), at Yad Vashem there was not even one corner dedicated to personal and Jewish remembrance. Yad Vashem indeed was developed as a national-secular site and was part of the view that characterized the years that followed the state's founding. Yad Vashem drew its power from its modern architecture and engendered among visitors a sense of a "large place," an alienating site, with no space for private remembrance. There was no place for private tears, no place to light a candle in memory of those who had perished or to remember in the traditional way, in the familial way, or, in effect,

---

31 Eric Hobsbawn, *Nations and Nationalism since 1780: Programme, Myth, Reality* (Cambridge: Cambridge University Press, 1990); Eric Hobsbawn and Terence Ranger, eds., *The Invention of Tradition* (New York: Cambridge University Press, 1983); Yossi Dahan and Henry Wasserman, "Introduction," in *To Invent a Nation*, ed. Yossi Dahan and Henry Wasserman (Raanana: The Open University Press, 2006), 11–28 [in Hebrew].
32 "The Chamber of the Holocaust and the Hall of Remembrance," *Herut*, April 9, 1964.

in the communal way. A desire had been expressed during the years of planning and building that the Mount of Remembrance bridge the gap between national, public, and personal remembrance; however, the institution's heads and planners were not up to the task, and ultimately it was built not for the survivors but rather for "the State of Israel." This remembrance was state, national, apolitical, greater than the many partisan disagreements that characterized Israeli society in the years that preceded and followed the state's founding.

It would be easy to criticize and disparage the original appearance of Yad Vashem, given the immense difference from its appearance today. Today, for example, the new historical museum gives greater weight to the place of the individual Jew, the family, and the community in the Holocaust. In historical Yad Vashem, in contrast, remembrance was general and national. In truth, the institution's founding and building constituted a tremendous achievement, bound up in a large financial investment, struggles, disagreements, many discussions, and countless people's hard work. It all began with the first hesitant steps made in the forties; with Shenhavi's revolution in the fifties, when he managed to drive the process that led to the Yad Vashem Law; with Dinur's ability to helm the institution in its early years; with the laying of the cornerstone for the archive building; and with the achievements of their successors in the years that followed, which led to the building and expansion of the geographical and symbolic boundaries of the Mount of Remembrance. In retrospect, Yad Vashem's success is clear as day. The protracted efforts led to the institution settling in the center of Israeli, Jewish, and global public life, in the local and international culture and space. Thus, despite the fact that more than seventy years have elapsed since the annihilation of the Jews in Europe, Yad Vashem and the Mount of Remembrance continue to serve as a meaningful memorial flame for the millions who perished in the Holocaust.

Bibliography

List of Archives

BGA	Ben-Gurion Archive
BLHA	Beit Lohamei HaGeta'ot (Ghetto Fighters' House) Archive
CAHJP	The Central Archives for the History of the Jewish People
HHA	HaShomer HaTzair Archive
HS	Herzliya Studios
ISA	Israel State Archive
JMA	Jerusalem Municipality Archive
KKLPA	Keren Kayemeth LeIsrael Photo Archive
KMHA	Kibbutz Mishmar HaEmek Archive
MGWAA	Munio Gitai Weinraub Architecture Archive
NPA	National Photo Archive
SSJFA	The Steven Spielberg Jewish Film Archive
YVA	Yad Vashem Archive

List of Newspapers

Al HaMishmar (before January 1948: *Mishmar*)
Davar
Haaretz
HaBoker
HaDor
HaTzofe
Herut
The Jewish Herald
Jewish Telegraphic Agency
Mishmar
Palestine Post
Yedioth Ahronoth

Secondary Sources

Azaryahu, Maoz. *State Cults: Celebrating Independence and Commemorating the Fallen in Israel, 1948–1956*. Sde Boqer: Ben-Gurion Research Institute, 1995 [in Hebrew].

Azaryahu, Maoz. "Innovation and Continuity: Jewish Tradition and the Shaping of Sovereignty Rites in Israel." In *On Both Sides of the Bridge: Religion and State in the Early Years of Israel*, edited by Mordechai Bar-On and Zvi Zameret, 273–94. Jerusalem: Yad Izhak Ben-Zvi, 2002 [in Hebrew].

Azaryahu, Maoz. "(Re)locating Redemption – Jerusalem: The Wall, Two Mountains, a Hill and the Narrative Construction of the Third Temple." *Journal of Modern Jewish Studies* 1 (2002): 22–35.

Azaryahu, Maoz. "Public Controversy and Commemorative Failure: Tel Aviv's Monument to the Holocaust and National Revival." *Israel Studies* 16 (2011): 129–48.

Azaryahu, Maoz. *In Their Death They Ordered: The Architecture of Military Cemeteries – The First Years*. Tel Aviv: Misrad Habitachon, 2012 [in Hebrew].

Azaryahu, Maoz. "Memory in the Landscape: Invisible Memorials – Three Test Cases." *Cathedra* 150 (2013): 211–38 [in Hebrew].

Azaryahu, Maoz and Batia Donner. *Beit Lohamei Haghetaot: The Yitzhak Katzenelson Holocaust and Resistance Heritage Museum, 1949–1999*. Lohamei HaGeta'ot: Beit Lohamei HaGeta'ot, the Yitzhak Katzenelson Holocaust and Resistance Museum, 2000 [in Hebrew].

Bar, Doron. "Holocaust Commemoration in Israel during the 1950s: The Holocaust Cellar on Mount Zion." *Jewish Social Studies* 12, no. 1 (2005): 16–38.

Bar, Doron. "Between the Chamber of the Holocaust and Yad Vashem: Martyrs' Ashes as a Focus of Sanctity." *Yad Vashem Studies* 38 (2010): 195–227.

Bar, Doron. "The Martyr's Forest, the JNF and Yad Vashem and the Commemoration of the Holocaust." *Cathedra* 140 (2011): 103–30 [in Hebrew].

Bar, Doron. "A Prayer House or a Memorial for the Holocaust? The Debate Over Yad Vashem's Synagogue, 1945–1964." *Yad Vashem Studies* 43 (2015): 179–209.

Bar, Doron. "Holocaust and Heroism in the Process of Establishing Yad Vashem 1942–1970." *Dapim – Studies on the Holocaust* 30 (2016): 1–25.

Bar, Doron. *Landscape and Ideology: Reinterment of Renowned Jews in the Land of Israel, 1904–1967*. Berlin: De Gruyter, 2016.

Bar, Doron. "The Hall of Remembrance at Yad Vashem: Israel's Holocaust Commemoration Monument." *The Journal of Holocaust Research* 34, no. 1 (2020): 24–48.

Bar, Doron. "Zionist Pantheons? The Design and Development of the Tombs of Herzl, Weizmann and Rothschild during the Early Years of the State of Israel." *Israel Studies* 25, no. 2 (2020): 72–94.

Bar-Gal, Yoram. *Propaganda and Zionist Education: The Jewish National Fund, 1924–1947*. Rochester, NY: University of Rochester Press, 2003.

Barnir, Sigal. "On Forests as Sites of Commemoration." *Itzuv Zikaron* 1 (1998): 86–97 [in Hebrew].

Barzel, Neima. "The Concept of Heroism Between Collective Memory and Privatized National Memory." *Dapim – Studies on the Holocaust* 16 (2000): 86–124 [in Hebrew].

Ben-Arieh, Yehoshua, ed. *Jerusalem and the British Mandate, Interaction and Legacy*. Jerusalem: Mishkenot Sha'ananim and Yad Izhak Ben-Zvi, 2003 [in Hebrew].

Ben Nahum, Izhar. *Visions in Action: The Life Story of Mordechai Shenhabi*. Dalia: Yad Yaari, 2011 [in Hebrew].

Ben Zur, Neomi. *Naftali Bezem: Holocaust and Heroism*. Jerusalem: Yad Vashem: n.d. [in Hebrew].

Bertrand Monk, Daniel. *An Aesthetic Occupation: The Immediacy of Architecture and the Palestine Conflict*. Durham: Duke University Press, 2002.

Brog, Mooli. "Besieged within Walls of Memory." *Alpayim* 14 (1997): 148–73 [in Hebrew].

Brog, Mooli. "'In Blessed Memory of a Dream': Mordechai Shenhavi and Initial Holocaust Commemoration Ideas in Palestine, 1942–1945." *Yad Vashem Studies* 30 (2002): 241–69 [in Hebrew].

Brog, Mooli. "A Memorial for the Fighters and Commemoration of the Victims: Efforts by the Va'ad Haleumi to Establish Yad Vashem, 1946–1949." *Cathedra* 119 (2006): 87–120 [in Hebrew].

Brog, Mooli. "'The Stone Will Scream from the Wall': Monumental Commemoration of the Holocaust in the Israeli Landscape." *Massuah Yearbook* 32 (2006): 93–109 [in Hebrew].

Brog, Mooli. *Who Should Be Remembered? The Struggle for Commemorative Recognition at Yad Vashem.* Jerusalem: Carmel, 2019 [in Hebrew].

Brutin, Batya. *Living with the Memory: Monuments in Israel Commemorating the Holocaust.* Kibbutz Lohamei HaGeta'ot: Beit Lohamei HaGeta'ot, 2005 [in Hebrew].

Carlyle, Thomas. *On Heroes, Hero-Worship, and the Heroic in History.* London: Chapman and Hall, 1852.

Cohen, Boaz. *Israeli Holocaust Research: Birth and Evolution.* Jerusalem: Yad Vashem, 2001 [in Hebrew].

Cohen, Yohai M. "Horror on the Wall: The Holocaust Image in Yad Vashem's History Exhibition, 1956–2005." PhD diss., Hebrew University of Jerusalem, 2018 [in Hebrew].

Cohen-Hattab, Kobi. "The Formation of National Identity in West Jerusalem During the First Decade after the Establishment of the State of Israel." *Zion* 72, no. 2 (2007): 189–217 [in Hebrew].

Dahan, Yossi and Henry Wasserman. "Introduction." In *To Invent a Nation*, edited by Yossi Dahan and Henry Wasserman, 11–28. Raanana: The Open University Press, 2006 [in Hebrew].

Dolev, Diana. "The Hebrew University's Master Plans, 1918–1948." In *The History of the Hebrew University of Jerusalem Origins and Beginnings*, edited by Shmuel Katz and Michal Heyd, 257–80. Jerusalem: Magnes Press, 1997 [in Hebrew].

Dolev, Diana. "An Ivory Tower in the National Precinct: The Architecture Plan for the University Campus in Giva'at Ram." *Zmanim* 96 (2006): 86–93 [in Hebrew].

Donner, Batia. *Nathan Rapaport: A Jewish Artist.* Jerusalem: Yad Izhak Ben-Zvi, Givat Haviva, Yad Yaari, 2014 [in Hebrew].

Don-Yehiya, Eliezer. "Statehood and Holocaust." In *In the Paths of Renewal: Studies in Religious Zionism*, edited by Avraham Rubinstein, 167–88. Ramat Gan: Bar-Ilan University Press, 1983 [in Hebrew].

Don-Yehiya, Eliezer. "Memory and Political Culture: Israeli Society and The Holocaust." *Studies in Contemporary Jewry* 9 (1993): 139–62.

Efrati, Shimon. *From the Valley of Tears: Responsa.* Jerusalem: Mossad Harav Kook, 1948 [in Hebrew].

Efrati, Shimon. *From the Valley of Death: Responsa.* Jerusalem: Yehuda, 1961 [in Hebrew].

Eisner, Jack. *The Survivor.* Edited by Irving A. Leitner. New York: W. Morrow, 1980.

Elon, Amos. *The Israelis: Founders and Sons.* London: Weidenfeld and Nicolson, 1971.

Englman, Adi and Dan Handel. *Dan Reisinger.* Jerusalem: Israel Museum, 2017.

Eshbal, Aminadav. *Hakhsharat ha-Yishuv.* Jerusalem: Hakhsharat ha-Yishuv, 1976 [in Hebrew].

Eshkoli, Hava. "Destruction Becomes Creation: The Theological Reaction of National Religious Zionism in Palestine to the Holocaust." *Holocaust and Genocide Studies* 17, no. 3 (2003): 430–58.

Even Shoshan, Shlomo. *Itzhak Katzenelson, Lament of the Holocaust.* Jerusalem: Ministry of Education, 1964 [in Hebrew].

Feldman, Jackie. "Now There's a Bridge Between Them: The Linking Path between Yad Vashem and Mount Herzl." In *Memory, Forgetting and the Construction of Space*, edited by Haim Yakobi and Tobi Fenster, 56–84. Jerusalem: Van Leer, 2012 [in Hebrew].

Friedlander, Saul and Adam B. Seligman. "The Israeli Memory of the Shoah: On Symbols, Rituals, and Ideological Polarization." In *Now Here: Space, Time and Modernity*, edited by Roger Friedland and Deirdre Boden, 356–71. Berkley: University of California Press, 1994.

Gil, Idit. "The Shoah in Israeli Collective Memory: Changes in Meanings and Protagonists." *Modern Judaism* 32 (2012): 76–101.

Golani, Motti. *Zion in Zionism: Zionist Policy and the Question of Jerusalem, 1937–1949*. Tel Aviv: Tel Aviv University and the Ministry of Defense, 1992 [in Hebrew].

Goldmann, Nahum. *Memories*. Jerusalem: Weidenfeld and Nicolson, 1969 [in Hebrew].

Gutterman, Bella. *Yad Vashem: 60 Years of Remembrance, Documentation, Research and Education*. Jerusalem: Yad Vashem, 2014 [in Hebrew].

Gutwein, Daniel. "The Privatization of the Holocaust: Memory, Historiography, and Politics." *Dapim – Studies on the Holocaust* 15 (1998): 7–52.

Handelman, Don. *Nationalism and the Israeli State: Bureaucratic Logic in Public Events*. Oxford, UK: Berg, 2004.

Handelman, Don and Lea Shamgar-Handelman. "The Presence of Absence: The Memorialism of National Death in Israel." In *Grasping Land: Space and Place in Contemporary Israeli Discourse and Experience*, edited by Eyal Ben-Ari and Yoram Bilu, 85–128. Albany: SUNY Press, 1997.

Harel, Dorit. *Facts and Feelings – Dilemmas in Designing the Yad Vashem Holocaust History Museum*. Jerusalem: Dorit Harel Designers, 2010.

Hashimshoni, Avyah, Tsiyon Hashimshoni, and Yosef Shavid. *Jerusalem Master Plan 1968*. Jerusalem: Municipality of Jerusalem, 1974 [in Hebrew].

Hecht, Reuben R. *Last Gentleman: Autobiography*. Or Yehuda: Zmora-Bitan, 2007 [in Hebrew].

Hershlag, Pua. *The Story of Yitzhak Zuckerman (Antek)*. Jerusalem: Yad Izhak Ben-Zvi, 2006 [in Hebrew].

Hevra Kadisha. *Hevra Kadisha, Jerusalem: Jubilee Book 1939–1999*. Jerusalem: Hevra Kadisha Jerusalem, 1992 [in Hebrew].

Hobsbawn, Eric. *Nations and Nationalism since 1780: Programme, Myth, Reality*. Cambridge: Cambridge University Press, 1990.

Hobsbawn, Eric and Terence Ranger, eds. *The Invention of Tradition*. New York: Cambridge University Press, 1983.

Horst, Hanske and Jörg Traeger. *Walhalla. Ruhmestempel an der Donau*. Regensburg: Buchverlag der Mittelbayerischen Zeitung, 1992.

Ingersoll, Richard. *Munio Gitai Weinraub: Bauhaus Architect in Eretz Israel*. Photographs by Gabriele Basilico. Milan: Electa, 1994.

Jockusch, Laura. "Breaking the Silence: The Centre de Documentation Juive Contemporaine in Paris and the Writing of Holocaust History in Liberated France." In *After the Holocaust: Challenging the Myth of Silence*, edited by David Cesarani and Eric J. Sundquist, 67–81. Abingdon, Oxon: Routledge, 2011.

Kabalek, Kobi. "The Commemoration before the Commemoration: Yad Vashem and the Righteous among the Nations, 1945–1963." *Yad Vashem Studies* 39, no. 1 (2011): 169–211.

Krakowski, Shaul. "Memorial Projects and Memorial Institutions Initiated by She'erit Hapletah." In *She'erit Hapletah, 1944–1948: Rehabilitation and Political Struggle*, edited by Yisrael Gutman and Adina Drechsler, 351–59. Jerusalem: Yad Vashem, 1990 [in Hebrew].

Liebman, Yeshayahu Charles. "Holocaust Myth in the Israeli Society." *Tfutzot Israel* 19 (1981): 101–14 [in Hebrew].
Lifshitz, Nili and Gideon Biger. *Forestry in Eretz Israel: First 100 Years 1850–1950*. Jerusalem: Ariel, 2000 [in Hebrew].
Linenthal, Edward T. *Preserving Memory: The Struggle to Create America's Holocaust Museum*. New York: Penguin Books, 1997.
Lishinsky, Yosef. "Yad Vashem as Art." *Ariel* 55 (1983): 14–25 [in Hebrew].
Lissovsky, Nurit and Diana Dolev, eds. *Arcadia: The Gardens of Lipa Yahalom and Dan Zur*. Tel Aviv: Babel, 2012 [in Hebrew].
Ludyga, Hannes. *Philipp Auerbach (1906–1952): Staatskommissar für rassisch, religiös und politisch Verfolgte*. Berlin: Berliner Wissenschafts-Verlag, 2005.
Mann, Yitzhak and Sarel Baruch. *A Memorial for the Holocaust and the Revolt*. Jerusalem: Keren Kayemet Leyisrael, 1953 [in Hebrew].
Marcuse, Harold. "Holocaust Memorials: The Emergence of a Genre." *American Historical Review* 115 (2010): 53–89.
Marily, Henry. *Confronting the Perpetrators: A History of the Claims Conference*. London: Vallentine Mitchell, 2007.
Markovitzky, Jacob. *Spirit of the Valleys: The Enterprise of the JNF as Stepping-Stones in the Development of the National Homeland (1920–1936)*. Tel Aviv: Misrad Habitachon, 2007 [in Hebrew].
Mayzel, Matityahu. "Introduction and A Few Remarks on Commemoration." In *Patterns of Commemoration*, edited by Matityahu Mayzel and Ilana Shamir, 7–10. Tel Aviv: Misrad Habitachon Press, 2000 [in Hebrew].
Merilyn, Henry. *Confronting the Perpetrators: A History of the Claims Conference*. Edgware, Middlesex: Vallentine Mitchell, 2007.
Minta, Anna. "Government Quarter, West-Jerusalem, 1950." In *Munio Weinraub Amos Gitai Atchitektur und Film in Israel*, edited by Winfried Nerdinger, 112–17. Munchen: Edition Minerva, 2008.
Nerdinger, Winfried, ed. *Munio Weinraub Amos Gitai Atchitektur und Film in Israel*. Munchen: Edition Minerva, 2008.
Neumann, Eran. "Monumental Holocaust Landscapes at Yad Vashem." *Dapim – Studies on the Holocaust* 21 (2007): 35–54 [in Hebrew].
Neumann, Eran. "Physical Presence of the Holocaust." *Massuah Yearbook* 35 (2007): 22–35 [in Hebrew].
Neumann, Eran. *Shoah Presence: Architectural Representations of the Holocaust*. Farnham, UK: Ashgate, 2014.
Ofer, Dalia. "How and What to Remember: The Holocaust in Israel in the First Decade." In *Independence: The First Fifty Years*, edited by Anita Shapira, 171–93. Jerusalem: The Zalman Shazar Center, 1998 [in Hebrew].
Ofer, Dalia. "We Israelis Remember, but How? The Memory of the Holocaust and the Israeli Experience." *Israel Studies* 18, no. 2 (2013): 70–85.
Ofrat, Gideon. *Origins of Eretz-Israeli Sculpture: 1906–1939*. Herzliya: Herzliya Museum, 1990 [in Hebrew].
Oren, Moshe. *Linking Trail*. Jerusalem: Yad Izhak Ben-Zvi, 2014 [in Hebrew].
Palombo, David. *David Palombo*. Jerusalem: David Palombo Museum, 1991 [in Hebrew].

Parciack, Rivka. *Here and There, Now and on Other Days: The Holocaust Crisis Seen through the Material Culture of Cemeteries and Monuments in Poland and Israel.* Jerusalem: Magnes Press, 2007 [in Hebrew].

Paz, Yair. "The Hebrew University on Mount Scopus as a Secular Temple." In *The History of the Hebrew University of Jerusalem Origins and Beginnings*, edited by Shmuel Katz and Michal Heyd, 281–308. Jerusalem: Magnes Press, 1997 [in Hebrew].

Paz, Yair. "The Botanical Garden and the 'Garden of the Prophets': Two Educational Projects in the Early Years of the Hebrew University." In *The History of the Hebrew University of Jerusalem, A Period of Consolidation and Growth*, edited by Hagit Lavsky, 443–72. Jerusalem: Magnes Press, 2005 [in Hebrew].

Ran, Daniela. *Mila Brenner.* Daliyya: Maarechet, 2003 [in Hebrew].

Rein, Arielle. "Historian as a Nation Builder, Ben Zion Dinur's Evolution and Enterprise, 1884–1948." PhD diss., Hebrew University of Jerusalem, 2000 [in Hebrew].

Rothem, Stephanie Shosh. *Constructing Memory: Architectural Narratives of Holocaust Museums.* New York: Peter Lang, 2013.

Safdie, Moshe. *Jerusalem: The Future of the Past.* Montreal: Optimum Pub. International, 1989.

Samuel, Edwin. *Tent of Remembrance at Yad Vashem.* Jerusalem: Yad Vashem, 1975 [in Hebrew].

Schwartz, Buky. "Monument of Bravery." *KAV* 8 (1968): 59–60 [in Hebrew].

Shaul, Michal. *Beauty for Ashes: Holocaust Memory and the Rehabilitation of Ashkenazi Haredi Society in Israel 1945–1961.* Jerusalem: Yad Vashem and Yad Izhak Ben-Zvi, 2014 [in Hebrew].

Stauber, Roni. "Confronting the Jewish Response to the Holocaust: Yad Vashem – A Commemorative and a Research Institute in the 1950s." *Modern Judaism* 20 (2000): 277–98.

Stauber, Roni. *A Lesson for this Generation – Holocaust and Heroism in Israeli Public Discourse in the 1950s.* Jerusalem: Yad Izhak Ben-Zvi, 2000 [in Hebrew].

Stauber, Roni. "The Debate in the 1950s Regarding the Establishment of a Holocaust Remembrance Day." In *A State in the Making: Israeli Society in the First Decades*, edited by Anita Shapira, 189–203. Jerusalem: The Zalman Shazar Center for Jewish History, 2001 [in Hebrew].

Tal, Miriam. "Sculptor Zvi Aldubi." *TAVI* 11 (1972): 71–75 [in Hebrew].

Tydor Baumel, Judith. "Commemorating the Holocaust by Communities and Individuals in the State of Israel." *Iyunim Bitkumat Israel* 5 (1995): 364–87 [in Hebrew].

Tydor Baumel, Judith. *Perfect Heroes: The Parachutists from Palestine during the Second World War and the Making of Israeli Collective Memory.* Sde Boqer: Sde Boqer and Ben-Gurion University Press, 2004 [in Hebrew].

Urbach, Efraim E. "The Laws of Idolatry in the light of Historical and Archaeological Facts in the Second and Third Centuries." *Eretz Israel* 5 (1958): 185–205 [in Hebrew].

Warhaftig, Zerach. *Refugee and Remnant during the Holocaust.* Jerusalem: Yad Vashem, 1984 [in Hebrew].

Wassermann, Henry. "Nationalization of the Memory of the Six Million." *Politika* 8 (1986): 6–7 [in Hebrew].

Weitz, Yechiam. "Shaping the Memory of the Holocaust in Israeli Society of the 1950s." In *Major Changes Within the Jewish People in the Wake of the Holocaust*, edited by Yisrael Gutman, 473–94. Jerusalem: Yad Vashem, 1993 [in Hebrew].

Weitz, Yechiam. "The Political Connection: Israeli Political Parties and the Memory of the Holocaust in the 1950s." *Iyunim Bitkumat Israel* 6 (1996): 271–87 [in Hebrew].

Weitz, Yosef. *Mount Herzl*. Jerusalem: Committee for Mount Herzl, 1968 [in Hebrew].
Yablonka, Hanna. "Survivor Meets the New Jew: Consciousness of Holocaust in Israel." In *The Age of Zionism*, edited by Anita Shapira, Jehuda Reinhart, and Jay Harris, 297–319. Jerusalem: The Zalman Shazar Center for Jewish History, 2000 [in Hebrew].
Yad Vashem. *Yad Vashem Exhibitions*. Jerusalem: Yad Vashem, 1960 [in Hebrew].
Yad Vashem. *Yad Vashem: Memorial Candle at the Tent of Remembrance*. Jerusalem: Yad Vashem, n.d.
Yaffe, Richard. *Nathan Rapoport Sculptures and Monuments*. New York: Shengold, 1980.
Yerushalmi, Yosef Haim. *Zakhor: Jewish History and Jewish Memory*. Seattle: University of Washington Press, 1982.
Young, James E. "The Biography of a Memorial Icon: Nathan Rapoport's Warsaw Ghetto Monument." *Representations* 26 (1989): 69–106.
Young, James E. *The Texture of Memory: Holocaust Memorials and Meaning*. New Haven: Yale University Press, 1994.
Zait, David. *Visions in Action: The Life Story of Mordechai Shenhabi*. Givat Haviva: Yad Yaari, 2005 [in Hebrew].
Zameret, Zvi. "Between Palestino-centrism and Judeo-centrism: Ben-Zion Dinaburg (Dinur) and the Holocaust of European Jewry." In *When Disaster Comes from Far: Leading Personalities in the Land of Israel Confront Nazism and the Holocaust, 1933–1948*, edited by Dina Porat, 263–95. Jerusalem: Yad Izhak Ben-Zvi, 2009 [in Hebrew].
Zerubavel, Yael. "The Death of Memory and the Memory of Death: Masada and the Holocaust as Historical Metaphors." *Representations* 45 (1994): 72–100.
Zerubavel, Yael. "The Forest as a National Icon: Literature, Politics, and the Archaeology of Memory." *Israel Studies* 1, no. 1 (1996): 60–99.
Zerubavel, Yael. "Between History and Legend: The Incarnations of Tel-Hai in Popular Memory." In *The Shaping of Israeli Identity: Myth, Memory and Trauma*, edited by Robert S. Wistrich and David Ohana, 198–202. Jerusalem: Van Leer, 1997 [in Hebrew].
Zuckermann, Baruch. "Yad Vashem's Idea." *Gesher* 4, no. 2 (1958): 70–79 [in Hebrew].
Zweig, Ronald W. *German Reparation and the Jewish World: A History of the Claims Conference*. Boulder: Westview Press, 1987.
Zweig, Ronald W. "Politics of Commemoration." *Jewish Social Studies* 44 (1987): 155–66.

Index

Subjects

10 Tevet 68, 70–71, 148

Agudat Yisrael 40, 81, 140
Association for Jerusalem's development 230
Association of Engineers and Architects 36, 48, 94

Binyanei Ha'uma (International Convention Center) 86
Bravery 191, 207, 211, 240

Center for the Commemoration and Documentation of the Holocaust (Centre de Documentation Juive Contemporaine) 60
Chief Rabbinate 24, 43, 67–68, 71, 142, 177, 200, 214
Claims Conference vii, 7, 9, 91, 104–109, 113, 115, 117–121, 133, 135–139, 150, 152, 158, 164–167, 182–183, 200, 206, 217, 241
Clandestine Immigration 82, 126, 213
Commemoration vii–viii, 1–8, 10–14, 18–27, 30, 32–34, 36, 38, 41–43, 45–47, 53–57, 59–60, 62–66, 68, 70–73, 75–78, 80–81, 84–85, 89, 91, 93, 95–101, 105, 108, 112–113, 116, 122–123, 125, 131, 135, 145, 147–148, 153, 155–161, 166, 168, 181, 183–184, 202, 209, 214, 224–226, 232–233, 235–239, 241–245
– Traditional Commemoration 100, 143, 147–148, 155–156
Conference on Holocaust and Martyrdom in Our Time 45, 47

Diaspora Jewry 2, 15, 86, 105, 126

Eichmann Trial 9, 179
El Malei Rahamim 106, 131–132, 151, 158–159, 162

Forest of the Jewish Soldier 17

Garden of the Prophets and Sages 39
Ghetto Fighters 18, 21–22, 24, 44, 76, 92, 95–96, 157–158, 160, 240–241
Global Conference of Jewish Fighters in the Second World War 191

Hapoel Hamizrachi 145
HaShomer HaTzair 17, 214, 230
Hebrew University 19, 22, 24, 29, 47, 49, 86
Hevra Kadisha 23, 46, 67, 144, 146, 163, 176
Hibbat Yerushalayim Association 87
Historic Committee (Linz) 65
Historical Society of Israel 118
Holocaust Memory 4, 8, 59, 95

IDF 6, 63, 200
International Association of Former Underground Fighters, Survivors, and Camp Inmates 93
Israel's Government 6, 62, 70, 74–75, 78, 80, 86–88, 98, 115, 121, 128, 137, 139, 142, 150, 167
– Ministry of Finance 117–118, 120
– Ministry of Defense unit for Soldiers' Commemoration 85
– Ministry of Education 62, 200, 217
– Ministry of Foreign Affairs 98, 141–142, 164, 193, 216

Jewish Agency 24–25, 35, 61, 66, 81, 92, 103, 121, 139, 150, 167, 216–217
Jewish Fighters 21, 26, 74, 96, 112, 191, 242
– Allied Armies 17, 96, 157, 190
– Jewish Brigade 44
Jewish Historical Institute in Warsaw 143
Jewish Museum (Berlin) vii
Jewish National Fund (JNF) 12–21, 23–25, 28, 32, 35, 37, 39, 41–44, 46, 50, 59, 62, 65,

72–77, 85, 87, 91–93, 97–98, 101–102, 119, 196–197, 199, 216, 218, 244

Kaddish 40, 106, 154
Keren Hayesod 25, 45–46, 244
Knesset 6, 10, 59, 67, 74–75, 77–78, 80–84, 87, 101–102, 132, 200, 217, 239

Landsmannschaften 30, 96, 157, 181, 196

Mapai 81
Martyrs' Ashes vii, 8, 23, 37, 59, 63–72, 97–101, 127–133, 135, 137, 139–149, 156, 163–164, 166, 172–173, 176–182, 187, 229, 232, 236, 239
Martyrs' Forest 5, 32, 41, 59, 65, 72–77, 85, 93, 101–103, 119, 216, 218
Memorial Day (Holocaust Memorial Day) 70
Military Rabbinate 177
Mount Herzl 1, 84–85, 87–88, 168, 180, 183, 232, 237, 239
– Herzl's Grave 1, 69, 85, 237
– Great Leaders of the Nation's Plot 1, 88, 237
– Military Cemetery 1, 85, 88, 168, 232, 237–240
Mount Zion 5, 59, 64, 71–72, 97–100, 135, 140, 142–144, 146–149, 155–157, 182, 196, 244
– Chamber of the Holocaust 5, 59, 64, 68, 70–71, 97–100, 140, 143, 145, 147–148, 155–156, 182, 196, 244
– Committee for Mount Zion 70, 97, 99–100, 142, 148–149, 156
– David's Tomb 70, 99, 142
Monuments viii, 1–5, 8–11, 14–16, 18–19, 21–24, 28, 30–31, 36–40, 43, 45–46, 54, 60–61, 63, 69, 75, 81–82, 84–85, 87, 94, 96, 109, 111, 114–115, 118, 120, 122, 126–128, 130, 136, 151, 158–160, 162, 166, 169, 171, 181, 184–191, 194, 197, 201–202, 207, 210, 213–230, 233–235, 237, 239, 241–242
Monumentality 38, 109, 214, 234

National Library 108

Painters and Sculptors Association 170
Palestine Land Development Company 28–29, 51
Pantheon 14, 69, 78, 166, 238
Paratroopers (Second World War) 44, 74, 158
Partisans 6, 44, 109, 157–158, 160, 189, 240–241
Partisans' Song 159
Pilgrimage 17, 46, 76, 126, 158, 166, 168, 171, 196, 237
Priests (kohanim) 176
Public Council for Commemorating the Soldier 140

Rachel's Tomb 52
Reparations Agreement 79–80
Righteous among the Nations 24, 43–44, 54, 110, 122, 151, 158, 184, 196–199, 213

Sculpture 2, 39, 81, 131, 175, 188, 206, 213–217, 219–223, 227, 231, 233, 235
– Alexander Zaïd 27, 39
– Figurative Sculpture 185, 214, 217, 234
– Mordechai Anielewicz (Yad Mordechai) 241
– Roaring Lion (Kfar Giladi) 27, 229
Six-Day War 191
Soap (burial and display) 68, 71, 99, 141
Solel Boneh 120

Tanach House 230
Tourism 1, 61, 63, 125, 183, 230

United States Holocaust Memorial Museum viii
UNSCOP (United Nations Special Committee on Palestine) 44, 48

WAGRO (Warsaw Ghetto Resistance Organization) 221
War of Independence 6, 21, 50, 62, 81, 84–85, 125–126, 143
World Zionist Organization 25, 87
– World Jewish Congress 69

- Zionist Congress 23, 34
- Zionist Executive 87
- Zionist General Council 23–24,

Yad Chaim Weizmann 127
Yad Vashem
- Archive 22, 28, 37, 54, 59, 82, 87, 95, 108, 110, 114–115, 118, 129, 166, 202, 206, 228
- Archive and Library Building 3, 91, 94–95, 104, 106–107, 109, 119–121, 130, 132, 135, 137–138, 151, 188–189, 200, 207–208, 224
- Avenue of the Righteous among the Nations 110, 184, 196–199, 213, 224, 227
- Basalt vii, 113, 125, 130, 151, 159, 171, 178, 180–181, 231, 234, 236
- Concrete viii, 113–114, 159, 178, 180–181, 185–186, 190, 192, 194, 206, 227, 231, 234, 236, 242, 242
- Connecting Path (Mount Herzl) 239
- Europe Field 28
- Gan Am (Nation's Garden) 13
- Grave of the Anonymous Victim 16, 28
- Grove of the Jewish Soldier 17
- Hall of Fighters 28
- Hall of Names 3, 53, 167, 184, 199–206, 213, 220–221, 225–228, 236
- Hall of Remembrance (Ohel Yizkor) 2–3, 8–10, 12, 91, 114, 127, 133, 135–137, 139–140, 142–146, 148–160, 162–185, 188–190, 192, 194–197, 201–202, 207–211, 213, 224–225, 227–229, 231, 234–237, 240
- Heroism Hall 29, 37–38, 41, 45, 54, 83, 94, 108–110, 112–113, 116–119, 121, 124, 151, 157–158, 168–169, 210, 241–243
- Holocaust Art Museum 3
- Holocaust Sanctuary 8
- Homeland Field 28
- Library 22, 42, 49, 83, 94, 108–110, 114, 129, 166, 206
- Memorial Plaza 28, 36, 151, 211, 221, 223–225, 227, 229, 234, 236
- Museum vii, 2–3, 10, 14, 19, 37, 40, 46, 82, 97, 110, 113, 116, 118, 122, 124, , 128–133, 136, 164–168, 183–184, 194, 199, 202–203, 206–213, 220–221, 225, 227–229, 234–235, 245
- Pavilion of the Jewish Soldier 17, 21
- Pavilion to the Missing 15
- Synagogue viii, 3, 10, 22, 28, 30–31, 40, 46, 54, 83, 94, 102, 104, 108, 110, 113–118, 120, 122, 124–125, 129–130, 132–133, 135–136, 139, 143, 145–146, 148–158, 161–162, 164–166, 168, 170, 182–184, 189, 193–196, 202, 204, 206–208, 210–211, 225–226, 228
- Valley of the (Destroyed) Communities 3, 197, 227, 240
Events
- Cornerstone Ceremony 2–3, 9, 79–80, 91, 105–107, 109, 132, 189, 197, 243, 245
- Symposium 91, 121–133, 135, 140, 207–208, 232
Exhibitions
- From the Collections of Yad Vashem 208
- Heroism and Rebellion 203
- Warning and Witness 209
Management and Organization
- Building Committee 112, 114, 123, 139, 153, 169, 173, 175–176, 184, 203, 211, 236, 239
- Commission for the Righteous among the Nations 199–121
- Council 92, 112, 119–122, 149–150, 157–159, 161, 165, 167, 169, 180, 188, 193, 209–210, 219, 231
- Management vii, 24–26, 36–39, 44, 46, 49, 55–56, 59, 61–62, 72, 77–78, 91, 231
- Martyrs' Ashes Committee 163
- Martyrs' Books 53, 199, 201–204
- Memorial Books 15, 21, 28, 30, 55, 74, 121, 199, 202
- Pages of Testimony 199–204, 225
- Yad Vashem's World Council 120, 149–150, 157, 159, 167, 180, 188, 193, 209–210
Publications
- Pinkas Kehillot books 104
- Yediot Yad Vashem 94
Sculptures and Monuments
- Cattle Car memorial 3, 227
- Children's Memorial 3, 188, 227

- Eternal Flame 8, 16, 28–29, 31, 77, 97, 111, 115–116, 124, 130, 158–159, 172, 174–176, 178–181, 183, 193, 229
- Gal-ed 158
- Holocaust Lamp 174
- Job (sculpture) 220
- Memorial Candle 31, 174–175
- Monument to Jewish Soldiers and Partisans 3
- Pillar of Heroism 3, 152, 178, 194, 191–192, 213, 225, 227, 237, 242
- Remembrance Tower 151, 166, 174, 186, 193
- Warsaw Ghetto Uprising Monument vii, 2–3, 9–10, 39–40, 159, 213–226, 228

Yad Vashem Law 7, 9–12, 57, 59, 74, 77–84, 87–89, 92–93, 95, 99, 101–103, 113, 116, 122, 132, 156, 200, 206–207, 231, 241, 243, 245
YIVO 93, 108
Yizkor (Berl Katznelson) 119
Yizkor (Prayer) 173, 181
Youth Aliyah (Aliyat Hanoar) 18

Zyklon (Gas) 148

Names

Agron, Gershon 123
Aldubi, Zvi 204
Alfenbein Shwergold, Miriam 231
Assaf, Simha 46
Arad, Yitzhak 191
Ardon, Mordecai 123, 217
Asher, Gad 167
Auerbach, Philipp 69
Auster, Daniel 156–157

Bardaky Israel 146
Baruch, Zwi Ophir 126
Bar Yehuda Idelson, Rivka 203
Ben-Gurion, David 25, 69–70, 75, 78–80, 89, 97
Ben-Zvi, Rahel Yanait 179
Ben-Zvi, Yitzhak 105–106, 132, 140
Bezem, Naftali 170, 212
Bialer, Yehuda 146, 148, 153–156, 163, 169–170, 176–179, 194, 219
Bogaard, Johannes 198
Brenner, Mila 204
Burg, Yosef 67
Burshtein, Moshe 20

Churchill, Winston 97
Cnaan, Nissan 190
Cohen, Idov 17, 33

Danziger, Yitzhak 170
Dinur, Ben-Zion VII, 7, 10, 50, 77–78, 80–82, 87–88, 91–93, 95–97, 99, 102–104, 106–108, 112–118, 120–124, 128–133, 135–138, 140, 142, 144–150, 152, 155–156, 158–159, 161, 164–166, 182, 207–209, 216–217, 231–232, 245
Dushkin, Alexander 180
Dworzecki, Mark 93, 140, 200

Eban, Abba 179, 189
Eck, Natan 157, 201
Efrati, Shimon 64
Eisner, Jack P. 221
El-Hanani, Arieh 7, 48, 53, 106, 114, 124–125, 130, 152–153, 159–161, 169, 175, 180–181, 190, 202, 205, 207–208, 226, 243
Eloul, Kosso 170, 175–176
Engel, Joel 119
Epstein, Abraham 14
Eshkol, Levi 103
Eytan, Walter 141–142

Feinberg, Nathan 131
Finkel, Shimon 120

Gafni, David 213
Gelber, Edward Elisha 153
Gitai (Weinraub), Munio VII, 15–16, 21, 26–28, 35–36, 41, 43, 48, 53, 86, 94, 114, 125, 150, 162, 180, 243
Goldmann, Nahum 103, 105–106, 108, 118–119, 121, 137, 139, 165
Gothelf, Yehuda 4
Granot (Granovsky), Abraham 14–15, 18–19, 25, 33, 49–50, 62, 74, 93
Greenberg, Aharon-Ya'akov 145

Hareuveni, Ephraim 39
Hausner, Gideon 179
Hecht, Reuben 69–70
Helman, Jacob 18
Henrik, Naomi 185–188, 190, 225
Herman, Abraham 125
Herzog Halevi, Yitzhak 40
Hushi, Abba 96

Idelson, Benjamin 93, 112, 180
Ish-Shalom, Mordechai 189

Jámbor, Ferenc-Iosef 166
Jarblum, Marc 216
Jolson, Anya 223
Jolson, Leon 204, 221, 223

Kahana, Aharon 173
Kahana, Shmuel Zanvil 67, 70, 72, 97–101, 141–144, 146–149, 155–157, 177
Kaplan, Eliezer 35
Karavan, Daniel "Dani" 170
Karl, William 141
Karmi, Dov 113, 123, 126
Katznelson, Berl 119
Katznelson, Yitzhak 46
Kauffmann, Richard 60
Kesse, Yona 81
Kol, Moshe 93, 96, 130–131, 154
Kovner, Abba 45, 123, 200
Krinitzi, Avraham 220
Kubovy, Arieh Leon 155–156, 166–169, 173, 176–177, 179–181, 184, 187–189, 193–195, 201–203, 211, 219
Kubovy, Miriam 190

Lauterbach, Arieh Leo 87
Levin, Yitzchak-Meir 40, 81, 140
Lishanski, Batya 170
Locker, Berl 216
Lubetkin, Zivia 73
Lurie, Zvi 34, 156

Maimon, Yehuda Leib 144–145
Mann, Kalman Jacob 163
Mansfeld, Alfred (Al) VII, 26–28, 35–36, 41, 43, 48, 53, 86, 94, 113, 150, 162, 180, 243
Maron, Nahum 208
Mark, Berl 143
Matrikin, Yaacov 154
Meir, Golda 198
Melkman, Josef 148, 156
Meridor, Ya'akov 204

Narkiss, Mordechai 217
Nissim, Yitzhak 176–177
Nurock, Mordechai 106, 178

Ogen, Gdula 205
Opozdower, Menshe 67

Palmon, Avraham 147–148, 218
Palombo, David 173, 175, 185–186, 188, 204
Pinkerfeld, Jacob 123, 126
Polus, David 39

Rapoport, Nathan VII, 2–3, 9–10, 39, 159, 184–186, 188, 204, 213–228, 237, 241
Reiser, Jacob 167
Reisinger, Dan 206
Remez, David 22, 24, 29, 38, 40, 43, 47–50, 60, 62–63, 73, 78
Rokach, Israel 65, 92
Rosenblatt, Gad 160
Rosenblum, Herzl 67

Safdie, Moshe 188, 235
Samuel, Edwin 180
Sarid, Yaakov 187
Schatz, Bezalel 173
Schatz, Zahara 174

Schechter, Yerachmiel 173
Schneersohn, Isaac 60, 62, 75, 78, 93, 97, 100, 108, 138, 140, 142
Schwartz, Buky 190, 225
Senator, David (Werner) 43, 50
Shag, Haim Avraham 140, 163–164
Shapira, Haim Moshe 80, 92, 143
Sharett, Moshe 92, 102
Sharon, Arieh 7, 48, 53, 93, 106, 113–114, 124, 128–130, 162, 167, 171, 174, 180, 203, 210, 243
Shatner, Mordechai 140, 156, 168, 170, 179, 194, 211, 239
Shazuri (Weber), Shmuel Aharon 43
Sheftel, Aryeh 125
Shemi, Yechiel 170
Shenhavi, Mordechai VII, IX, 7, 9, 12–26, 28, 30–57, 59–60, 62, 65–66, 69–70, 72, 74, 77–80, 84–87, 89, 91, 93–98, 102, 106–107, 111–112, 119, 124, 126–128, 157–158, 160–162, 166, 192–193, 196, 199, 206, 214–216, 218, 230–231, 233–234, 238–240, 242–245
Shlonsky, Avraham 181
Shragai, Shlomo Zalman 21, 24, 26, 93
Siegfried, Moses 218
Spector, Shmuel 191, 220
Sprinzak, Yosef 25
Steinbock (Shani), Yehoshua 123
Szold, Henrietta 18
Sztencl, Yonah 100

Tartakover, Arieh 24, 62, 69
Toledano, Ya'akov Moshe 155
Tuval, Meir 141

Tzur, Yaakov 100
Tzur, Dan 197

Ucko, Sinai 46
Unterman, Isser Yehuda 70
Urbach, Efraim Elimelech 131
Uveeler, Mark VII, 7, 107–109, 114–116, 118, 120–122, 133, 137–139, 148, 155, 165, 182, 206–207, 217–218
Uziel, Ben-Zion Meir Hai 40

Wachtfogel, Jacob 147
Warhaftig, Zerach VII, 37–38, 40, 49, 62, 81, 99
Weitz, Yosef 39, 41, 48, 51, 73, 85, 87, 88, 93, 100–101, 118, 127, 140, 146, 150, 160–161, 164, 197, 218
Weizmann, Chaim 25, 42, 44, 127
Wiesenthal, Simon 65–67
Wind, Moshe 114
Wittkower Werner, Joseph 167

Yadin, Yigael 123, 190
Yaffe, Arieh Leib 45
Yahalom, Lipa 197
Yosef, Dov 150

Zevin, Shlomo Yosef 176–177
Zuchovitzky (Zakif), Shmuel 46
Zilberg, Moshe 200
Zerubavel, Yaakov 169, 173
Zuckermann, Baruch 18, 24
Zuckermann, Yitzhak 46
Ziffer, Moshe 123, 170

Places

Auschwitz 141, 144, 173, 203
Anatot 23, 29

Bavaria 69
Beersheba 34
Beit Alpha 233
Bet Shean valley 178
Bucharest 141

Castel Hill 84

Ebelsberg 67
Efrata 68

Flossenburg 69–71

Places — 261

Germany 6, 17, 67, 69, 79, 103, 106, 213, 217
Gibeah 29

Haifa 15, 96, 200, 216
Har ha-Ru'ah (wind mountain) 35, 41
Hula Valley 10, 12, 15, 56

Jabel Abu Ghuneim 51
Jerusalem VII–VIII, 6, 10, 15, 18–19, 22–23, 26, 29, 32, 34–35, 43–54, 56–57, 59–63, 65–67, 69–70, 72–73, 75, 79–81, 84–89, 91, 93, 95–97, 101, 105–106, 108, 116, 123, 128, 138, 147, 149–150, 153, 156, 167, 169, 185, 196, 200, 205, 214–220, 232–233, 235–236, 238–239
– Givat Ram 86
– Mount of Olives 14, 23, 31, 64, 68
– Mount Scopus 19, 22–23, 29, 31, 46–47, 49, 51, 56, 243
– Old City 19, 23, 31, 50
– Sanhedria 64, 68, 71, 144
– Western Wall 31, 140
Jerusalem corridor 72, 116
Jezreel Valley 10, 15, 19, 31, 56, 233
Jordan Valley 15, 34

Kfar Giladi 27, 229
Khirbet al-Hamama 85, 88
Kiryat Anavim 29, 44
Ksalon 73, 76, 101
Krakow 125

Linz 65, 67
Lohamei HaGeta'ot 63, 91, 95, 119, 211, 241
London 23–24, 48

Ma'ale HaHamisha 10, 17, 26, 34–35, 38, 41, 44, 47–51, 60, 233, 243
Masada 190
Mauthausen 65, 67, 141
Mishmar HaEmek 15, 242
Mount Carmel 18

Negev 26
Neve Ilan 41, 44
New York 60–61, 93, 103, 108, 117, 125, 137, 139, 167, 204, 220–222

Paris 60–62, 75, 78–79, 91, 93, 97, 100–101, 108, 116, 138–140, 142, 160, 171, 215, 218
Poland 34, 96, 114, 143, 146, 215, 230, 233
Prague 125

Ramat Gan 23, 219–220
Ramat Rachel 10, 26, 50–54, 60, 197, 199, 243

Safed 13, 26

Tel Aviv 19, 57, 61, 63, 65–68, 70, 96, 200

United States 34, 221

Vilna 191
Vienna 141

Warsaw 63–64, 70, 73–74, 80, 96, 141, 143, 203, 212–215, 217, 219–224

Yad Mordechai 5, 119, 212, 241

www.ingramcontent.com/pod-product-compliance
Lightning Source LLC
Chambersburg PA
CBHW031424150426
43191CB00006B/381